THE OFFICIAL 1993 DEVOTIONAL BOOK

THE OFFICIAL 1993 DEVOTIONAL BOOK *for Super Kids*

Renée Coffee

Review and Herald® Publishing Association
Hagerstown, MD 21740

This book was
Edited by Richard W. Coffen
Designed by Bill Kirstein
Cover art by Helcio Deslandes
Typeset: 11/12 Clearface

PRINTED IN U.S.A.

97 96 95 94 93 92 10 9 8 7 6 5 4 3 2 1

Library of Congress Cataloging in Publication Data

Coffee, Renee. 1949–
The official 1993 devotional book for super kids / Renee Coffee.
p. cm.
Includes index.
1. Teenagers—Prayer-books and devotions—English. 2. Devotional calendars—Juvenile literature. I. Title.
BV4850.C563 1992
242′.63—dc20 92-38
CIP

ISBN 0-8280-0638-5 AC

This book is
DEDICATED TO

My parents,
Dave and Kathryn Kempf
Gilmer and Dorothy Coffee;

My mentor,
Elisabeth Spalding McFadden;

My best teachers,
my students at Alpena Junior Academy,
Pontiac Junior Academy, and
Gobles Junior Academy;
and

My school principal, proofreader,
inspiration, and general
all-around best pal,
Tom Coffee

Just Who Is Renée Coffee?

Renée Coffee has spent nearly all her life in school—17 years as a student and 20 years as a teacher.

Yet as far back as she can remember, teaching was never one of her goals. In fact, she once vowed that she'd never become a secretary or a teacher. But when she graduated from Andrews University in 1972 she graduated with a teaching degree in secretarial science.

Although it was her dream to teach in an academy, Renée's first job took her to a two-room church school in Alpena, Michigan. She liked teaching the younger children so much that she completed a graduate degree in elementary education.

Renée and her husband, Tom, who is also a teacher, are still in Michigan, team teaching grades three and four and grades nine and ten at Gobles Junior Academy.

Although teaching takes up most of her time, Renée finds time to share her stories at camp meetings and weeks of prayer. Recently she has become part of a speaking team that specializes in the subjects of worship and friendship.

Renée also enjoys skiing, reading, writing, music, reading, puzzles, flea markets, collecting Howdy Doody memorabilia, and reading.

JANUARY

1

Buried Treasure

I want you to know fully God's secret truth. That truth is Christ himself. And in him all the treasures of wisdom and knowledge are safely kept. Colossians 2:2, 3, ICB.

And to Edward, my youngest son, I leave my dearest possession of all, my Bible.' "

Edward couldn't believe his ears. He turned angrily to the lawyer. "You mean that's all Mother left me in her will? A Bible, a stupid Bible! She gave Beth the house. Ginny got the car and furniture. And all I get is an old book?"

The lawyer shrugged his shoulders. "I'm sorry, Edward. But that's what she put in her will. And when I talked with her last week, she stressed how important it was that you got the Bible—and this letter. Your mother loved you very much, Edward. I'm sure that there must be something special about this Bible."

The angry young man picked up his mother's Bible and stomped from the office. When he got home he ripped open the envelope and read the letter inside:

"Dear Son,

"Please take good care of my Bible. Read its words, and you will find a great treasure.

"Love, Mother."

Picking up the Bible, he shoved it next to his collection of mystery novels in his bookcase.

"I'll take care of it, Mother, but I won't read it."

Years passed. Edward's life went from bad to worse. Finally he remembered the Bible his mother had given him. Walking over to the bookcase, he pulled it out and began reading the story of Jesus. His heart softened, and he realized what a mistake it had been to turn his back on God.

As he turned the page, a piece of paper fluttered to the floor. Edward bent over to pick it up. He couldn't believe his eyes. It was a $100 bill!

How in the world did that get in this Bible? he wondered.

Curious, he turned the book upside down and shook it. Bills and more bills fluttered to the floor.

At last Edward understood why his mother had given him her Bible.

God has placed in the Bible a treasure for each of us that is better than money. If we just search His Word, we can find freedom from sin, friendship with Him, and a promise of eternal life in heaven.

Don't wait until you're old to get into God's Word. Read your Bible every day, and you will find the treasure God has waiting for you. Take time out to get to know the best Friend you'll ever have.

JANUARY

2

What You Give Is What You Get

In everything, do to others what you would have them do to you. Matthew 7:12, NIV.

What goes around comes around."

During World War II, the U.S. submarine *Tang* was sent on a mission off the China coast. Shortly after it had completed an assignment, the sub picked up some signals on its radar.

"A convoy of Japanese ships is heading our way," the radarman reported.

"Let's take her to the top," directed one of the commanding officers. It was late at night, so the enemy would not be able to see the submarine in the darkness.

After surfacing, the crew surveyed the large group of enemy ships in the distance. With only eight torpedoes left aboard the *Tang,* the sailors realized that there was no margin for error. Every torpedo must reach its target.

The crew hurried to their stations, and the attack began. The first torpedo made a direct hit and sank one of the Japanese ships. Aimed carefully, the next six underwater missiles took down six more enemy vessels. Only one torpedo remained.

The signal was given, and the last torpedo shot through the water. But as the sailors watched, they noticed that it wasn't traveling in a straight line. In fact, it started spinning in circles.

By the time the torpedo straightened out, it was not heading for a Japanese ship. It was heading right back toward the *Tang.*

The emergency alarm screamed a warning to the sub's crew. But it was too late to submerge. The torpedo slammed into the side of the submarine and blew it apart. Only nine men survived that terrible blast.

"What goes around comes around."

The treatment we give to others will return to us. Just like the submarine, whatever we send out will eventually come back our way. If we speak mean words to others, they'll speak them back to us. If we treat our friends unkindly, they'll treat us the same way. But if we encourage others, we'll receive encouragement when we need it. If we're considerate, people will treat us with consideration.

JANUARY

3

Copycats

You too, be patient and stand firm, because the Lord's coming is near. James 5:8, NIV.

Miss Brown stood in front of her classroom. "Today I'd like to give you a little math quiz on your multiplication tables," she said. "If you know the answer, raise your hand, but don't say anything out loud."

Turning around, Miss Brown wrote 5 x 7 = . The students quickly raised their hands.

"Keith, what is the answer?"

"Thirty-five," Keith responded.

"How many agree with his answer?"

Every hand went up.

Miss Brown wrote the next problem, 9 x 7 = .

"Who has the answer?"

Waving hands filled the classroom.

"Ginny."

"Sixty-three."

"How many agree?"

The whole class raised their hands.

"Now for the last problem," said the teacher. She wrote 6 x 8 = .

"Who has the answer? Rosa?"

"Forty-two."

The teacher surveyed the room. "How many agree?"

Twenty-five of the 30 students raised their hands. The five students who didn't looked around at all their friends and then slowly raised their hands in agreement. They didn't want to risk being different. So they went along with the crowd.

What they didn't know was that the other students and the teacher were in on an experiment. The people in charge of the experiment wanted to see if students would go against what they knew to be correct, or if they'd be willing to be different.

Last week at our Sabbath school, the primary leader played a guessing game with the class.

"Who was the doubting disciple?" he asked.

Three primaries said Thomas. But the rest said Timothy.

"How many say it's Timothy?" asked the leader.

Every hand went up. Those with the right answer went along with the crowd.

All through life you'll have to choose between right and wrong. Are you determined to do what's right even if it means being different?

Those who choose to follow God will never be in the majority. But they will always be on the right side.

JANUARY

4

Bruiser or Builder?

Be kind and compassionate to one another. Ephesians 4:32, NIV.

When I was growing up I didn't enjoy doing all my farm chores, but I loved gathering eggs. Each afternoon I'd take an egg basket to the chicken coop. Amid squawks, cackles, and flying feathers, I went from one nesting box to another, searching for the warm, brown eggs the hens had laid.

One day as I was heading for the chicken coop, I noticed the chickens picking on one of the smaller hens. Around the chicken yard they chased her, pecking at her with their beaks. Three days later I found the small hen dead. The other chickens had pecked her to death.

Sometimes boys and girls act like those chickens. They find someone who is smaller, slower, or just different. And then they begin to pick on him or her. They even invite their friends to join in on the "fun."

Tony, one of the ninth graders in our school, has a lot going for him. He's the tallest student. And the oldest. He gets straight A's. It would be very easy for him to be the school bully, but instead Tony uses his advantages to help others.

During class Tony helps the other students with their lessons. His classmates know he'll always take time to explain the English assignment or check over an algebra problem.

On Tuesdays our ski club spends the evening at Timber Ridge. Tony is always the first one to retrieve a runaway ski or help others get back into their bindings when they've taken a spill.

Bullying someone takes no talent. There will always be someone smaller or weaker to pick on. But it takes character and courage to give of yourself to help others.

Today you'll have opportunities either to hurt or to help someone else. How will you use your talents and abilities? Will you be a bruiser—or a builder?

JANUARY

5

Friends Forever

The wolf and the lamb will feed together, and the lion will eat straw like the ox. Isaiah 65:25, NIV.

A lion and a lamb living peacefully together? On earth? It sounds impossible. But it really did happen.

The place was a zoo in Osaka, Japan. A lioness gave birth to a cub, but as sometimes happens to animals in captivity, the mother rejected her baby. Afraid for the cub's life, the zookeepers decided to remove it from the cage and care for the little orphan themselves.

Lions are known to be great meat eaters. But for some reason the zoo workers fed the little cub lots of milk and vegetables and very little meat. The cub accepted the strange diet and grew quickly.

The lion soon became a favorite of both the zoo staff and the children who visited the zoo. Some of the staff even taught him to walk on a leash and obey certain commands.

The director, realizing that the lion was unusually gentle for a wild animal, decided to see just how gentle he was. So one day he opened up the lion's cage and set a goat inside.

As everyone watched, the big cat looked at the intruder, sniffed it, and then lay down for a nap.

A few days later the zookeepers brought a lamb and put it in the cage with the lion and the goat. The lion checked out his new roommate and then walked away.

Not only did the three animals live together in peace, but they became good friends—eating, sleeping, and playing together.

Someday we'll be with Jesus in heaven, where all animals and all people will live together in peace. Animals will not fear people. And we will not fear each other.

If we're going to live together in peace and happiness in heaven, wouldn't it be a good idea to start getting along with each other here on earth?

How is it in your home? Do you and your brothers and sisters pick on each other? Do you hurt each other with mean words? Or do you show love and encouragement?

Something to think about: You cannot change anyone else. But you *can* change yourself. What could you do to make your home more happy and peaceful?

JANUARY

6

Big Words

There is one thing worse than a fool, and that is a man who is conceited. Proverbs 26:12, TLB.

Back in 1877 prospector George Warren considered himself the fastest man around. No one could beat him in the 100-yard run. He became so sure of himself that he began to brag that he could even outrun a horse.

George's boasting made him the laughingstock of the town. "Outrun a horse?" the people snickered. "The man's got to be crazy."

But George refused to back down from his claim. "I know I can outrun a horse," he insisted. "And to show you I mean business, I'll put my entire interest in the Copper Queen Mine on the line."

The people couldn't believe their ears. George liked to make bets when he ran against other runners. He always won. But this time the wager was much bigger than a few dollars.

"If someone is willing to pay me $5,000 if I win, we've got a deal," he continued.

One of the townspeople took up the challenge.

On the day of the race people from far and near showed up in town. Everyone wanted to see if George really could run faster than a horse.

The race covered a total of 200 yards. One hundred yards to a post and then back.

George stepped to the starting line. Next to him waited the horse and its rider.

The crack of a pistol started the race. George shocked the entire crowd as he moved out in front of the horse. He reached the post and then started for the finish line. But try as he might, he couldn't keep up his pace. The horse passed him. And George came in second.

George the bragger had to give up his ownership in the mine. And his loss became the most expensive defeat any runner has ever experienced, for the mine was worth much more than the $5,000 George had hoped to win. Based on the amount of profit the Copper Queen Mine eventually produced, George's bet cost him $20 million.

When people boast, they are trying to make themselves look better than others. There's nothing wrong with being proud of the things you do well. But no one likes a braggart.

Bragging won't cost you $20 million like it did George. But it could cost your reputation, your friends, and your happiness.

JANUARY

7

Turn and Run

Flee the evil desires of youth, and pursue righteousness, faith, love and peace. 2 Timothy 2:22, NIV.

Art Smith, an electrician in our town, received a phone call from a couple who wanted him to do some work for them. They were in the process of restoring an old house and needed Art to fix up the wiring.

When Art arrived at the house, he surveyed the place, deciding just what needed to be done. Then he picked up his tools and headed for the basement.

He set his tools on the top of the old stone wall to his right and pulled out his flashlight. Just then he heard something hit the floor. Art looked down and saw his pliers lying on the cement. Reaching over, he picked them up and placed them back on the ledge. A few minutes later he heard them fall again.

Oh, well, he said to himself, *I'll just leave them there if they don't want to stay on the ledge.* So he continued his work. Not long afterward he heard another clink as something fell to the floor. This time it was one of his screwdrivers.

What in the world is going on? he thought. *Why do those tools keep falling?*

Art looked up just in time to see something wiggle across the ledge. Not just one something, but a whole bunch of them.

Snakes! And as Art listened, he heard a soft rattle. Rattlesnakes!

Art gingerly picked up his tools and dashed from the basement, never to return.

He knew rattlesnakes meant danger, and he wanted no part of them. Too bad Mr. Parker didn't feel the same way.

Mr. Parker lived in a Florida lagoon and kept a rattlesnake as a pet. For 20 years the man and his snake had lived together.

But Mr. Parker had a bad habit. He liked to tease the snake. Each morning when he came to breakfast, the man would stick his finger into the snake's cage just to get it angry. The snake would leap at the finger, missing every time. Well, almost every time.

Mr. Parker came down one morning and poked at the snake as he always did. But that morning the snake moved a little faster than usual. It sank its fangs into the man's finger, and in a few hours Mr. Parker was dead.

When you find yourself in the middle of a temptation, don't play around with it. Don't be like Mr. Parker and see how far you can push your luck. Learn a lesson from Art, the electrician, and *run!*

JANUARY

8

Make a Change

You shall not misuse the name of the Lord your God, for the Lord will not hold anyone guiltless who misuses his name. Exodus 20:7, NIV.

The boy probably shouldn't have joined the army in the first place. He was much too young to go to war. But he was there. And he was afraid.

At night he looked up at the stars and thought of home. He thought of the peaceful little village where his family lived. He thought of his brothers and sisters, mother and father. He longed for his mother's wonderful cooking. And his bed. Oh, he would give anything to be able to crawl into his own bed and fall asleep in the safety of his home! But he was a soldier.

After surviving one of the fiercest battles he'd ever fought, the boy decided that he had had enough. He was proud to be one of Alexander the Great's soldiers, but he was going back home to love and safety.

That night, after the other soldiers had fallen asleep, the boy quietly slipped out of his bedroll and disappeared into the woods bordering the camp. Feeling his way through the darkness, the young soldier hurried toward the town they had passed the day before. His plan was to find a barn where he could hide until the army moved on.

But just as he started across the wooden bridge, he felt a hand jerk him around. "Running away, are you?" asked one of the sentries.

The following morning the boy, along with a number of other deserters, was brought before Alexander the Great. The young soldier watched as the deserters were quickly tried and punished.

When his turn came, the boy was led up to the great military leader. Alexander looked down at the boy and felt a strange compassion in his heart.

"What is your name?" he asked.

The boy moved nervously. "Alexander, sir."

"What is your name?"

"Alexander, sir."

"What is your name?"

"Alexander, sir."

"You," said Alexander the Great, "will either have to change your name or change your conduct."

Some people feel that taking the name of the Lord in vain refers just to swearing. But it also has to do with the way we live as Christians. When we become Christ's followers, we take the name Christian. And with that name comes a responsibility to represent Jesus in all that we do.

Do you wear the name with pride? Do people know that you are one of Christ's followers?

JANUARY

9

Thar's Gold in Them Thar Hills

I am the Lord; those who hope in me will not be disappointed. Isaiah 49:23, NIV.

I don't know what his first name was, but his last name was Darby. And his initials were R.M. So for the sake of the story let's call him Rick.

Rick was just a young man when his uncle came banging on his door one afternoon. "Rick, open up! I've got some news, wonderful news."

Rick ran to the kitchen door and invited his uncle inside. "What are you all excited about?"

"Gold. I've found gold. See here?" The man handed Rick the rocks he held in his hand.

"I started diggin' around that old mine I bought, and this here's what I found. I had it checked, and it's gold, all right."

Rick shook his head in surprise.

"Well, that's great, Uncle. I hope you make a million."

"I will, but I need your help."

"My help? What do you need from me?"

The old man sat down at the table and leaned back in his chair. "Money. I need you to help me come up with some money. I've got to buy some mining equipment, and that stuff ain't cheap. But it's the only way we'll be able to get that gold out of the rock and into the bank."

"So what do I do?"

"Ask your friends to invest in the mine. They'll lend you the money for the equipment. When we start sellin' the gold, you can pay them back with interest. What do you say? Is it a deal, partner?"

Rick thought it over. He trusted his uncle. And it did seem like a sure deal. Reaching across the table, he sealed the partnership with a handshake.

Rick kept up his part of the deal. He borrowed money from his friends, and before long the mine was in full production. Everything was going great—until the gold supply disappeared.

As they drilled back farther into the mine, the rich vein of gold suddenly stopped. And the end of the gold meant the end of their dreams.

Have you ever been excited about something only to have it flop? It's hard to have your dreams come to an end. Someday Jesus will come and take us to heaven. And we'll never be disappointed again. But as long as we're on earth, things won't always work out as we expect them to.

Tomorrow we'll find out how Rick handled his disappointment.

JANUARY

10

Two Feet Down

A faithful man will be richly blessed. Proverbs 28:20, NIV.

Yesterday we left Rick with two problems. First, his dream of becoming rich ended when the mine stopped producing gold. Second, he still owed money to some of his friends. Unfortunately the mine had given out before he had paid back the loans.

So he took another job and began paying off his debts.

Rick's uncle, in the meantime, called in a junk dealer and sold the mining equipment. "Here," he said as he threw the deed of the mine on the ground. "You can have that, too."

The junk man handed him the money for the equipment, and Rick's uncle walked away from the mine. But the junk man didn't haul away the machinery. Instead he hired someone to check the mine to see if there might be more gold in it somewhere.

When the report came back, it said: "Dig two feet deeper, and you'll find another vein of gold."

The junk man drilled down just a little farther. And sure enough, he found more gold. Enough gold to make him a millionaire.

How do you think Rick felt when he heard about the "worthless" mine that his uncle had given away?

Most of us would be angry. We'd feel cheated. But not Rick. Instead of feeling sorry for himself, he decided to use his disappointment and learn something from it.

Rick started working as an insurance salesman. The work was time-consuming and often discouraging. But whenever a prospect said he didn't want to buy insurance, Rick didn't pack up his briefcase and leave. He'd remember the gold mine. And he'd tell himself, *Don't give up so soon. Don't take no for an answer. Just dig a little deeper.*

Rick's philosophy paid off. His business grew, and soon he was one of the top salesmen in the United States.

When you come face to face with a problem, don't give up. Like the second vein of gold, success may be within reach. All you need to do is to keep going and dig a little deeper.

JANUARY

11

Builders for God

Long life to you! Good health to you and your household! And good health to all that is yours! 1 Samuel 25:6, NIV.

Mr. Whitney unrolled the blueprints and smoothed them out across the desk. "What do you think, Carl?" he asked his assistant.

Carl looked over the house plans and nodded his head. "Nice design," he said. "Is that the next house we're going to build?"

"Yes, it is. But I have a favor to ask of you, Carl," said Mr. Whitney. "My wife and I want to do some traveling this summer. So I won't be around much. I want you to take charge of this new house. Go ahead and make all the decisions as to the color of siding, the carpeting, drapes—everything."

Carl couldn't believe his ears. He'd always wanted to build a house and use his own ideas, and now Mr. Whitney was giving him the opportunity.

"I'll certainly do my best," he said.

"I know you will," said his boss. "You always do."

Building the house wasn't as easy as Carl had expected. But Carl kept plugging away, working late in the evenings and on Sundays.

Months later Carl called Mr. Whitney and told him the house was ready for inspection.

Carl was sweeping off the sidewalk when his boss drove up. Mr. Whitney got out of the car and walked slowly around the house. "Let's look over the inside," the boss said.

The two men walked from room to room.

"You did a fine job, Carl," Mr. Whitney said.

Carl handed the house keys to his boss. "Well, I sure did enjoy working on it."

Mr. Whitney handed them back to Carl. "I don't think I'll be needing these."

"But the new owner will."

Mr. Whitney laughed. "I believe that the new owner already has them in his hand."

Carl looked up at his boss. "New owner?"

"That's right, Carl. This is your house. It's my gift to you for the good work you've done for me."

God has put each of us in charge of building a special house—our body. He lets us make the decisions about how we're going to treat it.

What kind of body are you building? Are you getting enough rest? Are you eating the right foods? Do you take time to exercise?

Do your best as you build your body home. For just like Carl, you're going to be the one who gets to live in it.

JANUARY

12

Thou Shalt Not Steal

For God will bring every deed into judgment, including every hidden thing, whether it is good or evil. Ecclesiastes 12:14, NIV.

One commandment that I never had a real problem with was number 8: "Thou shalt not steal." I can remember stealing only one thing in my life.

While shopping at the grocery store with my mother, I saw a piece of metal lying on the floor. It was just the same size as a penny. I put it in a gum machine, and it worked. Luckily, my mother found out what happened and made me give the store manager a penny to pay for my stolen goods. The embarrassment cured me of ever wanting to steal again.

So I've always felt pretty confident about my honesty. I wouldn't even think of taking something that belonged to somebody else. Stealing was not a problem for me.

Or so I thought.

During my worship time this week, I was reading about the thieves who were crucified on either side of Jesus. The author mentioned that we may not steal money or material possessions from other people, but we probably are thieves just the same.

Have you ever yelled at someone? Have you ever fought with your brothers and sisters in the back seat while your parents were driving you somewhere? Have you ever teased an animal? Then you're a thief. You've stolen someone else's peace and happiness.

Have you ever gossiped about a classmate? Then you're a thief. You've robbed from that person's reputation.

Have you ever thought impure thoughts about someone? Even though you may not think you have done anything wrong, you're still a thief. You've taken away the respect that the other person deserves.

Have you ever made fun of other people? Have you said or done anything to hurt their feelings? Then you're a thief. You've taken away an opportunity to show them what Jesus is like. And you may have pushed them further away from the Lord.

I don't know about you, but I think I have some problem areas that need help.

Unless we're in contact with Jesus every minute of the day, we're going to be stealing from others on a regular basis. We can't stop ourselves from hurting others. But if we ask Him into our lives, Jesus will live in us and for us. And when He does, we won't find pleasure in selfish taking. We'll find happiness in unselfish giving.

JANUARY

13

Who's in Control of Your Mind?

May the words of my mouth and the meditation of my heart be pleasing in your sight, O Lord, my Rock and my Redeemer. Psalm 19:14, NIV.

Have you ever wondered why you say some of the things that you do? Have you ever been surprised to find yourself swearing or using filthy language? or being disrespectful to your parents or your teacher?

A friend told me about an eye-opening experience he had after he joined the Adventist Church. And I've never forgotten his story.

"While I was in medical school, Dan, one of my classmates, started giving me Bible studies. I had been a Christian all my life, but when I heard about the seventh-day Sabbath, I decided to become an Adventist.

"After I was baptized, Dan and I started studying the Bible with Mike, another medical student.

"Week after week the three of us met together. One afternoon as we were studying, Mike began to criticize the Bible and make fun of religion. It caught me by surprise, because he had been so interested in learning about God.

"The longer the study went, the worse it got. I was just about ready to call it quits when I looked up and saw something that sent chills down my back.

"Right behind Mike stood a strange being. I realized that it was either Satan or one of his angels. The spirit bent over Mike, and opened its mouth, and out poured something that looked like honey. As soon as it touched Mike's head, Mike opened up his mouth and started speaking disrespectfully about God.

"As I sat there in a state of shock, the spirit looked up. When he saw me staring, he jumped back in surprise. He realized that I could see him. But after a few seconds he regained his composure and shrugged his shoulders as if to say 'So what.' "

To whom will you listen today? Will the words you speak reflect Satan's influence? Or will you place yourself on God's side and listen to the Holy Spirit's voice?

JANUARY

14

Being Like God

Your attitude should be the same as that of Christ Jesus: who, being in very nature God, did not consider equality with God something to be grasped, but made himself nothing, taking the very nature of a servant, being made in human likeness. Philippians 2:5-7, NIV.

A parable tells of a man who worked as a servant for a wealthy businessman and his family. Day after day Reilly worked around the Braidingtons' mansion, taking care of the family's needs. He fed and watered the children's pets. He kept the cars clean and shiny. He mowed the lawn and pulled the weeds in the flower beds. He ran errands for Mrs. Braidington.

Although the family paid him well, Reilly wasn't happy. "They treat me very well," he said to his wife. "And I sure can't complain about my salary. But I don't want to do this for the rest of my life. I want to be important."

Well, as it happened, Reilly's luck changed. One night he had a dream. And in it he was handed three envelopes. When he opened them, he found that each one contained a certificate good for one free wish.

In the morning he remembered the dream, and he decided to see if it would come true. So after thinking for a while, he said, "I wish that I could take over Mr. Braidington's job." Instantly he found himself sitting in Mr. Braidington's office, in Mr. Braidington's chair.

"It worked!" he cried. "I got my wish."

Leaning back in his desk chair, Reilly realized that he still had two more wishes left. *I'm not going to stop now,* he thought. *I can be more than just a company president. I think I'll become president of the United States.* So he closed his eyes and said, "I wish to become president of the United States."

In a split second he was sitting behind the desk in the Oval Office of the White House.

I've got one more wish left. I'm going to make this the best of all. Now, who is more powerful than even the president of the United States? Reilly thought for a moment and then he said, "For my last wish, I wish to become the most powerful person in the whole universe. I wish to become like God."

The next thing he knew, Reilly found himself back at the Braidingtons', trimming the lawn. A servant once again.

Of course, this is a made-up story, but it illustrates that all who wish to become like God are to be servants. When Jesus came to earth, He didn't take over the government, as the people hoped He would. Instead, He gave His life in service. And He wants us to do the same.

JANUARY

15

God's Creatures Deserve Kindness

Blessed is he who is kind to the needy. Proverbs 14:21, NIV.

People aren't the only ones who appreciate being treated kindly. Animals also respond to thoughtfulness. Mr. Strickland learned this a number of years ago while he was vacationing in Jamaica.

One morning Mr. Strickland started out from Kingston on a 42-mile bicycle trip. After about two hours of pedaling he came to a steep hill. He got off his bike and began pushing it up the incline. When he stopped to rest, a large brown dog came running toward him. At first the man panicked, but when he saw the dog's gentle eyes, he lost his fear.

"I felt so sorry for the poor animal. His ribs almost poked through his side. I knew he was hungry."

Mr. Strickland spoke kindly to the dog and patted him on the head.

"Soon the dog caught the smell of my lunch, which was tied to the handlebars of the bike. He sniffed the sack and then turned to me and wagged his tail. I knew what he was trying to say to me.

"When I asked him if he was hungry, he put one foot on the lunch and stared into my eyes."

The man opened his lunch and gave the dog half his sandwich. The poor starving animal ate it quickly. He even licked the ground where some of the crumbs had fallen.

"I handed him the rest of the sandwich. And when he finished that, I emptied the sack and gave him all the rest of the food inside."

When the dog finished eating, he walked over to Mr. Strickland and laid his head on the man's knee to show his thanks.

"After resting a little while longer, I walked the rest of the way up the hill. At the top I noticed a small store. I went inside and bought some milk and bread, which I shared with my animal friend.

"I said goodbye to the dog, then started again on my journey. The animal followed me for about two miles, but then he disappeared."

God gave us a special blessing when He created animals for us to love. If you have pets at home, do you always treat them kindly? Or do you tease and hurt them? Do you remember to feed and water them? Or do you forget to care for their needs?

Tomorrow we'll find out how the hungry dog repaid Mr. Strickland for his kindness.

JANUARY

16

A Kindness Returned

A kind man benefits himself. . . . But he who sows righteousness reaps a sure reward. Proverbs 11:17, 18, NIV.

After the large brown dog disappeared along the roadside, Mr. Strickland rode on alone toward Font Hill. Late that evening he reached his destination.

Four days later he began the 42-mile trip back to Kingston. The scenery was beautiful, and the miles seemed to speed by quickly. Then trouble struck. Just as Mr. Strickland neared the little roadside store where he'd stopped before, he heard loud barking. Looking up, he saw two black dogs blocking the middle of the road. He tried to shoo them away, but they wouldn't move. As he got closer, the animals lunged toward him and tried to bite his legs. He tried to escape from them, but the hilly road made it impossible for him to pedal any faster.

"Just when I thought things couldn't get any worse, I heard another dog barking. I looked up to see a brown dog bounding toward me at a terrific speed. I knew there was no way I could defend myself against three dogs. 'Lord, help me,' I prayed."

Sure enough, the third dog leaped into the air toward Mr. Strickland. But instead of sinking his teeth into the man, it attacked one of the other dogs, sending it yelping down the road. Within seconds the other black dog was also running for its life, with the brown dog close at its heels.

By then Mr. Strickland realized that his rescuer was none other than the poor, hungry dog he had befriended earlier that week.

After chasing the two black dogs away, the brown dog ran back to Mr. Strickland. "He wagged his tail and greeted me like an old friend. I jumped off my bike and threw my arms around him. He barked happily and licked my face.

"Together we walked to the little store. I bought some more food, and we shared a picnic dinner under the trees."

JANUARY

17

Wrong Signals

Trust in the Lord forever, for the Lord, the Lord, is the Rock eternal. Isaiah 26:4, NIV.

Back in the 1800s an Italian sailing boat got caught in a bad storm. The wind blew it hundreds of miles off course. Helpless, the 17 sailors aboard watched as they crashed into big rocks along the northeast coast of England.

Some people from the nearby town of Blyth had seen the boat as it headed into the dangerous waters. They knew the boat would sink once it hit the rocks. So they called for other townspeople to come, and together they hurried to the water's edge and began to plan their rescue operation.

If the rescuers tried to row out to the sinking ship, their boats would also be destroyed. So they brought out a special apparatus that they had used to rescue boats before. The long, heavy rope was attached to a weight. It would be shot through the air toward the boat. Once the sailors got hold of the rope, they would tie it to their mast. Then as the people on shore held on to the other end of the rope, the men could crawl to safety.

All held their breath as the rope shot through the air.

"Tie it to the mast," they shouted to the sailors. But the men on the boat didn't understand English. They thought the people were trying to kill them. So when the rope was shot toward their boat, they screamed in terror and dived for safety. Again and again the townspeople shot the rope over to the sinking boat. "Grab the rope," they yelled. But the men aboard refused to come out of hiding.

Today the graves of 17 Italian sailors lie not far from the coastline where their ship went down. If only they had understood what the people on shore were trying to do. If only they had realized that the people were trying to help them, not hurt them.

Sometimes we're like the sailors. When God tries to help us, we think He's just trying to hurt us. We run away from Him instead of following His guidance.

The next time your life hits a rut, don't turn your back on God. Reach out to Him, and let Him pull you safely through your problems.

JANUARY

18

Making a Difference

Do not withhold good from those who deserve it, when it is in your power to act. Proverbs 3:27, NIV.

"He who accepts evil without a protest against it is really cooperating with it."

Kate Kunze is a photographer. But she is also a hero. Kate works at a nightclub in Columbus, Georgia. She takes pictures of the people at the different tables and sells them as souvenirs.

As she came to work one night, she saw a sign advertising a new act: bear wrestling. A $500 prize was offered to anyone who could pin the bear to the floor.

When the bear was brought out onto the stage, Kate was shocked. The poor animal was almost totally blind. Its teeth and claws had been removed, and the leather muzzle was so tight the bear could hardly breathe.

Twenty men came on the stage and began to wrestle with the bear. They pulled her legs out from under her and jumped on her back.

Kate was angry. She took pictures of what was going on. And during the next few weeks found out all she could about bear wrestling.

She found that the bears are often drugged and intentionally blinded. And sometimes when their teeth are pulled out, the bears receive no painkiller. Some owners cut the bears' tendons so their paws are useless. And when the animals are maimed enough so they can't hurt people, they are then hauled from town to town in hot, dirty trailers.

Kate went to work to change the laws that allowed bear wrestling. First she got her hometown to ban it. Now she's expanding her fight. She's working to have similar laws passed in other cities and states.

Kate didn't solve the national debt problem, find homes for all the homeless, or win the war on drugs. But she saw something that bothered her and took action.

Don't wait until you're older to get involved. When you see a problem or a need, do something about it. Just like Kate Kunze, you can make a difference.

"I am only one, but still I am one.
I cannot do everything, but still I can do something.
I will not refuse to do the something that I can do."—Edward Everett Hale

JANUARY

19

Burning Martin

On the contrary: "If your enemy is hungry, feed him; if he is thirsty, give him something to drink. In doing this, you will heap burning coals on his head." Do not be overcome by evil, but overcome evil with good. Romans 12:20, 21, NIV.

Boy, would I ever love to punch that guy right in the face!" Stan was really steamed.

"Whoa," said Mother looking up from her sewing. "It sounds like you've had a bad day."

"I've had a bad day, all right. I had to sit in the same classroom as Martin McCall. That kid drives me crazy."

Stan opened the refrigerator and pulled out some orange juice. "Ever since school started, Martin has been making my life miserable. Yesterday he sent Trisha a love letter and signed my name to it. Today he tripped me when I was going up to work at the chalkboard. I fell flat on my face, and I felt like an idiot."

Stan opened the cookie jar and took out some Oreos. "Martin's parents just got a divorce this summer. That's why he moved to this area. I wish he'd have moved to South America or the North Pole."

"Do you think the divorce might have something to do with the way he acts?"

"I don't know," mumbled Stan. "It doesn't matter. He's still a jerk."

"That may be," said Mrs. Knight, "but it sounds to me like he's just trying to get some attention."

Stan knew his mom was right.

Mrs. Knight turned off her sewing machine. "Remember the Bible verse we read in worship a few weeks ago, about being kind to our enemies? Why don't you invite Martin over for supper Saturday night? We'll make some pizzas and play Monopoly."

"I don't know if I could stand being around him a whole evening."

"I know it'll be hard. But will you at least give it a try?"

"I guess so," Stan agreed reluctantly.

The next day at school during a game of basketball, Martin jabbed his elbow into Stan's stomach. Stan's first reaction was to give Martin some of his own medicine. But then he remembered what his mother had said. "Martin, how about coming to my house Saturday night? We're going to have pizza and play Monopoly."

"Me? You want me to come?" Martin asked.

"Yeah, sure. How about it?"

"That'd be great."

The bell rang, signaling the end of PE. As Stan went to the equipment room to put the ball away, Martin followed him. "Hey, Stan," said Martin, "uh, sorry about that jab I gave you during the game."

JANUARY

20

Mind Food

Whatever is true, whatever is noble, whatever is right, whatever is pure, whatever is lovely, whatever is admirable— . . . think about such things. Philippians 4:8, NIV.

Years ago the kea bird of New Zealand was harmless and peaceful. It fed on fruit and seeds, just as most birds do.

But when people began to spread out over the country, the bird's diet began to change.

The early settlers were mainly sheep farmers, so mutton was a large part of their diet. When the farmers killed the sheep for meat, they kept the parts that were edible and threw away the rest.

For some reason the keas started helping themselves to the meat scraps. Soon they lost interest in fruit and seeds, and developed a strong craving for the fat around the sheep's kidneys.

The mild-mannered bird began to change. Instead of waiting for handouts at the slaughterhouse, the keas became impatient. They started following the sheep as they grazed in the pastures. And when they had a chance, they'd attack the defenseless animals, tearing open their sides in search of their favorite food.

The farmers had to protect their flocks from the murderous birds. So they began shooting every kea they saw. The once-gentle bird had turned into a dangerous enemy. Feeding on sheep entrails had completely changed the birds' nature.

Just as the kea's diet changed his nature, so the diet you feed your mind will change your nature.

We have two different natures—a Christlike nature and a sinful nature. And the choices we make determine which nature we are going to strengthen.

If you want to become more and more like Jesus, you can't afford to waste your time on books, TV programs, music, and videos that feed your sinful nature. For what you fill your mind with will affect everything you do.

If you are serious about following God, then you'll want to make sure that the things you see and hear will increase your love for Him.

What kind of input are you feeding your brain?

JANUARY

21

Never, Never, Never Give Up

Whatever you do, work at it with all your heart, as working for the Lord, not for men. Colossians 3:23, NIV.

"Success comes in cans; failure in can'ts."

A young man walked into the editor's office at a Kansas City newspaper. Clutched in his hand were a number of drawings he had made.

"What can I do for you?" asked the editor.

The young man held out his pictures. "I understand you're looking for someone to work in your art department. I'd like to apply for the job."

The editor reached out for the papers. Leaning back in his chair, he leafed through them. "Sorry, but I don't think you're what we're looking for," he said as he handed them back.

"But I'd really like a chance—"

"Listen, I'll be frank with you, son. You really don't have what it takes to be an artist. Do yourself a favor and get into some other line of work."

The young artist walked out of the office, but he didn't give up. He applied at business after business. But nobody wanted his work. Finally he found a job drawing publicity material for churches. He rented an old mouse-infested garage and set up an office where he turned out his sketches. Not one to give up, he continued to try to sell his artwork to different businesses. Eventually he began to make some sales.

When he was 19 the young man got a job drawing movie cartoons. After four years he went to Los Angeles to see if he could get a job as a filmmaker. He failed at that, too, so he went back to drawing cartoons.

Then in 1928, when he was 27 years old, the young man who wouldn't give up turned one of his garage office mice into a star. And now Mickey Mouse and his artist, Walt Disney, are known all over the world.

Do you have dreams for your future? Or have you given them up just because others have laughed and said you'll never make it?

Don't ever be afraid to dream big. And don't be afraid to fail. Go after your dreams, and never stop until you reach them.

JANUARY

22

God Is on Our Side

Cast all your anxiety on him because he cares for you. 1 Peter 5:7, NIV.

Romans 8:28 says "All things work together for good to them that love God." That's hard to believe when bad things happen to you—like getting an F in math, or having your best friend move away, or getting a flat tire on your bike.

But when Jesus is in control of our lives, He can make sure that everything which happens to us works out for our good.

Let me explain.

Suppose you came over to my house and I invited you to stay for supper. I probably would serve my favorite meal: Choplets and gravy, mashed potatoes, broccoli, and carrots.

But how would you feel if when dessert came I handed you a bowl of sugar, three raw eggs, flour, soda, salt, and vanilla extract? You'd probably say, "No, thanks" and pass them right back to me.

None of those ingredients is very appetizing by itself—not even the bowl of sugar. But if I mix all those things together, cut them into different shapes, and bake them for eight minutes at 375° F, they come out as Christmas cookies. And I'm sure you'd be happy to eat a few.

In the same way, Jesus can take the different things that happen to us and make them into something positive and helpful. He is aware of everything that goes on in your life. In fact, since He knows the future, when you run into a problem, He has already planned on how He can use it for your benefit.

Instead of grumbling and complaining when things don't go as we wish they would, we need to accept them. Then we need to ask God to help us see how we can benefit from what has happened.

I don't want you to get the wrong idea, though. I'm not saying that, for example, if your brother hits you every day that you should let him keep doing it. When others do not treat us well, we should do what we can to stop them. But at the same time, instead of feeling sorry for ourselves, we should trust that God will use the problem to work for us, instead of against us.

JANUARY

23

Blind Spots

You, therefore, have no excuse, you who pass judgment on someone else, for at whatever point you judge the other, you are condemning yourself, because you who pass judgment do the same things. Romans 2:1, NIV.

"Too many people study their neighbors' faults closer than they do their Bible."

I want you to try something today. You'll notice below that there's a + and a ●. Carefully follow the instructions below.

+ ●

1. Hold this book and stretch your arms out straight.
2. Shut your left eye.
3. With your right eye, look directly at the +.
4. Start pulling the book slowly toward your face.
5. Keep focused on the +, but notice what happens to the ●, which you'll be able to see out of the corner of your eye.

If you did it right, the ● will disappear for a split second. If it didn't work, try it again. And remember to focus on the +.

The ● disappears because you have what is called a "blind spot." As you brought the book closer to your face, the ● eventually moved into the blind spot and seemed to disappear. It was still there; you just couldn't see it.

Carol had a problem with blind spots. She was very good at spotting everyone else's character weaknesses, but she could not see her own. At school Carol spent the majority of her time watching the other students so she could make a full report to the teacher when they did something wrong.

"Mrs. Foster, Jimmy didn't finish his reading assignment like you told him to."

"Mrs. Foster, Leslie had her eyes open during prayer." (I wonder how Carol knew that.)

"Mrs. Foster, Rachel hit Jeremiah with a spit wad."

Finally, Mrs. Foster had to have a talk with Carol. She explained that finding fault with others hurts both the person doing the criticizing and the person being criticized.

"Carol, instead of worrying about what others are doing wrong, we need to look at our own lives and see just what weaknesses we have."

Do you have a problem with blind spots? Do you see everyone else's faults but not your own?

Why not ask God to help you see where you need to make changes in your life?

JANUARY

24

Don't Get Burned

Keep a close watch on all you do and think. Stay true to what is right and God will bless you and use you to help others.
1 Timothy 4:16, TLB.

Jess wandered down the sidewalk as he tried to find something to do. He was bored. Then he remembered the matches he carried in his back pocket. Hurrying over to a big pile of leaves by the curb, he pulled out the matches and sat down. He looked down the sidewalk to make sure no one would see him. Then he struck one of the matches and set the leaves on fire.

The dry leaves burst into flames. Soon only ashes remained. Jess looked around and wondered what else he could burn. Then he saw it—the neighbor's car parked just down the street.

I wonder what would happen if I . . .

Mr. Burris was the grumpiest man on the block. He always yelled at Jess and the other kids when they ran on his lawn. Jess didn't like him at all.

Picking up his matches, Jess strolled over to the shiny black car. He found the gas cap and quickly unscrewed it. After striking another match, he started to drop it down the gas tank, but the wind blew it out. He turned his back to the wind and struck another match. It burst into flame. Jess threw it down the gas tank. And that's the last thing he remembered.

An explosion rocked the quiet street. The car blew apart, sending pieces of metal flying through the air. When Jess awoke he found himself lying facedown on the neighbor's lawn. Blood covered his shirt, and his body ached all over. Someone called an ambulance.

Fortunately, Jess only had two broken bones and a few cuts. But the neighbor's car didn't fare so well. It was totally destroyed.

Curiosity can be good. But too many times it leads to danger. When Eve ate from the tree of knowledge of good and evil, her curiosity helped cause her downfall. She became curious about the tree. She wondered why God had told her and Adam to leave it alone. When Lucifer appeared as a beautiful serpent, she became curious about the talking snake. And finally she was curious about what it would be like to know both good and evil. She found out.

When you find yourself becoming curious about something, make sure that you're not putting yourself in danger. Use your curiosity only for good things.

JANUARY

25

Take Responsibility

The Lord is not slow in keeping his promise, as some understand slowness. He is patient with you, not wanting anyone to perish, but everyone to come to repentance.
2 Peter 3:9, NIV.

It seems that nobody wants to take responsibility for his or her actions anymore. We'd rather blame other people. Here are some examples.

Two cattle rustlers were in the process of stealing some cows from a farmer. One of the thieves fell over a plow and broke his leg. He sued the farmer, and the farmer had to pay *him* money.

For years Rose Cipaloni's family begged her to quit smoking, but she refused. Even when the doctors removed her cancerous lung, she kept on smoking. Eventually she died. Mr. Cipaloni went to court and sued the cigarette companies. He told the judge that when she started smoking, cigarette companies didn't print health warnings on cigarette packages like they do now. He felt that the cigarette companies were to blame for her death.

It's true that the companies were somewhat to blame. But Rose made the choice to start smoking in the first place. And Rose made the choice to continue smoking, even after she developed cancer.

Do you remember Jess from yesterday? After he recovered from his accident, his parents filed a lawsuit against Mr. Burris. They blamed him for the car explosion. And I know you're not going to believe this, but the judge ruled in Jess's favor. He said that Mr. Burris shouldn't have parked his car out on the street where Jess could have access to the gas tank. Poor Mr. Burris not only lost his new car, but he also ended up having to pay thousands of dollars to Jess's family.

In each of these cases people blamed others for their own actions. They didn't take responsibility for what they had done.

When God confronted Adam and Eve right after they ate the forbidden fruit, they didn't want to take responsibility either.

Adam said, "It's not my fault. That woman You gave me—she gave it to me."

Eve said, "It's not my fault. That serpent tricked me."

When we do something wrong, we need to admit it. That's especially true when it comes to sinning. If we won't admit that we have sinned, God can't forgive us. The sooner we take responsibility, the sooner we can feel the happiness that comes from knowing that we're forgiven.

JANUARY

26

Doing Your Part

The more lowly your service to others, the greater you are. To be the greatest, be a servant. Matthew 23:11, TLB.

The sun was just beginning to spread its rays across the ocean. Scott slipped on his sandals and reached for his beach towel.

"See you later, Mom," he called as he headed out the door.

Scott loved living near the ocean. If he had his way, he'd stay there for the rest of his life. Each morning before breakfast he searched the shore for starfish. Scott wasn't collecting the five-legged sea creatures for his own profit like some people did. Starfish were popular items with tourists. If he'd wanted to, he could sell them to one of the many shell stores in town. But Scott looked for starfish every morning so he could save them. Sometimes the tide brought them up on the beach and left them stranded. If they stayed on the hot sand too long, they'd die. So Scott took it upon himself to be a committee of one to save as many starfish as he could.

That morning Scott met an older gentleman who was out early looking for shells.

"Hi, there," called the man. "How's the shelling this morning?"

"There are some nice ones just down the beach a ways," said Scott.

"Are you a collector?"

Scott reached over and picked up a small starfish that was sitting next to a pop can. "No, I come down here every morning before breakfast to look for starfish. I find the ones that have washed up on shore and throw them back into the water."

"You do that every day?"

"I try to."

The man shook his head. "Boy, that seems like a lot of work. Don't you ever get discouraged? I mean, what good does it do when there are probably thousands of them washed ashore along these miles and miles of beach? What difference does it make to save one here and there?"

Scott pulled back his pitching arm and heaved the little starfish back into the ocean. "Well, it made a difference to that one," he said.

Like Scott, we can't do everything that needs to be done. But we can do something. Even when we help just one person, we've made that life just a little bit better. We've made a difference.

JANUARY

27

Growing With God

So neither he who plants nor he who waters is anything, but only God, who makes things grow.
1 Corinthians 3:7, NIV.

As Paul walked toward the basketball court, the tallest of the players saw him coming. "Hey, shrimp, go play with someone your own size."

"Yeah," said another player, "go see if you can find some other pygmies to play with."

As Paul slinked back toward his house, he could hear the boys laughing at him. He hated being short. "Will I ever grow up?" he muttered to himself. His dad had assured him that he'd eventually be as tall as the other fellows. But Paul was sure he'd always be five feet tall.

Do you ever daydream about how great it would be if you could just hurry the growing-up process?

When James Garfield was president of a college in Ohio, the parents of one of his students came to his office with a request. "Our son is very bright," they said. "Isn't there some way that his education can be speeded up? There's no reason for him to waste his time taking the same courses as the other students."

Mr. Garfield, who later became the president of the United States, replied, "Certainly we can speed him through. But it depends upon what you want for your boy. When God wants to make an oak tree, He takes 100 years. But He requires only 60 days to make a squash."

Most young people are eager to grow up. Some are so impatient that they don't take the time to be themselves. You can usually spot the impatient ones by their actions and their dress. The girls will go overboard with makeup and hairstyles. They'll wear clothes meant for adults. The boys, on the other hand, will do things to prove they aren't kids any longer. They'll use bad language, smoke cigarettes, and even start drinking alcohol. They'll do daredevil stunts on their bikes or skateboards.

If you think it's taking a long time for you to grow up, consider what some insects have to go through. As soon as cicadas hatch out of their eggs, they dig down deep into the ground and give themselves some more time to grow up. God has put a special clock in their bodies, and they must wait 17 years before they're ready to emerge as adults.

Don't worry if you're not as tall as the other kids in your class. Don't worry if you're not as coordinated, as smart, or as sophisticated. Just be yourself. Give God time to help you develop according to His own time and way.

JANUARY

28

I Know Where I'm Going

For the living know that they will die, but the dead know nothing; they have no further reward, and even the memory of them is forgotten. Ecclesiastes 9:5, NIV.

An accident on Cleveland Avenue claimed the life of a 5-year-old girl. Kelly Coon, the daughter of Mr. and Mrs. Donald Coon, was fatally injured when she ran across the road into the path of an oncoming car driven by Fred Elgin of Berrien Center."

My sister Karen and I were riding home from school when we heard about Kelly, my best friend's little sister. A few days later Mother took Karen and me to Kelly's funeral. I remember the song a lady sang, and I remember seeing the man who had hit Kelly with his car. The man was crying so hard that two friends had to help him walk into the church.

We usually don't think much about death. It's a subject people would rather avoid. But it's important to know what happens when we die.

People hold many different ideas about where we go when we die. Some think the dead go right to heaven or hell. Others believe there's an in-between place called purgatory, where the dead have to suffer before they can go on to heaven. A few religions believe that we just live on as another person or maybe even an animal. Still others believe that there's no life beyond the grave. Once we die, it's all over.

But the Bible tells us different. Death is like a sleep. In Matthew 9:24, Jesus described the ruler's daughter as asleep, even though she was no longer alive.

I like the way God handles death. Instead of taking people to heaven when they die, He lets them rest in the ground. Instead of having them wait in heaven for their loved ones, He lets them pass the time without knowing what is going on.

Kent had to have some surgery on his leg. After the nurses wheeled him into the operating room, one of the doctors gave him some medicine that put him to sleep.

Kent closed his eyes for just a second. Then he opened them again. "When will the operation be over?" he asked.

A nurse patted his hand and said, "It's been over for almost an hour, Kent."

That's just how it'll be when Jesus comes. Those who have died will wake up, not even aware that they have been in the grave. When you think of death that way, it's not so scary.

JANUARY

29

Flashing Lights and a Pounding Heart

Blessed is he whose transgressions are forgiven, whose sins are covered. Psalm 32:1, NIV.

Steve loved his driver's ed class. He read his manual every night and studied extra hard for his tests. At the end of the class he received his permit. A few months later, on his sixteenth birthday, he got his driver's license.

"Now, remember to drive carefully," advised Mr. Nolan as he handed the car keys to Steve.

"I always do, Dad."

"But you've always driven with Mom or me. Now you're on your own."

"Just trust me, Dad."

Steve pushed the garage door opener and slid into the front seat. He grabbed the steering wheel and just sat there, enjoying the taste of freedom.

Turning the key, he started the engine and guided the car out onto the road. He flicked on the radio and tried to look confident and casual, although his heart was really hammering in his chest.

After stopping at the end of the road, Steve made a right turn and headed for town. He tapped his foot, enjoying the happy beat of the music. As he passed the Dairy Queen, he saw two girls from his class at school.

I hope they noticed me, he thought.

The girls didn't, but someone else did. Someone who drove a radar-equipped car with a siren.

Steve's heart dropped to the floor when he saw the flashing lights in his rearview mirror.

"Oh, no," he said as he pulled over.

The officer walked up to Steve and asked for his license and the car registration.

"So today's your birthday," said the policeman. "I take it that you just got your license, am I right?"

Steve nodded his head.

"Did you notice the sign back there that said 25 miles an hour?"

"No, sir, I didn't," Steve admitted.

"Well, you were driving 35. You should get a ticket for being that much over the speed limit, but I'm going to give you only a warning, son."

Steve looked up at the officer and smiled. "I'll sure do my best. And thanks for giving me another chance."

Something to think about: Do you think the policeman made a wise choice when he decided not to give Steve a ticket? Do you think Steve drove more carefully after that? What spiritual lessons could you draw from Steve's experience?

JANUARY

30

Free to Obey

I will praise you, O Lord my God, with all my heart; I will glorify your name forever. For great is your love toward me; you have delivered me from the depths of the grave. Psalm 86:12, 13, NIV.

As Steve drove home after his encounter with the policeman, you can be sure that he didn't see how many stop signs he could run through or how fast his car would go. Being pardoned by the officer didn't mean he had permission to go out and break the law again. In fact, Steve was so appreciative that the policeman had forgiven him that he did his best to drive carefully.

Steve's story has a spiritual lesson in it. And it has to do with keeping God's law. When we do break the commandments, all we have to do is ask God to forgive us. And as long as we are truly sorry for what we have done, He'll remove our sins from our record. But does that give us the right to turn around and sin all over again?

In class one day we were talking about temptation and sin. I asked my students what they do when they're tempted to do something wrong.

"Well, I just go ahead and do it," said one boy. "God has forgiven me before. He'll forgive again. In fact, I sometimes ask God for forgiveness as I'm getting ready to sin."

This student had a wrong attitude about forgiveness. When we're really sorry about what we have done, we won't be eager to do it all over again. We'll be so appreciative of God's pardon that we won't want to let Him down. We'll want to do what's right. We'll want to obey God's law because we've learned from experience that it's the only way to freedom and happiness.

Our salvation is not determined by our actions. Salvation is a free gift that Jesus offers to each of us. We can never be good enough to earn it. What really matters is whether or not we have given Him control of our lives.

The more we get to know Jesus, the less we'll want to sin. We'll find out that obeying God's law is much more enjoyable than breaking it.

JANUARY

31

Hidden No Longer

And the peace of God, which transcends all understanding, will guard your hearts and your minds in Christ Jesus. Philippians 4:7, NIV.

Ricky Rodriguez and his four friends climbed over the fence and raced toward the abandoned grain silo. "Last one there's a rotten egg!"

The boys knew they weren't supposed to trespass. They knew that the fence meant *keep out!* But they wanted to have some fun. And besides, the silo had been shut down for more than 10 years. They wouldn't hurt anything.

Someone found a way to break in, and the boys climbed 15 flights of stairs to get to the top.

"Hey, this is great!" they yelled as they jumped on the conveyor belts that stretched across the silo.

One of the boys took a stone from his pocket and tossed it over the edge. The boys heard a faint chink after it fell 120 feet and finally hit the floor.

"Boy, that's a long way down," someone said.

"So, are you chicken?" laughed Ricky.

"Nah, are you?"

The boys got up and started chasing each other. Then they heard Ricky scream.

"Ricky, where are you?" one of the boys called.

No one answered.

With dread in their hearts, the boys ran down the stairs to the bottom. There they found Ricky. Dead.

"Ricky's dead, and we're going to get blamed for it," someone said.

The boys ran out of the silo and headed for home. They promised to tell no one of Ricky's accident.

For five months the boys kept their dark secret. They lived in terror that the police would find out what had happened and blame them. At night they had a hard time sleeping. And when they did fall asleep, they often had nightmares.

Finally the truth came out.

The boys' parents took them to the police station. After the boys told their story, the police assured them that no one blamed them for what had happened.

If only the boys had gone to their parents right after the accident, they could have saved themselves five months of misery.

Do you ever carry troubling thoughts in your mind? If something is worrying you, don't keep it to yourself. Talk it over with your parents, a teacher, a pastor, or a counselor.

Once you get the problem out in the open you'll feel a lot better. And you'll be taking the first step toward solving your problem.

FEBRUARY

1

Working Hand in Hand

Each one should use whatever gift he has received to serve others, faithfully administering God's grace in its various forms. 1 Peter 4:10, NIV.

"Help!" screamed Sir Edmund Hillary.

Tenzing, the mountain guide, instantly dug his ice ax into the ice and grabbed hold of the rope, Hillary's only lifeline.

Hillary disappeared from sight as he plunged into a hidden crevasse. But because of Tenzing's quick action, Hillary slid only 15 feet before the rope stopped his fall. Completely helpless, the mountain climber waited while his guide slowly pulled him back to the surface and to safety.

That night around the campfire, Hillary told the other climbers how Tenzing had saved his life. But the Sherpa guide refused to take any credit. "Mountain climbers always help each other," he replied modestly.

Edmund Hillary and Tenzing Norgay continued to climb together. In May of 1953, they became the first men to conquer Mount Everest. As they planted the flag at the summit, they realized they couldn't have reached their goal without working together. Hillary knew how to climb giant mountains, but Tenzing knew Mount Everest. He knew the peaks and the crevasses. He knew the best places to climb and the best sites to pitch camp. By working together, they accomplished what many considered to be impossible.

Cooperation always makes things go smoother. Cooperation helps businesses succeed. Cooperation builds family togetherness. Cooperation improves students' attitudes and grades.

A few summers ago workers in Berrien Springs, Michigan, finished building the town's new library. It was time for them to move in. But if you've ever had to move from one house to another, you know that moving isn't easy. You have to pack up everything, load it onto a truck, take it off the truck, unpack, and put everything into the new house.

Just think how long it would take to pack, load, and unpack thousands of books.

But the townspeople came up with a clever idea. They joined together and formed one long line from the old building to the new one. Then they passed the books from person to person until they ended up on the shelves of the new library.

Each of us has special abilities. Instead of doing our own thing, we need to work together to improve our homes, schools, and churches. Be willing to do your part.

FEBRUARY

2

Promises to Keep

It is better not to vow than to make a vow and not fulfill it. Ecclesiastes 5:5, NIV.

The year was 1633. The little town of Oberammergau in Germany heard the awful rumor: a plague was spreading across Europe and heading their way. The plague, now known as the bubonic plague, had killed nearly 150,000 people in London alone.

The townspeople of Oberammergau turned to God, pleading with Him to protect them. And God spared them. To show their thanks, they made a vow to the Lord. And to this day they have kept their promise.

Every 10 years the residents of Oberammergau present the Passion Play, a six-hour play that portrays the suffering of Jesus during the last few days before His death. The play runs for four months and requires 1,200 performers (nearly a fourth of the town's population).

My husband, Tom, and I visited Oberammergau in 1978. We were there during an off year, but we did have an opportunity to go behind the scenes and see the outfits that the actors wear and many of the props, including the cross.

The residents of Oberammergau made a promise to God, and they along with their descendants have kept that promise for more than 350 years. Thousands have been blessed because of their faithfulness.

When you make a promise, do you always follow through? Can your family and friends depend on you to keep your word? More important, can God depend on you?

It's easy to make big promises to God when you're in a tough situation. Maybe you once promised to give your life to Him if He'd help you get the new bike you always wanted, or get you out of trouble, or bring your family back together.

But too often we forget our promises once we receive what we want.

Promises are important to God. And promises made by young people are just as serious as those made by adults. Before you make a promise to God, think it through carefully. Don't make any promises that you cannot keep.

FEBRUARY

3

Are You a Gifted Person?

The Lord your God will bless you in all your work and in everything you put your hand to. Deuteronomy 15:10, NIV.

"Use the talents you possess, for the woods would be very silent if no birds sang except the best."

Have you ever heard of Leslie Lemke? Leslie is a gifted pianist who travels around the world giving concerts. A few years ago I heard Leslie play at the Michigan camp meeting. The gymnasium was packed. People stood in the aisles. Everyone wanted to get a glimpse of the famous young musician.

After Leslie played a number of selections, his sister Mary threw out a challenge. "Leslie has the ability to listen to a song once and then play it back from memory. Is there anyone out there who would like to play a song for Leslie to copy?"

Ken, an accomplished pianist from one of the academies, came forward. He sat down at the grand piano and began a difficult composition by Brahms. His fingers flew up and down the piano keys. Leslie just sat nearby listening intently.

When Ken finished, Leslie returned to the piano. Placing his fingers over the keys, he started playing the Brahms composition note for note. He even included the mistakes that Ken had accidentally made!

Leslie's ability to reproduce music is impressive. But when you realize that Leslie is blind, crippled, and mentally retarded, his accomplishments seem unbelievable.

Leslie has the mental ability of a baby, and he can't even carry on a conversation. But God has given him a special gift that he can share with others.

God gives each of us talents and abilities. Some have many; some have a few.

Can you identify which special gifts God has given to you? Has He given you the ability to

play a musical instrument?
excel in sports?
work hard?
do well in school?
care for small children?
get along with other people?
write stories?
cook?

If you aren't sure about your abilities, ask your parents or teacher. Maybe they can give you some insight into your special gifts.

Whatever your talents may be, don't hide them. Develop them to the best of your ability. And then use them to bless the lives of the people around you.

FEBRUARY

4

Curiosity Kills the Cat

No temptation has seized you except what is common to man. And God is faithful; he will not let you be tempted beyond what you can bear.
1 Corinthians 10:13, NIV.

One summer Tom and I stopped at a local shopping mall to buy a wedding gift for a friend. We noticed a large crowd of children seated around a center stage. They seemed to be enjoying some type of show.

We walked over just in time to see a handsome man with pure white hair shake hands with a 10-year-old boy. The man walked away, but the boy's hand continued to move up and down. The children all laughed.

The man turned back to the boy, shook hands with him again, and said, "Thanks for being such a good sport, Kevin. Let's give him a hand, everybody."

The audience applauded, and the boy turned to walk off the stage. But his feet remained glued to the floor.

"I—I can't move," he said. Fear spread across his face as he tried again to leave the stage.

Tom and I looked at each other and back at the white-haired man. We realized that the man had taken control of the boy by hypnotizing him. Something told us that we were in the devil's territory. We knew we should leave. Yet at the same time our curiosity almost glued our feet to the floor. We felt almost as trapped as the hypnotized boy. It was all we could do to walk away—we actually felt a power drawing us closer to the stage. But we pulled ourselves away and hurried off in the opposite direction.

Satan uses the attractions of the world to get our attention. And we find ourselves thinking, *I wonder what it would be like to . . .*

Most young people don't fall into the devil's traps because they want to be bad. They just become too curious about the things they've been warned against. They want to find out for themselves what life outside the church is like. Unfortunately, by the time Satan has them in his trap, he has no intention of letting them go.

Play it safe. Don't let curiosity kill your chances for a happy life.

FEBRUARY

5

Service With a Smile

A kindhearted woman gains respect. . . . A kind man benefits himself. Proverbs 11:16, 17, NIV.

When Agnes Bojaxhiu was 18 years old, she decided to become a missionary. Her first job took her to Calcutta, India. There she taught geography to girls from wealthy homes.

But 15 years later God impressed her to leave her comfortable surroundings and live among the poor. So Agnes, whom we now know as Mother Teresa, began her work in the slums of Calcutta.

* * * *

Around the corner from the temple of the Indian god Kala stood the long, low building that Stephen Kovalski had been searching for. "Home for Dying Destitutes," the wooden sign read.

Stephen had come to India to help the poor. But before he started a care center for the people in his district, he wanted to see how other facilities were set up. And what better place to visit, than one of Mother Teresa's refuges?

He walked into the building and tried to adjust to the strange smell that hung in the air. The dimly lit room was filled with rows and rows of thin mattresses. On the beds lay 110 dying Indians.

Stephen's eyes searched over the lines of patients until he spotted Mother Teresa. She was kneeling next to a young man who appeared to be close to death. The skin on his wasted body stretched tightly, outlining the protruding bones beneath. Mother Teresa talked to him softly as she gently bathed his wounds. The expression on his face was one of peace and security.

As soon as Mother Teresa sensed Father Kovalski's presence, she spoke a few more words to her patient and then stood up. After greeting Stephen, she gazed over the room at her dying charges. "What they give us is so much more than we can ever give back to them," she said simply.

The kind of love that she has for the poorest of the poor is a love that only God can give.

Is it any wonder that Mother Teresa is one of the most loved and respected women in the world?

As you go through your day, look for ways to give your love to others, especially to those who are not easy to love.

Something to think about: How could Mother Teresa find great happiness in such depressing surroundings?

FEBRUARY

6

United We Stand

Be completely humble and gentle; be patient, bearing with one another in love. Make every effort to keep the unity of the Spirit through the bond of peace. Ephesians 4:2, 3, NIV.

He is the happiest, be he king or peasant, who finds peace in his home."—Goethe.

One Sabbath I invited Cara and Doreen over for an afternoon of music. Cara played the piano while Doreen and I played flute and cello.

After tuning up, we looked through our music books for something to play. "How about page 30?" I asked.

Cara played the introduction, and Doreen and I joined in. After we'd played for just two lines, I put down my cello bow. "Hold it, hold it," I said. "That didn't sound too good. Let's try it again from the top."

So we started over. The second time was no better than the first. This time Doreen called us to a halt. "For some reason that doesn't sound like Bach."

"Wait a minute," I said. "Doreen, are you sure you're playing both sharps?"

"Sharps? What sharps?"

"What do you mean, 'What sharps?' The song is in the key of D."

"No, it's not," retorted Doreen. "It's in C. My music—wait a minute. What page are you on?"

"Thirty."

Doreen started giggling.

"I'm on page 13. No wonder we sounded so disgusting."

After we had a good laugh, Doreen found page 30, and we tried again. That time the song sounded like Bach.

Just as a group of musicians must play together in harmony, so a family must work together in unity if it is to be successful.

Are you a team member, or do you insist on doing your own thing: playing your music so loudly that your brothers and sisters can't study, making extra work for your mom because you don't pick up after yourself, borrowing your dad's tools without permission?

Don't look around at the other family members to see how they could improve. Take it upon yourself to find ways that you can make life more enjoyable for the others who share your home.

FEBRUARY

7

The Big-Mouth Frog

For whoever exalts himself will be humbled, and whoever humbles himself will be exalted. Matthew 23:12, NIV.

"There is no limit to the good a man can do if he doesn't care who gets the credit."

Once upon a time there was a frog. Frog lived in a mucky little swamp, but life was very boring. So Frog decided to leave his swamp and see the world.

After jumping out of the swamp, Frog started down the dusty little country road. Day after day he hopped along, until he arrived at a beautiful blue lake.

How will I ever get across the water? he thought. *This is much bigger than my little swamp.*

Just then two geese went honking by.

"Hey, geese," yelled the frog. "Come down here. I want to talk to you."

The geese circled around, then dropped down into the water.

"What do you want, Frog?"

"I need your help. I'm on a trip to see the world, but I can't get across the lake. Will you help me?"

"It all depends," said the other goose. "What must we do?"

Frog pointed to a long, thin stick. "All you have to do is fly this stick across the lake. I'll hold on to the middle and ride across with you."

So each of the birds took an end of the stick in its beak. The frog stood between them and grabbed the stick with his rubbery, green mouth.

As the birds and their passenger traveled across the lake, two people in a sailboat watched them go by. "Why, look at that," said the lady to her husband. "Those two geese are carrying a frog across the lake. What clever birds!"

Frog, hearing the lady's comment, puffed up with pride and called out, "This was *my* idea." But as soon as he opened his mouth, he slipped off the stick and into the water. End of trip.

Do you insist on getting credit for all the things you do at home or at school? Or do you find contentment in being able to help others? When we brag about what we do, we always end up the big loser. Just ask Frog.

FEBRUARY

8

Counter-feits

Guide me in your truth and teach me, for you are God my Savior. Psalm 25:5, NIV.

While I was looking through a box of watchbands at a flea market, I overheard the owner of the booth trying to make a sale to another customer.

"Now, this Rolex band isn't new. But it's in good shape, and I'm asking only $125 for it." The seller reached into a paper envelope and brought out a thick silver watchband.

I didn't know much about Rolex watches, but I knew that they are among the most expensive watches a person can buy. I moved in closer so I could see what a $125 watchband looked like.

"Let me check it over," the buyer said as he reached across the showcase. He frowned as he studied the metal band. "I think you got taken. This is a fake."

"Why, it can't be!" protested the seller. "I bought it from a watch dealer in Detroit."

The man next to me pulled back his shirtsleeve to uncover the Rolex on his wrist.

"Look at the insignia on my band. Now look at the one on yours. They aren't the same. I'm afraid that someone sold you a counterfeit."

Rolex watchbands aren't the only things that dishonest people try to counterfeit. There are fake antiques, coins, works of art, and designer clothes. Unless you know the genuine, you can be tricked easily.

From the beginning of time Satan has used counterfeits to draw people away from God. He offers the world cheap imitations of the blessings that God has provided:

God gave us the Sabbath. Satan says, "Worship on Sunday in honor of the Resurrection."

God gave us marriage. Satan says, "Who needs a marriage license? Go ahead and live together."

God gave us the Ten Commandments to guard our happiness. Satan says, "The commandments were done away with. Don't be such a legalist."

Bank employees become expert at identifying counterfeit money. They study the genuine so closely that they are able to spot the counterfeit bills. By knowing the true, they can easily detect the false.

Don't settle for Satan's cheap imitations. Study God's Word so you'll know the truth.

FEBRUARY

9

The Salt of the Earth

You are the salt of the earth. Matthew 5:13, NIV.

One afternoon I got in a baking mood and decided to make some chocolate chip oatmeal cookies. In fact, I was in such a strong baking mood that I doubled the recipe.

After the cookies had cooled, I took a plateful to Tom, who was sitting in the living room correcting algebra assignments.

"Is this a new recipe?" he asked after his first bite.

"No, it's the same one I always make."

"Well, there's something wrong. This cookie tastes pretty bad."

I tried one. "Oooooh, you're right. They're terrible," I said. "They taste like dry glue."

I ran the recipe through my mind.

Shortening, sugar, salt—oops! So *that* was what I'd done. I'd forgotten to put in the salt. But it didn't seem that a half teaspoon of salt would make that much difference. After all, a half teaspoon is insignificant when compared to the other ingredients: a cup of shortening, a cup of sugar, a teaspoon of vanilla, three cups of rolled oats, a cup of walnuts, two cups of flour, and a bag of chocolate chips. But that tiny bit of salt made all the difference in the world.

The next day during lunch I asked my students if anyone would like some chocolate chip cookies. All the students grabbed a handful and returned to their desks.

I didn't say anything. I just watched.

All reacted the same way. First they took a bite. Then they chewed. Next they got a strange look on their faces.

"Well, how do you like them?" I asked.

"They're, uh . . . What kind of cookies did you say these were?" asked Anita.

I finally told them I had left out the salt. We had a good laugh over the cookies. And I think we learned a lesson that afternoon.

We're all like that salt. We may feel pretty unimportant at times, but the part we play is essential. There are certain people whom only you can help. Maybe you're the only Christian these people will ever come in contact with.

Don't wait until you're grown up to find ways you can serve the Lord. You're an important part of God's church right now.

Something to think about: Can you name at least two people whom you could help today?

FEBRUARY

10

What Traps Do You Fall For?

As fish are caught in a cruel net, or birds are taken in a snare, so men are trapped by evil times that fall unexpectedly upon them. Ecclesiastes 9:12, NIV.

I've got a problem, and I need your help." Mr. Stevens, the junior leader, set down a box on the piano bench. "This week my wife discovered that a whole family of flies has invaded our house. And she gave me the job of getting rid of them.

"I've brought along a large collection of traps," he continued, "and I need you to help me decide which one to use."

Reaching into the box, Mr. Stevens brought out a mole trap. "What do you think about this one?"

The class laughed as they imagined Mr. Stevens trying to catch flies with the heavy metal trap he held in his hands.

"I think it's a little too big for the job," Kevin spoke up.

"Hmmm. I think you may be right," Mr. Stevens said as he replaced the mole trap. "I think we need something a little smaller." He reached into the box again and pulled out a mousetrap. "How about this?"

"That's smaller, but it still won't work," said Beth.

Mr. Stevens scratched his head. "Boy, this is harder than I thought. Well, why don't I just show you the rest of my traps and let you decide which one I should use?" With that, he poured out the contents of his box: a beaver trap, a fishing lure, an ant trap, and some flypaper.

"Flypaper!" everyone called out. "Use the flypaper."

"What a great idea," said Mr. Stevens.

Picking up the small cylinder, Mr. Stevens lifted off the top and pulled out the sticky, coiled paper inside.

"You can't use just any trap to catch an animal or an insect. You have to choose a trap that is specially designed for each one. And that's exactly what Satan does when he tries to trap us.

"He knows our weaknesses, so he knows which traps to use on us. He traps some of us with lying or cheating. Others he catches with things like harmful TV shows, jealousy, or disrespect to parents. We need to make sure that we stay close to Jesus so we don't fall for the devil's traps."

As you go through your day, be on the lookout for Satan's traps. Don't let him take you by surprise.

FEBRUARY

11

Avoiding the Traps

Free me from the trap that is set for me, for you are my refuge. Psalm 31:4, NIV.

Yesterday we talked about how Satan uses special traps to catch each of us. Today we want to look at some of the things you can do to avoid falling into his traps.

The most important step you can take is to place yourself on God's side every day. Start your morning with prayer, giving your life to God for the next 24 hours. Don't be like people who pray only when they're in the middle of a temptation. It's usually too late by then. Prayer is not a magical charm that helps get you out of tight spots. It's a way of getting to know God better so that when you are tempted your love for Him will help you choose to do what's right.

Second, ask God to give you the power to say no to temptation. Only with God's help can you avoid the traps that Satan puts in your way.

Third, take notice of the different temptations that Satan uses on you. After watching you since the day you were born, he has a pretty good idea how he can get you to sin. He knows not only which traps to use, but also what "bait" to lure you with. Do what you can to avoid getting into situations that make it easy for you to sin.

Fourth, take good care of yourself. Make sure that you eat balanced meals, take time for exercise, and get a good night's sleep. When you feel good, you'll have an easier time saying no when temptation comes your way.

Finally, be careful with the information that you're feeding into your brain. Are the programs you see on TV strengthening your character? Are the magazines and books that you read helping you become a better person? Do the videos you watch portray Christian values?

As long as you live, Satan will continue to set out traps for you. But when your life is in God's hands, you won't get caught.

Something to think about: Which of the suggestions above would you like Jesus to give you extra help with?

FEBRUARY

12

The Paintings No One Wanted

For we are God's workmanship, created in Christ Jesus to do good works, which God prepared in advance for us to do. Ephesians 2:10, NIV.

Vincent wanted to be a painter more than anything else. He tried other lines of work, but he always returned to painting. Unfortunately, no one liked his artwork. In fact, most people made fun of it.

Vincent's brother, an art dealer, tried to promote Vincent's paintings by displaying them in his art gallery. But Vincent's works were ignored by wealthy art collectors, who preferred to purchase paintings done by other, more famous artists.

Vincent wasn't discouraged, though. During the last five years of his life he painted more than 800 pictures. But it seemed nobody wanted them.

Day after day Vincent stopped by the art gallery, hoping that someone had bought one of his paintings. But Theo could only shake his head.

Vincent took the continual rejection personally. He became deeply depressed and ended up in a mental hospital. The doctors tried to help him, but in the end he took his own life.

It's too bad Vincent isn't alive today to see how different things turned out. Few know all the names of the artists who were popular in Theo's gallery. But most of the world now knows the name of Vincent Van Gogh.

In Amsterdam, Holland, the Dutch people erected an art museum in his honor. And in 1987 Vincent's painting entitled *Irises* broke all records when it was sold for $53.9 million, the highest price ever paid for a single painting. Not bad for a man who sold only one painting during his entire lifetime.

Van Gogh's story illustrates the fact that people are often poor judges of value. What we consider of little worth one moment is considered almost priceless the next.

Don't let people's opinions of you shape your feelings of self-worth. Instead of measuring your value on a human scale, look to Jesus and recognize how valuable you are in His sight.

FEBRUARY

13

Roots

During spring vacation, Tom and I went to Washington, D.C., for a few days of sightseeing. After visiting the FBI Building, Ford's Theater, and the Washington Monument, we headed for the museums of the Smithsonian Institution.

At the Museum of Natural History we walked through an exhibit on the evolution of man. I was curious to see what kind of evidence scientists had collected to base their beliefs on.

Tom and I followed the dimly lit display, studying the skulls of the various prehistoric people and reading about what life was supposed to have been like hundreds of thousands of years ago. The more I read, the more depressed I became. *Why am I feeling like this?* I wondered.

Just as we turned the corner to the archaeology demonstration, I knew the answer. I had never studied evolution before. I had always believed that we were created in God's image. Seeing this explanation on how life began made me feel insecure.

This is ridiculous, I said to myself. *I know exactly where humans came from. And I know how special we are.* Suddenly the dark feelings vanished, and I felt a warm sense of peace and confidence.

Many evolutionists describe life as an accident. How contrary that idea is to the Bible's explanation of how life began. We came about because of a deliberate plan, not as the result of an accident or explosion. The Bible clearly reveals everything we need to know about how things began—and even more important, how they will end.

How fortunate we are to be able to learn the biblical truth about ourselves. How blessed we are to have God as our Creator, Saviour, and Friend!

Then God said, "Let us make man in our image, in our likeness." Genesis 1:26, NIV.

FEBRUARY

14

The Greatest Gift

Greater love has no one than this, that he lay down his life for his friends. John 15:13, NIV.

Screaming bombers roared over the peaceful Vietnamese town, blasting the little village below. When the smoke had settled, the local orphanage lay in ruins. A doctor and nurse who were sent to the scene by the U.S. Navy quickly checked the wounded to determine who needed attention first. The most critically injured included an 8-year-old girl.

The nurse did a quick blood test and found that neither she nor the doctor could give blood to the child. Turning to the uninjured orphans, the nurse tried to explain that the little girl needed some blood. "If she doesn't get some soon, she'll die. Would any of you be willing to share your blood with her?"

The children looked at each other. Finally a small boy slowly lifted his hand.

"Oh, thank you," said the nurse. "What is your name?"

"Heng."

After checking the boy's blood type, the doctor picked him up and laid him on a blanket. The nurse swabbed his arm with alcohol and carefully inserted the needle into his vein.

Suddenly the little boy let out a sob. The doctor rushed to his side. "Does it hurt, Heng?"

The boy shook his head no and tried to cover his face with his free arm. The sobs grew into steady, silent crying.

Again the doctor asked Heng if he was in pain. But the boy just shook his head and continued to cry.

Soon a Vietnamese nurse arrived. Seeing the little boy's distress, she spoke to him in Vietnamese and listened to his reply. As they talked, the boy slowly relaxed. The nurse patted his arm and turned to the Americans. "He thought he was going to die. He misunderstood. He thought you were going to take all his blood and give it to the little girl."

"And he was willing to die for her? Why would he do that?" asked the Navy nurse.

The Vietnamese nurse turned to Heng and repeated the question. His answer was short and simple. "She's my friend."

Today on Valentine's Day, think of some way that you can show love to someone else.

FEBRUARY

15

Puppy Love

Each of you should look not only to your own interests, but also to the interests of others. Philippians 2:4, NIV.

Love is not a gift given only to humans. Many animals are capable of showing affection not only to people but also to each other.

Some years ago a hound dog by the name of Tennessee fell into a large rock crevice. Her mate, Pete, was the only one who knew where she was.

Unable to get either food or water, Tennessee was doomed to a lonely, painful death. But Pete saved her life. Each evening when Pete was fed, he ate only a small portion of his food. He saved most of it and took it to where Tennessee was trapped in the rocks. Carefully he dropped his supper down to his friend. Pete carried food to Tennessee for 10 days before a search party discovered where she was and rescued her.

Another story of animal devotion comes from London, England.

During World War II, Adolf Hitler, intent on controlling Europe, sent his Nazi bombers into London. Whenever German planes came near the city, sirens screamed to warn the British to take cover.

Darby and Joan, two Belgian shepherds, came to fear the sirens as much as the people of London did. Each time the sirens sounded, Joan would run to her sleeping box. Darby, following close behind, would throw himself over Joan and protect her until the air raid was over.

One day the Nazis dropped a bomb directly over the part of the city where the two dogs lived. When rescuers made their way through the burned homes, they came upon Darby, who had been killed in the blast.

"Look here," shouted one of the rescuers. "There's something moving under this dog."

Sure enough, as the men watched, Joan crawled out from under Darby's body. Darby had sacrificed his life to protect his best friend.

Even in the animal kingdom God has given us reminders of how we should treat each other. Why not look for ways you can show kindness to the people you meet today.

FEBRUARY

16

Lending a Helping Hand

You, my brothers, were called to be free. But do not use your freedom to indulge the sinful nature; rather, serve one another in love.
Galatians 5:13, NIV.

"Serving others is the ultimate way to achieve joy and fulfillment for Christians."—Anthony Campolo.

While we were touring Europe some years ago, Tom and I had the opportunity to visit many beautiful churches. Coventry Cathedral in Coventry, England, was our favorite.

During World War II, German bombs destroyed 85 percent of the town's 600-year-old church. After the war, the people of the town decided to rebuild their cathedral.

The man chosen to design the building was an English pilot who had taken part in the bombing of Germany. He felt so bad about the damage he had done during the war that he wanted to make up for it by building a church.

People from all over the world donated time, money, and objects to be used in the construction. The German Evangelical churches sent over stained glass windows for one of the chapels. The baptistry was hewn out of a boulder that was taken from a valley near Bethlehem.

Coventry Cathedral is an example of what can happen when people reach out to help others.

John Wesley, founder of the Methodist Church, had the following saying as his rule for life:

"Do all the good you can,
By all the means you can,
In all the ways you can,
In all the places you can,
At all the times you can,
To all the people you can,
As long as ever you can."

We can't keep bad things from happening to others. But we can follow Jesus' example and stand by them in their time of need.

FEBRUARY

17

Too Late to Be Sorry

How can a young man keep his way pure? By living according to your word. Psalm 119:9, NIV.

At one time billions of passenger pigeons flew across North America. But not one is alive today. What happened?

More than 180 years ago, in 1810, Alexander Wilson, an ornithologist, saw something he could hardly believe. It was a flock of passenger pigeons. Not just your normal flock of birds, but a group that he estimated to be 240 miles long. If his calculations were correct, that one flock contained more than 2 billion birds. Three years later John James Audubon, the naturalist, reported seeing a flock so thick that it actually darkened the light from the sun. And as the birds flew by, their beating wings sounded like thunder.

Since the pigeons were so plentiful, they soon became a popular target for hunters. Some people killed the birds for food. Others shot them for profit, sending the bodies to large cities and selling them for a penny or two. Many farmers fed them to their hogs.

By 1908, only seven passenger pigeons remained in the whole world. People began to realize that something had to be done. A $2,000 reward was offered to anyone who could find a passenger pigeon nest in the wild. But all the efforts to increase the bird population failed.

Finally, on September 1, 1914, Martha, the last remaining passenger pigeon, died at the Cincinnati Zoo at the age of 30. Her body was taken to the Smithsonian Institution in Washington, D.C., where it was placed on display.

The passenger pigeon, probably the most numerous bird in America's history, is extinct. We can do nothing to bring it back.

It's the same way with sexual purity. When you become careless and give it away before marriage, there's nothing you can do to get it back. Although God will always forgive you, He can't change the fact that you have given away a special part of yourself.

Decide now to save yourself for the person you're going to marry. If you follow God's instructions and keep sex for marriage, you'll never be sorry.

FEBRUARY

18

The Secret to Brain Power

I guide you in the way of wisdom and lead you along straight paths. Proverbs 4:11, NIV.

"Come on in, Henry. Have a seat. I want to let you in on some good news."

Henry Day pulled up a chair and sat down in front of the personnel manager's desk. He couldn't figure out why he had been called away from his job.

Mr. Culver looked up from a stack of papers. "We've been getting some good reports about you. The men in your area of the factory like working with you. And you do excellent work. So we'd like to offer you a job as a supervisor."

"A supervisor? You want to make *me* a supervisor?" asked Henry.

"We sure do."

"What would I have to do?"

"Well," began Mr. Culver, "you'd be in charge of 20 other men, checking their work, making sure they have the necessary materials, and keeping records. And you'll have a small office and a raise in pay."

"Sounds pretty good. When do I start?"

Mr. Culver shuffled his papers. "Well, there's a small hitch, Henry. All supervisors must have a high school diploma. Company policy. And in checking your file, I find that you never finished school."

"Well, it wasn't because I didn't want to. My father got hurt in a farm accident, and I had to get a job to help pay the bills. Does that mean that the offer for the new job is all off?"

"No, no, no. We do have an alternative. You can take a test called the GED. If you pass it, then the job is yours."

Mr. Culver made arrangements with the testing department at a local university, and Henry took the test.

When his scores came back, the head of the testing department called Henry into his office.

"Mr. Day, I want to congratulate you on doing such a good job on the test. But I'm curious. Did you take some special classes to prepare for the test?"

"No. I haven't been to school since I quit the eighth grade 30 years ago."

"Well, then, you must have reviewed some textbooks on the different subjects."

"No. The only reading I do is from the Bible."

If you're having a difficult time with your school work, why not put more time into studying God's Word? Learn from experience how God's Word can help you be a better student.

FEBRUARY

19

Digging Deep

I love all who love me. Those who search for me shall surely find me. Proverbs 8:17, TLB.

Some people feel that reading the Bible is going to make great changes in their lives. It can, but it all depends on your definition of reading.

One of the requirements for becoming a Master Guide is to read the entire Bible through. So when I worked on my Master Guide badge, I set a goal of reading 10 chapters a day. I started at Genesis. That went pretty well, but I got bogged down in books like Leviticus, Chronicles, and Ezekiel. It was only through self-discipline that I ever made it to Revelation.

Although I can say that I've read the Bible all the way through, it didn't do much for me spiritually. I was so busy rushing to get to Revelation 22:21 that I didn't take time to put myself in what I was reading.

If you are interested in making the Bible come alive as you read it, here are a few suggestions:

1. Read your Bible every day. (Try to read in the morning if possible. Your mind will be sharper. If you put it off until evening, it'll probably get crowded out by homework or your favorite television shows.)

2. Plan to spend a certain amount of time. Begin with 10 or 15 minutes, then increase your time gradually.

3. Offer a short prayer in which you ask the Holy Spirit to guide your mind as you study.

4. Concentrate most of your reading in Matthew, Mark, Luke, or John. Put yourself into the stories—see Jesus through the eyes of the rich young ruler, imagine that you're the young girl Jesus raised from the dead, picture yourself as Peter when he walked on the water.

5. End your study in prayer. (We'll talk more about prayer tomorrow.)

Bible study is the greatest way of getting to know God better. It is also the best way to prepare yourself for each new day of your life.

FEBRUARY

20

Prayer—As Easy as A-C-T-S

For the eyes of the Lord are on the righteous and his ears are attentive to their prayer. 1 Peter 3:12, NIV.

Tammy has a hard time praying. "It's not that I don't like to pray; it's just that my mind wanders. I start thinking about other things. What can I do?"

Phil has a different problem. "When I pray at night, I always end up saying the same thing. God must get pretty tired of listening to my prayers. They even bore *me.*"

Most people are like Tammy and Phil. It's not that they don't want to pray; it's just that prayer doesn't seem to be very enjoyable for them.

Today I want to share some ideas with you that are guaranteed to make your prayer time more meaningful and enjoyable.

Some time ago a friend shared something called the A-C-T-S method of prayer. Each letter represents a special part of personal prayer time:

A—Adoration. In this first part of the prayer time, pick one of God's qualities and praise Him for it. For example, you might say, "Today, Lord, I want to praise You for Your power. You're in charge of the entire universe."

C—Confession. Next, spend a few minutes thinking over the past 24 hours. What temptations did you have? What sins did you commit? Be specific. Don't just say "Forgive me for all my sins." Face up to your weaknesses, and ask God to give you the power to represent Him better.

T—Thanks. Now it's time to thank God for all the blessings He's given to you. Think of at least five things that you're thankful for. Don't forget the things we often take for granted, like eyesight, food, friends, good health, and a warm bed.

S—Supplication. That's a big word for "request." This is the time to talk to God about the things you would like Him to do for you and others.

The A-C-T-S method of praying helps you focus your mind on what you are doing. It also keeps your prayer from becoming just a memorized recitation.

Isn't it exciting to get a letter or a long-distance phone call from a friend who lives far away? Well, God, too, loves to have us communicate with Him. And He's always available whenever we want to talk to Him.

It's not important that you follow certain steps when you pray. What is important is that you take time every day to open your heart to your Father in heaven.

FEBRUARY

21

Playing a Deadly Game

Discretion will protect you, and understanding will guard you. Wisdom will save you from the ways of wicked men. Proverbs 2:11, 12, NIV.

"What are you going to have?"

"I don't know. What about you?"

The group of men studied the menu.

"Hey, how about some fugu?"

"Yeah, let's live a little."

Mitsugoro Bando, the famous Japanese actor, motioned to the waiter. "Bring us some fugu," he called out.

The waiter hurried back to the kitchen and gave the chef the men's order.

Fugu is a type of puffer, or blowfish, that usually weighs between three and seven pounds, but sometimes grows up to 30 pounds. In Japan fugu is a delicacy. An expensive delicacy. People pay up to $200 for one serving of the specially sliced raw fish.

But everyone who eats fugu is playing a type of Russian roulette. You see, the puffer fish is highly poisonous. If not properly prepared, it will kill. In fact, the poison found in fugu is 1,250 times more deadly than cyanide, and the amount of poison in a large puffer can kill up to 30 people.

Mitsugoro and his friends knew that fugu is dangerous, but that didn't stop them from eating it. In fact, someone dared Mitsugoro to eat some fugu liver, the most deadly part of all. Mitsugoro took the dare. Five minutes later he dropped dead.

Why would people eat fugu? Why would they deliberately put their life in danger?

One reason is that it's fun to take chances. Another reason is that most people think bad things happen only to other people.

When kids try their first cigarette, they don't ever expect to die from lung cancer or emphysema. People who drink alcohol never plan to become alcoholics, and they don't intend to cause an accident when they drive intoxicated. Those who take drugs think that they can experience the highs without permanently damaging their minds and bodies.

Each year between 70 and 100 people die from eating the deadly fugu. None of them need to die. But they do. None of them want to die. None of them expect to die. But they do. They find out that they're just as vulnerable as anyone else.

God wants you to avoid the problems that come from drugs, alcohol, and tobacco. Will you follow His direction? Or will you be one of those unfortunate people who have to learn the hard way?

FEBRUARY

22

Not a Kimono in Sight

Do not show partiality in judging; hear both small and great alike. Deuteronomy 1:17, NIV.

All of us have preconceived ideas about other people. I certainly had some when Tom and I landed at the Narita Airport in Tokyo, Japan.

As we left the plane and entered the terminal I looked around, expecting to see the Japanese ladies in their elegant kimonos. To my disappointment, I found out that the Japanese women dressed just like I did.

Well, although I was wrong about the kimonos, I was sure about one thing: All Japanese children played the violin. Wrong again. Although the famous Suzuki method for learning stringed instruments did originate in Japan, playing the violin is not Japan's national pastime.

By the end of the summer, I had seen only three ladies dressed in kimonos and one child carrying a violin.

I was not the only one who had problems with stereotyping. (Stereotyping means labeling people according to the groups they are in. For example, some people think that redheads are hot tempered.)

Yumi, one of the students I got to know in Japan, dreamed of someday visiting the United States. "Oh, I would love to come and see your country," she said. "But I am much too afraid."

"Afraid?"

"Oh, yes. I would be so scared to be in a country where everyone carries a gun."

"Where did you ever get the idea that all Americans carry guns?" I asked in surprise.

"On the television. We see programs from the United States, and all the people have guns."

I assured her that some people do own guns, but only a very few are allowed to carry them.

The ideas that Yumi and I had about each other's countries did not hurt our friendship, but stereotyping can build barriers between us and other people.

Stereotyping is not new. Even back in Jesus' time, people had the habit of labeling others according to the group they were in, not viewing them as individuals. Nathanael had heard about Nazareth, and as far as he was concerned that town could produce nothing but criminals. If Jesus came from Nazareth, He couldn't possibly be the Messiah.

Don't let your preconceived ideas about people keep you from getting to know them. Learn to appreciate people for themselves.

FEBRUARY

23

The Magic Ring

Do not say, "I'll pay you back for this wrong!" Wait for the Lord, and he will deliver you. Proverbs 20:22, NIV.

The tale is told of an ancient ruler who sent one of his servants to find a special ring. "The ring," said the king, "has the ability to make a happy man sad, and a sad man happy. Go search the world for it, and," he added, "don't come back until you've found it."

Hadab, the servant, journeyed from village to village in his search for the special ring, but everyone just laughed at him. "There's no such ring," they all said. "The king is playing you for a fool."

Weeks and months passed. Hadab had walked hundreds of miles and visited scores of towns and was still empty-handed. Finally he stopped at a village tucked behind a range of mountains. He went straight to the town's goldsmith. "Have you a ring that will make a happy man sad, and a sad man happy?" he asked.

The goldsmith was just about to say no when a smile spread across his face. "Why, I believe I do. Let me get it for you." The man hurried back into his workroom and emerged about an hour later. "Here it is," he said, handing Hadab a plain band of gold.

"But why would this make a happy man sad, and a sad man happy?" the servant asked.

"Read the inscription," the goldsmith replied.

Hadab held the ring up to the light and read the engraved words: "This too shall pass."

At last Hadab had found the special ring. When a happy man read the words, he would realize that his happiness would not last forever, and that would make him sad. But when a sad man read the words, he would realize that his sadness was only temporary, and knowing that, he would become happy.

Do you ever feel so sad that you're tempted to do something drastic? Each day 3,288 young people run away from home, 1,512 drop out of school, and 6 commit suicide. No doubt they are all unhappy with life, but the way they choose to deal with their problems creates only more problems.

When life gets hard, don't do something you'll regret. Tell Jesus how you feel. He always has time to listen. If you're tempted to do something that will only make the situation worse, wait awhile. Give yourself some time. Remember: "This too shall pass."

FEBRUARY

24

What's in It for Me?

Let us not become weary in doing good, for at the proper time we will reap a harvest if we do not give up. Galatians 6:9, NIV.

Three men traveling to a neighboring town on foot became lost in a freezing blizzard. Grasping hands, they struggled on together through the blinding snow, until one of the men fell and couldn't get up.

John, knowing that his friend would die if left alone, reached down and with his last bit of energy, slung the man over his shoulder.

"Leave him," the third man shouted. "If you try to carry him, you'll both die. Leave him there and save yourself."

But John refused.

"I can't just walk away and let him die."

"Suit yourself," his companion returned. "But I'm not waiting for you." And with that he forged ahead, leaving John to carry his burden alone.

The minutes seemed like hours. Intent on saving the life of his friend, John continued plodding through the drifts.

Eventually the storm lost its fury. The wind stopped blowing, and the sun peeked through the clouds, lighting up the sky. To his joy, John caught sight of a small town just over the ridge. As he started down the hill, John saw a familiar figure lying alongside the road. His other companion, who had insisted on saving himself, had frozen to death.

John, in caring for the needs of someone else, had expended enough energy to withstand the cold that killed the other man. In seeking to save the life of his friend, John had also preserved his own.

And that's exactly what happens when we witness. We not only help others know Jesus better, but we also strengthen our own relationship with Him. "It is in working to spread the good news of salvation that we are brought near to the Saviour" *(The Desire of Ages,* p. 340).

FEBRUARY

25

Be a Winner!

Blessed is the man who perseveres under trial, because when he has stood the test, he will receive the crown of life that God has promised to those who love him. James 1:12, NIV.

Many people become discouraged when they find out that Christians are not free from temptation. Somewhere along the way they got the idea that when we accept Jesus, all our problems disappear. But that's just not so. In fact, when people become Christians, they often experience more temptation than before.

Every four years the world enjoys the excitement of the Olympic Games. I'm always impressed by the sacrifices that the participants are willing to make in order to compete for the Olympic medals. Many put off their schooling. Others leave their families in order to be near their coaches. Most have to pay their own expenses. And all must spend countless hours in training.

I've never known of an Olympic athlete who didn't have to make sacrifices. I wonder what the Olympic Committee's reaction would be if someone showed up on registration day and said, "Hey, I was watching a soccer match on television last week. It looked like a lot of fun, so I just bought myself a new pair of soccer shoes. Do you know of any team that could use an extra player?"

Sounds ridiculous, but aren't we like that sometimes? We want the reward that Christ offers, but we don't want the self-discipline that goes with it. We want to gain spiritual muscle without having to exercise our power of choice to overcome temptation.

When Satan tries to get us discouraged by suggesting that we take the easy way, we should put our faith in God, view our problems as opportunities to grow, and, in the words of Sir Winston Churchill, "never give in, never give in, never, never, never, never."

FEBRUARY

26

Re-deemed

Do you not know that your body is a temple of the Holy Spirit, who is in you, whom you have received from God? You are not your own; you were bought at a price. Therefore honor God with your body.
1 Corinthians 6:19, 20, NIV.

Each year my parents look forward to their annual vacation trip to Montana. To pass the time during the long drive, they stop along the way to browse through antique shops and flea markets. Dad usually finds some treasures to add to his antique collection back home.

After coming home from one of their trips, Mom emptied the suitcases and started doing the laundry.

"That's strange," she said.

"What's strange?" asked Dad.

"I can't find my red blazer."

"I don't remember you wearing it on our trip."

"I didn't, but I'm sure I took it along."

"Maybe you just thought you took it."

Mom decided that Dad was right. She'd probably run across it the next time she put away some ironing.

Spring came. Then summer. Mom forgot about the missing blazer. When fall blew in with its cool temperatures, my parents packed their things and again drove to Montana.

Three days later, they arrived at the Mountain Inn. When they had settled their things into the room, Dad suggested that they take a trip into town.

"I'd like to get a newspaper and stop at that resale shop across from the bank."

As Dad pulled into a parking space in front of the resale store, my mother couldn't believe her eyes.

"Dave, that's my red blazer in the window. The one I lost last year."

"Are you sure?"

"Well, I know how I can find out."

Mom hurried inside the store and checked the stitching on the hem of the sleeves. Sure enough. There was her special hem stitch she'd used when she'd shortened the sleeves.

Later when Mom told me the story she said, "Although I had paid for the blazer once before, I liked it so much that I was willing to buy it back."

And didn't Jesus do the same for us? When He created Adam and Eve, they belonged to Him. But by sinning, they chose to place themselves in Satan's hands. And since then, the human race has been separated from God. But God loved us so much that He decided to pay the price so He could have us back again.

FEBRUARY

27

Seeing Over the Mountain

Listen, my son, to your father's instruction and do not forsake your mother's teaching. Proverbs 1:8, NIV.

I hated practicing the piano. Every few days I'd try to talk my mother into letting me quit. Her answer was always the same: "No." Then she would say, "When you grow up, you'll thank me for making you practice the piano." That was one prophecy I was *sure* would never come true! But now, 20-some years later, I have to admit that Mother was right.

Today, music is one of my greatest joys. I even teach piano. (By the way, I *have* thanked Mom many times for making me stick with it. And now I use her someday-you'll-thank-me pep talk on my students.)

When I was younger, I was unable to see into the future the way my mother could. She knew that eventually I would come to love music, and she was willing to prod me through years of reluctant practicing.

I'm sure that you aren't always appreciative of your parents' counsel. You probably have at times felt that they really don't know what they're talking about. It's not that parents have higher IQs than their children. It's just that they've already had a chance to live through the experiences you're going through. They can see dangers and problems that you aren't aware of.

A race-car driver, traveling in California, missed a hairpin turn and flew over the side of a mountain. For three days he lay pinned under his truck. Finally a helicopter pilot spotted the wreckage and alerted the police.

Because of the high octane racing fuel that the driver had been hauling, the paramedics couldn't rescue him. They had to wait until the fuel was removed.

A special crane was brought in and placed at the edge of the mountain road. The crane operator couldn't see down the mountain. So he had to listen to one of the rescue workers tell him where to drop his hook and when to lift it up. Working together, the rescue workers, paramedics, and police removed the fuel and saved the injured man's life.

If you'll listen to your parents' directions, you'll avoid a lot of unnecessary problems. Taking their counsel will make your life much happier. (Just remember to thank them someday!)

Something to think about: Read Ephesians 6:1-3 and find three reasons young people should obey their parents.

FEBRUARY

28

Riding the Roller Coaster of Sin

Therefore do not let sin reign in your mortal body so that you obey its evil desires. Romans 6:12, NIV.

"The trouble with sin is that it starts out as fun."

Karen and her girlfriend Beth walked around the amusement park. "Let's try the roller coaster," suggested Beth.

Karen eyed the rickety-looking ride. "I don't know. I've never been on one before."

"Oh, you'll love it. Come on." Beth headed toward the ticket booth. "Don't be a chicken," she called over her shoulder.

Karen looked at the roller coaster one more time. She watched other kids lining up for tickets. *Oh, well,* she thought. *Why not? Everybody else is doing it.*

After paying for their tickets, the two girls got into car 7. An attendant walked by and slammed the safety bar into place. Pretty soon the car began to roll forward.

"Hey, this is kinda fun," Karen said to Beth as they creaked up the track. As she looked out across the park, the people got smaller and smaller. "I wonder how fast—"

The first drop lifted the girls right out of their seats. Karen opened her mouth to scream, but nothing came out. *Lord, make it stop,* she prayed silently. *Please make it stop.* But with no thought for its terrified captive in car 7, the Bullet careened around the track.

Sin is a lot like Karen's roller coaster ride. When we first dabble in sin, it seems pretty harmless. Satan starts us out on small things. He doesn't want to scare us away. But before we realize it, we've lost control of our lives, and Satan pulls us along into things we never thought we'd do.

When you're tempted to do something wrong, push the thought out of your mind. Don't give Satan a chance to control your life. Don't let him take you for a ride.

MARCH

1

It's the Little Things That Count

Whoever can be trusted with very little can also be trusted with much, and whoever is dishonest with very little will also be dishonest with much. Luke 16:10, NIV.

"Honesty is the best policy."—David Tuvill.

Richard ran into my classroom and interrupted my English lesson. "Mrs. Coffee, the space shuttle blew up!"

"Is this a joke, Richard?"

"No, it's true! We were just watching it on TV in Mr. Coffee's room."

The students put their books away, and we joined the other class. And for the rest of the day we sat glued to the news broadcasts, watching again and again the footage of the smooth takeoff and the silent (to us) explosion.

People had many theories as to what happened to cause the death of the seven people aboard. But eventually the commission studying the explosion reported that some synthetic rubber rings in one of the rocket boosters failed to seal properly. Such a small thing, but such devastating results.

Do you ever find yourself becoming careless with the little things in your life? For example, does the sheet hang down six inches below the bedspread when you make your bed? When you mow the lawn, do you leave patches of uncut grass?

Right after Phil got out of college, he applied for an accounting job at a large Adventist hospital. On the day of his interview, he arrived an hour early. After walking around the hospital, he decided to try the cafeteria food. As he walked through line, he took some lasagna, green beans, Jell-O, and bread. Lifting up the slice of bread, he slipped a pat of butter underneath.

At 1:00 p.m. Phil took the elevator to the Accounting Department. Mr. Hilbert, the head of the department, greeted him warmly. "Phil, I was very impressed with your résumé. In fact, I was planning to hire you today. But I'm afraid I can't."

"Why not?"

"Well, you weren't aware of it, but I was right behind you in the cafeteria line. I saw you hide the butter under the bread. Phil, if you're dishonest with something as small as a pat of butter, I'm afraid we could never trust you handling the thousands of dollars that go through our office every day. I'm really sorry, Phil, but we can't hire you."

Phil learned the hard way that little things do matter.

MARCH

2

Working Together in Harmony

How good and pleasant it is when brothers live together in unity! Psalm 133:1, NIV.

In the town where I grew up, the Memorial Day parade is a big event. One year the local academy was asked to play in the parade. Normally the chosen band marched down the street, but the academy didn't have a marching band. So the group rode on two different flatbed trailers that were pulled along by cars.

The director stood at the front of the first trailer, gave the band a few preparatory beats, and signaled for the song to begin. At first everything went fine. But somewhere in the middle of the song, the first group got slightly ahead of the second, and things went downhill from there. When the first group reached the last note, the second group still had a measure or two left to play. So group one ended, and group two kept playing until they reached their final note. I may be wrong, but I don't think the academy was ever asked to play again.

In order for a band to perform well, the players must work together in unity. It's the same for sports teams and businesses. Unity is necessary for success.

One of the reasons Japan has made such tremendous strides in technology during the past few years is that the Japanese people believe in team effort. Instead of trying to get ahead of the next guy, employees pool their knowledge and work together.

Unity is also important in a home. All family members must work together to make their home a success. It means watching out for one another. It means protecting the feelings and the rights of all family members. It means being willing to sacrifice at times for the sake of the group.

Something to think about: Are you working as a team member in your family? If not, what can you do today to unify your family and help make it a success?

MARCH

3

Looking for Happiness in All the Wrong Places

Be careful and guard against all kinds of greed. A man's life is not measured by the many things he owns. Luke 12:15, ICB.

When I was in grade school, I fell in love. Not with one of the boys in my class, but with a horse.

My family lived out in the country, near a horse farm. Every day after school I jumped onto my bike and rode over to Meadowbrook Farm. For the next two hours I sat on the corral fence and dreamed what it would be like to own a horse like Duke, the chestnut gelding.

At home I spent hours pouring over catalogs, deciding what kind of saddle I'd buy and which bridle would work best. I was so horse-crazy that my friends at school groaned whenever I got up to read a composition. "Oh no. Not another horse story," Bob would moan.

Then something happened that ruined my fantasy. Dad bought me a horse. I came home from school one afternoon and saw a saddle by the barn door. "A horse!" I screamed. "Dad got me a horse!"

I jumped out of the car and raced to the stall. Sure enough, there munching a bale of hay was a beautiful quarter horse! My dream had come true!

But owning a horse was not half as much fun as thinking about owning a horse. I had to feed Queen every day. I had to clean her stall and haul water from the house.

And Queen was far from gentle. She kicked me three times in one week. Twice she ran away—with me on her back. And another time she bucked off my 6-year-old sister, Karen, and almost killed her.

Toward the end of summer Dad called a local horse trader. When Mr. Livengood took Queen away, I didn't feel bad at all.

I learned early in life that the happiness that comes from owning things is only temporary.

People who don't know Jesus spend their lives trying to fill their emptiness with things or people. There's nothing wrong with having possessions or friends, but they can never substitute for God.

Don't waste your time searching for happiness in worldly things. Jesus is ready to give you the best life you can ever imagine.

Something to think about: Have you made a full commitment to follow the Lord, or are you still looking for things to bring you happiness?

MARCH

4

Am I Valuable?

And so we know and rely on the love God has for us. God is love. Whoever lives in love lives in God, and God in him.
1 John 4:16, NIV.

I hate myself."

Have you ever heard someone make that comment? Have *you* ever said it?

Sometimes we don't like ourselves very much. We know all too well how far we are from being perfect. Our self-esteem, or self-worth, is based on who we think we are and how we feel about it.

Unconsciously we make a list in our head of what we assume makes a person valuable: good looks, intelligence, popularity, the right clothes, athletic ability, and various other talents. Then we compare ourselves with the list. If we meet all the requirements, we feel pretty good about ourselves.

If we fall short, we see ourselves as failures.

Our self-esteem affects the way we react to life. It colors our perspective toward the things we experience. For example, let's say that your family has to move to a new state. On the first day of classes at your new school, you walk up the steps and enter the building. You make your way down the hall and into your first class. All day long the other students ignore you. At the end of the day you walk home alone.

A person with good self-esteem would say, "I sure wish we hadn't moved. It's hard to make new friends. But I'm sure that I'll eventually get to know the other students here." On the other hand, someone with low self-esteem would think, *I'm a real loser. No one talked to me. They probably were laughing behind my back all day.*

It's important for each of us to have a true idea of our value. It's important to realize that our value has nothing to do with the list we make for ourselves.

Tomorrow we're going to find out why people don't feel good about themselves.

MARCH

5

Why Don't I Like Myself?

How great is the love the Father has lavished on us, that we should be called children of God! 1 John 3:1, NIV.

If you don't feel good about yourself, you're not alone. Low self-esteem began a long, long time ago—way back in the Garden of Eden.

When God gave life to Adam and Eve, He placed them in a perfect environment. And in order to preserve their happiness, God warned them to stay away from the tree of the knowledge of good and evil (Genesis 2:17).

Do you remember how Adam and Eve reacted when they sinned? Notice how their actions illustrate their lack of good self-esteem:

1. They tried to cover up their sin by making clothes for themselves.

2. They were no longer comfortable in God's presence, so they hid.

3. When God gave them an opportunity to confess, they refused to accept the responsibility and tried to push the blame onto someone else. (Eve went so far as to blame God indirectly for allowing the serpent to be in the garden.)

Poor self-esteem is the natural result of separation from God. Getting a new outfit or being voted class president may help us feel good for a while. But soon we'll be back to feeling insecure again. The only way that we can keep our self-esteem is to reunite ourselves with our Creator.

God gives us value by living in us through His Holy Spirit. Read Romans 5:8 and find two more reasons why we are valuable.

If we had been in God's place when Adam and Eve disobeyed, we probably would have destroyed them and then started over. But human beings, even in their sinfulness, were and are still valuable in God's sight.

Jesus died for you. He wants you to realize how valuable you are to Him. You *are* somebody. You're a child of the King. And it doesn't get any better than that!

MARCH

6

Safe and Secure

Fight the good fight of the faith. Take hold of the eternal life to which you were called when you made your good confession in the presence of many witnesses. 1 Timothy 6:12, NIV.

Climb on up to the top of the mast and see if we're nearing land," said the captain of the ship to the new sailor. "And here, take my telescope with you."

The sailor, aware that the rest of the crew would be watching, started climbing as fast as he could up the rope ladder. Up he climbed until he reached the crow's nest.

Lifting the telescope to his eye, he surveyed the horizon. Nothing but water and more water. Miles and miles of it.

"No land in sight, sir," he called down to the captain.

The captain waved back. Tucking the telescope into his shirt, the sailor started back down the rigging.

Suddenly his feet slipped, throwing his body off balance. The crew below watched in horror as the boy fell off the rope ladder.

Thinking quickly, the young sailor reached out with both hands and grabbed one of the ropes that hung from the rigging. A cheer went up from the men below. "He's saved!" they cried.

But their happiness was short-lived. For the rope that the boy had grabbed wasn't fastened to anything. And within seconds the young sailor's body hit the deck, ending his life instantly.

Like the sailor, each of us is heading toward certain death. Because we are sinners, death is all we deserve. But Jesus has made a way of escape for us. He gave His life so that we can live forever.

But too often young people don't accept the lifeline that Jesus has offered to them. Instead, they choose a rope that isn't anchored. Some believe they'll be saved because their parents were good Christians. A few depend on their church membership to save them. Others work hard to do all the right things, hoping that good works will earn them eternal life.

The only security we can safely grab onto is a personal relationship with Jesus. It's the only way to salvation.

Won't you reach out in faith to Jesus today and ask Him to live in your heart? Don't settle for a substitute. Take hold of the real thing.

MARCH

7

Forgive and Forget

Be gentle and ready to forgive; never hold grudges. Remember, the Lord forgave you, so you must forgive others. Colossians 3:13, TLB.

The only safe and sure way to destroy an enemy is to make him your friend."

When Frank and Elizabeth Morris saw the policeman at their front door, they knew that he wasn't there to deliver good news. The patrolman told them as gently as possible that their son, Ted, had been in an automobile accident. Less than two days later, on Christmas morning, Ted died.

As the Morrises began to face the death of their only child, hate took over their hearts—hate for Tommy Pigage, the 24-year-old drunk driver who had caused the accident.

Frank and Elizabeth hoped that Tommy would be charged with murder and forced to spend the rest of his life in prison. When their son's killer got off with only five years of probation, their hatred grew.

The Morrises became obsessed with punishing Tommy. They attended every court appearance. They went to the jail to make sure that he was there on the weekends. And they watched his apartment, hoping to catch him violating his probation guidelines.

But God stepped in and changed everything.

When revenge didn't bring them satisfaction, the Morrises decided to forgive Tommy and help him rebuild his life. They realized that for their own good, they had to get rid of their anger before it destroyed them.

Now the Morrises have a son again. They have opened their hearts to Tommy, who is now an unofficial member of their family. Twice a week they attend church together. And Tommy often stops by their house for dinner. Not only has Tommy quit drinking, but he also speaks to other young people, encouraging them to live free from alcohol and drugs.

"The Morrises have given me a better life," he said. "They've made it much easier for me to live with myself and forgive myself."

Many people would argue that the Morrises had a right to hate Tommy. But Jesus knew best when He told us to forgive those who hurt us. He knew that anger destroys. Putting away our right to resent others gives us the freedom to be happy. And it also makes a difference in the lives of the people around us.

MARCH

8

Money—The Root of All Evil?

Keep your lives free from the love of money and be content with what you have. Hebrews 13:5, NIV.

Jesus spent a lot of time telling stories. And He often talked about money.

True or false: The Bible says that money is the root of all evil. Check your answer by reading 1 Timothy 6:10.

The issue here is not money, but the *love* of money. Anytime God does not hold first place in our lives, we are headed for trouble.

Money represents the ability to buy things, and with this ability comes a sense of power. One of the problems with money is that the more a person has of it, the easier it is for him or her to lose dependence on God.

Another problem that money can cause is dissatisfaction and greed. In a research project, people of all economic levels were asked, "How much money would it take to make you happy?" The answer was the same. All, no matter if they earned $8,000 a year or $350,000 a year, gave the same answer. They all said, "I'd be happy if I made just a little bit more." Not one person said he or she had all the money he or she needed.

There's nothing wrong with having money and things as long as we don't value them more than we should.

Jesus knew that money would keep many people from going to heaven. The rich young ruler was a fine, upstanding church member. He had kept the commandments and lived a good life. But his money was his god. Jesus pointed that out to him, and then encouraged him to make God first in his life. But the young man could not turn his back on all his possessions. Instead, he turned his back on Jesus and walked away.

Is there anything in your life that is more important than God? If there is, ask Jesus to help you rearrange your priorities. For money and things will never bring you happiness. You'll always want a little bit more.

MARCH

9

Letting Go—and Letting God

Now glory be to God who by his mighty power at work within us is able to do far more than we would ever dare to ask or even dream of. Ephesians 3:20, TLB.

The most difficult thing I've ever done was to get down on my knees and say, "Jesus, I'll do whatever You ask me to do."

Most of us like to be in control. We'd rather make our own decisions. It's hard to give control of our lives over to someone else.

During Bible class, one of my students said, "Mrs. Coffee, I'm afraid to trust God with my life. I just know that if I let Him control my life, He'll ask me to marry somebody that's really ugly."

I remember feeling that same distrust of God myself. I was sure that once God took over my life, He'd ruin it, and I'd be miserable.

Right after I decided to let God run my life, I waited for the bomb to fall. I just knew He was going to ask me to do something I hated. Instead He told me He wanted me to be a writer. I was shocked! That day I wrote in my prayer journal: "Lord, you can't be serious. Why, I love writing more than anything else. Do you mean that You've been waiting for me to trust You so that You could use my writing to help other people? All this time You've been waiting to give me a chance to do what I enjoy doing!"

What was Jesus' purpose for coming to this earth? (See John 10:10.) Jesus doesn't want to give you just good things. He wants to give you the best.

Trusting God with your life is what faith is all about. It's being able to say, "I'm willing to follow You even though I don't know how this is all going to turn out."

The important thing is to keep in touch with God every single day. As we give our lives to Him each morning, He will work out what is best for us.

Giving God control of your life may be the hardest thing you'll ever do. But once you've made the decision to trust Him, you'll never regret it.

MARCH

10

The Power of Praise

And we know that in all things God works for the good of those who love him, who have been called according to his purpose. Romans 8:28, NIV.

Praise is a positive, scriptural way to make everything in your life work for you instead of against you."—Merlin Carothers.

If I were to pick out one book that has made the greatest impact on my life (other than the Bible), I would probably choose the book *Power in Praise.* In it the author tells about the importance of praising God in every situation.

At first the whole idea seemed ridiculous. Why in the world would anybody want to praise God for the bad things in life? When things go wrong, we're supposed to blame the devil, not praise God. But I decided to give it a try. And was I ever surprised! When I started praising God for everything that happened to me, I couldn't believe what a change it made in my life.

No longer am I afraid of what might happen to me in the future. No matter what comes along, God can turn it into something good. My job is to praise and thank Him for the opportunity to watch Him turn something bad into something good.

Another benefit I've gotten from learning to praise God is that I feel so much closer to Him now. I know that He's my friend and that He's in total control of everything that goes on in my life. If something bad happens, then I know that He has allowed it for my own good. And every time I replace my grumbling with praise, I come out a winner.

Carrie, one my students, loves to cross-stitch. One day she showed me a recent project she had been working on. As she unrolled the fabric, all I could see was a tangled mess—different colored threads going every which way. But as soon as she turned over the material, a beautiful picture appeared.

Life is like that. At times it doesn't make any sense at all. But if we trust the Lord and praise Him for everything, we'll begin to see the beautiful results that He'll work out for us.

MARCH

11

The Stolen Business

Be strong and courageous. Do not be afraid or terrified because of them, for the Lord your God goes with you; he will never leave you nor forsake you. Deuteronomy 31:6, NIV.

Peter was angry, bitter, and filled with resentment. And from a human standpoint, he had good reason to be.

When Peter was 20, his parents owned a small bakery in Brooklyn, New York. They worked hard to support Peter and his two brothers.

One day a church member suggested that Peter's parents expand their bakery. "You could offer more products and increase your income. Then you could hire someone to help you. You shouldn't work yourselves so hard."

So they decided to take the advice of their friend. Further talks with the man revealed that he would even lend them the money they would need.

A month later the owners of the bakery made their first payment on the loan. When they got home that night, they decided to sit down and figure out just how long it would take them to pay back their debt.

"This can't be," said Peter's father. "We made our first payment, but it didn't decrease the amount we owe. Instead, we owe more than we borrowed in the first place."

The family made a phone call to the church member who had lent them the money. "There must be something wrong," said Peter's father. "Our debt is growing instead of getting smaller."

"I'm sorry, but that's what you agreed to. You signed the papers, and it's all legal."

The family struggled to make their payments. But their debt continued to grow month after month. Finally they lost the entire business to the church member who had taken advantage of them.

Since the family no longer had any income, Peter had to go to work as a taxi driver. His anger and bitterness grew year after year. "I lay awake at night thinking up things I could do to that church member who had robbed my parents. The only reason I didn't do anything to him was that I could never think of anything bad enough for what he had done to us."

Peter became so angry that he refused to have anything to do with God. If a passenger started a conversation about God, Peter would pull over to the curb and say, "If you want to talk about religion in my cab, then you'd better get out."

As far as Peter was concerned, God had let him down. But had He really? Don't miss tomorrow's story.

MARCH

12

The Rest of the Story

Oh that men would praise the Lord for his goodness, and for his wonderful works to the children of men! Psalm 107:8.

Peter refused to allow anyone to speak to him about God. So God used a book to get through to Peter's heart. One day a passenger left one of Pastor Carother's praise books, *Prison to Praise,* on the seat of Peter's cab.

Prison, thought Peter, *is exactly where that church member should be for cheating my parents out of the bakery.*

Because he had nothing better to do, Peter began to read the first few pages. The plot interested him, so he kept reading until a new passenger got into the cab. Throughout the day Peter continued to read the book, and the Holy Spirit touched his heart. Before he went home that night, he bowed his head and asked God to forgive him for his own sins.

"O God, for 10 years I've had only hate in my heart for that man. I see now that you've used him to bring me to Christ. Please forgive me and him. Thank You for what he did."

For the first time in years Peter felt at peace.

That evening after supper, Peter sat in the living room with his parents. He prayed that God would help him share what he'd learned about praising God in all situations.

Just then someone rang the doorbell. Peter opened the door. There stood the man who had stolen the family business. It was the first time in 10 years that they had seen him.

The man walked inside the house and came right to the point. "God has made me so miserable and guilty that I have come to beg your forgiveness."

Peter couldn't believe his ears. Within just a few hours from the time he had praised God for losing the bakery, the man showed up at their house asking forgiveness. But the man had more to say. "Your bakery is doing very well. It is worth several times what it was when I took it 10 years ago. But God has told me that I must give it back. Here are the papers. It is yours."

Peter now works in the bakery again, and business is booming. But even more important, Peter's family has learned a lesson about praising God even in bad situations.

MARCH

13

Good Things From Bad

This is the day the Lord has made; let us rejoice and be glad in it. Psalm 118:24, NIV.

"To praise God for a difficult situation means literally that we accept and approve of its happening, as part of God's plan for our lives."—Merlin Carothers.

Have you ever felt as though everyone else had it all together? Have you ever felt as though you were a real loser?

It's no fun being different from other people, but when you're born with a handicap, it's even harder to accept yourself just as you are.

It's one thing to be able to thank God when you get a bad grade on a test or when you don't get what you want for Christmas. But how can people praise God when they have to live with a physical problem all their lives, especially one that's never going to get any better?

I'd like to share with you a letter written by a teenager to Pastor Carothers.

"Your book *Power in Praise* is right on. I'm a junior in high school, and am really turned on for Christ. When I read your book about praising God for everything that has happened, I could hardly believe it. When I was born, I suffered brain damage that affected my ability to walk. I couldn't see how I could praise God for that. I sure hadn't in the past! I always wondered why God let me be born if I had to be a cripple. Even after I was a Christian, I wished I hadn't been born.

"When I tried doing what you said to do—boy, I couldn't believe what happened to me. I got so excited I could hardly stand it. When I thanked God for my problem, I started feeling like I was the luckiest person in the whole wide world. That was several months ago, and I'm still on cloud nine. I used to have to try to cheer myself up, but now I have to hold my laughter down. I feel so great I can hardly stand it!"

Would you like that kind of happiness in your life? Then begin today to praise God in everything that happens. Your life will never be the same again.

MARCH

14

Praise Him in All Situations

Speak to one another with psalms, hymns and spiritual songs. Sing and make music in your heart to the Lord, always giving thanks to God the Father for everything, in the name of our Lord Jesus Christ. Ephesians 5:19, 20, NIV.

When I first heard about the idea of praising God in all situations, I just couldn't accept it completely. One reason I had a problem accepting it was that I couldn't believe I should praise God when I sinned. It seemed pretty strange to do something wrong and then praise God about it. After all, God's primary goal for us is that we live a perfect life, isn't it?

No, God's goal for us is summed up in Matthew 22:37-39. When Jesus was asked which was the greatest commandment, He said, " 'Love the Lord your God with all your heart and with all your soul and with all your mind.' This is the first and greatest commandment. And the second is like it: 'Love your neighbor as yourself' " (NIV).

The most important thing to God is our love for Him. Love for other people is next in importance. If we really love Him, we can praise God even when we sin.

If we praise God when we do something wrong, then that means we're in contact with Him. Praising God shows that we've established a trusting friendship with Him. It shows that we have faith that He can turn our problem into something good.

When we sin, we are also better able to identify our weak areas. If, for example, you find yourself repeatedly lying, then you can see that as a warning signal that you have a weakness when it comes to dishonesty. You can praise God that He has used your sin to point out where you need to make changes with His help.

Finally, when we sin we can praise God because our mistakes show us that we need to stay close to Jesus. We can't live a righteous life without having the Holy Spirit guiding us every moment of the day.

Isn't it exciting to realize that God can make something good even out of our sins? If you haven't already, why not begin today to practice praising God for everything that happens to you? And then watch as He turns your problems into pluses.

MARCH

15

Pass It On

You will be his witness to all men of what you have seen and heard. Acts 22:15, NIV.

One thing I really like about praising God is that it's a great way to witness to other people. I've always wanted to be able to tell others about Jesus, but I didn't know how to go about it. I have tried giving Bible studies, but that doesn't seem to be one of my talents. I've given studies to four different people, and not one of them has even finished the lessons. I've had to realize that God may have different ways for me to witness.

Although I'm not very successful with giving Bible studies, I've found that I can tell others about the importance of praising God. It takes only a few minutes, and it's something that people of all ages and all denominations are happy to hear about.

Last Christmas Tom and I spent our vacation skiing in Vermont with our friends Jim and Ruth. One night Ruth and I were talking about praising the Lord. Ruth's daughter, Teri, sat listening to us, but she didn't say much.

A few weeks later Teri, a registered nurse, called her mother long-distance.

"Mom, it works!" she said excitedly.

"What are you talking about?" Ruth asked.

"Praising God, Mom. It really works, just like you and Mrs. Coffee said. Last night at the beginning of the shift, we were swamped. We practically ran from patient to patient. And then I got a call asking me to work on a different floor. I thought to myself, *Oh, great. That's all I need, more pressure!* But then I remembered what you two had been saying about praising the Lord. So I decided to give it a try.

"I took the elevator to second floor and praised the Lord as I went. When I got to my new area, I helped the patients settle in for the night. Within an hour everything was done, and I had the easiest shift I've had in weeks. Praise really works!"

Why not share with your friends how they can praise the Lord for everything that happens? You'll find it an easy and exciting way to witness for Jesus.

MARCH

16

Putting Praise Into Practice

He who sacrifices thank offerings honors me, and he prepares the way so that I may show him the salvation of God. Psalm 50:23, NIV.

These past few days we've been looking at how our praise to God allows Him to bring about positive results in our lives.

Right now let's take a look at some real-life situations that young people face. See if you can come up with at least one good thing that could come out of each negative experience.

1. Kathy wants to go to church school. She prays that God will send her the money for tuition. But He doesn't answer her request with a yes. What good might come from her having to go to public school instead of church school?

2. Josh has a hard time with swearing. He tries his best to keep his language free from wrong words, but his brother starts teasing him one day, and Josh swears at him. What is there to praise God about since he sinned?

3. Brad's parents have decided to get a divorce. Brad is devastated that his family is breaking up. He prays that God will get his parents back together. But the divorce goes through. What good could come out of it?

4. Heidi has a learning disability that makes it hard for her to read. She doesn't do well in school, and she's embarrassed at her poor grades. What good could come out this problem if she praises the Lord for her learning disability?

5. Lisa's guitar is her pride and joy. One day her little brother plays with it and puts a big scratch in it. What could Lisa praise the Lord for?

6. Ed moves to a new city and has to go to a new school. After a whole year he still doesn't fit in with the other kids. What good could come from feeling so lonely and out of place?

If you can't come up with an idea for each situation, that's OK. Because when we praise God, His blessings will not always be evident. But that shouldn't stop us from praising Him. Even though we can't see good coming from the bad, we must still believe that God is working everything together for our good.

I hope that you'll start making praise to God a part of your life. It's the most exciting thing you'll ever do!

MARCH

17

Happy, Happy Home?

Those who have served well gain an excellent standing and great assurance in their faith in Christ Jesus. 1 Timothy 3:13, NIV.

Some of the best memories I have from my church school years were the times I spent at Vicki Hainer's home. Vicki was an only child. So her parents liked having me come over to spend time with her.

When I was at Vicki's, I loved helping out. Her parents appreciated everything I did around the house. They praised me and made me feel important.

After coming home from a weekend at the Hainers', I usually gave my mother a rundown of everything we did.

"Well, you sure seem to enjoy helping around the house at Vicki's," my mother used to comment.

"It's fun over there," I said. "They notice the things I do, and they appreciate me."

"Why don't you like doing the dishes here at home?"

"It's just not the same, Mom. I *have* to do them here. But I can choose to do them at Vicki's."

Do you find yourself feeling the same way? Do you consider your chores a real bother? Do you grumble when you have to help out around your house?

I'd like to tell you about Jennie Larsen, one of my ninth graders. She is one young person who isn't afraid of taking on responsibility. Last year when she was in eighth grade, she was in charge of organizing the school's hot lunches each week. One day during parent-teacher conferences, I mentioned to her mother about what a great help Jenny was.

"And she's the same way at home," her mother replied.

"Tell me about it," I said.

"I don't know what I'd do without her," Mrs. Larsen said with pride in her eyes. "I work full-time, and when I get home in the evening, she has the house cleaned and supper on the table."

It's good to be helpful to people outside our families. But don't forget how much your parents depend on you to help your own home run more smoothly.

Something to think about: What kind of attitude do you have when you're asked to help out in your home? Do you do your jobs cheerfully, or do you resent your duties?

MARCH

18

The Grass Isn't Always Greener

Honor your father and your mother, so that you may live long in the land the Lord your God is giving you. Exodus 20:12, NIV.

Sherry Hill was one of my very best friends during my elementary school years. I loved spending time at her house. Her parents were a lot more fun than mine. Her dad took us roller skating, and her mother always had us laughing. Sherry's parents let her do just about anything she wanted. My parents always said no. I often imagined how great it would be if her parents could have adopted me into their family.

Beth Kline was another good friend. She lived down the street. Her parents loved to have me come over. Mrs. Kline would fix us snacks while we played Monopoly in her bedroom. Once in a while her dad took us bowling. On Thursdays Beth took riding lessons. As I watched her jumping her horse over the bars, I wished God had given me great parents like hers.

Now that I'm older, I'm thankful that I didn't get what I'd wished for. I found out that life wasn't all that great at my friends' homes. I found out that I didn't realize what good parents I really did have.

One day during spring vacation I went over to Sherry's house early in the morning. We were planning to ride our bikes to town and spend the day shopping.

When I walked into Sherry's room, I found her crying on her bed. "He hit me again," she sobbed. "Dad got mad and threw me against the refrigerator. He hit my mom, too. Why does he do that?"

I had no answer for my friend. I didn't know parents did things like that to their children.

I also found out a few years ago that Beth's life was far from happy. Her parents were both alcoholics. They were glad to have me over. When Beth was busy, they didn't have to worry about her. And they could spend their evenings drinking in the kitchen.

Instead of wishing for different parents, why not appreciate those God has given you? Could it be that maybe your parents are the ones your friends wish they had?

Something to think about: Name five things that you like about each of your parents.

MARCH

19

Untying the Apron Strings

The master answered, "You did well. You are a good servant who can be trusted. You did well with small things. So I will let you care for much greater things." Matthew 25:21, ICB.

One of the hardest jobs a mother or father faces is learning to let go. After being so involved in your life from the day you were born, it's difficult for Mom and Dad to give up the control over your life.

Although I'm 40 years old, my mom still likes to mother me. When I come to visit, she tells me how I should wear my hair and spend my money.

I was once telling a friend at church about how frustrating it was that my mother still treated me like a child at times.

Mrs. Stafford shook her head knowingly and laughed. "I don't think that parents ever get over being parents. My mother is 83, and she still insists on bringing food when she comes to our home for dinner. I'm a grandmother, but in her eyes, I'm still her child."

You can't force your parents to give you more freedom, but you can do two things that will make it easier on them: you can act in a responsible manner and always deal honestly with them. If your parents know that they can trust you, they will be more likely to increase your freedom.

Can your parents believe everything you tell them? Can they give you important responsibilities and be assured that you'll carry them out? Can they release you to new experiences, knowing that you'll use good sense?

If you have let down your parents in the past, don't expect them to trust you overnight. Trust is like a good reputation—it's easier to keep it than it is to lose it and have to win it back again.

Give your parents a reason to believe in you, and you'll find yourself on the first step toward independence.

Something to think about: Are you trustworthy? Can your parents believe everything you say?

MARCH

20

Room for One More

Him that cometh to me I will in no wise cast out. John 6:37.

The Baggett family had been looking forward to their Florida vacation. It was a cold December in Michigan, and they could hardly wait to spend the Christmas holidays under the Florida sun. But most of all they looked forward to a trip to Disney World.

On Sunday morning they loaded up the car and headed out. But after they had been only four hours on the road, something went wrong with the car.

An hour later a tow truck hauled the car into a repair shop.

"Looks like the transmission is shot."

"Well, how long will it take to fix?" asked Mr. Baggett.

"I'm afraid it'll take a few days."

So the family left the car and rented a motel room.

It didn't take them long to find out that they were sharing the room with cockroaches.

Mr. Baggett stayed up all night killing the bugs, while his wife and six children tried to get some sleep.

Finally, on the fourth day of their vacation, the car was ready, and they continued the trip.

But when they arrived in Florida, they were greeted with cold, rainy weather. So they spent most of their time sitting in the motel.

Fortunately, on the last day of their vacation the family woke up to a bright, sunny sky.

"Hey, Dad," called Steve excitedly, "it's *great* outside! Let's get going to Disney World!"

Everyone seconded the motion, rushed through breakfast, and piled into the car.

When they were only 25 miles from Disney World, Mr. Baggett noticed that traffic was slowing down.

"There must be an accident up ahead," he said.

Soon all the cars came to a complete stop. Unknowingly the family became part of a 22-mile backup. For three and a half hours they inched along toward their destination.

Finally, as they pulled up to the parking lot at Disney World, they saw a sign that read "Sorry, but We're All Full."

All they could do was turn around and drive back to the motel.

If your goal is to reach heaven, you'll never have to worry about being turned away. Jesus is just waiting for you to accept His offer of eternal life. In fact, He's got a special place all ready for you. Have you made your reservations?

MARCH

21

Not My Will, but God's

Teach me to do your will, for you are my God.
Psalm 143:10, NIV.

Have you ever said to yourself, "I have absolutely no willpower"? Most of us feel this way at times, but the truth of the matter is that we always have willpower—but sometimes we use it to make wrong decisions.

Erwin Lutzer says that "your emotions express how you feel, your mind says what you know, but your will tells what you want." Let me give you an example of how this works. Let's say that it's 6:30 a.m. You're sleeping peacefully, all snug in your bed. That is, until your alarm rings at 6:31. You know that you need to get up and get ready for school. But you're still tired. So what happens?

Imagine it this way. Instructions are sent to the brain that say *I need to get up.* The message is backed by 40 millivolts of energy. But at the same time, you get another thought. *Boy, it sure would feel nice to sleep just a little bit longer.* This message is also sent to the brain, but since you feel more strongly about this choice, it is backed with 60 millivolts of energy. Your brain does some quick arithmetic and figures out that there are 20 more millivolts in favor of sleeping in. So sleeping wins. You shut off your alarm and snuggle back under the covers.

The daily decisions you make are determined by what you consider valuable and important. In the preceding illustration, if you were hoping to get a perfect attendance certificate at the end of the school year, you would have gotten up right away when the alarm went off. Sleeping in might have been pleasant, but it wouldn't have been as important as getting to school on time.

It's the same with spiritual issues. When serving God is our number one goal, we will be able to say no to sin even if it is appealing. It all depends on what we want most.

Something to think about: What are some of the areas in which you have a hard time making the right decisions? Friendships? The way you spend your money? Things you watch on TV and videos? Being kind to others? Obeying your parents? Honesty? Jealousy? The food you eat? Getting your homework done? Why not ask the Lord to help you today to use your power of choice to make the right decisions?

MARCH

22

Freedom—Within Limits

Be happy, young man, while you are young, and let your heart give you joy in the days of your youth.
Ecclesiastes 11:9, NIV.

How would you like to live in a country where people can do anything they like?

Whenever I ask my students that question, they respond with applause and cheers. "That would be great!" they all agree.

Is complete freedom good? Is it even possible? Are there times when a person should not be given freedom?

Read through the following list and decide which people should be free to do as they wish.

____ a 6-year-old girl who doesn't want to brush her teeth
____ a 12-year-old boy who doesn't want to go to church
____ in a restaurant, the couple sitting next to you who want to smoke while you eat
____ a woman who wants to drink but neglects her children when she's drunk
____ a man who wants to drink and drive
____ your friend who cheats when he plays Monopoly
____ a 16-year-old who wants to quit school
____ an AIDS patient who wants to sell some of his blood to earn money
____ a 10-year-old who would rather watch TV than study
____ your neighbor who wants to start a junkyard next to your house

As you can see, complete freedom for everyone would cause a lot of problems. Rules are necessary so that people can live more peaceably together. We need rules so that the freedom of one person doesn't take away the freedom of another.

Rules also help us learn good habits. Your parents and teachers have set up certain rules that can help you be happier and healthier. They're hoping that by learning to do things right when you're young, you'll continue doing them when you get older.

Instead of resenting rules, learn to appreciate them. Be thankful that your country, your school, and your parents care enough about you to protect your happiness by giving you guidelines for living.

MARCH

23

Put on a Happy Face

Happy is that people, whose God is the Lord. Psalm 144:15.

As a man "thinketh in his heart, so is he" (Proverbs 23:7).

It all started out as a joke. During my junior year in academy, Cathy, my best friend, and I decided to see if we could get one of the girls in our dorm sick.

No, we didn't cough on her or give her spoiled food. We used something even more potent—our words.

We planned the whole thing during breakfast. "When Christy comes to Bible class, you ask her if she's feeling all right," I directed.

"What are *you* going to do?" Cathy asked.

"Well, she and I have chemistry together, so I'll casually ask her if she's getting the flu."

"This is going to be a riot," laughed Cathy. "I bet she'll be on the sick list before lunch."

At Bible class that morning, I saw Cathy talking to Christy. A few minutes later Cathy turned around and gave me a wink.

After class I followed Christy to the chemistry lab. "Hey, Chris. Are you OK?"

"Well, I think so," she said. "Why do you ask?"

"Oh, nothing. I just . . . well . . . to tell you the truth, I thought maybe you were coming down with the flu or something."

"No, I'm fine. I think."

"Oh, don't worry about it. You're probably OK."

Well, that's all it took. After chemistry Christy spent the rest of the day in bed.

I am not proud of the trick we played, but I did learn a valuable lesson: Our thoughts affect the way we feel.

When we think depressing, negative thoughts, we're going to feel tired, unhappy, and sick. But when we think cheerful, positive thoughts, we'll feel full of life.

There's a whole new field of research being done on how laughter affects the body. It is believed that laughing may help cure some types of diseases.

Scientists have discovered that when a person smiles, the blood flow to the brain increases. Make a big smile. Did you feel your face getting warmer? That's the extra blood on its way to your brain.

Christians should be the happiest people on earth. Because we have Jesus living in our hearts, we can enjoy life no matter what our circumstances.

So put on a happy face. You'll feel better, and so will everyone else around you!

MARCH

24

Monkey See, Monkey Do

Don't let anyone look down on you because you are young, but set an example for the believers in speech, in life, in love, in faith and in purity.
1 Timothy 4:12, NIV.

Have you ever noticed how children like to copy their parents? You may have watched your little sister or brother step into Father's shoes and go clumping down the hallway. We all tend to copy those whom we admire.

As a member of a family, you need to be aware of the impression that you're making on your brothers and sisters, especially if you're older.

When I met John the first time, he had been a Christian for only a few years. During his first 22 years, he'd dropped out of school, sold drugs, spent some time in jail, and in general lived a rebellious life.

As he was telling me about the changes that God had made in him, he paused, and then added, "I only wish I could do something for my brother."

"What do you mean?"

"Well, I've tried so hard to witness to him. But he won't listen. He's really into drugs now, and when I tell him he needs to give them up, he says, 'Don't go preaching to me, John. You're the one who got me started on them in the first place.' I know he's right. But now I'd give anything to be able to undo the damage I've done to him."

It's easy to think that just because you're young you don't have much of an influence on others. But the things you say and do influence all around you, and that includes your brothers and sisters.

What kind of impressions are you making on the people around you? Are you leading them closer to God—or further away from Him?

Something to think about: What attitudes and actions in your life are having a positive influence on your family? Do you have some habits that your brothers and sisters shouldn't copy? Are you willing to give them up?

MARCH

25

The Big Squeeze

Do not gaze at wine when it is red, when it sparkles in the cup, when it goes down smoothly! In the end it bites like a snake and poisons like a viper. Proverbs 23:31, 32, NIV.

Greg wanted to be cool. He wanted to be sophisticated. He wanted to stand out in a crowd. So Greg decided to join the party scene.

Greg's motto was "Party Till You Drop," which really means "Drink Until You Pass Out."

One evening after attending a drinking party, Greg decided to walk home and save himself the cab fare. But the longer he walked, the more tired he became. The alcohol that had put his thinking powers to sleep was also putting his body to sleep.

As he shuffled down the sidewalk, Greg noticed a small hut off to the left. He wandered over to it and crawled through a small door.

"If I could just get a little nap, I'd feel a lot better," he mumbled to himself as he dropped down onto a soft cushion. "Ah, this feels good."

Sometime later a loud noise interrupted Greg's peaceful rest. *What's going on?* he thought. As he tried to look around, he realized he couldn't see anything. He tried to rub his eyes, but he couldn't move his arms. In fact, he couldn't move at all.

Again Greg heard the loud noise. And then he felt himself being squeezed. Squeezed so hard that he could hardly breathe.

Greg tried to scream, but something was covering his face. And boy, did it stink!

Another loud roar. Panic snapped Greg out of his drunken stupor. Where was he, anyway?

This place smells like a garbage dump, he thought. *That's it. I'm in a pile of garbage!*

And that he was. Greg's little hut had turned out to be a dumpster. Before daylight a garbage truck had come by, picked up the garbage—and Greg. Now the truck was on its way to the city dump, where bulldozers were waiting to crush the incoming loads.

When the truck reached the dumping ground, Greg screamed his head off. Fortunately someone heard him and came to his rescue.

The next day when the papers carried the story of Greg and the garbage, he didn't feel cool. He didn't feel sophisticated. But he did stand out in a crowd, much to his embarrassment.

When people drink alcohol, they can't think clearly, and they end up doing some pretty stupid things. Don't abuse your brain. Use it.

MARCH

26

When God Doesn't Make Sense

"For I know the plans I have for you," declares the Lord, "plans to prosper you and not to harm you, plans to give you hope and a future." Jeremiah 29:11, NIV.

Yesterday I had to do something that I absolutely hate. I had to take my dog, Teddy, to the veterinarian.

First Dr. Main checked her for heartworm. I held her as he drew blood from her neck. She looked at me with her doggy eyes as if to say, "How could you let him do this to me?"

Just as I was about to take her off the examination table, Dr. Main said, "I see by her records that she's supposed to have her yearly vaccination next month. Why don't I save you a trip and give it to her now?"

After the shot, I picked up Teddy and went to pay the bill. Just as I was writing a check, the doctor stuck his head around the corner.

"Did you know she's going to need a rabies shot this summer?"

Back to the examination table.

When we finally got into the car to go home, Teddy crawled to the other side of the front seat—as far away from me as she could go. And I began to understand how God feels when I resent the problems He allows in my life.

While Teddy was suffering at the vet's, she had no way of understanding that I brought her there because I love her. She had no way of knowing that the pain she felt would help her be healthier and happier in the future. And she had no way of knowing that I suffered alongside her.

I've been angry at God for letting bad things happen to me. I remember one time when I actually raised my fist at Him and said, "I *hate* You." But now I realize that the things I went through were really good for me. And I'm glad He let them happen.

The next time I'm tempted to complain about the trials God allows in my life, I hope I'll remember yesterday. I hope I'll remember that He's really on my side.

MARCH

27

The Worthless Pardon

Let the wicked forsake his way and the evil man his thoughts. Let him turn to the Lord, and he will have mercy on him, and to our God, for he will freely pardon. Isaiah 55:7, NIV.

Have you ever heard someone say "I'll never forgive myself for what I've done"? People are often harder on themselves than they should be.

Jesus offers to free us from guilt. All we have to do is ask for forgiveness. But too many people think that God's way is too simple. They'd rather try to pay for their own sins. So they reject God's pardon.

Back in 1829, hanging was a popular way of dealing with lawbreakers. One particular criminal named George Wilson was captured and tried for robbery and murder. When the jury found him guilty, he was sentenced to hang.

But right before his day of execution, President Andrew Jackson gave him a pardon.

"I won't accept it," George replied.

"What!" cried the government officials. "You *must* accept it. You can't turn down a pardon."

George remained set in his decision. "I can't be pardoned unless I accept the pardon. And I refuse to do so."

No one knew just what to do with George. But eventually his case went all the way to the Supreme Court. In the end, Chief Justice John Marshall decided that "a pardon is a paper, the value of which depends upon its acceptance by the person implicated. It is hardly to be supposed that one under sentence of death would refuse to accept a pardon, but if it is refused, it is no pardon. George Wilson must be hanged."

When you come to Jesus with your sins, are you willing to let Him forgive you? Or do you hold on to your guilt and refuse His pardon?

Jesus has promised to forgive our wickedness and remember our sins no more if we'll only turn them over to Him.

If you haven't been able to forgive yourself for something you've done in the past, why not accept the pardon that Jesus offers you today? No sin is too big for Him to handle.

MARCH

28

Love Under Construction

Be devoted to one another in brotherly love. Honor one another above yourselves. Romans 12:10, NIV.

When a wolf enters a sheepfold, the sheep instinctively run toward each other and pack together as tight as possible. The wolf, which had hoped to run off with one of the stragglers, finds himself facing one big mound of wool. That is, unless he's already been trampled to death by the flurry of sheep hooves.

The sheep offer a beautiful lesson for families. Instead of just caring for ourselves, we need to band together to support one another. Not only do we need to make sure that the family members' physical needs are met, but we also need to show concern for one another's self-esteem.

Every day families leave their homes and enter the stresses of school and work. When they return at night, the home can provide the encouragement and security that will help them be ready to face a new day.

The following are some suggestions on how you can build togetherness in your family.

1. Show an interest in what the other family members are doing. If your sister has a piano recital, be there in the audience. If your brother plays softball, offer to play catch with him.

2. Offer encouragement. Instead of making cutting remarks or teasing your brother and sister, look for reasons to compliment them.

3. Do things with your family. Participate in activities that everyone can enjoy. Watching TV doesn't count! In fact, why not turn off the TV once in a while and play a game, take a walk, or do yardwork together, or just talk to each other?

4. Keep confidences. Some things that are said at home should never go outside the family. Protect everyone's privacy by carefully watching your words.

Something to think about: Make a list of three things that you would enjoying doing together with the other members of your family.

MARCH

29

A Race to the Finish

Therefore, since we are surrounded by such a great cloud of witnesses, let us throw off everything that hinders and the sin that so easily entangles, and let us run with perseverance the race marked out for us. Hebrews 12:1, NIV.

The day was clear and sunny. Excitement hung in the air. After lunch everyone at Gobles Junior Academy was taking part in the final event in the President's Physical Fitness Test—the one-mile run.

It was difficult for the students to concentrate, but Joann Roosenberg was having a particularly hard time of it. Joann had managed to pass every test so far, but the one left was the mile run. That was the hardest of all, in her opinion. Would she be able to do it?

At 1:00 p.m. the entire student body lined up around the outdoor track. Mr. Coffee organized the first group of 10.

"Now keep a nice steady pace. Don't push too hard at the beginning," he warned them. "All right. On your mark, get set, *go!*"

At the sound of the gun, the runners started around the dirt track. Each time they passed the starting line, recorders shouted out the number of laps they had completed.

When the first group finished, Joann and nine of her classmates spaced themselves across the starting line.

"On your mark, get set, go!"

Joann started out the race with a nice even stride. She concentrated on exhaling so she wouldn't get a sideache.

The students along the sidelines cheered each time Joann finished a lap.

"Only two more to go," the recorder yelled.

"I don't think I can make it two more laps," gasped Joann.

All eyes focused on Joann as she crossed the line the sixth time and began her final lap.

"Come on, Jo!" yelled her friends. "You can do it!"

Joann's muscles felt like they were being torn apart. She pushed herself for all she was worth.

Only one more lap. Only one more lap, she thought to herself.

The finish line was in sight. Joann pushed herself across the line as her friends cheered.

"Good race, Joann," said Mr. Coffee.

"Did I make it?" she asked.

"I'm sorry, Jo," the principal said, "but you were one second over."

Have you ever failed at something you really wanted to accomplish? What would you do if you had been Joann? Don't miss tomorrow—and the rest of the story.

MARCH

30

Winners Never Quit

When Joann found out that she had been just one second short of getting the President's Physical Fitness Award, she lay on the grass and sobbed.

"But I tried so hard, Mr. Coffee."

"I know you did, Jo. And that's why I believe that if you try it again tomorrow you'll make it."

"I can't do it again. It's just too hard. I already did my best. Can't you just give the award to me anyway?"

Mr. Coffee shook his head. "Joann, if I gave you the fitness award, it wouldn't mean a thing to you because down in your heart you'd always know that you hadn't really earned it. Tomorrow we're going to have one final run. Give it one more try."

By the next morning Joann's courage was a little stronger. She knew that Mr. Coffee was right. She wouldn't take any pride in the fitness award unless she earned it fair and square. She decided to try again.

Right after school started, the sky clouded over. Soon the rain came pouring down.

By afternoon the rain had stopped, but little puddles lined the entire athletic field. The students gingerly walked down to the track to watch the final race.

"Everyone who wants to be retested should line up at the starting line," called out Mr. Coffee.

Joann took her place next to three other students.

"On your mark, get set, go!"

Joann's first few strides sent water splashing everywhere. But she ignored her soggy tennis shoes.

Everyone cheered the runners.

On Joann's sixth time around, her older brother, John, started jogging alongside her. "How are you doing?" he asked.

"I'll never make it," she panted.

"Sure you will," John said. "Just don't give up."

John continued running with her.

"Only one more lap to go," shouted Mr. Coffee as he checked her time. "Give it all you've got!"

Joann pushed herself as fast as she could go. *I'm going to make it. I'm going to make it.*

As she headed toward the finish line, the students screamed with excitement, "You're almost there, Jo! You're going to make it!"

With her last bit of energy Joann crossed the finish line and fell to her knees in the mud.

"You did it!" shouted Mr. Coffee. "You were 20 seconds faster than yesterday! Congratulations, Jo."

The most important thing is that I complete my mission. Acts 20:24, ICB.

MARCH

31

Real Winners

Do not neglect your gift. . . . Be diligent in these matters; give yourself wholly to them, so that everyone may see your progress.
1 Timothy 4:14, 15, NIV.

What makes a person a winner? Some people would say that winners are those who do something outstanding, such as taking first place in a contest or making good grades or sinking the winning basket.

Yesterday you read about Joann Roosenberg running the mile the second time and cutting 20 seconds off her previous time. Joann made her goal and earned the President's Physical Fitness Award. She was definitely a winner.

But what if Joann hadn't run fast enough? What if she had run the race the second day and didn't make her goal? Would that have made her a loser?

Before you decide, I'd like to tell you about two of my former students.

Trisha has the IQ of a genius. She is one of the quickest learners I've ever known. But she doesn't take college too seriously. She skips her classes whenever she feels like it. And she rarely turns in homework. But because she does so well on her tests, she gets almost all A's and B's on her report card.

Sarah is another college student I used to teach. But for Sarah, school isn't a breeze. From the time she was a preschooler, Sarah has had trouble reading. Because of a learning disability, some words and letters appear backward when she reads. But Sarah hasn't let her reading problem stop her from succeeding. Although she works hard to get C's, she's determined to get a college degree. In addition to taking her classes, she also works almost 20 hours a week to help pay for her tuition.

Something to think about: Who do you think is the real winner—Trisha or Sarah? Finish this sentence: A winner is someone who __________. If Joann had not finished the race in time, would you have considered her a winner or a loser? Why or why not?

APRIL

1

No Two Alike

Don't be afraid, because I have saved you. I have called you by name, and you are mine. Isaiah 43:1, ICB.

Last Monday at a writers' workshop a man stopped me as I was walking to the parking lot. "Did you ever live in California?" he asked.

"No," I admitted, "I was there only for a few hours while I changed planes at the airport."

"Well, you look just like a girl I went to school with a few years ago."

The next day a lady tapped me on the shoulder as I walked down a hallway. She asked me the same thing.

"I can't believe it," she said. "You look just like a girl at Loma Linda University. She must be your twin."

This sort of thing happens to me on a regular basis. (I must have a generic face.)

Maybe someday I'll see another person who looks like me. But I know the resemblance will be only external. My "twin" will have a different personality. She'll have different abilities, goals, attitudes, and fears. She may look like me, but she won't *be* me.

One school year Tom had two sets of twins in his classroom. Kelly and Ken were easy to tell apart. But it took me until the end of first semester before I could tell the difference between Linda and Rhonda. They were the most identical-looking twins I've ever seen. But my husband, who spent six hours a day with them, noticed their differences right away. Their personalities were not at all alike. And once I got to know the girls, I was able to see them as totally different individuals and not carbon copies of each other.

When we see ourselves as God's special creation, we'll be comfortable with who we are. And we'll make the most of the talents and abilities that God has given us.

Something to think about: What makes *you* special? What talents and abilities has God given to you?

APRIL

2

Nothing Is Impossible With God

What is impossible with men is possible with God. Luke 18:27, NIV.

One day before a World Series baseball game, Lou Gehrig, the famous Yankee first baseman, visited a hospital for crippled children. As he passed through the wards, greeting his excited young fans and signing autographs, he encouraged them never to give up trying to walk again. "If you really want to do something bad enough, you can do it," he told them.

One little boy surprised Lou by turning the tables on him. "Mr. Gehrig, would you knock in two home runs at the game today?"

Lou, not wanting to discourage the boy, said, "I'll tell you what. I'll make two home runs if you'll promise me that you'll walk someday." The boy agreed to the deal and shook hands with the famous ballplayer.

Lou, true to his promise, hit the two home runs that afternoon.

Some years later as Lou was entering the stadium for a game, he felt a hand on his shoulder. Turning, he saw a tall, handsome young man behind him.

"Do you remember me?" the stranger asked.

"I can't say that I do," Lou replied honestly.

"Well, we met once when I was a boy. And I just wanted you to know that I can walk now."

Can people accomplish every goal they set for themselves? Probably not. But one thing we know for sure is that we can accomplish nothing unless we do set goals.

Donna Otto, a time management expert, says that if you make goals for yourself without writing them down, you will reach about 20 percent of them. But if you write down those same goals, your rate of accomplishment will jump to almost 90 percent.

As you set goals for yourself, don't forget to include God in your plans. He'll give you the ability to keep going when things get difficult. With Him on your side, all things are possible.

APRIL

3

Self Talk

The Lord detests the thoughts of the wicked, but those of the pure are pleasing to him. Proverbs 15:26, NIV.

How would you respond if you were to spill a glass of milk all over the table during breakfast tomorrow morning? While you were frantically mopping up the mess with a handful of napkins, would you be thinking something like *Nice going, dummy. You're always doing stupid things like this. What's the matter with you?*

You've probably never realized it before, but you carry on a running conversation with yourself the whole time you're awake. Everyone does. Dr. David Stoop says that while we speak between 150 and 200 words a minute, our self-talk can run to more than 1,000 words a minute. Unfortunately, most of the things we say to ourselves aren't very positive. It's no wonder that most people have a problem with poor self-esteem.

During my typing classes I warn my students about the unconscious little negative messages they're giving their minds. I encourage them to think only positive thoughts as they type. If they think, *I just know I'm going to make a mistake,* they *will* make a mistake. But if they tell themselves that they are doing a good job, they will relax and make fewer errors. What they think will determine how they type.

It's the same way with all our other activities, too. Those continual messages that we run through our minds all day long influence everything we do. They either strengthen or tear down our self-esteem. And they help determine whether we'll be a success or a failure.

Train your mind to think positive, uplifting thoughts. And you'll be able to be a positive, uplifting person.

Something to try: During the next 24 hours, listen to the things you think about yourself. Each time you think something discouraging, replace the thought with a positive, encouraging message.

APRIL

4

Are You in Control of Your Words?

A good person has good things in his heart. And so he speaks the good things that come from his heart. But an evil person has evil in his heart. So he speaks the evil things that come from his heart. Matthew 12:35, ICB.

It is with a word as with an arrow—once let loose, it does not return."

Our local newspaper carried a shocking story about a well-respected citizen in our town. The man was being accused of immoral conduct. Only a week later the paper ran a second story about the man. This time the article reported that after an investigation, all charges had been dropped. The story had been a lie.

Although the man has been declared innocent, his name will never be completely cleared. Some people who read the first article never saw the second one. As far as they know, he's still guilty. And many of those who did hear of his innocence will continue to question his character.

Once something is said about another person, it can't be taken back.

During a church potluck dinner I was helping several of the ladies carry food to the serving tables. Gina made a cutting remark about Beth, without realizing that Beth was standing right behind her. When Gina turned around and stood face-to-face with the person she had just criticized, she just laughed and said, "Oh, just forget I ever said it."

That's easier said than done.

Gossip is another problem area. I'll be the first to admit that gossip is fun. There's something exciting about watching the shocked expression on another person's face as you share with him or her some exciting bit of news. But is it really worth it? Is it worth it when you've hurt another person's feelings? Is it worth it when you've passed on information that turns out to be false? Is it worth it when people lose their respect for you?

The best policy is to think twice before you speak. Control your words. As the old proverb goes: When you have spoken the word, it reigns over you. When it is unspoken, you reign over it.

Something to think about: How could you kindly discourage someone who wants to tell you some gossip?

APRIL

5

The General and His Son

But God demonstrates his own love for us in this: While we were still sinners, Christ died for us. Romans 5:8, NIV.

The year was 1936. The place, Morocco, Spain. Army units had revolted against the Spanish government and begun a civil war that would last for three long years and cost hundreds of thousands of lives.

One of the greatest stories to come out of this war was that of a father and his son.

A group of Rebel soldiers had taken over an old fort in Toledo, Spain. The Communist-dominated Loyalists surrounded the fort and began their attack, which continued day after day.

Then the Loyalists made a move that gave them the upper hand. They captured the Rebel general's son. Convinced that victory was sure, they telephoned the general. "We have your son, General. You may as well surrender. For if you don't, you'll never see him alive again."

And to prove that they were serious, they put the telephone to the son's ear and forced him to speak. "They tell me, Father, that unless you surrender the fort to them, they will kill me."

There was a long silence on the father's end of the line as he wrestled with his choices. Should he save his son—or do what was best for the country?

At last the general spoke. "My son, commend yourself to God. Cry 'Long live Spain' and die like a patriot. Goodbye, my son."

"Goodbye, Father."

The general hung up the phone and quickly left the room. He found a quiet corner and knelt in prayer. As tears streamed down his face, he heard the shot of a gun, and then a sickening silence.

Nearly 2,000 years earlier another Father received word that His Son was in the hands of the enemy. But God the Son was not a helpless prisoner of war. Even before the Garden of Eden, Jesus had offered to die in the place of sinners. He died so that you and I can look forward to eternal life.

God could have rescued Jesus. But if He had, you and I would have been lost forever.

What great love the Father and Son showed, and are showing, for us! And all that They ask is that we love Them back.

APRIL

6

It's Not MY Fault

Who is a God like you, who pardons sin and forgives the transgression of the remnant of his inheritance? Micah 7:18, NIV.

One of the major auto insurance companies once printed a list of explanations people gave for being in an accident. Here are a few of my favorites.

"To avoid a collision, I ran into the other car."

"I blew my horn, but it wouldn't work because it had been stolen."

"A pedestrian hit me and went under my car."

"I can give no details of the accident, as I was somewhat concussed at the time."

"I knocked over a man. He admitted it was his fault, as he had been run over before."

"Coming home, I drove into the wrong house and collided with a tree I don't have."

"The other man changed his mind, so I had to run over him."

We laugh at these excuses. But when it comes to sin, making excuses is serious business.

Have you ever heard people make some of these?

"Well, there's nothing I can do about my bad temper. That's just the way I am."

"I wouldn't have had to cheat on that history test if the teacher wasn't such a hard grader."

"It's not my fault that I swear. Everyone in my family talks that way."

However, we don't have to be controlled by sin. Jesus has given us His promise that He'll free us from our evil habits and tendencies. But He can't do that unless we admit we have problems.

In the nineteenth century Napoleon, the emperor of France, gave a Russian prince an unusual opportunity. Napoleon offered to let the prince visit a French prison and pardon one of the convicts.

The prince spoke to each of the men, asking them what they had done. Every prisoner claimed to be innocent of the charges brought against him.

"I was set up," said some.

"I was blamed for someone else's crime," others maintained.

Finally the prince found one man who didn't try to make excuses. "I'm in here because I broke the law," the repentant man admitted.

The prince smiled as he shook the man's hand. "Well, I have brought you pardon in the name of the emperor. You are a free man!"

We too can receive pardon, from the Emperor of the universe. All we have to do is admit that we've sinned and ask Him to forgive.

APRIL

7

Look to Jesus

Be on your guard; stand firm in the faith; be men of courage; be strong.
1 Corinthians 16:13, NIV.

"Watch out!"

Tom slammed on the brakes, while I covered my face with my hands. After we had screeched to a halt, I peeked between my fingers. The mother mallard and her six ducklings marched across the highway just a few inches in front of our tires. Getting run over by an eight-passenger van was the least of their worries.

As I watched them scamper into the underbrush at the side of the road, I was reminded of how adults, like the mother duck, sometimes lead the younger generation in the wrong direction.

I remembered one man who lived in the town where we first began teaching. Whenever he needed things at the store, he'd take his two children to the shopping mall. Then while he waited in the car, he sent the kids inside, where they stole the items that he needed.

Most of the time the children didn't get caught, but when someone did see them shoplifting, little could be done. The children were too young to prosecute.

I grew up during a time when children were taught to obey adults without question. But unfortunately that's not a safe rule to live by anymore. Some people do not think clearly and don't have your best interest in mind.

I'm not saying that you can't trust anybody. What I'm saying is that if anyone should ever do something to you or try to get you to do something that makes you uncomfortable, stand up for your rights. (Having to give a report in class or singing for special music at church doesn't count! We're talking about situations that would dishonor God and cause you to think less of yourself.)

I hope that you will never have to deal with a problem like this. But it's always good to think about what you would do, just in case.

If a problem should ever come up and the warning bells in your head go off, get away from the situation as fast as you can. And find an adult who will listen to you and help you.

Don't ever be afraid to stand up for what's right.

APRIL

8

How Do People See You?

Be imitators of God, therefore, as dearly loved children and live a life of love, just as Christ loved us. Ephesians 5:1, 2, NIV.

Have you ever heard your voice after it's been taped on a camcorder or a tape player? Most people when they hear what they sound like say, "That doesn't sound like me at all."

How you see yourself is also probably different from how others see you. You may see yourself as shy, while your friends consider you to be outgoing.

One day the manager of a printing company called a new employee to his office. "Allen, I want you to drive to the airport and pick up our company president. Mr. Reilly has been gone on business for a week and he's supposed to get in this afternoon. He'll be on Flight 411, which should arrive about 2:30. Go ahead and use my car. It's the black BMW."

Allen was eager to do as he was told, but he hesitated as he started to leave.

"Is there something wrong?" asked the manager.

"Well," stammered Allen, "I just wondered how to identify Mr. Reilly when I see him. I mean, uh, we've never met before."

"No problem. All you have to do is look for a man who is helping someone else."

"That's it? That's all the description I need?"

"Trust me. You'll know him when you see him."

That afternoon Allen slid behind the steering wheel of the BMW and drove to the airport. He arrived a few minutes early, so he bought a newspaper and sat down in the waiting area.

"Flight 411 arriving at gate 2."

People began streaming into the waiting room.

How in the world am I going to pick him out? thought Allen.

Then he saw a tall dark-haired man escorting a frail grandmotherly lady through the doorway.

"I'll get your suitcase," Alan heard him say. "Just sit here until your son arrives."

The man was starting to walk toward the baggage claim area when Allen stuck out his hand. "Mr. Reilly, my name is Allen Densmore. I'm here to take you back to the office."

Mr. Reilly looked at the young man in surprise. "How did you know who I am?" he asked.

Allen smiled. "It was easy. Before I left work, the office manager gave me your description."

How do other people see you? Would they describe you as a caring individual? When we make Jesus our example, people will know that we are Christians by our love.

APRIL

9

Hidden Treasure

When John bought the 25 acres of farmland, he had no real idea what he was getting. He did notice that the ground had a lot of gravel on the surface. But that was no problem. Hay grows well in rocky soil.

Later that spring, John was putting in a circular driveway in front of his house. As he was about to order a truckload of gravel, he thought of his new hayfield.

I wonder if I could get some gravel out of that field I just bought? It wouldn't hurt to try. So John drove his excavator over to the field and started digging. And digging. He couldn't believe his eyes. The gravel was not just on the surface of the field. As far as he could tell, it went down deep.

As soon as he finished investigating, John rushed home. "Ann," he said to his wife, "we may have a gold mine in our new field. I did a few rough calculations and figured out that there could be more than a million dollars' worth of gravel buried on that property!"

John has not yet called in the experts to evaluate his field, but he believes that he may soon become an accidental millionaire.

John's exciting discovery reminds me of one of Jesus' parables. In the story, a man accidentally finds a buried treasure while plowing a field. Since he only rents the land, he sells all his possessions, buys the property, and then claims the treasure as his own.

God has given each of us a field with a hidden treasure. The field is the Bible. And when we dig down deep and really study, we'll discover the valuable treasure of God's truth.

Don't let your Bible sit on the shelf. Get into its pages and search for the riches that are available to all who are willing to dig deep.

The kingdom of heaven is like treasure hidden in a field. When a man found it, he hid it again, and then in his joy went and sold all he had and bought that field. Matthew 13:44, NIV.

APRIL

10

A Book of Great Value

The precepts of the Lord are right, giving joy to the heart. . . . They are more precious than gold, than much pure gold. Psalm 19:8-10, NIV.

If you looked around your house right now, you'd probably find at least one Bible for each member of your family. Many homes have even more. Bibles are so inexpensive that most anyone can own one. And often we own several different versions, such as the King James Version, the New International Version, or the Revised Standard Version.

But it hasn't always been that way. Before the printing press was invented, all books had to be copied by hand. So copies of the Bible and other books were rare and expensive. Many times the only Bibles people ever got to see were those that were chained to reading stands in the large cathedrals. In the tenth century the countess of Anjou bought a book that was written in longhand. For it she gave 200 sheep, a load of wheat, a load of rye, a load of millet, and several furs.

But even more recently we have seen others who were willing to pay a high price to own a book. Back in September of 1989, the Russian government allowed Christian booksellers to sell Christian literature for the first time in their country. At a large booksellers' fair, copies of the New Testament went on sale for 100 rubles, which is about one month's wages for the Russian worker. (Regular Russian books sell for two or three rubles.)

People stood in line to buy copies of the New Testament. Soon all 10,000 Testaments were sold out. And the booksellers took orders for 17,000 more.

In Cuba it is illegal for people to bring Bibles into the country. It's hard to imagine, but on this island that is less than 100 miles from Florida, Bibles are so rare that the Seventh-day Adventist churches put them in the church libraries so members can check them out for a few weeks.

The next time you're tempted to view your Bible as just another book, remember how valuable it would be in Russia or Cuba. Start studying it for yourself. And then you'll understand why others value it so highly.

APRIL

11

Happiness—It's Your Choice

I have learned to be content whatever the circumstances. Philippians 4:11, NIV.

"Events are less important than our responses to them."

Imagine with me for a moment that it's your birthday. After you blow out your candles and open your gifts, your mother hands you a letter.

"It's from Aunt Becky," you say as you read the return address. You rip open the envelope and find a birthday card and a check for $25. How would you feel?

♦ ♦ ♦

Imagine again with me that it's your birthday. After you blow out your candles and open your gifts, your mother hands you a letter.

"It's from Aunt Becky," you say as you read the return address. Aunt Becky had promised you that this year she was going to send you $100 so you could buy the new bike you've been dreaming of. You rip open the envelope and find a birthday card and a check for $35. How would you feel?

♦ ♦ ♦

Why was it that you were probably happy with the $25 and disappointed with the $35?

These two situations illustrate that the events in your life are not as important as your attitude toward the events. In the first scene you were surprised and excited about getting the $25. In the second scene you were probably disappointed and maybe even a little angry. Your aunt had let you down.

As you can see, your attitude, not the size of the gift, determined whether or not you were happy.

Too many young people miss out on happiness because they have the wrong attitude. When they don't get what they want, they feel sorry for themselves. When there's nothing exciting going on, they're bored. When they run into a difficulty, they give up and quit.

Viktor Frankl was a Jewish psychiatrist during World War II. Hitler's Gestapo captured him and sent him to a concentration camp. On his arrival, the Nazis ordered the new prisoners to hand over their personal possessions.

As Viktor removed his watch and his wedding ring, he said, "There is one thing you can never take from me, and that is my freedom to choose how I react to whatever you do to me."

Like Viktor, we can't control everything that happens to us, but we can decide how we'll react.

APRIL

12

What's Tying You Down?

But now you are free from sin and have become slaves of God. This brings you a life that is only for God. And this gives you life forever. Romans 6:22, ICB.

Have you ever seen an elephant up close? You probably were surprised at how gentle it was. How is it that a person can control a huge elephant that could easily crush him or her under one foot?

When an elephant is first captured, it isn't tame. The hunters have to keep it from running away. So they secure a heavy chain around the elephant's foot and tie the other end to a banyan tree. The elephant, eager to escape, pulls and pulls on the chain. But the chain and the banyan tree won't budge. Finally, after some time the elephant realizes it is captured. And it stops trying to escape.

When the hunters see that the elephant has given up, they remove the chain from the tree and tie it to a small iron stake pushed into the ground.

Although the elephant could easily lift its leg and pull out the stake, it never tries. It never catches on that things have changed.

All of us have been born captives of Satan. And as long as we remain his slaves, we are under his control. But when we come to Jesus and accept Him as our Saviour, we don't have to give in to sin. The Holy Spirit, who lives in us, will give us the power to be like Jesus. But we often react like the elephant. We think we're still hopelessly chained to bad habits and past mistakes. So we just give up and remain Satan's captives.

When we come to Jesus and ask Him to save us, He does two things: He forgives us for our past sins, and He begins to change us so we'll reflect His character. He does the changing by giving us the Holy Spirit. The Spirit will speak to our minds, telling us what we should do and giving us the power to choose the right way.

If you have asked Jesus to come into your life, then you don't have to obey your sinful urges. The Holy Spirit is living in you. Make use of His power today—and every day.

APRIL

13

Are You Hooked?

Dear friend, I pray that you may enjoy good health and that all may go well with you. 3 John 2, NIV.

The ninth and tenth graders at our school give drug education programs to elementary students in our area. During the program we give a quiz to the students. One of the questions is "True or false, the most widely used drugs in America are marijuana and cocaine." How would you answer?

Most of the groups we see know that the answer is false. The most widely used drugs are nicotine, which is in tobacco; alcohol, which is in alcoholic drinks; and caffeine, which is in coffee, tea, and cola drinks.

Most of the time we visit public schools, but a few weeks ago we gave a program at one of our church schools. When my students mentioned that caffeine is a drug, a collective moan came from the group.

"Hey, I don't care what anybody says," said one student, "I like Mountain Dew and Coke."

"Yeah," said another, "what's the big deal? Caffeine isn't that bad."

When I was a freshman in college, I had a part-time office job at an electronics company. And every morning the servicemen would start the day with coffee and doughnuts. I had never tasted coffee before, but one day I decided to be one of the gang and try it.

After all, I told myself, *I really don't think coffee is all that addicting. I can control myself.*

But a week later I found out different. As I walked into the office, I heard myself say, "Where's the coffee? I'm not starting work without it." All of a sudden I realized that I was hooked.

That's it, I told myself. *No more. I'm not going to be controlled by caffeine.* So I went cold turkey that day. It was hard. I wanted to feel that caffeine "lift," but I wanted my freedom even more.

So what's the big deal about caffeine?

Here are some of the problems it can cause. It makes the heart beat faster; raises the blood pressure; causes headaches; makes a person more nervous, jumpy, and irritable; increases depression; and makes it harder for people to sleep at night.

But the most dangerous problem with caffeine is that it can lead a person into trying stronger drugs. One health educator has called it the Adventist "gateway drug."

If you regularly drink coffee or caffeine drinks, you may want to think about making a change. It's up to you.

APRIL

14

Hiding God's Word in Your Heart

But his delight is in the law of the Lord, and on his law he meditates day and night.
Psalm 1:2, NIV.

One of the best ways to keep your mind filled with good thoughts is to memorize Bible verses. Then throughout the day you can use these verses to give you encouragement. Bible verses are also a great way to shove out bad thoughts when they pop into your brain. It's much easier to get rid of bad thoughts when you have something good to replace them with.

I don't know about you, but I have a terrible time memorizing things. When I decided to start learning Bible verses, I was afraid I'd never be able to do it. But I found a few tips that have helped make memorization easier.

1. Choose verses that mean something to you. For instance, if you have a problem with fear, memorize a verse or two that talk about the courage we can have through Jesus. Choose specific verses that deal with your problems. The best way to find a verse is to use a concordance. If you have never used one before, ask you parents, teacher, or Sabbath school leader how to use it.

2. Choose a version of the Bible that you are comfortable with. You may want to check out two of the newer translations, the New International Version and the New Century Version. They use modern words that make the Bible easier to understand.

3. Write down word for word on 3 x 5 cards the verses you want to learn. On the back of the cards, copy just the first letter of each word.

4. Punch a hole in the upper lefthand corner of the cards, and hold them together with a metal ring or brad.

5. Read through your cards every morning. As you get to know the verses better, turn the cards over and try saying the verses by using only the first letters of each word to prompt you.

6. When you have a verse learned, review it at least once a week.

7. You may also like to make an extra set of cards that you can take with you. When you have some spare time, read through them a few times.

As you begin to learn Bible verses, you'll find that it will get easier and easier. You'll also notice that God will bring them to your mind when you need them most.

APRIL

15

Are You a Procrastinator?

I tell you, now is the time of God's favor, now is the day of salvation. 2 Corinthians 6:2, NIV.

Better to do it than to wish it had been done."

I think we should proclaim today National Procrastinator's Day in honor of the people all over the United States who put off filling out their tax forms until the last minute.

You probably don't have to worry about paying taxes, but I bet you still have a problem with procrastination.

Why do we put off doing things? Well, it's usually because we think the experiences will be painful in some way. Students put off doing their homework because it's not fun. Adults put off going to the dentist because they're afraid they'll have to get a tooth filled. Teachers put off grading papers (boy, don't I know that!). Piano students put off practicing their music. Mothers put off washing windows . . . But none of these situations are as harmful as putting off our decision to give ourselves to God.

We know that becoming a Christian is the right thing to do. But we're afraid that it will be painful. We think about all the things we'll have to give up. We imagine the unpleasant things that God might ask us to do. And so we say, "Not now. I'll do it later, after I've had a chance to have fun. I'll come to God when I'm old. I want to live a little first."

But there's a lot of danger in that kind of thinking. For starters, we do not know how long we will live. Life is just too uncertain, even for young people. The only time we can be sure of is today.

Another problem is that only a small percentage of people become Christians when they're older. Christian psychiatrist Paul Meier states that 85 percent of all people who accept Jesus do so by the time they're 18. That means those who become Christians after age 18 account for only 15 percent of the church body.

Don't put off your opportunity to become one of God's children. While you're still young, get to know the best Friend you'll ever have.

If you've never invited Jesus into you heart, won't you do it right now?

APRIL

16

Once Is Not Enough

Create in me a pure heart, O God, and renew a steadfast spirit within me. Psalm 51:10, NIV.

Asking Jesus to come into our lives is not a one-time commitment. We need to give ourselves to Him every single day.

Pastor Donaldson had hoped to clean out his garage that Sunday afternoon, but a phone call changed his plans. "Are you the minister at the Seventh-day Adventist church?" asked the caller.

"Yes, I am," the pastor replied.

"Well, some truck driver has driven his rig into your parking lot at the church. I think he's drunk. But he keeps asking to talk to a minister. So I thought maybe you'd come over."

"Sure, I'll be there in about 10 minutes."

Hanging up the phone, Pastor Donaldson called Ray Conrad from Alcoholics Anonymous and asked Ray to meet him at the church.

When the pastor reached the church, he saw a man leaning against the cab of his truck. Walking over to him, the pastor stuck out his hand and said, "Hi, I'm Pastor Larry Donaldson. What can I do for you?"

When the man began to talk, Larry realized he was drunk. But he patiently listened as the man droned on and on about all his problems.

A few minutes later Ray drove up.

Together he and Larry tried to encourage the man. "What you need is Jesus," Larry said after a while. "He can help you find meaning in life. Have you ever asked Him to be your Saviour?"

"Yeah, I did that once when I was a kid."

"Well, why don't you ask Him again right now?"

Suddenly the man body's was thrown to the ground by an unseen force. Larry recognized immediately that he was dealing with Satan's forces. He and Ray started praying out loud for the man, who gradually regained his strength and stood back up.

"Listen," said the pastor, "Satan is trying to control your life. Call on Jesus to save you right now."

"I already did that once," the man said. As soon as he spoke, his body slammed to the ground again.

Satan and his angels are a very real force in our world. They don't always take control of a person's body, but they live in the minds and hearts of all who don't belong to God.

Every day we need to ask Jesus to live in us through His Holy Spirit. We can't depend on the decision we made yesterday. We must recommit ourselves each day to follow our Saviour.

APRIL

17

Our Present Help in Trouble

God is our refuge and strength, an ever-present help in trouble. . . . The Lord Almighty is with us; the God of Jacob is our fortress. Psalm 46:1-11, NIV.

When we left Pastor Donaldson yesterday, he was trying to encourage the stranger in his church parking lot to ask Jesus into his heart. But again and again the man refused, saying he'd already done it once before. And again and again the man was thrown to the ground by a supernatural force. Neither Larry nor Ray was ready for what happened next.

Suddenly a strange look came into the man's eyes. When he opened his mouth again, he spoke with an eerie, hollow voice. "I know all about you," he said, pointing to the pastor. "I know things about you that nobody knows." And then the demon speaking through the man began to list the minister's specific weaknesses and sins.

It was too much for Ray, who had a bad heart. He hurried away to his car and got inside. But the pastor stood his ground. He knew he was sinful, but he also knew that Jesus had promised to cover him with His perfect righteousness.

The demon-possessed man's rage fueled hotter. Reaching out, he tried to grab the pastor's neck. But his hands froze in midair, restrained by an invisible force.

"You're just lucky!" he screamed. "Because if Jesus wasn't standing next to you, I'd kill you on the spot!"

Pastor Donaldson almost fainted. *Jesus* was standing next to *him?*

The pastor knew that Jesus is not omnipresent like the Holy Spirit. Because Jesus has retained His humanness, He has lost His ability to be everywhere at one time. Was it possible that Jesus had come from heaven and was actually standing by his side, offering protection from Satan and his evil angels? The thought seemed more than the pastor could comprehend.

Unfortunately, the story doesn't have a happy ending. Within a few minutes the police arrived, and the man was taken away. He never did ask Jesus to release him from Satan's power.

But Pastor Donaldson has never forgotten that day—the day Jesus made a special trip to stand by him in his hour of need.

APRIL

18

God's Invisible Hand

For I am the Lord, your God, who takes hold of your right hand and says to you, Do not fear; I will help you. Isaiah 41:13, NIV.

"All right, everybody, time to clean up," I called to my sewing class. "We need to get back to the school in 10 minutes, so gather up your things and get ready to go."

On Thursday evenings the Pathfinders met for opening exercises at the school gym. After that I took the sewing class girls across the street to my house, where they worked on the outfits they were making.

In a few minutes everyone was ready to go. Betty Harris (one of the counselors), her son Donnie, and I followed the girls down the long, dark driveway.

Betty picked up 4-year-old Donnie so she could carry him across the highway. The girls started across the road, and I followed. Just then I looked up and saw a pair of headlights racing straight toward me.

The driver must see us crossing the road. Surely he'll slow down, I thought.

But as I neared the center line, I heard the driver gun the engine. The car seemed almost on top of me. I screamed and lunged ahead for safety, dropping my jacket in the process.

Oh no, I thought, *Betty's behind me, and she's carrying Donnie. She'll never make it.*

The next thing I knew, the car streaked past, running over my jacket. I looked up, trying to find Betty in the moonlight.

"Oh, Renee," she gasped, "I thought he was going to kill us. I was only halfway across. I couldn't run with Donnie in my arms. But all of a sudden I was on this side of the road. It was like something just picked me up and set me down."

When I was young I used to worry all the time about living through the time of trouble. How would I survive? How would I make it if I was separated from my family? How would I find food and shelter?

After seeing how God saved Betty and Donnie that night after the sewing class, I know that He's capable to taking care of every situation I find myself in. My job is not to worry about the time of trouble, but to get to know the One who will meet all my needs now and then.

APRIL

19

God's Big Surprise

I could hardly believe my eyes last week when I looked out my classroom window and saw snowflakes pelting the grass. *What is going on?* I thought to myself. *It's the middle of April. Michigan has strange weather, but this is crazy! If "April showers bring May flowers," I wonder what April flurries bring?*

The snow was the big topic of the day. We joked that maybe the seasons were turning around, and that soon we'd be having snow during summer vacation. By Sunday the mystery of the April flurries was solved. It all started with an 8-year-old boy named Jeffrey Fleckenstein. Jeffrey, who lives in Phoenix, Arizona, suffers from a weak artery in his heart. And unless he has a heart-lung transplant, he won't live very long.

The Make-a-Wish Foundation heard about Jeffrey and, as they have done with many other children with life-threatening conditions, granted him a wish. His request was to fly to southwestern Michigan to see family members in the area—and to feel some snow.

A few days before his arrival, Jeffrey's grandmother called our local ski resorts to see if they might have some snow left. But because of the beautiful warm weather we've been having, she couldn't find a single flake.

The first day after Jeffrey's arrival, he began visiting some of his many aunts, uncles, and cousins. On the second day he went shopping with his mother and grandmother. And as he walked out of the mall, the sky opened up, and down came the first snowflakes Jeffrey had ever seen.

Did God send the snow for Jeffrey? I think He did. God is like that. He loves to give us special gifts.

As you go through your day, remember that you have a heavenly Father who loves you and who cares about not only your needs but also your wants.

If you, then, though you are evil, know how to give good gifts to your children, how much more will your Father in heaven give good gifts to those who ask him! Matthew 7:11, NIV.

APRIL

20

Using the Power

Finally, be strong in the Lord and in his mighty power. Ephesians 6:10, NIV.

An old farmer walked into the tool department at the local hardware store.

"May I help you?" asked the clerk.

"I'm lookin' for a new saw, young man."

"Just what kind of saw do you need? What do you plan to use it for?"

The old man scratched his head. "Well, I suppose I'll be needin' it mainly for cuttin' firewood."

"Right over here," the clerk said as he led the man through the aisles. "This," he said, pointing to a chain saw, "would be just what you need."

"Never did use one of those," said the old man. "Is it faster than a handsaw?"

"There's no comparison. In fact, I bet you could saw 20 trees with this chain saw in the time it took you to saw one with a handsaw."

So the old farmer bought the chain saw and left the store. Two weeks later the clerk was surprised to see him back with the chain saw in hand.

"Well, what do you think?" the clerk asked.

"It's the worst saw I've ever used. I've been tryin' to cut down one tree for almost two weeks. And I'm still cuttin'. I'm returnin' this and buyin' myself a handsaw."

"Let me take a look at it," said the clerk as he picked up the chain saw. Stepping back from the counter, he pulled the starter rope and the saw roared into action.

The old farmer nearly jumped from under his straw hat. "Land sakes, where did that noise come from?"

Of course this story isn't true, but it does illustrate a point.

The farmer had the ability to cut down trees in just seconds, but because he didn't use the power that was available, he ended up wearing himself out and being hard on his chain saw. I can just see him sawing back and forth against the tree trunk.

We often do the same thing when it comes to sin. We try to change ourselves using our own power, but all we're doing is scratching the surface. We may look a little different on the outside, but we're still the same on the inside.

But with the help that Jesus offers, we can say no to temptation. As long as we look to Him, He'll give us the power we need.

When you meet temptation today, don't try to meet it on your own. Turn on the power.

APRIL

21

Accepting Responsibility

He who conceals his sins does not prosper, but whoever confesses and renounces them finds mercy. Proverbs 28:13, NIV.

It was Friday. The eighth-grade class was serving spaghetti for hot lunch that day.

Walking past the kitchen during the first break, I noticed that there wasn't any food sitting on the counter. Calling Ken, the class president, aside, I asked him who was making lunch.

"Oh, no," he said, putting his face in his hands. "I forgot to get the food last night."

"Ken, this is the second time this has happened," I said. "What's the problem?"

I expected Ken to blame his mother, or maybe the biology teacher for scheduling a test on Friday, or even me for giving him the responsibility. His answer caught me off guard.

"I'm sorry, Mrs. Coffee. There's no excuse. I've just been careless."

When Ken admitted his fault, I was no longer upset. I wanted to help him work things out. As soon as I had some free time, I drove to the store and got the food.

Why is it so difficult to admit it when we're wrong? I think it has to do with pride. We want to think well of ourselves, and we want others to respect us, also.

Let me give you a little quiz. Pretend that you're drying the dishes after supper. Your mother is in the other room. Suddenly she hears a loud crash and calls out, "What happened?"

What do you say? (Stop here and decide what your answer would be.)

Was your response something like, "The glass broke" or "The glass fell"? If you answered either way, you're pretty normal. Did you notice who was responsible for the accident? The glass. Instead of saying "I dropped the glass," you blame a poor, innocent piece of dinnerware.

The next time you're tempted to blame someone else for something you've done, accept the responsibility. You'll be surprised at how forgiving people will be. And you may even be surprised at how good you'll feel about yourself.

APRIL

22

The Joy of Giving

One man gives freely, yet gains even more. . . . A generous man will prosper; he who refreshes others will himself be refreshed. Proverbs 11:24, 25, NIV.

There never was a person who did anything worth doing, who did not receive more than he gave."—Henry Ward Beecher.

When Daniel Pearson died penniless, he was a happy man. As a boy Daniel had very little. His family couldn't afford much for their son. So when he went away to college, he had to support himself. He lived in an attic and cooked his own meals in order to save enough to pay his tuition.

After graduation he took a job as a teacher. Some years later he went into farming, and then eventually into the lumber business. Things went well for Daniel and his wife. In fact, they made so much money that they decided to start giving it away. So they began making large donations to different institutions.

One of Daniel's special interests was students who wanted a college education but couldn't afford it. He must have remembered his own struggle as a young man. In order to help industrious young people reach their dreams, he set up student education funds in 47 different colleges.

Once he was asked why he gave so much money away instead of keeping it for himself. He said, "I have had more fun than any other rich man alive. They are welcome to their automobiles and yachts. I have discovered that giving is the most exquisite delight in the world. I intend to die penniless."

By the time Mr. Pearson reached his ninety-first birthday, he had given away his entire fortune, which amounted to more than $6 million.

When Jesus told us that giving is better than receiving, He knew what He was talking about. The enjoyment that comes from having things lasts only a short time. But the happiness that we get from giving to others comes back every time we think about it.

Daniel Pearson died penniless, but you can be sure that he enjoyed every penny he gave away.

APRIL

23

A Promise of Blessings

"Bring the whole tithe into the storehouse, that there may be food in my house. Test me in this," says the Lord Almighty, "and see if I will not throw open the floodgates of heaven and pour out so much blessing that you will not have room enough for it." Malachi 3:10, NIV.

A few years ago a minister got up one Sunday and preached a sermon on tithing. He told how God has promised to bless all those who return to Him one tenth of their income.

The concept was new to the congregation. But a number of the families decided to give it a try. A month later one of the men in the congregation brought a lawsuit against the minister. The man claimed that God had not blessed him, so he wanted his money back. And since he couldn't sue God, he sued the minister. But another church member gave the man the money he demanded, saying he'd be glad to take the man's blessings, since he didn't want them.

Many people have the idea that God's blessings come only in the form of money: an inheritance from a long-lost relative, a raise in pay, or a winning lottery ticket. They want God to be like a game show host who passes out prizes to those who come up with the right answers.

But God's blessings are not limited to money and material things. He gives good health, protection from accidents, a clear conscience, friendships, contentment, and best of all, friendship with Him.

Paying tithe is not just the privilege of adults. Young people can also trust God with their tithe and be blessed. Figuring out your tithe is easy. Let's say you receive $12.00 for your birthday. Move the decimal over one place to the left. The number will look like this: $1.200. Cross off the right end number (the last zero). Your tithe is $1.20. Put the money inside a tithe envelope, then drop it in the offering plate next Sabbath.

If you haven't given your tithe to God before, why not put Him to the test. There's no reason you shouldn't get in on God's blessings! He has plenty.

APRIL

24

The Fire Shall Not Destroy

For the Lord loves the just and will not forsake his faithful ones. They will be protected forever.
Psalm 37:28, NIV.

One thing to remember about God's blessings is that they aren't always obvious. In fact, we may have to wait until we're in heaven to find out some of the ways God blessed us while we were on earth. But many times God does work special miracles for those who faithfully return their tithes to Him.

In 1902 Alexander Kerr decided to pay tithe even though he owed money on a number of large debts. Not long afterward, he took money out of his small bank account and began a small business in San Francisco. Soon the Kerr Glass Manufacturing Company became one of the largest producers of canning jars in the country.

During the next four years, the business grew. Then on April 18, 1906, San Francisco was hit with one of the worst disasters in United States history. An earthquake rocked the city, collapsing buildings and spreading fires everywhere. For three days fires burned out of control. Finally fire fighters had to dynamite entire city blocks in order to control the blazes.

About 700 people died; 250,000 lost their homes. More than 28,000 buildings were destroyed, leaving the city in shambles.

Mr. Kerr was not in San Francisco during the earthquake. He had no idea what had happened to his factory. His family and friends were sure that it had been completely wiped out with the rest of the city.

A week later a telegram arrived for Mr. Kerr. It read: "Everything for a mile and a half on all sides of the factory burned; but your factory was miraculously saved." As it turned out, the fire had burned up to the wooden fence surrounding the factory and then stopped. Employees checking the building found that not one of the jars inside was even cracked.

The next time you see a Kerr canning jar, remember how the Lord rewarded Alexander Kerr's faith.

APRIL

25

You've Got the Smarts!

The unfolding of your words gives light; it gives understanding to the simple. Psalm 119:130, NIV.

Charles Talleyrand was a highly respected French statesman during the time of Napoleon. Talleyrand was also one of the great intellectuals of his day.

The story is told of a group of scientists who came to him one day with a strange request. "Talleyrand," they said, "we would like permission to study your brain when you die."

"Study my brain?" asked the surprised man.

"That's right. We want to find out how your brain is different from the average person's. If we could figure out the answer, we might be able to help people become more intelligent."

Talleyrand thought over the request and then gave the written permission they requested.

In 1838, at the age of 84, the famous man died, and his brain was donated for research. Scientists eagerly began studying Talleyrand's brain to see if they could find the secret to his great intelligence. At the end of the day, the scientists placed it on a slab at the end of the laboratory table. They planned to continue their work when they returned the next day.

Sometime later a lab assistant came into the room with a brain he had been studying—the brain of a common man. Seeing Talleyrand's brain on the lab table, he decided that the slab must be where all brains were to be placed when not in use. So he set the brain he was studying next to Talleyrand's.

When the scientists arrived the next morning, they were shocked to see not one but two brains sitting on the table. Quickly they hurried over to retrieve Talleyrand's brain, but try as they might, they couldn't tell which was which. The brains looked just alike.

Every marking period when grades are passed out, I hear students say things like "Well, if I had John's (or Megan's or Lisa's) brains, then I'd get good grades too." Or "Well, it's not my fault that I'm dumb." Most students who get low grades blame their poor grades on a lack of brainpower, but what they're really lacking is willpower.

Not all students can make straight A's. But all can put time and effort into their work and learn to take their education more seriously.

If you're having a hard time in school, don't give up. God has given you a powerful brain. Make the most of it.

APRIL

26

God's Not Against Fun

The prospect of the righteous is joy, but the hopes of the wicked come to nothing. Proverbs 10:28, NIV.

Satan is the father of lies. He uses them to ruin human relationships, and he also uses them to separate us from God.

One of Satan's favorite falsehoods is "God is against fun." This lie works great on young people. You don't want to live a boring life. You want plenty of good times. Satan tells you that Christian fun is limited to prayer meeting, singing bands, and Ingathering. No wonder some kids say "No, thanks."

God isn't against fun. He just wants you to do things that will make you feel better about yourself. He wants you to have good memories instead of bitter regrets. He wants to build your future. Satan does all he can to make sure you don't have a future.

Last week three high school students from our area decided to have a little fun during a heavy windstorm. They walked out onto a pier to watch the waves. But one of the waves washed them into Lake Michigan. Rescuers pulled the girls to safety, but divers are still searching for the boy's body.

Angela gets her thrills in a different way. She likes to drink. Part of the excitement comes from hiding her habit from the dean at her boarding academy and from her parents. Her boyfriend had to leave the academy in the middle of the year so he could go to an alcohol rehabilitation center. But she's sure she'll never become addicted. Maybe she won't. But she's destroying brain cells every time she takes a drink. And because alcohol makes it harder for us to say no, she'll be more likely to experiment with other drugs or give in to sexual pressure. And if she drives after drinking, she could kill someone else—maybe even herself.

Whatever fun we choose lasts only for a short time. But the consequences of the wrong kinds of fun always last a long time, sometimes even for the rest of our lives.

Get all the fun out of life that you can. Just be sure you use your head. Remember, you'll building for two futures—life on earth and eternal life in heaven and the new earth.

APRIL

27

Chained

Another one of Satan's lies is "If you choose to follow God, He'll take away all your freedom."

Everybody wants to feel free to make his or her own choices. Nobody likes to take orders from someone else. As soon as we're able to talk, we start saying things like "Do it myself, Mommy."

Satan knows how we love freedom, so he tells us that once we become Christians and surrender our lives to God, we lose our freedom of choice and become puppets. But it is Satan, not God, who is the master puppeteer.

Let's see how he controls just a few of the people who have fallen for his type of freedom.

1. Liars. Liars may be free to say anything they want to, but their lies hold them captive. They have to continue making up stories to cover the untruth they've already told. They are not free to tell the truth.

2. Overeaters. These people don't let anyone tell them what they can and cannot eat. So they stuff themselves, enjoying every last bite. But they end up being held captive in a body that doesn't look good or work right.

3. Smokers. They are free to inhale the 200 chemicals found in cigarettes. All those warnings about cancer and emphysema don't scare them. But when the doctor sees a dark spot on their lung X-ray, they'll find out just how imprisoned they really are.

4. The sexually free. These people ignore God's warnings against immorality. They think good feelings are more important than good judgment. But all those who go after this kind of freedom will eventually find themselves in a prison of regrets—regrets for the self-respect they have lost; regrets for the unplanned babies that are born or aborted; regrets for the sexually transmitted diseases they have picked up and maybe passed on, some of which can never be cured.

Every relationship involves give-and-take. When Satan controls your life, he gives a few good times, but takes away your freedom.

On the other hand, when Jesus is Lord of your life, He gives you His righteousness and takes away your sins. Sure, He'll ask you to stay away from the things that hurt you, but the choice is always yours. You are always free to have your own way.

They promise them freedom, while they themselves are slaves of depravity—for a man is a slave to whatever has mastered him. 2 Peter 2:19, NIV.

APRIL

28

God's First Choice

Live as free men, but do not use your freedom as a cover-up for evil; live as servants of God. 1 Peter 2:16, NIV.

We find freedom when we find God; we lose it when we lose Him."—Paul Scherer.

Yesterday we looked at Satan's lie about freedom. It reminded me of a statement Chris Blake, editor of *Insight,* made sometime ago. When I first heard the idea, I said, "Impossible"—it was so different from what I'd always been taught. But I thought it over and finally had to say, "I think he's got something there."

Chris Blake said that freedom is more important to God than salvation.

Let's go back in time. Way back before even the angels were created. If God had wanted to make sure that the angels would never rebel against Him, He would have made them without the ability to sin. But He didn't do that. He wanted to share His love with His heavenly family, and He wanted to receive love back from them. But He knew that a loving relationship is possible only when both parties are free to make a choice. So He gave the angels the power to choose to follow His rules or to go against them.

Now let's go to the Garden of Eden. Because God wanted a special friendship with human beings, He created Adam and Eve with the power of choice. They too were free to obey or disobey.

And what about us? Aren't we free to decide for or against God? Although He gives us plenty of warnings against sin, He won't force us into obedience. God gives us the opportunity to choose what we want to do. He wants us to be free to make up our own minds.

And what about the future? If Jesus valued our salvation more than our freedom, then when He comes again, He'd force everyone to go to heaven, whether he or she wanted to or not. But that's not God's way, for He knows that heaven would be worse than death for those who never learned to love Him.

Christians are the freest people in the world. We're free to follow whomever we choose. But once we really get to know God, we'll never want to leave His side.

APRIL

29

There's Always Hope

If you, O Lord, kept a record of sins, O Lord, who could stand? But with you there is forgiveness. Psalm 130:3, 4, NIV.

The last of Satan's lies that we're to look at comes in two parts. The first part is "Doing it this once won't hurt."

Most Christian young people know the difference between right and wrong. So Satan had to come up with another angle to entice them into experimenting with sin.

When you're tempted to do something you know is wrong, Satan probably says "Go ahead and try it. Doing it this once won't hurt." Satan knows that most Christians won't jump into sin with both feet, so he talks us into just dipping our toes into it.

And then what happens? As soon as we do something wrong, the tables turn, and our old buddy Satan jumps back from us in horror. "Oh no!" he cries. "Look at what you've done! What a rotten, dirty sinner you are!"

Now here comes the second part of the lie.

"If you think God is going to forgive you," he continues, "then you'd better think again. You're too sinful to be forgiven. God wants nothing to do with the likes of you."

And some people believe Satan. Instead of coming to Jesus right away and asking for forgiveness, they decide to give Him time to cool off. Others just give up and decide that living a Christian life is impossible.

That's the whole problem with sin. It separates us from God. Our guilt, instead of bringing us back to Jesus for forgiveness, often keeps us away from Him.

Satan has it all backward. Doing something wrong just once *does* hurt. Sin, no matter how small, always hurts. But we're never too sinful for God to forgive.

The next time Satan gets you to do something wrong, turn to Jesus right away. Don't be fooled into thinking you're beyond hope. Your hope is in Jesus—if you'll only ask.

APRIL

30

Fighting the Lazies

All hard work brings a profit, but mere talk leads only to poverty. Proverbs 14:23, NIV.

Some people are like blisters. They never appear until the work is done."

The sloth has to be one of the strangest animals in the world. It can stay in one place for hours without moving a muscle. And it sleeps at least 15 hours a day. Almost 99 percent of its life is spent upside down. As it moves in a tree, the sloth advances upside down, hanging from the branches by its hooklike claws.

A sloth may spend its entire life in one tree. In fact, the sloth is so slow-moving that algae often begin to grow on its hair. And sometimes the algae get so thick that the animal turns bluish green.

The only reason a sloth leaves its tree home is to find more food, and if food isn't close by, the animal will die of starvation because it moves so slowly. One adventuresome sloth did leave home and travel four miles. But it took a month and a half to reach its destination.

Do your parents ever mistake you for a sloth around your home? Do you just hang around the house, eating and sleeping, without making a contribution to the family?

It's easy to get the lazies at school, too. Have you ever found yourself putting off your homework because you just didn't feel like doing it?

Laziness is a hard habit to break because it's pleasant, at least for a while. When you're lazy, you can avoid the things you don't want to do. You feel in control of your life. But as it is with all other bad habits, you'll eventually pay the price.

The price could be failing math because you didn't study. It could be messing up during special music because you didn't practice. Or it could be getting fired from your part-time job because the boss can't depend on you.

When you feel like avoiding responsibility, don't give in to the urge to be lazy. Get your work done right away. You'll feel like you've accomplished something, and you'll feel good about yourself.

MAY

1

Be Yourself

Do not conform any longer to the pattern of this world, but be transformed by the renewing of your mind. Romans 12:2, NIV.

Some young people spend a lot of time trying to be like everyone else.

During a high school graduation last year, I overheard a man talking to his wife. "It's really strange," he said. "All the girls look alike." He was right. In their white robes and with identical hairstyles, they did look very much alike.

It's easy to go along with the crowd. Instead of enjoying our specialness, we stick to what is safe and accepted. And too often we miss out on the chance to develop into the person we were intended to be. And even worse, sometimes we get ourselves into trouble because we'll do anything to belong.

The Metropolitan Life Foundation found that more than half of all elementary school students do things they don't want to because of peer pressure. They're afraid to say no.

Have you ever done something because you didn't want to be different from everybody else?

We get the idea that peer pressure is having someone try to force us to drink a can of beer or smoke a cigarette. But peer pressure is usually just an urge to do what everyone else is doing, and it involves much more than drugs and alcohol.

Peer pressure happens when the cool kids at school listen to heavy metal rock music. They don't force you to listen, but you find yourself changing radio stations and buying new tapes because you don't want to be different.

It even happens when others begin to pick on certain kids and make fun of them. You don't want to hurt anyone's feelings, but you don't want to be different, either. And besides, if you don't do what the group is doing, the group might start picking on you. So you join in on the fun.

Peer pressure isn't all bad. I've seen students putting pressure on their classmates to take their schoolwork more seriously. That's positive peer pressure.

The important thing is to make your own decisions. Don't let others pressure you into doing something that could destroy your health or your self-respect. Decide what's best for you. Dare to be different.

MAY

2

Pride Always Goes Before a Fall

If anyone thinks he is something when he is nothing, he deceives himself. Each one should test his own actions. Then he can take pride in himself, without comparing himself to somebody else. Galatians 6:3-5, NIV.

"It is not the capabilities you now possess or ever will have that will give you success. It is that which the Lord can do for you."—E. G. White.

Cellist Emil Maestri was a teenager when he learned an important lesson about pride. While he was playing his cello in a cathedral in Barcelona, Spain, Emil noticed a large crowd gathering. And more people kept streaming in.

They've come to hear my music, he said to himself. *I will show them what a fine musician I am.* So leaning back in his chair, he closed his eyes and began playing with all his heart. When he drew his bow across the strings on the final chord, he looked up, expecting to see appreciative nods from his vast audience. Instead, he saw nothing but an empty church.

Setting his cello down, he hurried over to the elderly minister who was standing in the doorway. "Where did everyone go?" he asked. "When I started playing, people were crowding to the front just to hear me. But now they are all gone."

The kindly old man put his hand on Emil's shoulder. "Emil, they were not here to listen to you play. They were here waiting for food. Once a week we pass out free food to the poor. They were waiting for the bread line to form."

There are two kinds of pride. Good pride is taking pleasure in doing something well. We feel good about ourselves and what we do.

Bad pride, on the other hand, is comparing ourselves to others, hoping that we'll come out looking better than everyone else. This kind of pride is a form of selfishness in which we try to draw attention to ourselves.

Whatever we do, we need to remember that our gifts and talents are all gifts from God. Instead of using them to show off, let us use them to bring glory to His name.

MAY

3

No Easy Answers

I have told you these things, so that in me you may have peace. In this world you will have trouble. But take heart! I have overcome the world. John 16:33, NIV.

My brother-in-law, Tim, got some interesting mail recently, and I'd like to share it with you. Here's the first letter:

"I, Madame Daudet, solemnly make this promise: I have a wonderful new life planned for you. The kind of perfect life without any money worries. Without depressing thoughts. A life filled with love and laughter. A life in which every day will be filled with sunshine.

"But I must be frank: I can help nice people like yourself only for the next few months while you are into that special 'Golden Wave' time of your life. That brief time period when you—personally—are in a lucky magnetic field every breathing moment of each day and night."

Madame Daudet goes on to explain that if Tim would just send her $19.95, she'd rush his "Golden Wave" revelations. And then he could begin to gain great sums of money, attract love, and find the happiness he wants and deserves.

Tim also got a letter from world consultant June Penn, who says: "Timothy, your 'Time of Power' is coming up. A time when the possibility exists for you to amass a great deal of money.

"For a very short time period you have the chance to acquire all the money you want. All the success you want. All the love and happiness you want for yourself in life."

All Tim needs to do is send her $20, and he'll receive his personal Time of Power Action Plan.

Knowing some "Golden Wave" revelations or our "Time of Power" won't give us a life free of problems, with all the money, love, and happiness we want. What these people are promising does not exist on earth.

As long as we live in a sinful world, we're going to have problems. But as Christians we know that God will help us work them out.

"If we surrender our lives to His service, we can never be placed in a position for which God has not made provision" *(Christ's Object Lessons,* p. 173).

Don't look to other people for the answer to your problems. Look to Jesus.

Something to think about: What problems would you like Jesus to help you with today?

MAY

4

You Get What You Give

Remember this: Whoever sows sparingly will also reap sparingly, and whoever sows generously will also reap generously. 2 Corinthians 9:6, NIV.

Back in the days of the circuit-riding preachers, most churches saw their minister only a few times each season. Churches were far apart, and transportation was slow. So the congregations had to rely on their elders or other visiting ministers while their pastor made his rounds.

One Sunday morning a guest speaker traveled to a neighboring village to deliver the sermon. His young son rode along with him on the front of the saddle.

When they arrived at the church, the man tied his horse to the hitching post and helped his son from the saddle. The visiting preacher was ushered through the sanctuary up to the pulpit. And for the next 30 minutes he delivered a moving sermon to the congregation.

After the closing song and the benediction, the man walked to the back of the church and shook hands with the people as they left. When he finished, he put on his hat and coat and started to leave. But then he remembered that no offering had been taken.

Always one to bring a gift to the Lord each week, the minister dropped a dime into an offering box, which stood next to the entrance door. And then he and his son went outside.

Just as they were about to mount the horse, the church treasurer hurried over. "Pastor, we want to thank you so much for coming and giving us the message today. It is the custom at our church to give the speaker all the money that is put into the offering box after the service." With that, the treasurer handed over a dime—the same dime the pastor had put in the box.

The man's son looked up at his father and said, "Daddy, if you'd given more, you would've gotten more, wouldn't you?"

We all get out of life just what we put into it. If we give away happiness, we'll get it back. If we spread around unhappiness, we'll get that back, too.

It's the same at school. If you put time and effort into your studies, you'll learn a lot. But if you do no more than occupy a desk, you won't make much progress.

MAY

5

It's All in a Name

We are therefore Christ's ambassadors, as though God were making his appeal through us. 2 Corinthians 5:20, NIV.

Actions speak louder than words—it is by our deeds that we are known."

What comes to your mind when you hear the words Rigoletto, J. J. Thunder, Normark, and Dritz? Nothing? Well, try these: Levi, Kodak, Nike, Hershey, and Schwinn. Do they sound a little more familiar? The names are all different brand names, or trademarks. A trademark represents the company that stands behind it. Companies hope that you will learn to trust their brands and keep coming back to buy their products.

I love to buy my clothes at resale shops. After I find something that I like, I always check the tag to see if it has a good brand name. During college I worked at a ladies' dress store. I got to know which companies make high-quality products. So I'm always on the lookout for clothing with a good name.

When we decide to follow Jesus, we take on the name Christian. By the way we live, we represent to the world what Jesus is like.

Jacob Braude in his book *Human Interest Stories* tells of a Muslim trader in India who approached a European. "Could you please get me a Bible?" he asked.

"A Bible? Why would you want a Bible? You don't believe in Jesus."

"That's true," said the Muslim. "But I want one, one that is written in English."

The European scratched his head. "I don't get it. You want a book you don't believe in, and you even want it in a language you can't read. What are you going to do with it?"

"Well, you see, I do much business with European traders. When one comes to me, I will set the Bible in front of him. If he treats it with respect, I know I can trust him. If he makes fun of it or shoves it aside, I will refuse to deal with him because I will know that he's a man of dishonor."

Although the Indian man did not believe in the Bible, he knew that those who did were people with high standards.

What does the name Christian mean to the people in your town? What does it mean to your next-door neighbors? Have you lived in a way that causes other people to respect and admire the trademark?

MAY

6

Let It Shine

Let your light shine before men, that they may see your good deeds and praise your Father in heaven. Matthew 5:16, NIV.

Karen and Kevin loved their father, but one thing bothered them. He smoked. They were just preschoolers, but they knew that smoking hurt their father, Pete. So they started begging him to quit.

"Please, Daddy," Karen said. "Smoking isn't good for you. Please, say you'll never smoke again."

"We don't want you to die and leave us all alone," added Kevin.

Pete couldn't get to sleep that night. He remembered the hurt in his children's eyes.

It really is stupid to smoke, he thought. *I'm wasting my money and killing myself.*

When Pete got up the next morning, he gathered up his cigarettes and threw them into the trash. That was 12 years ago. He hasn't smoked since.

Adam Conrad and his parents took Bible studies from an Adventist minister. But when Pastor Nilsen presented the lesson on unclean meats, Adam's mother objected.

"Pastor, this time you've gone too far. No one is going to tell me what I can and cannot eat. We just filled our freezer with pork and seafood. We're going to eat it all."

The pastor didn't argue with the angry woman. He decided to give her some time to think over what they had studied. "Well," he said, "I can understand your feelings. Why don't we just put that on the back burner for now."

So the subject was dropped.

At supper the next evening Mrs. Conrad served her family her special stuffed pork chops. Adam looked at the meat on his plate and thought about what Pastor Nilsen had said about pigs. He pushed the meat aside and ate his vegetables.

"And what's wrong with the meat?" asked Mrs. Conrad. "I thought you liked pork chops."

"I used to," admitted Adam. "But I don't think I can eat them anymore."

Mr. Conrad agreed. "I don't think I can eat mine either."

Mrs. Conrad looked at her husband, her son, and the plate of pork chops. "Well, I'm not going to eat all that meat by myself. I may as well go along with the crowd," she laughed.

Karen, Kevin, and Adam didn't shine their lights around the neighborhood. They let them shine in their own homes. Don't ever underestimate your ability to be a good influence on your own parents.

MAY

7

How to Be Popular

A man that hath friends must shew himself friendly. Proverbs 18:24.

"You can make more friends in two months by becoming interested in other people than you can in two years by trying to get other people interested in you."—Dale Carnegie.

Feeling lonely is no fun. Ask anyone who has had to move to a new town or start classes in a new school. We want to fit in with the people around us. We want to be accepted; we want to have friends. But sometimes making friends isn't easy.

Of all the students I've taught in the past 16 years, I think Rob was the most popular. And it wasn't that Rob was just popular with his classmates. Everyone liked him—from the senior citizens down to the preschoolers.

What was his secret? Well, he was nice looking, but there were a number of other boys who were just as handsome as Rob. His grades were above average, but he wasn't the best student. He enjoyed sports, but many of the others played as well as he did. Then why was he so popular?

There were three reasons Rob was so well liked.

First, he always had a smile on his face. Everyone loved to be around him because he was always happy. His cheerful attitude drew people like a magnet and put everyone else in a good mood.

Second, he was enthusiastic. He got involved with whatever was going on. And his enthusiasm spread to those around him.

Third, and most important of all, Rob liked people. During class his classmates felt comfortable asking him for help. Rob was always willing to work out a math problem or explain the reading assignment. And when it came to PE, he went out of his way to encourage the smaller students and those who didn't do well in sports.

Everyone liked Rob because he liked them. He was so busy liking people that he didn't have time to worry about what everybody thought about him.

When it comes to friendship, what are you most concerned about—what you can get from the friendship, or what you can give?

If you want to have more friends, be a friendly person and find ways to care about other people.

MAY

8

What's on Your Mind?

Search me, O God, and know my heart; test me and know my anxious thoughts. See if there is any offensive way in me, and lead me in the way everlasting. Psalm 139:23, 24, NIV.

I read a story about a man who decided to terrorize some of the people in his town. He went through the phone book and randomly picked out some names. Then he sent each person a letter with just one sentence: *I know your secret.* Everyone panicked.

Did the man know bad things about these people? Of course not. He didn't even know who they were. But he knew that we all have secret areas in our lives that we don't want others to find out about.

We may not do lots of bad things. But sometimes what we think about is not too good.

Sometimes Satan puts sinful thoughts into my head. It's not my fault when they pop into my mind, but it is my fault if I let them stay there.

A few years ago I started having trouble with little food moths. I found my first one in our whole wheat flour. I scooped him out and washed him down the drain. But that wasn't the end of my problem. Pretty soon I started finding moth larvae all over—inside the graham cracker box, on the bottom of a can of mushroom soup. So I waged all-out war on the little insects. "Now, *that* should take care of the problem," I said to my husband. "I checked every single thing in the pantry."

But the moths didn't disappear. In fact, they seemed to multiply even faster. One morning when I opened the pantry, a cloud of them flew right into my face.

"I think you're going to have to throw out everything except the food in cans and jars," said Tom.

"But what a waste," I moaned.

Tom shrugged his shoulders. "It may be a waste, but that's the only way you'll get rid of them."

So I cleaned out my pantry and threw away almost everything. And it did get rid of the moths.

It wasn't my fault that the moths got into my cupboard. (We discovered later that they had been in some oatmeal I had bought through a food cooperative.) But once I discovered them, it was my responsibility to remove them.

When Satan puts bad thoughts in your mind, don't let them sit there and multiply. Push them out right away and replace them with good thoughts.

Something to think about: The words from Christian songs are great mind fillers. Can you think of other things that could replace bad thoughts?

Dying of Embarrassment

A good man may be bothered by trouble seven times, but he does not give up. Proverbs 24:16, ICB.

Scott fidgeted in his seat. He had a terrible time sitting in one place for more than a few minutes. He checked his watch—11:45. Would he make it until noon? When the minister finished his sermon?

Scott leaned over toward his mother. "Can I go out and get a drink?" he whispered.

Mother turned to him with a frown and shook her head no.

"Why not?"

"You'll just disrupt the service. You can wait until church is over."

Why did I even bother to ask? Scott thought. *She never lets me leave. Eddie's parents always let him go out during church.*

Later, as Scott and his parents rode home from church, Mrs. Miller brought up Scott's request. "You know how I feel about people getting up and leaving during the sermon," she said. "It's very distracting to the minister and those listening to the sermon."

"Yeah, but everybody else does it. Sometimes Eddie goes out twice."

"I realize that, but I'm not his mother. But, speaking of Eddie, his mother asked me to remind you that you're supposed to have special music next week."

"I know. I've been practicing at school. Mr. Case has been helping me. I'm going to play 'Blessed Assurance.' "

By the following Sabbath Scott knew his song almost by heart. After the offering was taken, Scott walked to the platform, laid out his music, and lifted the trumpet to his lips. As he neared the chorus, he got ready to play a difficult run. And then something caught his attention, and he looked up.

When he looked back down, he couldn't find his place. He tried to keep playing, but the notes were all wrong. He thought he heard someone in the congregation laugh.

When he finally found his place, the song was almost over. He played the last few notes and then fled from church.

Have you ever been humiliated in front of other people? When it happens, you're sure life will never be the same again.

But even embarrassing moments can turn into good lessons. Tomorrow we'll find out what Scott learned from his musical disaster.

MAY

10

It's Not the End of the World

Observe my Sabbaths and have reverence for my sanctuary. I am the Lord. Leviticus 19:30, NIV.

Scott was so embarrassed that he went outside and sat in the car for the rest of the church service.

I'll never get up front again, he vowed. *I'm through playing trumpet.*

It seemed like hours before church ended and people began making their way to the parking lot. Scott slid down in the back seat, hoping no one would see him.

Finally his parents opened the car doors and got in.

"We were a little worried when you disappeared after your solo," said his father.

Scott just stared at the floor.

"It's hard to mess up in front of people, isn't it?"

Scott nodded as he fought to hold back the tears that threatened to spill out onto his face.

Mrs. Miller patted his shoulder. "I know you won't believe it, but someday you'll laugh about this."

"I doubt it," Scott said. He blew his nose and wiped his eyes.

"What happened?" his mother asked. "You knew the song perfectly."

Scott shrugged. "I thought I did too. But someone walked through the doors at the back of the church, and without thinking, I looked up to see who it was. The next thing I knew, I'd lost my place."

"Now you know why Dad and I want you to stay in your seat during church."

"What do you mean?"

"Well, when people walk in and out of the sanctuary, they distract the attention of both the speaker and the congregation. You found out from personal experience how hard it is to concentrate when people are moving around."

"You can say that again!"

At school on Monday morning, a few of Scott's friends kidded him about his new arrangement of "Blessed Assurance," but by Tuesday the incident was forgotten. Scott, however, has never forgotten what he learned from his awful experience.

First, he found out that failure doesn't last forever. He decided not to give up playing the trumpet. And by his junior year in academy he was playing first chair in the concert band.

The other lesson Scott learned was the importance of being reverent in church.

MAY

11

Adopted Into God's Family

Wherefore thou art no more a servant, but a son; and if a son, then an heir of God through Christ. Galatians 4:7.

A young mother, carrying her new infant son in her arms, walked out of the hospital. Hurrying over to the rubbish pile, she set the baby on a garbage can and disappeared into the streets.

Shortly afterward some little girls walked by and heard a strange noise. At first they thought it was an injured animal. But as they searched through the trash, they found the two-pound infant, its face covered with ants.

The baby was taken to Casa de Ninos, an orphanage and day-care center that housed more than 350 children. Because he was small, the baby spent his first three months of life in an incubator.

One of the people who supported Casa de Ninos financially was a man by the name of Oscar. Although he and his wife, Francoise, were never parents, he always had a great love for children.

Shortly after his wife died, Oscar saw the abandoned baby, who was the tiniest and the weakest of all the children in the orphanage. During his visits, Oscar spent time with the child, and before long he decided to adopt the little boy.

The child, named Moses—after the Moses in the Bible who was rescued by Pharaoh's daughter—has no idea of what is in store for him. The man who adopted him was the world-famous clothing designer Oscar De La Renta. Not only was Mr. De La Renta going to give Moses a home, but he was also making him the heir to a $250 million clothing business.

It would be easy to be a little jealous of Moses' good fortune. But each of us has riches far beyond what Moses will receive, for we have been invited into the family of God, to be adopted as His sons and daughters. And if we accept the offer, we too will inherit a fortune. And what God promises us will be billions of times greater than any fortune on earth.

Jesus has gone to heaven to prepare us a home so that we can spend eternity with Him. The Bible says that no one has ever seen or even imagined the great things God has waiting for those who love Him. Have you accepted His offer of eternal life? Have you become His child?

MAY

12

Don't Leave Home Without It!

Put on the full armor of God so that you can take your stand against the devil's schemes. Ephesians 6:11, NIV.

Ivan McGuire could hardly sleep. Whenever he got ready for a jump, the anticipation kept him from thinking of anything else. Ivan and a number of other skydivers were planning a mass jump the next day. Ivan would be in charge of filming the stunt.

When the alarm clock finally went off at 7:00 the next morning, Ivan showered, ate, and drove to the airport. The other divers arrived one at a time. Each one checked his parachute and made sure it was ready.

Ivan strapped the voice-activated camera onto his helmet and boarded the plane along with the other divers. As the plane climbed into the clouds, the team members mentally rehearsed their jump. By the time they reached an altitude of 10,500 feet, they were lined up at the side of the plane and ready for some action.

One after another they dived out of the plane and sailed through the air. When it was Ivan's turn, he switched on the camera, leaned forward, and let gravity pull him away from the plane.

By the time Ivan caught up with the others, they were already getting into formation. Ivan maneuvered his body toward the chain of arms and grabbed on.

Once the trick was completed and caught on film, the divers pushed away from each other and opened their parachutes. Ivan reached back for his rip cord. But it wasn't there. Frantically he clawed the air, only to discover that he wasn't even wearing a parachute. In his excitement about the jump, he had forgotten to put one on.

Like Ivan, the busyness and excitement of each new day sometimes causes us to forget what is most important.

Do you spend time with Jesus each morning? Do you establish a lifeline to Heaven before you start your day? It's only as we put ourselves on God's side and trust Him to fight our battles with sin that we'll be able to resist temptation.

We all need God's protection. Don't leave home without it!

MAY

13

Don't Get Even—Take Control

Do not take revenge, my friends. . . . Overcome evil with good. Romans 12:19-21, NIV.

When you are angry for one minute, you lose 60 seconds of happiness."

This week I got a catalog in the mail that offered materials that help a person get revenge. One was *That'll Fix 'Em.* The book explains how to get even with people who steal parking places, greedy landlords, rude salespersons, mean neighbors, etc. Another book includes 100 sample letters designed to ruin your enemy's life. You can even buy a video that shows interviews with people who tell how they got even with their enemies.

We've probably all had the urge to get back at someone who has hurt us. But revenge never solves problems. It just makes things worse.

An example of this happened in Rio de Janeiro, Brazil, on December 17, 1961. While attending a circus, a man became angry at the way some circus employees treated him. He was so infuriated that he decided to get even. He made his plans, and then he waited until the next performance. When the spectators had all taken their seats and the show had begun, he set the tent on fire. By the time the blaze was extinguished, more than 300 innocent people had lost their lives.

How different was Jesus' advice on getting even. He told the disciples, "Do not resist an evil person. If someone strikes you on the right cheek, turn to him the other also. And if someone wants to sue you and take your tunic, let him have your cloak as well. If someone forces you to go one mile, go with him two miles" (Matthew 5:39-41, NIV).

Jesus was saying that when a person does something mean to you, you should take control of the situation. Not by taking revenge, but by choosing to do more than the person is demanding. When you react with kindness, you'll stay calm. And it will completely baffle your enemy.

Something to think about: Is there someone at school or in your neighborhood who treats you unkindly? What could you do to show him or her kindness?

MAY

14

Don't Be Sorry

Let the wise listen and add to their learning, and let the discerning get guidance. Proverbs 1:5, NIV.

Do you have a dream for the future? If you're a sports fan, you just may be hoping to become a professional ballplayer when you get older. It's fun to imagine what it would be like to be a football or basketball star. But getting into the world of professional sports is very difficult.

Lots of students have the opportunity to play on different teams during high school. But it's a little harder to get on a team when you enter college. And it's in college that most players are chosen.

Only 8 percent of college ballplayers are drafted. And of those drafted, only 2 percent ever get on a pro team. That means out of 1,000 college ballplayers, fewer than two will make it to the big time.

I'm not writing this to discourage you, but you need to realize that very few people will become professional athletes.

During my 16 years as a teacher, I've had a number of students put all their spare time into sports. They felt that a good education wasn't important because they planned to play professional ball. As a result, they didn't learn to study, and because they didn't get a good education, they ended up with low-paying, uninteresting jobs.

In a survey, adults were asked what they regretted most in life. The number one answer: I wish I had taken my schoolwork more seriously.

You may not know right now what you want to do when you get older. But you can prepare yourself for later life by putting your best effort into your schoolwork. Learn everything you can, and dedicate your life in service to God. He's interested in every part of your life. And if you ask Him, He'll help you find a job that is just right for you.

MAY

15

Self Surgery

A few years ago I did something that wasn't very smart. I decided to operate on myself.

It all started when Tom said that the mole on my arm was ugly. I decided that if he felt that way, I'd have it taken off. His birthday was only two weeks away, so it would be a great surprise.

The next morning, I started to call the doctor for an appointment. Then I got an idea. I could take the mole off myself. It was so small. It would be easy.

I'll spare you the details, but I cut it off. The only problem was that it grew back in a week. Then all my friends started telling me how stupid my plan had been. They started talking about cancer. I decided to see a doctor.

When Dr. Cook looked at it, he said, "I don't want to take any chances. I think you'd better go see a surgeon."

When the surgeon looked at it, he said, "I think we'll have to go to the hospital to take it off."

So I ended up in the operating room a few days later. The nurses covered my eyes so I couldn't see what was going to happen. Then they gave me a shot to numb my arm. So when the doctor said he was going to give me some stitches, I was surprised. "Stitches?" I said. "You mean you had to cut that deep?"

"I sure did. Most people don't realize that there's a lot more to a mole than what you see on the surface. I had to go quite deep to get it all out."

Whenever I think about my attempt to remove my mole, it reminds me of how we sometimes try to remove sin from our lives. Instead of going to Jesus, the Great Physician, we think we can handle the problem ourselves. We're sure that if we just try harder, we can make ourselves better. And maybe for a while it may look as though we've succeeded, but before we know it, our old habits return.

If you're battling sin, don't try to fight it on your own. Don't even spend time looking at all the things you're doing wrong. Instead, put your energy into spending more time with Jesus. Give Him control of your life every day. Let Him remove the sin.

If we confess our sins, he is faithful and just and will forgive us our sins and purify us from all unrighteousness. 1 John 1:9, NIV.

MAY

16

Free at Last

In all these things we are more than conquerors through him who loved us. Romans 8:37, NIV.

In 1947 Ivan Bushilo, a 25-year-old veteran of the Russian Army, went too far. He spoke out against Joseph Stalin's secret police.

Stalin, dictator of the U.S.S.R. from 1929-1953, was known as one of the most brutal leaders who ever lived. He ordered his secret police to track down everyone who opposed him. Millions were executed or sent to prison camps. And because he trusted no one, he even killed or imprisoned most of the men who had helped get him into office. He was afraid they might try to take away his power.

Ivan realized that his life was in danger. So he fled to the Byelorussian woods. Having no gun, he lived off the land by trapping and fishing and scouring the woods for wild fruits. He survived the vicious Russian winters and never got sick. He lived his life in total seclusion, hardly ever seeing another human being. On rare occasions relatives ventured into the forest to bring him clothes, newspapers, and food.

Even after Stalin died in 1953, Ivan refused to leave the woods, and it was not until 1989 that he finally believed that it was safe for him to return to society. After 42 years of hiding, he finally walked out of the woods and returned to his home village in Byelorussia.

Many Christians live a life similar to Ivan's. They fear Satan's power. They believe that Satan is in control of the world. Instead of realizing that Jesus has won the great controversy, they act as though Satan runs the world.

It's true that Satan has some power, but compared to God he's a weakling. I love this sentence from *The Great Controversy:* "Satan is well aware that the weakest soul who abides in Christ is more than a match for the hosts of darkness" (p. 530).

As long as we put ourselves in God's hands, Satan is powerless to control us. He may tempt us and make life miserable at times, but as we've learned already, God can use even the hard times for our benefit.

Don't be a coward. Our King is in control.

MAY

17

"I Think That's Leah Morris"

May the Lord make your love increase and overflow for each other and for everyone else. 1 Thessalonians 3:12, NIV.

For Kevin Ishmael it was just another workday. He started the motor of his Greyhound bus and backed it out of the parking lot. His assignment was to drive a church group to Chicago for a day of shopping.

An hour into the trip, he turned on his CB just as a message was crackling over the airwaves. "Hey, anybody out there know first aid? We've got an accident just south of the South Haven exit."

Kevin drove along until he caught sight of a group of people standing on the other side of the highway. Bringing the bus to a stop, Kevin grabbed his first aid kit and sprinted across the road. After pushing his way through the crowd, Kevin saw the overturned car lying in a drainage ditch at the bottom of the embankment. He sidestepped his way down the incline and hurried over to the wreckage. A burly truck driver was kneeling next to two arms that stuck out from beneath the car.

"Any sign of life?" asked Kevin.

The man shook his head. "I tried to get a pulse, but I'm afraid she didn't make it."

"Let me give it a try," said Kevin as he knelt down. He picked up the woman's wrist and felt for her pulse. "You're right," he said as he laid her hand back down. "Why don't you get on your CB and radio for an ambulance, but tell them they don't need to hurry."

"I think that's Leah Morris." Kevin looked up, noticing for the first time a young woman who had been standing near the car. "I think that's Leah Morris," she repeated. "In fact, I'm sure it is. We work at the same factory."

Kevin's body sprang into action. He jumped up and started pushing against the car. "Help me," he screamed to the truck driver. "We've got to move this car. We've got to save her. Leah Morris is my sister."

When Kevin heard that his sister was the person under the car, his rescue attempt took on a new meaning. That wasn't just some stranger under there. That was his sister. And he was willing to do anything he could to save her life.

It's easy to become insensitive to the needs of others when they're not part of our family or our circle of friends. But we need to remember that we're all a part of Jesus' family.

The next time you find yourself thinking unkind thoughts about someone else, remember that he or she is one of God's children too.

MAY

18

A Place for Everyone

In him we were also chosen, having been predestined according to the plan of him who works out everything in conformity with the purpose of his will.
Ephesians 1:11, NIV.

With superhuman strength, Kevin and the truck driver tipped the car over and back on its wheels. Turning the young lady over, Kevin began CPR—two quick breaths and 15 chest compressions.

O God, please don't let her die, he prayed. *She's only 20 years old.*

Kevin kept up his lifesaving attempts. And then—

"A heartbeat!" he called out to the crowd. "Her heart's beating! Call the ambulance."

Within minutes the ambulance siren could be heard screaming its way toward the scene of the accident. The paramedics jumped over the embankment with their equipment. Kevin helped them secure his unconscious sister to the stretcher and then carry her up the hill.

"You go ahead to the hospital. I'll drive my bus," he said to the ambulance driver.

Two other drivers drove their trucks across the road and stopped all traffic, so Kevin could do a U-turn and follow the ambulance.

At the emergency room, the doctor examined Leah and called for a helicopter to fly her to a trauma center. Kevin telephoned Leah's husband, Brian. Then he called for a replacement driver to take his passengers on to Chicago.

Just as the helicopter touched down, Brian drove up. Kevin jumped in the car with him, and they started the 40-minute drive to Borgess Hospital.

When Leah reached the trauma center, the staff ran her through a battery of tests to find out the extent of her injuries. X-rays revealed only two broken ribs and a chipped shoulder blade. What worried the doctor was the injury done to her brain. Sometime during the accident her brain had been knocked against the skull.

It wasn't until 2:30 the next morning that Leah finally regained consciousness. And it was three more days before she could start to remember things again. Nevertheless, after a nine-day stay in the hospital, Leah went home.

When Kevin looks back on the accident, he realizes it wasn't chance that brought him past Leah's accident that day. "God timed everything just right so that I'd be there to save my sister's life."

God has a special purpose for your life, too. He wants to use you to do great things. And He will, if you're willing to follow His direction.

MAY

19

What's That in My Soup?

As servants of God we commend ourselves in every way: . . . in purity, understanding, patience and kindness. 2 Corinthians 6:4-6, NIV.

Homemade soup. That's what I decided to make for supper one Sunday night. I pulled out my recipe file and thumbed through it until I found my chicken noodle soup recipe.

I measured six cups of water into my cooking pot and turned on the burner. After dicing up the celery, onions, and vegetarian chicken, I dumped everything, along with some spices, into the water. In a few minutes the soup was boiling. I added the noodles and turned down the heat.

By the time I had finished making a salad and some sandwiches, the soup was ready. I set the table and called Tom for supper.

After prayer, I dished up a bowl of soup for each of us.

"Hey, we haven't had chicken soup for a long time," said Tom as he broke some crackers into his bowl.

"Well, there's enough that you can take some to school for lunch tomorrow," I said.

Just as I was about to take my third spoonful of soup, I noticed something floating along the surface.

I looked a little closer and noticed that it was a worm.

"Oh, gross," I said. "There's a worm floating in my soup. I think I'm going to be sick."

Tom checked his soup and found that he had not only one but two worms in his. We checked the pot on the stove. Same story.

I went to the cupboard and pulled out the bag of noodles.

"Here's the culprit," I said to Tom. "I guess they've been sitting around too long."

We could have just fished them out, but somehow we lost our appetite for chicken noodle soup.

Although the worms were just a small part of the soup, they ruined the whole pot.

The world is made up of many things that are basically good. The soup was 99.99 percent pure, but the worms made it unfit to eat.

How many movies, records, books, and magazines are essentially decent, except for occasional swear words, vulgar language, and indecent scenes? Is the enjoyment you might receive worth the damage that is done to your character?

Don't let Satan contaminate your life. Choose things that are 100 percent worthwhile.

MAY

20

Beware! Someone May Be Watching

In everything set them an example by doing what is good. Titus 2:7, NIV.

"The first great gift we can bestow on others is a good example."—Thomas Morell.

The newspaper carried a tragic story. It told about an accident that should never have happened.

Mrs. Lacy was on her way to the doctor. Her little son, Jonathon, was due for his 6-month checkup.

Mrs. Lacy dearly loved Jonathon. She felt that he was a special gift from God. Two years earlier the Lacys' first child, Benjamin, had been born with a defective heart valve. He lived only a few days. So when Jonathon came along, a year and a half later, the Lacys feared that he too might have heart problems. But Jonathon proved to be a healthy little fellow.

So it was that Mrs. Lacy strapped him into his car seat that day and started for the doctor's office. She drove carefully through town, keeping her eyes on the blue Escort in front of her. What a deadly mistake. For the driver of the blue car drove right through a stop sign. And Mrs. Lacy followed him.

Brakes squealed as a car coming from the right slammed broadside into the Lacys' car. Baby Jonathon's car seat was torn loose and hurtled through the window. He was killed instantly.

I'm sure that the driver in front of Mrs. Lacy meant no harm in running the stop sign. He was probably just careless, but his bad example resulted in the death of a precious baby.

When you disobey rules set down by your parents, the school, or God, you are not just hurting yourself. You are also hurting others who may be watching. While your bad example may not cause someone else's death, it could easily influence that person to make wrong decisions.

As a member of the human race, you have a responsibility to do what you can to be a good example to others. Before you do something that could lead others in the wrong direction, stop and think it over.

You never know who may be watching.

MAY

21

Coming On Too Strong

Let your conversation be always full of grace, seasoned with salt, so that you may know how to answer everyone. Colossians 4:6, NIV.

A few years ago I invited some new friends over for supper. I don't remember what we had for the main course, but I remember the dessert. I don't make cheesecake very often because it's expensive and fattening. But I decided to go all out for my guests.

That evening after our meal, I cut four large pieces of cheesecake and set them on my best china. As I took my first bite, my eyes almost bulged out of the sockets. The cheesecake was so salty that I could hardly stand it. I was too embarrassed to say anything, so I just held my breath and ate it as fast as I could. I noticed that my guests didn't finish theirs.

The next morning at breakfast Tom poured some cereal into his bowl. Out plopped two unshelled Brazil nuts.

"What in the world?"

"Let me see that," I said, reaching for the box. Looking inside, I saw walnuts and pecans nestled among the Rice Chex.

Tom picked the nuts out of his cereal. "I wonder if the academy kids who stayed at our house last week had anything to do with this." (While we were gone, we had opened our home to the traveling choir and their director.)

"The sugar!" Tom said.

I hurried over to the sugar container and stuck my finger in it. "Salt! No wonder that cheesecake was so terrible. It had a cup of salt instead of a cup of sugar."

A little salt makes food pleasant to eat. But too much makes it unbearable. Jesus said that Christians are like salt. They preserve the world and make it a better place to live. But like salt, we can sometimes come on too strong.

Donnie was an elementary school student who spent his recess time preaching. Day after day he threatened his fellow students that if they didn't repent, they'd burn in hell. Instead of attracting them to Jesus, he turned them off.

Donnie had the right idea—we should urge others to come to Jesus. But we need to do it in a kind, loving way.

Something to think about: When you witness to others, do you ever come on too strong?

MAY

22

Going Down the Tubes

We take captive every thought to make it obedient to Christ.
2 Corinthians 10:5, NIV.

If you're feeling bored, lonely, or depressed, the best thing to do is to sit down and turn on the TV. Right? Wrong. Watching TV can be one of the worst things you can do for yourself.

After studying television viewers for more than 13 years, two psychologists found out that TV watching doesn't help people feel better. In fact, the longer they watch, the more likely they are to become sleepy, bored, sad, lonely, and hostile.

So why do people watch TV? Probably the biggest reason is to escape. Have you ever sat down to a pile of homework and suddenly felt a terrible urge to watch TV instead? Why agonize over a whole page of math when you can escape to the land of the Huxtables or the Simpsons? The only problem is that TV is only a temporary escape. When your program is over, those math problems are still sitting on the page, waiting to be figured out. You haven't avoided the work. You've just prolonged the agony.

Another reason people watch TV is because they're bored. They have nothing exciting to do. So they turn on a show and watch other people do things instead of getting involved themselves.

Watching TV every now and then probably isn't harmful, as long as you're careful about what you watch. But it's easy to become addicted to TV.

A few years ago I realized I had an addiction. I got in the habit of watching TV while I made supper and did the dishes. It didn't matter what was on. I just liked having the noise in the background.

Then our portable TV died. For a few days I made dinner in silence. But finally I couldn't stand it any longer. I started hauling our large TV into the kitchen every day. That's when I realized I had a problem.

I tried to kick the habit on my own, but I couldn't. Finally I asked God to help me. And do you know what He did? He gave me something better. He got me involved in listening to a Christian radio station that plays really great music. I don't even miss the TV now.

If you'd like to cut back on your television watching, ask the Lord for help. Then look for new hobbies and activities that can replace some of your TV time. You may never feel bored again!

Something to think about: What are some things you could do instead of watching TV?

MAY

23

When Skies Turn Black

I will say of the Lord, "He is my refuge and my fortress, my God, in whom I trust." Psalm 91:2, NIV.

I'm sorry to have to tell you this, Mrs. Barboza," said the doctor, "but you have savage fire."

Mrs. Barboza and her husband didn't want to believe what they were hearing. "Isn't there anything we can do?" asked Pastor Barboza.

The doctor shook his head. "I'm sorry, but there's no cure for savage fire."

Savage fire was a well-known disease in Brazil. People who came down with it suffered a slow, painful death. Their bodies broke out in open sores that burned like fire. The sores also smelled so bad that hospitals refused to accept patients with the disease.

As the couple got up to leave, the doctor pulled Pastor Barboza aside. "As the disease gets worse, she won't be able to sleep on a regular bed. The sheets will stick to her sores. My advice is to gather up some banana leaves and let her lie on them. They are naturally oily and won't cause further discomfort. I'm sorry. I wish I could do more to help."

Alfredo nodded his head. "I understand what you are saying, Doctor. But I can't just sit back and watch her die. I must find a cure."

So Alfredo began his search. Leaving their children in the care of friends, Alfredo and his wife traveled to São Paulo. They located a place to stay. And after finding someone to care for his wife, Alfredo began visiting every doctor and every hospital in the city.

But he found no cure. And Mrs. Barboza got steadily worse.

Finally one day she called her husband to her bedside and made a request. "Alfredo, I will live only a few more days. Would you go get the children? I want to see them one more time before I die."

"Of course I'll get them," he answered. "I'll leave tomorrow."

When sickness, death, and other disappointments come into our lives, it's easy to become discouraged. We wish that God could protect us from evil and just let the bad things happen to bad people, but that doesn't happen. Yet, as we learned earlier, He *can* bring something good out of our bad times. We just need to trust Him.

MAY

24

Disappointment With God

"For my thoughts are not your thoughts, neither are your ways my ways," declares the Lord. Isaiah 55:8, NIV.

Alfredo knew that he had no time to lose. Traveling by the ancient train would take two solid days. He had to find an airplane. Friends told him to inquire at the military base to see if they had any planes going to Campo Grande. If a plane was not full, civilians were occasionally allowed to ride along.

"O Lord, please impress them to give me a ride," he prayed as he walked into the office at the air force base.

Alfredo explained his predicament to the officer in charge. "My wife has savage fire and she will not live more than a few days. Her last request is to see our children before she dies. I'm afraid that if I take the train, we won't make it back in time. That's why I have come here. I was wondering if you would be so kind as to let me get a ride to Campo Grande in one of your planes."

The sympathetic man looked through the plane schedules. Picking up the telephone, he called another office and then turned to the pastor. "Come tomorrow morning at 6:00. Plane 314 is going your direction. You can ride along."

Alfredo was so happy he felt like singing. The Lord had answered his prayer. He hurried home to his wife and gave her the good news.

"I will hold my children in my arms one more time," his wife said, weeping for joy.

But when Pastor Barboza woke up the next morning, the Lord impressed him not to take the plane.

Have you ever felt that God let you down? Have you ever been disappointed with Him? Whenever we pray, God always answers our prayers. He can say yes, no, or wait. Tomorrow we'll find out why God said no to Pastor Barboza's request for a plane ride.

MAY

25

When the Pieces Fall Together

He will call upon me, and I will answer him; I will be with him in trouble, I will deliver him and honor him. Psalm 91:15, NIV.

God, why didn't You want me to ride the airplane? Alfredo grumbled. *I thought You were going to answer my prayer.*

Bitterly disappointed, Alfredo hurried over to the train station. After purchasing a ticket, he boarded the rickety old train. Taking his place on the uncomfortable wooden seat, he prepared himself for the trip.

As the hours passed, Alfredo continued to ask God Why? Why did his wife have to die? Why did he have to take the train instead of the plane?

Toward afternoon the train slowed down and finally stopped. *O Lord, not another delay,* thought Alfredo. *I'll never get my children back to see their mother before she dies.*

Pastor Barboza, along with some of the other passengers, left the train to see what was holding up the trip. Just ahead he saw a crumpled airplane. And on the wing was the number 314.

Alfredo bowed his head. *Now I understand why You told me to take the train, Lord. Forgive me for doubting You.*

Two days later the train finally reached Alfredo's hometown. He picked up his suitcase and started for the center of town. Just then he noticed the strangest sight he'd ever seen. There, getting into a taxi, was a woman with a black coating on her face.

Running over to the cab, he caught her attention. "Miss, why is your face all black?"

"Well, I have savage fire, and this is the medicine I take for it."

Alfredo's heart began to race. "Does it help?"

"I'm getting better all the time."

Alfredo excitedly explained how he had been looking for a cure for his wife. The woman directed him to the pharmacist who had helped her. When Alfredo finally found him, the man was close to death. But after hearing why Pastor Barboza was there, the man generously shared his special formula.

Alfredo hurried back to his wife, not with the children, but with the medicine. And within a short time she was completely free from the deadly disease.

Today the Adventist Church has a hospital in Campo Grande that treats savage fire with a success rate of nearly 100 percent.

The next time God says no or wait to your prayers, don't get discouraged. He has something better in mind for you.

MAY

26

Keep on Running

But one thing I do: Forgetting what is behind and straining toward what is ahead, I press on toward the goal to win the prize for which God has called me heavenward in Christ Jesus. Philippians 3:13, 14, NIV.

"Adversity causes some men to break, others to break records."—William A. Ward.

Snooks Dowd was an unknown football player for Lehigh University in 1934. But the final game of the season changed all that. During one of the plays, the tackles from the rival team broke through the Lehigh lines. Snooks, who had possession of the ball, was caught off guard.

The goal line. Run for the goal line, he said to himself. He poured on the speed and shot across the field for a touchdown. But after crossing the goal line, he realized that he had just made a touchdown on the wrong side. So he turned around and headed back the other direction. Running the entire length of the football field, he scored another touchdown—this time, one that would count.

Snooks' 210-yard touchdown remains today as the longest ever recorded.

Snooks made a big mistake, all right. But once he discovered it, he didn't give up. He just changed directions and started running again.

One winter my sister Kim became all excited about downhill skiing after watching the Winter Olympics. The following Sunday she and some friends drove to a ski lodge and got ready for a day of fun and excitement.

But skiing wasn't as easy as it looked. After putting on the boots and snapping them into the bindings, she poised herself on the edge of a hill. Pushing herself forward with her poles, she started down. But her skis turned to the side, and she wiped out. Kim pulled off her skis, trudged down the hill, and went home. I don't think she's ever skied again.

Those who give up may protect themselves from further disappointment, but they also miss out on opportunities to grow. As someone once said, "the men who try to do something and fail are infinitely better than those who try to do nothing and succeed."

When you are faced with obstacles, problems, or disappointments, how do you react? Do you give up or gear up?

MAY

27

What to Do With Guilt

Sometimes people let guilt ruin their lives. Willard Hershberger is one example of someone who let it get the best of him.

Back in 1940 the Cincinnati Redlegs were one of the hottest baseball teams around. In fact, they won the World Series that year.

Willard Hershberger, the team's catcher, had been playing major league ball for three years. His future looked bright. Not only could he catch, but he also had a .300-plus batting average.

Toward the end of the season, the Redlegs found themselves in a tight game with one of their rival teams. It was the bottom of the ninth. The score was 4-3, in favor of the Redlegs. There were two outs and a runner on base.

Hershberger leaned over and signaled to the pitcher. But he signaled the wrong pitch. As soon as the ball came whizzing across home plate, the batter slammed it over the field into the stands for a home run. And the Redlegs lost the game.

For days Hershberger brooded about the mistake he had made. No one else blamed him for his error in judgment, but he couldn't forgive himself.

On August 3, 1940, Hershberger didn't show up for the scheduled game. The manager sent someone back to the hotel to pick him up. But when the hotel clerk opened Hershberger's room, he found Hershberger's corpse. He had killed himself over one simple mistake.

This story reminded me of the last few hours of Jesus' life. Both Judas and Peter made a very big mistake. They betrayed the Saviour. But they chose two very different ways to handle their guilt.

Judas hanged himself.

Peter gave up on himself. When Peter looked into Jesus' face, he realized how deeply he had hurt his best friend. And at that point Peter became truly converted.

The purpose of guilt is to bring us to repentance. Once you have made things right, let go of guilt and get on with life.

You know my folly, O God; my guilt is not hidden from you. . . . But I pray to you, O Lord, in the time of your favor; in your great love, O God, answer me with your sure salvation. Psalm 69:5-13, NIV.

MAY

28

Paying the Price

You are forgiving and good, O Lord, abounding in love to all who call to you. Psalm 86:5, NIV.

For some reason human beings aren't comfortable with God's method of forgiveness. God says that He's paid the price for our sins. All we have to do is ask Him for forgiveness. But that sounds too easy. We'd rather pay the price ourselves.

Before Martin Luther understood that righteousness comes from faith in God, he used to beat himself until he was unconscious. He felt that he could pay for his sins by inflicting pain on his body.

Today people have a little more civilized way of trying to make themselves right with God. They may put a little extra in the offering plate. Or maybe they devote their lives to serving others. Although these things are nice, they don't take away our sins.

I took a different route. I agonized over everything I did wrong. Sure, I asked forgiveness, but I refused to let go of my guilt. I preferred to make myself feel miserable about what I had done. Then one day someone pointed out to me that I was human and that there has never been a human being who lived a perfect life. Somehow I had missed that. I had always thought that if I was real careful, I could live a sinless life, and so for some time I did pretty well. But then I found out that sin involves more than just a person's actions. It also involves thoughts. So much for perfection!

The day that I stopped trying to be my own savior was one of the happiest days of my life. No longer did I have to stare at the ceiling at night as I thought of all the things I'd done wrong and hated myself for it. I was finally free to take my sins to Jesus and leave them at His feet.

If we could have saved ourselves, Jesus never would have had to come and die. But there was only one way we could be freed from sin and its guilt. How thankful we can be that Jesus paid the price and now offers to take our sins in exchange for His perfect character!

MAY

29

The Great Impostor

You are precious and honored in my sight. Isaiah 43:4, NIV.

Fred Demara was one of the strangest people who ever lived. For most of the time he wasn't Fred Demara. At one time he was Martin Godgart, a high school teacher. He was also known as Dr. Robert Linton French, a college dean; Dr. Cecil B. Hamann, a law student; and Brother John, a Catholic monk. In addition, he worked as a hospital chaplain, a Hollywood actor, and most unbelievable of all, a surgeon aboard a Canadian navy destroyer.

Demara was probably the greatest impostor of our time. On stolen school stationery he wrote to different universities, requesting the records of certain former students. Then he would present these records as his own when he applied for a job. All he had to do was take the name of the person he was pretending to be.

Demara tried to be someone other than himself, and young people often do the same thing. It appears that Demara did it just to see what he could get away with. But teenagers have a different reason for hiding their real selves.

When you're young, it's easy to see the world as black and white. Things are either wonderful or terrible. There seems to be no category for average. So if your grades aren't the best in the class, you're stupid. If you don't have perfect skin and beautiful hair, you're ugly. If you lose a class election, you're a failure. No wonder so many kids put on an act and pretend they're someone they aren't.

As you get older, you'll find out that no one has it all together. Everybody has certain strengths and weaknesses. And it's OK to have pimples or straight hair or average grades. It's OK if your best friend becomes eighth grade class president and you're nothing.

You can't do everything, and you can't be everything. But you can be the best that you can be. Make the most of *your* abilities and strengths. Learn to live with *your* weaknesses. And let the world get to know the real *you*.

MAY

30

Keeping Your Job

From the fruit of his lips a man is filled with good things as surely as the work of his hands rewards him. Proverbs 12:14, NIV.

I'm sure that some of you hope to find a job for the summer. It's nice to have a little spending money. But it's not always easy to find work when so many others are also job-hunting.

I can't help you find work, but today I'd like to give you some ideas on how you can keep a job once you get one.

1. Be on time. I once had a boss who used to say, "If you're not at least five minutes early, you're late." Being on time tells your employer that you take your work seriously.

2. Keep busy. While we were building our house, two part-time workers on the construction crew caught my attention. Ron spent most of his time entertaining the crew. He leaned on his shovel and told jokes while the rest worked. When the electrical inspector came by, Ron followed him around asking questions about electrical problems he was having with his own house. I wasn't surprised when the boss fired him a few weeks later.

Tony was just the opposite. He kept busy every minute he was on the job. When he completed one task, he didn't wait around for the boss to tell him what to do next. He found something to do. I wasn't surprised when the boss told me he planned to hire Tony full-time.

3. Do more than is expected of you. If you earn money by mowing lawns, trim around the trees and sweep off the sidewalk when you're done. Baby-sitters could dust and vacuum the house or wash dishes.

4. Be dependable. Don't miss work if at all possible. And do a job that you can be proud of. Happy is the employer who doesn't need to check all the time to see if a job was done correctly.

5. Be honest in all areas. If you work by the hour, keep an accurate time card. And don't help yourself to things that don't belong to you. If you're baby-sitting, stay out of the refrigerator unless your employer has given you permission to help yourself.

There may be a shortage of jobs available, but workers who give 110 percent will always be in great demand.

MAY

31

Hidden Treasure

But seek first his kingdom and his righteousness, and all these things will be given to you as well. Matthew 6:33, NIV.

One Christmas a few years back, Tom's brother, Tim, got a metal detector. He didn't do much with it until spring. Then he started taking it in the car with him, running it over the ground at playgrounds and ball fields. He found only a few coins.

That summer while on vacation, Tom and I drove to Ohio to spend a week with his family. One afternoon Tim suggested we go treasure hunting.

We had great fun. We'd walk along the foundations of old houses and barns while Tim swung the detector back and forth. As soon as we heard a beep, we'd pinpoint the "hot" spot and start digging. We found a belt buckle, a chain, and a few bottles.

When Tim came to visit us that fall, he brought the metal detector along with him. We borrowed it and took it to school. At that time we lived in Alpena, Michigan, a small secluded town on Lake Huron. We hoped that we could find some things left behind by the early settlers. All 20 of our students in grades 1-8 gathered around as we started searching along the ground behind the school. Nothing happened for a while, but suddenly we heard a loud beep.

"Bring the shovels!" Tom called out.

The beeping continued as Tom walked across the field.

"There must be something really big underneath," said Darren.

"I can't wait to see what it is," added Brian.

The boys started digging, and it wasn't long before we found our buried treasure. Except it wasn't what we expected. It was something left behind, all right. But not by early settlers. Our treasure turned out to be all the paint cans left behind by the men who had built the church a few years earlier.

What a disappointment! But we had a good laugh, covered everything back up, and returned to our schoolwork.

Everyone is searching for something. Some people look for ways to make money. Others try to find success and fame. But what we're all hoping to find is happiness. We just look for it in different places.

The Bible tells us that there is only one way to happiness. And that's through knowing Jesus and doing His will.

Don't spend your life looking for things that only bring temporary happiness. Go after that which will really satisfy.

JUNE

1

Resting in God's Care

Know that the Lord is God. It is he who made us, and we are his; we are his people, the sheep of his pasture. Psalm 100:3, NIV.

When I was 6 years old, our family moved to a small farm. During the next few weeks, Dad brought home some chickens for our henhouse, kittens for the barn, and a springer spaniel for the doghouse. But what excited me the most was a pair of sheep that soon munched contentedly in our pasture.

Although my sister Karen and I were small, the sheep didn't frighten us. We loved digging our fingers deeply into their thick wool coats and patting their smooth black faces.

The summer months turned into fall, and fall into winter. One cold morning in December, Mother woke us up and told us to get dressed. "Put on your coats and boots. There's a surprise out in the barn."

We trudged out through the snow and opened the stable door.

"Look," said Karen, pointing to a dark corner. There stood Sheba and a pair of newborn lambs.

Some months later I found another surprise out in the barn. I went out to do my morning chores and couldn't find the sheep. But I did find the corral gate standing wide open. I hurried back to the house and reported to my parents that the four woolly inmates had made a mad dash for freedom. Dad, figuring that I was responsible for the open gate, gave me orders to track down the escapees and return them at once.

It wasn't hard to find the sheep. I just followed the hoofprints. There they were on the other side of Maiden Lane, enjoying the grass around the Lentzes' vineyard. Finding them was easy. Getting them back home wasn't. I pushed and shoved, moaned and groaned, but they chose to stay right where they were. Finally Dad had to bring the pickup truck and haul them back to the barn.

My childhood experiences with our pet sheep gave me an idea of what it must have been like for David when he cared for his father's flock some 3,000 years ago.

For the next few days we're going to take a look at Psalm 23 and see if we can learn something new about the old art of sheepherding and God's care for His children.

JUNE

2

The Good Shepherd

He tends his flock like a shepherd: He gathers the lambs in his arms and carries them close to his heart; he gently leads those that have young. Isaiah 40:11, NIV.

The Lord is my shepherd; I shall not be in want" (Psalm 23:1, NIV).

How would you describe ice cream to someone who had never tasted it? You'd probably say, "Well, it's cold and sweet. Something like pudding, but not as smooth."

The only way that you can describe an unknown thing is to compare it with something the other person is acquainted with.

At lunch yesterday, my husband tried some kiwi fruit for the first time.

"What's it like?" I asked.

"Well, it's slimy like a green grape, but it tastes something like a banana." He compared the kiwi fruit to something I had eaten before, something I could understand. Now if he had said it tasted like a mango, I still wouldn't have known what kiwi tasted like because I've never tried a mango.

When David wrote Psalm 23, he wanted to explain to people what God was like. So he created word pictures that his readers could understand.

I can imagine him sitting out on a hillside in Judea . . .

The Lord is . . . is. . . . Now how can I describe Him? He's powerful, yet kind and loving. He's fearless, yet patient.

As his eyes scan the acres and acres of pastureland, he sees sheep grazing in the distance. Shepherds walk among the animals to make sure all is well.

That's it! The Lord is my shepherd.

After spending a good part of his life caring for sheep, David knew the love the shepherd had for the animals under his care. He knew that the shepherd would lay down his life to protect his flock. He knew that God would someday do the same.

Something to think about: If you were going to describe the way God takes care of His people, what would you compare Him with in today's modern society?

JUNE

3

Still Waters

I will listen to what God the Lord will say. Psalm 85:8, NIV.

He makes me lie down in green pastures, he leads me beside quiet waters" (Psalm 23:2, NIV).

As a shepherd leads his sheep through the fields, he has one main thought: I must find a safe drinking place for my flock.

In the area where David tended his sheep, water was very scarce. And often when water *was* found, the sheep were unable to reach it because the banks along the gullies were too steep.

Another problem encountered by the shepherd was the danger of fast-flowing streams. Sheep are afraid to drink from fast currents, for if they lose their balance and fall into the water, they will most likely drown. Once they lose their footing, the current will carry them down the stream, and there is little the shepherd can do to rescue them. In order to create "still waters" (KJV), the shepherd must find a suitable bend in the stream. There, by blocking it off with a little dam, he creates a quiet pool for the sheep to drink from. Then he calls for the animals to come.

The sheep know their shepherd's voice and never respond to another shepherd who might be in the area. The animals come in groups and take turns enjoying the water their leader has provided for them.

The sheep know their shepherd's voice because they have spent time with him. They rely on him for all their needs.

The more time we spend getting to know God through prayer and Bible study, the better able we will be to hear His voice as He speaks to us. And the more we get to know Him, the easier it will be for us to rely on Him for all our needs.

Something to think about: Do you know God's voice when He speaks to you? Are you listening for it?

JUNE

4

Safe Paths

In love he predestined us to be adopted as his sons through Jesus Christ, in accordance with his pleasure and will. Ephesians 1:4, 5, NIV.

He restores my soul. He guides me in paths of righteousness for his name's sake" (Psalm 23:3, NIV).

There's always the temptation to find out what life is like on the "other side of the fence." Television, movies, and magazines lead us to believe that as Christians we're missing out on a whole lot of fun and excitement. So some young people (and even adults) walk away from God and begin to experiment with the things that God has warned them about.

When a person crosses the border into Satan's territory, he or she finds that entering is easy. Exiting is not. A sheep has no trouble leaving the safety of the flock, but once separated, it can't find its way back home.

Most of the fields of Judea were open to anyone who wanted to use them. But there were also private fields, gardens, and vineyards that were off limits to trespassers. If a sheep was caught straying into private property, it automatically became the property of the landowner.

When God created Adam and Eve, He did not force them to obey Him. He gave them the freedom of choice.

In each of the inhabited worlds, God placed a tree of knowledge of good and evil. At these trees Lucifer was allowed to come and state his side of the great controversy between himself and God. Lucifer was not free to follow individuals around and bother them. He could only try to win them to his side if they willingly came to the tree.

So when God created the Garden of Eden, He placed in it a tree of knowledge of good and evil, just as He had in the other worlds. If Adam and Eve had stayed away from the tree, sin would have never entered our world. But as soon as they walked into Lucifer's territory and rebelled against God, Lucifer claimed humanity as his captives.

It was for this reason that Jesus died on the cross. By paying the price for our sins, Jesus bought us back from the enemy. And He restored us to His family.

Something to think about: Have you accepted God's offer to pay the price for your sins? Are you a part of the family of God?

JUNE

5

Living in the Shadows

The Lord upholds all those who fall and lifts up all who are bowed down. Psalm 145:14, NIV.

Even though I walk through the valley of the shadow of death, I will fear no evil, for you are with me; your rod and your staff, they comfort me" (Psalm 23:4, NIV).

The people living in David's time often named certain places with fitting descriptions, such as "The Valley of the Robber" or "The Ravine of the Raven." In fact, that custom continues in some places even today.

When he can, a shepherd keeps his sheep far away from the dangerous areas, but at other times he can't avoid them. Sometimes he has no other choice. Yet when he takes his sheep through risky areas, he watches them even more carefully than usual.

The shepherd has three special tools that he uses when guiding his flock.

The rod he carries is a tree branch with a large knob on the end. He uses it like a club to protect the sheep against wild animals and robbers.

The staff is a crooked cane about five or six feet long. It helps the shepherd guide the sheep. And if one of the lambs falls off the path, he uses the curved end to pull it back to safety.

The shepherd also uses his voice as a tool. When a wolf sneaks into the flock, the sheep become wild with fright, taking off in every direction and making it impossible for the shepherd to protect them. At that moment, the shepherd runs to a rock, calls out to the sheep, and gets their attention. When they hear his voice, the sheep draw close together. The wolf ends up in a tight squeeze and is often crushed to death.

When we go through difficult times, God is there right at our side. He doesn't remove our problems, but He calls us to look to Him for the strength to get through. And if we keep our eyes on Him, we'll make it every time.

Something to think about: Have you gone through a difficult experience lately? Did you ask God to walk through this "dark valley" with you? If so, how did He help you?

JUNE

6

The Perfect Host

With God we will gain the victory, and he will trample down our enemies. Psalm 108:13, NIV.

"You prepare a table before me in the presence of my enemies. You anoint my head with oil; my cup overflows" (Psalm 23:5, NIV).

You would think that bringing a herd of sheep to a new feeding ground would be easy. But whenever the shepherd comes to a new pasture, he has a whole new set of problems to deal with.

First, he must check the entire area for different poisonous plants that grow along with the grass. The sheep will avoid most of the harmful plants, but a few varieties look very appealing to the animals. If the shepherd isn't careful, hundreds of his sheep can die just from eating the wrong plants.

Of course, he must also contend with the wild animals: the jackals, wolves, hyenas, and panthers that live in the holes and caves on the hillsides. But even more threatening are the snakes that hide in the fields. They lie in shallow holes, just waiting to bite the noses of the grazing sheep. The shepherd must walk ahead of his flock and make sure the area is free from the harmful reptiles.

At the end of the day, the shepherd leads his flock back to the sheepfold. As the sheep enter one at a time through the gate, he checks each one. He searches the face and legs for bruises and scratches. If a sheep has been hurt, the shepherd treats the injury with olive oil or cedar tar.

When an injured sheep is too weak to stand on its own, the shepherd will bring water to it. He dips a large two-handled cup into the water reservoir and then holds the cup as the weary sheep drinks.

The shepherd takes special interest in the comfort and safety of each sheep. God's care for us is just as loving and kind.

Something to think about: What enemies is God trying to protect you from today? Are you following His leading, or are you stubbornly refusing His guidance?

JUNE

7

Happy Endings

Surely goodness and love will follow me all the days of my life, and I will dwell in the house of the Lord forever" (Psalm 23:6, NIV).

I always like stories with happy endings. The shepherd's psalm ends with the sheep all safe and secure in the shepherd's fold.

Life on earth isn't very safe and secure. In fact it's just plain hard at times. I think of my cousin Mark, who fell when some scaffolding collapsed. That was seven years ago. Mark has never walked since. And he faces the rest of his life in a wheelchair.

I think of Kyle, one of my former students. His father, an engineer for one of the automotive companies, went in the hospital for some minor surgery. But because of someone's carelessness, Kyle's dad came out of surgery with severe brain damage.

I think of Archie. When he was only 5, he was taken from his home and placed with foster parents. His own parents had mistreated and neglected him. After two years with his foster parents, he met a Christian couple who wanted to adopt him. But because of certain adoption rules, he was adopted by a different family. A year later, his new family decided that they didn't want him. And they returned him to a different foster home.

Life is difficult. How thankful we can be that life on earth is only temporary—that there's something much better waiting for us in the future.

When the shepherd brings his flocks home at the end of the day, they can rest through the night, knowing that they are safe and secure, protected from the dangers that lurk around them.

It's just a matter of time before our Shepherd will come to take us home. What He has planned for us will more than make up for the sadness we've had on earth. When we see Him coming in the clouds, the happy ending to our lives will be just the beginning.

Something to think about: What will make heaven special to you?

I am going there to prepare a place for you. And if I go and prepare a place for you, I will come back and take you to be with me that you also may be where I am. John 14:2, 3, NIV.

JUNE

8

The Forgiving Prince

Then Peter came to him and asked, "Sir, how often should I forgive a brother who sins against me? Seven times?" "No!" Jesus replied, "seventy times seven!" Matthew 18:21, 22, TLB.

The French Revolution, which began in 1789, was one of the most brutal revolts in the history of the world.

By 1791 the hatred against the royal family had increased. King Louis XVI, Queen Marie Antoinette, and their son and daughter dressed up in disguises and attempted to flee from their home in Paris. But they were recognized and stopped.

A year later the opposition forces threw the king and his family into prison. The cruel guards took the young prince away from his family and put him into a solitary cell. Day after day young Louis sat alone. He was allowed no fresh air or exercise. What little food he received was always tossed on the floor by his guard, Simon.

Simon was a member of the Jacobin Club, the most fanatical political group during the revolution. Because of his hatred for the king and queen, Simon took special pleasure in heaping cruelty on the innocent little boy. He even refused to let the prince wash himself. And for more than a year the little boy was not even allowed to change his clothes.

Despite the inhumane treatment he received, Prince Louis did not feel hatred for his brutal jailer.

At one point it appeared that a counterrevolution was going to break out. And if the government forces would be successful in regaining control, the young prince would no doubt be crowned king and given the throne of France.

Simon began to wonder what his fate would be if the prince indeed became king. "I hear that you could end up as king of France, Louis," he said to the boy. "So just what would you do with me if you did get out of prison?"

Louis thought for a while and then simply answered, "I would pardon you."

There may be people in your life who have done mean things to you in the past. Or maybe someone is making life miserable for you right now. Although you may not have the power to get out of a bad situation, you aren't helpless. You have the ability to choose your reactions. You can choose to forgive.

JUNE

9

Let Go

I removed the burden from their shoulders; their hands were set free. Psalm 81:6, NIV.

"Tess, how many times have I told you not to get into my perfume?"

Sarah shooed her little sister out of her room and went back to the bottles of perfume that were lying all over the carpet. After putting their caps back on, Sarah set the bottles back on her dresser. "Little sisters," she muttered. "Always into things that don't concern them!"

When Sarah came home from school the next day, she found Tess in her room again. "Now what are you up to?" she asked.

Tess looked up with tears in her eyes. "Get it off," she pleaded.

"Get what off?"

Tess held up her right arm. On the end where her hand used to be was a beautiful antique vase.

"Oh, great," fumed Sarah. "You weren't satisfied playing with my perfume. Now you've gone and put your hand in the vase Aunt Josephine gave me."

Sarah stomped into the kitchen. "Mother, Tess has been in my room again, and she's got Aunt Josephine's vase stuck on her hand."

Mother hurried back to Sarah's room. "Why is your hand inside the vase, honey?" she asked the little girl.

"I dropped my two dimes into the vase, and I tried to get them out."

Mother took hold of the vase and tugged gently. "Can you push your fingers out straight and make your hand real skinny?" she asked.

Tess shook her head. "I want my dimes."

"But Tess, you can't get your hand out unless you let go of the money."

"No, no, no," the little girl cried. "I want my dimes."

Have you ever insisted on holding on to something that kept you from being free?

Like Tess, we often hold on to things that imprison us—things like jealousy, anger, and grudges. Some people spend their whole lives trapped by these bad attitudes.

Don't let bad feelings take over your life. Let them go.

JUNE

10

Someday I'll—

They rejoice in your name all day long; they exult in your righteousness. Psalm 89:16, NIV.

Katy and Jan were two very different students.

Katy wore a continual frown on her face. She rarely got enthusiastic about anything. When I'd announce a field trip, she'd roll her eyes up into her head and sigh. When we took the class on a campout, she complained all the way home about how bored she had been. It seemed that no matter what was going on, Katy was miserable.

Jan, on the other hand, loved life. She saw it as a big adventure and squeezed out of it every bit of fun there was.

Both girls came from good homes. Both were talented and smart. And both were nice-looking. Then why were they so different?

I think the answer is that Katy had the habit of thinking negatively, while Jan always thought positively.

Abraham Lincoln once said, "People are generally about as happy as they make up their minds to be." Our happiness is not based on what happens to us but on what we *think* about what happens to us.

Too many people plan to be happy in the future—when life is perfect.

Billy couldn't wait until he could go to school like the big kids. "I'll be happy then," he said. But once he got in school he found out it involved a lot of hard work.

"Boy, I'll be glad to get out of here and get a job," he decided. So after high school, Bill became a salesman at a computer store. But working was boring too.

"What I need is a wife." So Bill married Jennifer. But being married didn't make him happy either.

"Kids. That's it. We need a family. That will make me happy." But Bill found out that there's a lot of work to raising children. And getting up in the middle of the night to change the baby's diaper wasn't fun.

"Retirement. That's when I'll be happy. I'll have time to do what I really want to do. The kids will be on their own. I won't have to go to work. Yep, that's when I'll be happy." But when Bill retired early at 55, his free time drove him crazy.

"Maybe," he said to his wife one day, "I should go back to school."

Don't put off your decision to be happy. Make the most of today. Look for reasons to be happy. Don't wait for tomorrow. Because tomorrow never comes.

JUNE

11

Home, Sweet Home

I know what it is to be in need, and I know what it is to have plenty. I have learned the secret of being content in any and every situation. Philippians 4:12, NIV.

Mr. and Mrs. Simons were tired of their house. They'd lived in the same place for more than 20 years. It was time to find something bigger and better.

They decided to put their house on the market right away. The sooner they sold their property, the sooner they could buy a new house. So Mr. Simons called one of the real estate companies and invited a realtor over. At the end of their visit, the Simonses gave Mr. Davis permission to put their house on the market.

During the next few weeks, the Simonses began the search for their new home. Every Sunday they got in the car and drove along the back roads, looking for a house that might catch their interest. During the week they combed the "House for Sale" advertisements in the newspaper. But they just couldn't find what they were looking for.

Then one day Mrs. Simons excitedly called her husband on his lunch hour. "I think I found a house we might be interested in," she said. "Listen to this. 'Well-kept four-bedroom ranch home in quiet country setting. Two and a half baths. Room for garden.' Should we make an appointment to see it? It's listed with our realtor."

"Sure. I'll be home at 5:30. Call and find out if someone can show it to us after 7:00."

So Mrs. Simons called the real estate office.

"Which house are you interested in?" asked Mr. Davis.

"The one advertised in the paper today. The four bedroom house in the country. Could we see it tonight?"

Mr. David started laughing. "Mrs. Simons, I've never had this happen before, but the house you're calling about—well, it's the one you're living in right now."

Do you appreciate what you have, or are you always wanting something different? Jesus warned us not to covet what other people have. He wants us to be contented with what we already have.

JUNE

12

A Bad Case of the Gimmes

Let the morning bring me word of your unfailing love, for I have put my trust in you. Show me the way I should go, for to you I lift up my soul. Psalm 143:8, NIV.

When I was in church school, my grandmother liked to have me spend the night at her house. While she'd work on her flower bed, I'd mow the lawn and do some trimming around the trees and the sidewalk.

After supper I'd help her wash dishes. And then I'd check out the junk drawer. Now, I'm sure every home has a junk drawer—the place where you put all the odds and ends that don't belong anywhere else.

One day I found some really great things that I thought I couldn't live without. So I decided to see if she'd give them to me.

"My, you sure have a bad case of the gimmes, tonight, Renee," she said.

Are you ever guilty of having the gimmes? Maybe you don't ask other people for things, but do your prayers ever resemble more of a shopping list than a conversation with a friend?

God wants us to ask Him for things. But too often we try to see what we can get from God, rather than what we can give to Him. How would you feel if the only time your friends called was when they needed something? After a while you'd probably realize that they were just using you.

Sometimes we use God in the same way. We spend time with Him only if we need something.

The story is told of a worldly man who, while hunting one day, got lost in the woods. For eight hours he wandered around in circles. Finally, in exhaustion he fell to the ground. "O God," he prayed. "I need Your help. I'm lost. Please help me get out of the woods. And if You do, I promise that I'll never bother You again for the rest of my life."

The poor man had it all wrong. God loves spending time with us. He doesn't consider our prayers a nuisance. But He wants our prayer time to be an opportunity when we can get to know Him better, not just a time when we present Him with our wish list.

JUNE

13

Are You Listening?

Be still, and know that I am God. Psalm 46:10, NIV.

"Prayer is conversation with God."—Clement of Alexandria.

One of the girls I went to academy with just loved to talk. In fact, she got into trouble a lot because she talked so much in class. Lisa talked so much that she never took the time to listen to what others were saying. Communication requires sending messages *and* receiving messages. Lisa knew only how to send them.

I remember one conversation I had with her that went something like this.

"Hey, Renee, how did you do on your tryouts for band?"

"Real well, I—"

"Boy, I was really worried when I had to go in. I hadn't practiced my scales. How far did you get on scales?"

"Well, I did all right except—"

"And that one march we had to play. Wasn't it awful? I sure hope that I did as well as Frank. I don't want to have to play third chair this year. What chair do you think you'll get?"

"First, as long—"

"Hey, I've got to get to geometry. Does the teacher have the tests graded yet?"

Lisa heard absolutely nothing I said. All she was interested in was what she had to say.

When we pray, we need to be careful that our prayers aren't one-sided conversations. It's important that we share our thoughts with God, but it's also important that we let Him share His thoughts with us. At the end of your prayers, sit quietly and give God an opportunity to speak to you. He may put a special Bible text into your thoughts. He may ask you to do something—or He may warn you against something you shouldn't do. He may take that time to assure you of His love and care. And some days He may not speak at all. But we still need to keep our minds open to His voice.

This week as you pray, spend a minute or two letting God communicate with you. Make your prayertime a two-way conversation.

JUNE

14

Going Down for the Last Time

And everyone who calls on the name of the Lord will be saved. Acts 2:21, NIV.

When he was a boy, Watchman Nee, a well-known Christian writer, used to love to gather with his friends at the local swimming hole. The swimming hole provided not only a place for entertainment, but also a chance to cool off after a hot day.

On one particular day, one of Nee's friends suffered a severe leg cramp while he was out in deep water. The boy tried to get to safety, but couldn't do it.

"Help," he cried out. "I can't swim. Somebody help me."

The other boys froze in fear. All they knew how to do was dog paddle. None of them could swim—except for the oldest boy. Turning, they looked toward the swimmer, expecting him to jump in and save their drowning friend, but he just stood there watching.

"Do something," someone shouted.

The older boy didn't move.

The others went wild, screaming at the boy to help their friend in distress. Eventually the boy with the cramp quit struggling and sank below the surface.

Instantly the swimmer dived into the water. With strong strokes he sped toward the drowning boy. Reaching down, he grabbed the boy's hair and pulled him back to the surface. Within a few seconds he had him over to the edge of the water, where the others pulled him out and turned him face down on the bank. The dazed boy coughed a few times and then took in a big breath of air.

The angry group turned toward the hero. "Why did you wait so long to save him? He almost drowned."

The hero explained. "If I had tried to save him while he was still struggling, we both would have gone down. I had to wait until he gave up."

Sometimes Jesus has to do the same with us. As long as we're so intent on saving ourselves, He can't do it for us. So He waits until we get to the end of our rope. When we finally give up on our own ability to run our own lives, He steps in and takes over. He knows that we'll never learn to trust in Him until we've given up on ourselves.

JUNE

15

The Power of Positive Thinking

For as [a person] thinketh in his heart, so is he. Proverbs 23:7.

"If you aim at nothing, you will hit nothing."

The human brain is beyond understanding. We are only beginning to realize just how powerful it really is.

Scientists wanted to find out if people's thoughts have anything to do with their performance. So they asked a group of college students to try an experiment. The students were divided into three groups. All three groups went to the school gym, where they took turns throwing a basketball through a hoop. After each person had made 100 free throws, the scores were recorded.

Next, the scientists gave each group specific instructions that were to be carried out for 20 days:

Group A was not to touch a basketball during the time.

Group B was to go to the gym every day, and each member was to make 25 practice shots.

Group C was also to go to the gymn, and its members were to make 25 practice shots each, but instead of actually throwing the ball, they were to just think about throwing it through the hoop.

After the 20 days, the groups were brought back into the gym and retested.

The people in group A, those who didn't do anything to improve their score, increased their score by 1 percent. Group B, those who practiced making free shots in the gym, did 24 percent better. (Just as the scientists expected.) But what surprised them were the results of those in Group C. After practicing their free throws in their minds, they improved by 22 percent, a score just slightly less than that of those who had gone to the gym and actually practiced their free throws.

Do you see what the results of this experiment say about you and your possibilities for success? Are your negative thoughts keeping you from doing better in school or in sports? Do you imagine yourself as a success—or a failure? God is not honored when we waste our talents and abilities. He wants to help us use them to bring glory to His name and to make our lives happier.

Why not face your challenges with a positive attitude? See yourself as a winner. And you'll be a winner.

JUNE

16

Fiery Words

Likewise the tongue is a small part of the body, but it makes great boasts. Consider what a great forest is set on fire by a small spark. James 3:5, NIV.

Eric and Skip knew they weren't supposed to play with matches. If their dad had warned them once, he'd warned them 50 times. But they didn't listen.

One afternoon they got bored watching TV, so they went outside to play in the woods that surrounded their house on three sides.

"Hey, let's build a fire," suggested Eric. "I've got some of Dad's matches."

"Well, we'd better be real careful so Mom won't see us," said Skip. "We'll be in big trouble if she finds out."

So the boys hid themselves a safe distance from the house. After they had gathered a pile of sticks, they stood them on end—tepee fashion, as they had learned in Pathfinders. Eric struck a match and held it carefully until it burned brightly. Leaning down, he touched it against one of the smaller twigs. The match died out. "We need some dried leaves," he suggested.

Skip gathered up a few and set them inside the sticks. Eric tried another match. This time it lasted long enough to kindle the leaves. The two brothers continued adding leaves and dead grass until the wood started to burn.

Then all of a sudden one of the burning leaves floated out of the fire and up into the air. It traveled a few feet and landed on some dry grass, which ignited before the boys' eyes.

"Quick, we've got to get some water!" shouted Eric.

The two boys jumped up and ran for the house. They grabbed two paper cups and filled them with water. Back to the fire they went, throwing their meager water supply on the burning grass.

Mrs. Kitsen, hearing the commotion, came up from the basement just as Skip was refilling his cup.

"What's going on, Skip?" she asked.

"Oh, Mom, there's a fire, and we can't put it out."

Mrs. Kitsen hurried to the phone and called the fire department. Fortunately the men arrived before any buildings were destroyed. But you can be sure that the boys had some explaining to do when Dad came home that night.

Our words are like fire. Once sparked, there's little we can do to keep them from spreading damage. Before you speak, make sure that your words will help—not hurt.

JUNE

17

You Sow, You Reap

Do not be deceived: God cannot be mocked. A man reaps what he sows. Galatians 6:7, NIV.

When my mother was in nurse's training, one of her duties was changing the bed sheets. Every day the student nurses practiced making up the beds—often while the patients were still in them.

One particular day, my mother's best friend, Joan, was assigned to help out on the surgical floor. Just as she was finishing making up the bed in Room 216, an orderly brought in a new patient. Joan pulled back the sheets and then helped the orderly transfer the patient from the gurney to the bed.

A few hours later Joan stopped by the room to see how the new patient was doing. To her surprise, she found the lady dead from a heart attack. She went to the nurses' desk and reported the death. Within an hour the body was removed and taken to the morgue.

Joan was supposed to remove the sheets from the bed and replace them with new sheets, but she didn't. She figured that she'd just save herself some work. After all, no one would know the difference. So she quickly smoothed out the sheets and fluffed up the pillow. "There," she said to herself. "It'll be my little secret."

Joan went on with her work. At 3:00 p.m. she and some other nurses went down to the cafeteria for a sandwich. But halfway through her meal, Joan felt a stabbing pain in the middle of her abdomen.

"Oh, no," she moaned. "I think I'm going to die."

Her friends took her to the emergency room, where the doctor gave her a quick examination.

"I want to run some blood tests to be sure, but I suspect that you're having an appendicitis attack, Joan," he said. "I think we'd better get you ready for surgery."

As soon as tests confirmed the doctor's suspicions, Joan was hurried in to surgery, where the doctor took care of her problem. Then she was taken to second floor. And put in bed 216.

When Joan woke up and found out where she was, she wanted out. But there was nothing she could do but lie there. She found out the hard way that our actions have a strange way of catching up to us.

We may get away with some things, but in the end we reap what we sow.

JUNE

18

A Hard Road to Walk

The law of the wise is a fountain of life, to depart from the snares of death. Good understanding giveth favour: but the way of transgressors is hard. Proverbs 13:14, 15.

Although many people believe that sinners have a happier and more exciting life than the righteous, the reverse is actually true. Those who choose to follow Satan are the ones who have it rough. They may have it easy at first, but ignoring God's guidelines results in regret and disappointment.

From 1907 to 1927 beautiful girls competed to become one of the chorus girls in the world-famous Ziegfeld Follies. Kenneth Wood in his book *Meditations for Moderns* tells about an incident that involved six of the girls.

One day the girls were approached by a wrinkled old woman who was selling face cream and other cosmetics. As she talked with the girls she shook her head sadly and said, "Twenty years ago I was just as beautiful as you are."

This shocked the girls so much that they vowed never to let themselves deteriorate as that woman had. And to seal their pledge, they decided to meet exactly 20 years later to prove their point.

Twenty years later Kathryn Lambert, one of the six, appeared at the restaurant specified. But she was the only one. All the others were dead. One had committed suicide in a Paris hotel 16 years before. Another had died in Hollywood at the age of 34, after breaking her health through strenuous dieting. A third had died in a fire after someone accidentally dropped a cigarette into the ruffles of her evening gown. The fourth was killed in a brawl in a New York nightclub. The fifth died penniless, an addict to drugs and alcohol. All had achieved world success—one had been known as "the best-dressed woman on the screen"; another was the leading lady of a popular play; the third had married a millionaire. But they had left God out of their lives, with inevitably tragic results (Adapted with permission from Kenneth H. Wood, Jr., *Meditations for Moderns* [Washington, D.C.: Review and Herald, 1963], p. 320).

Following God isn't easy. It requires self-denial. We have to say no to the things that can hurt us. But in the end, we always come out ahead.

Something to think about: What are some of the things that God asks us to avoid for our own good?

JUNE

19

Fight or Flight?

The Lord is my light and my salvation—whom shall I fear? The Lord is the stronghold of my life—of whom shall I be afraid? Psalm 27:1, NIV.

Six years ago we lived in a big apartment complex that was located right next to the junior academy where we taught. The complex was almost like a small city.

In the Sunday paper I had read a story about two men who had beaten and robbed a lady only a few buildings down from us. I decided that I was not going to be a helpless victim. I would prepare myself in case someone tried to attack me.

I remembered an idea that I'd seen during a self-defense demonstration, and I thought I'd use it. The instructor had put her key chain in her hand and pulled the keys up between her fingers. When she made a fist, the keys stuck out like sharp little fingers. When the attacker approached, she scratched his face and sent him running.

Two nights later, our music teacher and I worked late. It was dark by the time we locked the school door and headed for home. I arranged my keys between my fingers. Holding up my weapons, I said to Sue, "See this? If anyone tries to steal my purse, I'm ready for him."

Just then a man walked out of the shadows around the corner of the school. Sue and I both screamed. My knees decided not to hold me up, and I fell down on the sidewalk. My keys fell to the ground. (We sure did give the poor man a scare!)

The experience taught me that no matter how well we plan, we can never eliminate fearful situations or anticipate how we're going to handle them. No amount of self-defense will take the place of God's protection.

Of course, we need to take precautions and use good sense, but we should never allow Satan to intimidate us into living in a state of fear. God wants us to be filled with His confidence and His power.

JUNE

20

Don't Go It Alone

Higgins wasn't the highest-ranking officer aboard, but the young ensign caught the attention of the captain. "That young man is going to be a real credit to the Navy," said the captain. "Why don't we give him a chance to see how well he can run the ship?"

So orders were sent to the sailor that he was to take charge and prepare the boat for departure. In record time Ensign Higgins had the ship on its way out of the harbor. He sat back, proud of a job well done.

A knock at the door roused him from his moment of glory. "Captain Stevens would like a word with you."

Higgins straightened his uniform and followed the messenger to the captain's office. He looked forward to hearing the praise that the captain was sure to give him. But when he entered the office, the captain wasn't around. The messenger just pointed to the telephone on the desk.

"Hello," said Higgins. "Captain Stevens?"

"Yes, Higgins. I just wanted to commend you on a job well done. You readied the ship in record time. But you overlooked one thing. Next time, make sure your captain is aboard *before* you set sail."

Every morning we need to make sure that the Captain of our lives is with us before we begin to sail through a new day. We may be efficient and skilled, but without His direction, we're headed for trouble.

There are two basic reasons that we start a day without God.

Sometimes we don't want His companionship. We know that the things we have planned are against His will. And we don't want Him to step in and try to change our direction.

But most of the time we're just careless. We let other things distract us from praying and reading the Bible. We may feel that worship is a nice thing to do but that it isn't all that important. So we put it on the back burner—something to do if we have the time.

Do all you can to take the Captain with you each day. It will take some of your time, but the benefits you'll receive will be well worth it.

In everything you do, put God first, and he will direct you and crown your efforts with success. Proverbs 3:6, TLB.

JUNE

21

Irritations

Whoever loves his brother lives in the light.
1 John 2:10, NIV.

After the friendship of God, a friend's affection is the greatest treasure on earth."

Pearls are some of the most beautiful and most expensive gems money can buy, but instead of being mined from the earth, they are formed underwater by oysters.

The oyster's inner shell is lined with a hard, shiny substance called nacre. This is the same material that makes up a pearl. When a grain of sand or some other irritant gets inside the oyster's shell, the oyster covers it with a thin layer of nacre. Layer after layer is added, and eventually a pearl is produced. And pearls come in many different colors: white, cream, pink, orange, gold, and black.

When oysters can't get rid of the sand inside their shell, they don't get angry. They don't give up. They just use their irritations as a foundation to produce something beautiful.

My father considered one of the other workers in his factory a real irritation. Len wasn't a loudmouth or a troublemaker, but Dad just didn't care to be around him. Then one day my father visited with him during a break. Later that week he ate lunch with Len. He found out that Len wasn't so bad after all, and the more he got to know him, the more he liked him. Eventually Len became one of his closest friends.

There may be people in your life whom you could live without. You may even daydream about how great things would be if they would move away or go to a different school. Instead of letting them irritate you and make life miserable, take a lesson from the oyster. Look for ways to make something beautiful out of your bad relationship. Don't wait for the other person to do something about it. Decide to make the first move yourself.

Something to think about: What one irritating person could you make into a friend? What could you do today to take the first step toward that goal?

JUNE

22

Surprise, Surprise, Surprise!

You may be sure that your sin will find you out. Numbers 32:23, NIV.

Crickets chirped an evening serenade as the Quinn family slept peacefully inside their motor home that August night in 1991.

They had no idea that at that very moment a thief was stalking through the shadows, and he was headed straight toward their campsite.

The thief, a teenage boy, was searching for something—the gas tank for the motor home. He planned to help himself to a free tank of gasoline. No use paying for it when he could steal it. Besides, the sleeping occupants would never know what happened.

After locating the tank, the boy headed back to the road where he had left his car. Starting the engine, he drove slowly to the motor home and parked as close as he could to the tank.

Before siphoning the gas, the boy surveyed the area to make sure no one was watching. When he was satisfied that the coast was clear, he opened the car door and pulled out a flashlight and a long rubber hose.

With a quick twist of the wrist, he removed the cap. Then he took one end of the rubber hose and threaded it down into the tank. His plan was simple. He'd put the hose into the tank of the motor home, then by sucking on the other end he'd draw the gas up through the hose. (The action is similar to a person using a drinking straw in a glass of milk.) Once the gas would start flowing, he'd take the hose out of his mouth and let it drain into the fuel tank of his car.

Putting the hose into his mouth, he started to suck the gas up through the hose. But instead of getting a mouthful of gasoline . . .

A loud noise just outside the motor home awakened Mr. Quinn. He grabbed a flashlight and hurried out to investigate.

There curled up on the ground was the teenage thief. Next to him lay the rubber hose, which was pouring sewage all over the ground. What he thought was the fuel tank turned out to be the holding tank for the motor home's sewage.

When the police came to investigate, Mr. Quinn decided not to press charges. He decided that the boy had already learned his lesson. I think Mr. Quinn was right, don't you?

JUNE

23

Nearer, Still Nearer

What does the Lord your God ask of you but to fear the Lord your God, to walk in all his ways, to love him, to serve the Lord your God with all your heart and with all your soul, and to observe the Lord's commands. Deuteronomy 10:12, 13, NIV.

When I was in eighth grade, my best friend was not a member of our church. In fact, I don't think Beth ever went to church at all.

One day her parents invited me to a horse show. Beth took riding lessons, and she would be riding in a number of events. I was all excited. Then I found out that the show was going to be on Sabbath. "I'm sorry, I can't," I told them. "I go to church on Saturday."

"Well, that's no problem. The horse show is in the afternoon. You go to church in the morning, don't you?" Mrs. Kuhn asked.

"But we keep Sabbath all day," I replied.

Beth was very disappointed that I couldn't come. "Can't you just talk to your minister and get permission to go?"

I explained that the Sabbath wasn't my minister's rule. It was God's commandment, and nobody could give me permission to disobey any of God's rules.

God's rules. Have you ever wondered why He gave them to us in the first place? It's not that God wants to take away our fun. It's just that He has a special plan for our lives—He wants to help us grow to be more like Him.

When Adam and Eve were first created, they were perfect. But as soon as they chose to disobey, they became sinful. It has been God's plan ever since to bring the human race back, as much as possible, to what Adam and Eve were like before sin. He doesn't just want to save us from our sins; He also wants to remake us into His image, so others can see Him through us.

God's law is a reflection of His character. If we want to be like Him, we'll do whatever He asks.

JUNE

24

More Power to You!

But as for me, I am filled with power, with the Spirit of the Lord, and with justice and might. Micah 3:8, NIV.

David and Emmie are the nicest neighbors anyone could have. Since they are both retired, they give of their time to others. David mows our school's enormous lawn. Emmie is always stopping by with some braided bread, German pastries, or vegetable soup.

So when Emmie called needing some help with her VCR, Tom was more than happy to go over to see how he could help. "What seems to be the problem?" he asked.

David took him over to the VCR. "I just can't figure out what's wrong," he said. "It was working perfectly last night. But now we can't even get it to turn on."

Tom fiddled with the controls, but nothing worked. "Did you blow any fuses?" he asked.

David shook his head no.

"Wait a minute," Tom said slowly. Turning to me, he said, "Flick on that light switch behind you." I did, and the VCR lit right up.

Tom had remembered that in our living room the bottom plugs in the electric outlets can be turned off and on from the light switch. Emmie and David thought their VCR was broken when all they needed to do was to turn on the power.

Even more powerful than electricity is the power of the Holy Spirit. Through His power we're able to overcome our bad habits. Through His power we're able to do whatever the Lord asks us to do. And through His power we can become brand-new people.

When I was younger, I used to think that the Holy Spirit was a special force coming from God. But now I know that He is a being just like God and Jesus. I realize He is the one who stays with me 24 hours a day. It is His voice I hear speaking through my conscience.

Before Jesus comes again, the Holy Spirit will work with God's people in a way far greater than ever before. He will help us give the last warning to the world, and He will work in the lives of each of God's followers to prepare them to receive the seal of God.

The Holy Spirit's power is available to you today. Are you willing to receive it? It's your decision to turn on the switch.

JUNE

25

Making Your Decision

Choose for yourselves this day whom you will serve. Joshua 24:15, NIV.

At the conclusion of one of his evangelistic meetings in Brazil, Pastor Henry Feyerabend, along with a number of other pastors, held a large baptism. There were so many people wanting to be baptized that they had to stand in a long line that snaked outside the church and by the school building.

A few days after the baptism, an irritated man came to talk to Pastor Feyerabend. "I've come to find out just why you baptized my son," he said. "He wasn't prepared to join the church."

The pastor didn't know which boy the man was speaking of. "I'm sorry, but we had such a large group. Maybe you should ask him why he made the decision."

So the man went home that night and questioned his son. "Why did you get baptized without even telling your mother or me?"

The boy shrugged his shoulders. "Well, I saw all those people lined up, so I got in line with them. The next thing I knew, I was baptized."

Are you an accidental Christian? Do you go to church because that's what everybody else is doing? Or have you made a commitment to follow Jesus?

Going to church each Sabbath may be a rule at your house. If it is, you can be thankful that your parents are helping you develop a good habit, but someday you're going to be on your own. Someday you'll have to decide whether or not you'll remain in God's family.

You may be thinking about being baptized in the near future. If this is the case, why do you want to join the church? Are you doing it to please your parents? Are you doing it because of your friends? Or are you joining because you want to turn your life over to Jesus?

Joining the church is an important step. Think it over carefully before you take it.

Something to think about: In your opinion, what steps should be taken before a person becomes a church member?

JUNE

26

Don't Trust Your Eyes

For your love is ever before me, and I walk continually in your truth. Psalm 26:3, NIV.

A half-truth is a dangerous thing, especially if you have got hold of the wrong half."—Myron Boyd.

On Spook Hill in Lake Wales, Florida, you can put a car in neutral, and it will roll uphill. You can place a tennis ball on the ground, and it too will roll uphill. Or so it seems.

According to the city manager, the strange sights are really optical illusions. Objects really roll downhill—it just appears that they're going uphill. The laws of physics assure us that gravity pulls things downward.

There are many strange beliefs that are being promoted today. If they were completely false, they'd be easier to judge. But because they are mixed with truth, they seem more believable. Just like Spook Hill, they look genuine.

Last week one of my piano students came for a lesson. As she played through a song she'd gotten the week before, I noticed that she was playing it in the key of C. The song was written in F, which meant she should have been playing a B flat all the way through.

When I pointed out her mistake, she said, "But, Mrs. Coffee, it sounded all right."

To most people, the beliefs of the New Age movement sound fine too. New Agers encourage self-improvement, exercise, good nutrition, and meditation. These are things Christians believe in.

But as you dig deeper into the philosophy of the New Age movement, you find some very dangerous beliefs. New Agers are told to kneel down and worship themselves, since they are God. They are encouraged to get in contact with the dead. They are also told that they may have had previous lives.

If we didn't have the Bible, we could be taken in easily by this tool of Satan. The Bible is God's truth, and when we use it as our standard of right and wrong, we'll be able to judge whether something is from God or from the devil.

Don't ever settle for a new idea just because it looks good or sounds good. Put it to the test.

JUNE

27

Shattered Lives

Count yourselves dead to sin but alive to God in Christ Jesus. Romans 6:11, NIV.

I love to watch people juggle. When Tom was in college, his PE teacher taught him how to do it. And now every once in a while he'll pick up some oranges or apples and do a little juggling just to keep in practice. When I try, I cause severe fruit damage.

I've seen people juggle knives, torches, and even chairs. But the most unforgettable juggler I've ever seen was a man I watched on television when I was a little girl. The juggler, for his final act, brought out a tall stack of glass dinner plates, which he set on a table. Then he began placing thin wooden poles into stands that were lined up in rows across the stage. As the music began, he took a plate and placed it on the end of one of the poles. With a quick spin, he set the dish whirling like a top. Down the rows he went, adding one plate after another, until he had 30 going at the same time.

The audience went wild with applause. But their cheers soon turned to nervous moans as one of the plates began to wobble. The juggler jogged over to it, moved the pole back and forth, and set the dish spinning again. But no sooner had he taken care of the problem plate than another began to wobble. Frantically the juggler ran between the rows of plates, trying to keep all 30 on an even keel. But no matter how hard he tried, the plates lost their spin and one by one shattered on the tile floor below.

So it is with us when we try to handle sin on our own. Just as soon as we think we have one problem under control, something else goes wrong.

Instead of concentrating on all the things we do wrong, we need to concentrate on getting to know Jesus better. Instead of wearing ourselves out by trying to be good, we need to trust Jesus to change us. When we give our lives to Him each day, He will give us the ability and the "want to" to follow His example.

JUNE

28

What Are You Putting Into Your Checking Account?

Commit to the Lord whatever you do, and your plans will succeed. Proverbs 16:3, NIV.

Five-year-old Toby and his father pushed the grocery cart up to the checkout counter. They unloaded their purchases and watched as the cashier rang up the prices. "That will be $46.32," she said.

Dad pulled out his checkbook, wrote a few words, and then handed a check to the lady.

Wow, thought Toby. *Dad didn't have to give her any money. All he had to do was write something on a piece of paper.*

During supper that night, Toby decided it was time to get his own checkbook. "Dad, I want to go to the bank and get a checkbook tomorrow."

His parents looked at each other in surprise. "Oh, really?" asked his father. "Just what do you need a checkbook for?"

"So I can buy things. If I had a checkbook, I could buy things."

Without saying anything, Mr. Peters walked over to the closet. He reached inside and pulled out his checkbook, which was in his overcoat. "Well, Toby," he said as he returned to the table, "I think you may have the wrong idea about checks. You see, they're only worth something if you put money in the bank ahead of time."

Mr. Peters opened up the checkbook and showed Toby the check register. "You see right here? Well, this shows that I have $500 in the bank. I put that money in an account some time ago. The grocery store will take my check to the bank, and the bank will give them $46.32 from my $500."

Toby was disappointed. "You mean you can't buy just anything you want with a check?"

"That's right. You can spend only as much money as you've put in your account."

So it is with many areas of life. We must put something in an account before we can make withdrawals.

Students must put time and effort into their studies before they can expect to get good grades.

Athletes must spend hours practicing in order to do their best when they compete.

Musicians must go over their songs, practicing the different passages again and again before they are ready to perform in public.

Nothing worthwhile is accomplished without effort. What deposits do you need to make today for your future?

JUNE

29

Putting On Christ's Armor

Therefore put on the full armor of God, so that when the day of evil comes, you may be able to stand your ground, and after you have done everything, to stand. Ephesians 6:13, NIV.

Yesterday we read how we must put time and energy into our goals if we expect to reap the benefits. We have to make periodic investments in order to accomplish anything in the future. And what is true for students, athletes, and musicians is also true for those who want to resist temptation.

Lee had a terrible time with his temper. At school he was known as a real hothead. One day Gary, his biggest rival, intentionally tripped him while they were playing basketball. Lee took a nosedive and slid halfway across the gym floor.

"That does it!" he screamed. "I'm going to smash you, you jerk." Jumping up from the floor, he tackled Gary. By the time Coach Benton separated the boys, Gary's nose was bleeding and Lee had a black eye.

When Lee got home that afternoon, he dreaded telling his parents that he had been suspended. So he waited until right before bedtime. Dad was relaxing in the recliner when Lee handed him the note from the principal. After reading it, Dad asked Lee to sit down. "I'm really worried about your temper, Lee," he said. "It seems that you have no control over it."

Lee hung his head and said nothing.

"Son, have you asked God to help you?"

"Sure, Dad. Lots of times. But it never works. Like today. As soon as Gary tripped me, I said, 'Lord, help me.' But He didn't. I still got into a fight."

Mr. Rollins shook his head knowingly. "I understand what you're saying, Lee. I used to do the same thing when I was tempted, but I found out that God can't do much to help me if the only time I come to Him is when I'm in trouble. You see, God helps us resist temptation by changing us. And that can't happen unless we're spending time with Him."

"You mean reading the Bible and praying?"

"Right. We can't say no to sin unless God's Spirit is living in us. And that only happens when we keep in constant contact with Heaven."

Don't wait until you're in the middle of temptation to turn to God. Go to Him each day and let Him surround you with His power.

JUNE

30

The Only Thing That Matters

You shall have no other gods before me. Exodus 20:3, NIV.

Zacchaeus didn't care anymore. He didn't care if he lost all remaining dignity. He didn't care if the whole town laughed at him for sitting up in the tree. He didn't care if they started telling "short" jokes. He had only one thought: *I've got to see Jesus.*

Money was the only friend he had. It didn't make fun of him like his neighbors did. Money didn't betray him. And it provided him with a few pleasures to fill his lonely life. But it wasn't enough. He needed a real friend. He needed Jesus.

Jesus knew about the deep longing in Zacchaeus' heart, and He could hardly wait to add him to the family of God. But He also knew that Zacchaeus needed to make a clean break from the one thing that controlled his life.

Jesus didn't need to scold Zacchaeus about the way he had cheated the people out of their money. The Holy Spirit had already been at work convicting him of his sin. So when Zacchaeus came face-to-face with Jesus, he was willing to give up everything just for assurance of God's acceptance.

He knew that Jesus couldn't be Lord of his life while money was still his god. So he pledged half his wealth to the poor, and to those he had cheated, he promised a fourfold repayment. Although Zacchaeus had been a very rich man, he willingly gave up his fortune. He knew that a friendship with Jesus was all that really mattered.

Are there some things that have come between you and God? Have you given Him only second, third, or fourth place in your life?

You may not have problems with money, but have you made a god out of sports, popularity, television shows, movies, clothes, or music? It doesn't matter to Satan what you choose, as long as you don't choose God.

Who or what sits in first place in your life today?

Something to think about: If Jesus were to ask you to give up one thing in your life, what do you think He would choose?

JULY

1

Echo Valley

Add to your faith goodness; and to goodness, knowledge; and to knowledge, self-control; and to self-control, perseverance; and to perseverance, godliness; and to godliness, brotherly kindness; and to brotherly kindness, love. 2 Peter 1:5-7, NIV.

Louis Agassiz was a Swiss scientist who lived in the late 1800s. A brilliant man, he taught both zoology and geology at Harvard University. But Agassiz was much more than an educator. He was also a kind and loving individual.

When he was just a little boy, he learned a great lesson about the importance of words. One day his mother took him to a place called Echo Valley. As they stood on the edge of the valley, Louis's mother told her son to say something.

Louis didn't know exactly what to say, so he just said, "Who are you?"

"Try again, son," said his mother, "but this time say it as loudly as you can."

Louis opened his mouth wide and cried out, "Who are you?"

Back came the words "Who are you?"

Louis had never heard an echo before. He thought for sure that some other little boy was standing on the other side of the valley, copying his words. And he didn't like it one bit. In fact, it made him angry to think that someone was mimicking him.

"I don't like you," he shouted back angrily.

"I don't like you," the echo replied.

Hearing the mean words shouted back at him scared Louis. No one had ever treated him so unkindly before. Hiding his head in his mother's lap, he began to cry.

Louis' mother put her arm around her little son. "Why don't you say something nice? Maybe then the voice on the other side will also speak kindly."

So Louis called out, "I want to be your friend."

Back came the echo "I want to be your friend."

Louis learned that the words we speak are usually returned to us.

JULY

2

Who's in First Place?

Come, let us bow down in worship, let us kneel before the Lord our Maker; for he is our God and we are the people of his pasture, the flock under his care. Psalm 95:6, 7, NIV.

The two great religions in Japan are Shintoism and Buddhism. Many Japanese practice both religions. During the summer Tom and I taught in Japan, we learned a lot about the customs of the Japanese people. We visited their temples and watched the different ways they worship their gods.

When we visited the different religious centers, we saw the people brushing holy smoke across their foreheads, drinking holy water that ran off the roofs of the temples, and sticking coins into cedar trees.

Along the country roads where we lived, people erected little shrines to honor their gods. They would leave money, flowers, food, and beer inside. A few days later the items would disappear. I always wondered what happened to them.

Religious customs make up a great part of the Japanese culture. For example, nearly 90 percent of the people consider themselves Shintoists, and nearly the whole population takes part in Shinto ceremonies and practices.

Winning the Japanese people to Adventism can be very frustrating work. For one thing, all young people go to school Monday through Friday and a half day on Saturday. So it is difficult for them to keep the Sabbath.

Another problem is that the Japanese have a hard time breaking away from the religions of their ancestors. After hearing the gospel, new converts will claim to accept Jesus as their Saviour, but they often continue in their old forms of worship. So one person may end up practicing Christianity, Buddhism, and Shintoism—all at the same time. Many Japanese see no need to give their loyalty to only one God.

As Christians we realize that we can't mix one religion with another. God does not allow us to worship anyone else but Him. And for good reason. He is the only true God. All other gods are either something He created or a figment of the imagination.

We don't have a problem with worshiping idols, but sometimes it's easy to let other things become more important than God. Just as it's impossible to be a Christian and a Buddhist at the same time, so it's also impossible to worship God and material things.

Who or what will have first place in your life today? It's up to you to decide.

JULY

3

The Price of Freedom

I will walk about in freedom, for I have sought out your precepts. Psalm 119:45, NIV.

April 1975, Saigon, South Vietnam.

It was only a matter of time, and not much time at that. The Communists were taking over the country. The Seventh-day Adventist General Conference voted to send Elder Don Roth to Vietnam. His job was to help evacuate the Vietnamese workers from the Adventist mission, the publishing house, and hospitals.

Although the workers were citizens of Vietnam, they were still in jeopardy. Because of their association with Americans, they would be considered enemies of the new government. And that meant they would be in danger of torture and death.

Elder Roth's first group of refugees consisted of 36 women and children. The men had decided to stay behind. They wanted to keep the hospitals open as long as possible.

On April 23 Elder Roth took his group to a bowling alley, where they spent the night with 1,000 other refugees. The night was long. The fear of the unknown kept almost everyone from getting much sleep. The accommodations weren't too great either. Pastor Roth ended up sleeping across a bowling lane. (He used his camera bag for a pillow.)

By the next morning tension filled the air. Group after group was called forward for inspection. Papers were checked and baggage searched. Elder Roth's group just sat and waited. Finally at 3:00 in the afternoon, they were called forward. When the inspection ended, the group boarded a bus.

Just as they arrived at the airport gate, the bus stopped. A policeman stepped aboard. He looked out over the rows of passengers and surveyed each face. Then he motioned for the mission president's 17-year-old son to come forward.

Pastor Roth's heart began to pound. He knew that no male citizens of military age could leave the country. Would they have to leave him behind? Would he be forced to join the army? Was he about to lose his hope of freedom?

For those of us who live in a free society, freedom is a way of life. We don't have an opportunity to see what life is like in many other places in the world. Don't take your freedom for granted. Be thankful for it every day of your life. Don't wait until it's gone before you learn to appreciate it.

JULY

4

Freedom Isn't Free

Proclaim liberty throughout the land to all its inhabitants. Leviticus 25:10, NIV.

The policeman questioned the young man for a short time and then looked up at Elder Roth and smiled. A smile came over the face of the uniformed man. He sent the youth back to his seat and walked off the bus. A soldier got on board and signaled for the bus driver to continue.

When the bus pulled up to the C-130 military cargo plane, Pastor Roth walked to the front of the bus and stood behind the soldier who was blocking the aisle. The Vietnamese man tilted his head back and spoke in perfect English. "American money for the policeman and me, or the boy does not get on the plane." With that, the soldier left the bus.

The stunned pastor reached for his wallet. When he opened it up, all he found was a $10 bill. He checked his pockets and found nothing more. Would $10 buy the boy's freedom?

Elder Roth stepped down out of the bus and walked over to where the soldier was standing. Quietly he handed over the money.

As the refugees came streaming out of the bus, Elder Roth stood next to the soldier, waiting to see what would happen. The Vietnamese teenager came through the door of the bus. The soldier stepped forward. Lifting his hand, he waved the boy toward the plane. Turning toward Pastor Roth, the soldier offered a snappy salute, made an about-face, and reboarded the empty bus.

Elder Roth was able to buy the teenager's freedom for only $10, but the freedom you and I enjoy today cost much more. It was paid for with the lives of tens of thousands of people who were willing to die for liberty. Because of their unselfishness, you and I can enjoy a country in which we can live and worship as we choose.

Something to think about: Which of the following freedoms that you possess right now do you value the most? Freedom to say what you believe, freedom to follow your religion, freedom to choose the things you want to buy, freedom to choose what job you would like to have.

JULY

5

Jumping to Conclusions

Do not be quickly provoked in your spirit, for anger resides in the lap of fools. Ecclesiastes 7:9, NIV.

It was my birthday, and I had to take a written driver's test in order to renew my license.

My husband dropped me off at the license bureau and promised to return in a half hour. He needed to go to K Mart and get some cleaning supplies for the school.

I went inside and took my test. I paid my $4, and someone directed me over to the place where they take those awful-looking pictures.

The paperwork completed, I sat down to wait for Tom. At 5:00 the door was locked, and I had to stand outside in the cold. *Where in the world is he?* I thought. *It can't take an hour to pick up a few cans of cleanser and some sponges.*

As the minutes ticked by, my body got colder, but my temper grew hotter. *I can't believe how inconsiderate he is, leaving me to stand out here in the cold while he's killing time at the store.*

Finally at 5:30 I saw our car coming down the highway. Tom pulled into the parking lot and gave me a little wave.

Look at him. He doesn't even care that I've been standing out here in the cold for the past half hour. I walked over to the car, opened the door, and got in.

"Sorry I'm late," said Tom.

I gave him the silent treatment. I was just waiting for him to ask me what was wrong. Then I was going to let him have it.

"I need to drive by the Hockings' house. I need to borrow some tools from Greg," he said.

I just sat looking straight ahead.

When we got to our friends' house, I followed Tom inside. I couldn't wait to tell Dolly about how I'd stood outside in the cold for 30 minutes.

"Happy Birthday," said Tom as we walked into the kitchen. There stood our friends setting the table for my surprise birthday supper.

Tom went back to the car and came back to the kitchen carrying a brightly wrapped present. "I'm sorry I took so long, but I had a terrible time trying to wrap this in the car."

Now every time I look at the beautiful Kitchen Aid mixer on my counter I think of how quick I had been to judge Tom.

Before you jump to conclusions, find out the facts. Most of the time people have a good explanation for what they do. If you wait to hear their side of the story, you'll stay calmer, and you'll save yourself a lot of embarrassment.

JULY

6

Where Never Is Heard a Discouraging Word

An anxious heart weighs a man down, but a kind word cheers him up. Proverbs 12:25, NIV.

Herschel Binderloff had big dreams. He wanted to be an architect. Herschel moved to New York City and began studying architectural drawing. He put every ounce of his effort into his studies.

Eventually his health began to suffer. At first he thought he had a cold. But when he failed to get better, he decided to make an appointment at the clinic.

After the doctor checked him over and ran some tests, he gave Herschel the bad news. "I'm sorry, son, but you've got tuberculosis. Your chances of fully recuperating are not real good. If I were you, I'd move to Arizona. The climate might help you feel better, but I can't give you any guarantees."

Herschel walked out of the doctor's office in a daze. His great hopes of becoming an architect were all gone. Leaning against the building, he closed his eyes and tried to fight back the tears.

A taxi driver waiting at the corner noticed the young man. *Something must be wrong,* he thought.

The man opened up the door to his cab. "Get in," he said to Herschel. Herschel obeyed.

"Where do you need to go?" the man asked.

"To the apartments on State Street." As they drove along, Herschel shared with the cabby the doctor's diagnosis.

Just before the man let Herschel off at his apartment, he turned around and said, "Listen, son, everybody has problems. But if you keep up your courage and keep fighting, you'll come out a winner."

Within a few days Herschel was on his way to Arizona. He found a room at a ranch. The warm, clean air did wonders for Herschel. He felt better every day.

When he heard about a new highway that was being built through the mountain area, Herschel began studying civil engineering. He applied for a job. He started drawing plans for bridges and highways. His reputation as an architect and engineer spread. And before long, Herschel was not only successful, but also healthy once again.

Herschel never forgot the taxi cab driver. "If he hadn't encouraged me, I would probably have given up and never reached my dream."

There are hurting people everywhere. Don't miss an opportunity to encourage them. Take the time to say something. You never know when your words might change their lives.

JULY

7

The Missing Ingredients

Blessed are those who keep my ways. Listen to my instruction and be wise; do not ignore it. Proverbs 8:32, 33, NIV.

Bridget loved to cook. Whenever she could talk her mother into letting her take over the kitchen, she'd pull out a recipe book and make something new.

One Sabbath Aunt Donna and Uncle Dave invited them all over for dinner. Aunt Donna let Bridget set the table while she and Mother put the finishing touches on the meal. Bridget loved eating at her aunt's. Aunt Donna always used fancy china dishes and linen napkins, and Uncle Dave would put on some nice music that they could listen to while they were eating. But best of all, Aunt Donna insisted that Bridget and her brother Derrick didn't have to eat any food they didn't like.

After the families finished their meal, Aunt Donna disappeared into the kitchen. When she returned, she had carried a tray filled with plates of dessert. "You're going to love this," she said as she placed the glass dish on the table. "It's called Party Pumpkin Dessert."

As soon as Bridget received her dessert, she picked up her fork and took a bite. "Boy, is this good!" she said. "Aunt Donna, could I have the recipe? I'd like to try making this sometime."

"Sure," said her aunt. "In fact, I'll copy it for you right now before I forget."

So when Bridget and her family went home that day, she took with her a copy of the pumpkin dessert. Two weeks later Mother had some errands to do. So she asked Bridget to make the dessert for Sabbath.

Bridget pulled out Aunt Donna's recipe and started gathering the necessary ingredients. Then she mixed everything together and put it in the freezer as directed. But when she served the dessert to her family the next day, she was very disappointed. "This doesn't taste at all like Aunt Donna's dessert."

"Did you follow the instructions exactly?" asked Mother.

"Well, sort of," said Bridget. "I was supposed to put in some nutmeg, but I couldn't find it. So I left it out. And I used peanuts instead of walnuts. And we didn't have any ginger snaps, so I used graham crackers."

Mother laughed. "Well, if you don't follow the recipe, then you can't expect things to turn out like they're supposed to."

It's the same way with life. God has given us a special recipe—the Ten Commandments. As long as we follow His plan, we'll have a happy life.

Are you following the recipe?

JULY

8

Think Twice

A patient man has great understanding, but a quick-tempered man displays folly. Proverbs 14:29, NIV.

After school Rod came home and threw his books onto the table. Just as he was heading out to play ball, his mother walked into the kitchen. "Rod, I need you to go into town and pick up some groceries."

Mrs. Phillips handed her son a shopping list and the checkbook. "Dad isn't feeling too good today. He'll need your help when he feeds the animals tonight. So don't stay in town too long."

Rod walked out the door and got into the car. He liked having the privilege of driving the family car even though he was only 16. Most of his friends weren't allowed to drive by themselves. But since Dad had gotten sick some months back, Rod had taken on a lot more responsibility around the house.

By the time Rod had driven to town and done the shopping, it was nearly 5:00. He knew Dad would start feeding the cattle any minute. So he headed straight for home, but when he drove back to their farm, he was surprised to see the cows all waiting for their supper. Rod hurried into the house and pulled on his overalls and boots. As he went out the door, he saw his dad sleeping on the couch.

Rod kicked a rock as he headed for the barn. *It's not fair that I get stuck with all the work,* he said to himself. *Tonight after supper I'm going to tell Dad just how I feel.* But the more he thought about it, the more he realized that he shouldn't feel sorry for himself. His dad was probably tired. He decided just to forget the whole thing.

That evening as Rod was doing his homework, his father came into the room. "Rod, you're the best son a man ever had. I'm really sorry that I left you with all the work, but I haven't been feeling good."

"Oh, that's OK, Dad," said Rod. "I'm glad I could help out."

The next afternoon Rod's father died. The weakness he had felt the previous evening had been the beginning of the end. For the rest of his life, Rod never forgot his father's words of appreciation. In telling the story, Rod said, "I can still remember the anger I felt when I came home and found the chores left undone. How terrible it would have been if I had lost my temper and told my dad off. I would never have forgiven myself. Now I have forever the memory of his farewell words. I'm so thankful that I thought twice before speaking."

JULY

9

Thrills and Chills

Those who live according to the sinful nature have their minds set on what that nature desires; but those who live in accordance with the Spirit have their minds set on what the Spirit desires. Romans 8:5, NIV.

Reading is one of my hobbies. I just love books. When I was in the fourth grade, I won an award for reading more than 100 books during the school year. I think fourth grade was also the year I started my addiction.

People get addicted to all sorts of things—alcohol, cigarettes, gambling, etc. When I was 10, I became addicted to mystery books. Someone lent me one of the books from the Bobbsey Twins series. After reading about their exciting adventures, I had to have more. I ended up reading almost every book in the series.

From there I went on to other mystery books. I just couldn't get enough of them.

If you've ever read books like the Bobbsey Twins or the Hardy Boys, you know that the books don't go against Christian standards, yet they still had a bad influence on me. They didn't encourage me to do something wrong, but they did discourage me from doing something right. The problem with the mystery books was that I got so involved with them that I didn't have time to read anything else. I didn't take time to read character-building stories or books on nature.

I also developed another problem. For a few years afterward I found it difficult to concentrate on books if they weren't thrilling. My steady diet of mystery books had made me crave excitement. I especially had trouble reading my Bible and my Sabbath school lesson. I didn't want to think; I wanted to be entertained.

It took a long time before I was able to start enjoying good reading material. I had to force myself to concentrate, but eventually my love for mystery stories was replaced by a love for good books and magazines.

One of the ways we learn about God is through reading. So Satan will do his best to keep us from reading good things. Don't let him attract you to the wrong kinds of books and magazines. Read only things that will help you be a better person.

JULY

10

He Sees Everything

"Come now, let us reason together," says the Lord. "Though your sins are like scarlet, they shall be as white as snow; though they are red as crimson, they shall be like wool." Isaiah 1:18, NIV.

The story is told of a famous sculptor who was commissioned to create a statue that would be placed inside a great cathedral. For more than a year he worked on it. He took his time; he was in no hurry. He wanted the statue to be his best work ever. He wanted it to be perfect.

Occasionally, his friends would stop by and visit while he worked. One afternoon they noticed how carefully he was working on the back of the statue's head. With great pains he chiseled out soft curls from the hard stone.

"Why are you wasting your time working so much on the hair?" called out one bystander. "That statue is so tall that once it's put in place, no one will ever see the back of its head."

The sculptor put down his tools and looked down at the man. "Oh, but you're wrong, my friend. God will see."

God always sees. He sees everything we do. He hears everything we say. We can fool our friends and our parents, but we can't fool God.

Achan learned that lesson a little too late. Right after God's people marched around the walls of Jericho and conquered the city, God gave them special orders. He told them to gather up all the silver, gold, bronze, and iron for the Lord's treasury. Everything else was to be burned.

All the people obeyed God's orders. All the people, that is, except Achan. As he was going through the city looking for the different metals, he spotted a beautiful robe. He grabbed it up and hid it under his own robe. He also found 200 shekels of silver and a wedge of gold, which he carried off to his tent. After digging a hole, he buried his treasures.

No one will know what I have done, he thought. And no one did. No one, that is, except God.

Within a short time everyone in the camp of Israel learned of Achan's disobedience. And because of his sin, he and his entire family lost their lives.

If you are hiding some sin in your life, I'd like to encourage you to go to God for forgiveness. He already knows all about you. He knows your weaknesses, and He's ready and willing to help you have victory. All you have to do is ask.

JULY

11

Price and Value

Better a little with reverence for God, than great treasure and trouble with it. Proverbs 15:16, TLB.

Back in the "good old days" I could drive into a gas station and not even have to leave my car. The attendant would greet me with a smile and ask, "Fill 'er up?" If I said yes, he would fill my tank for—are you ready for this?—$5 or less. While he filled the tank, he'd wash the windows and check the oil. Then the attendant would give me a set of drinking glasses as a bonus for doing business at his station.

Today when drivers pull in, they pump their own gas and wash their own windows. If they need air for the tires, they'll probably have to put a quarter into the air machine. The only thing many stations offer for free is water for the radiator. Water doesn't have much value when compared to gasoline, especially today during this time of high fuel prices.

But suppose that you're out with some friends hiking through the mountains. After a long, hot climb to the top, you reach for your canteen, only to discover that you'd forgotten to fill it before you left home. In that situation gasoline would have absolutely no value, but you'd probably be willing to give your entire savings account for just one glass of cool, clear water.

When you walk into a store or look through a catalog, you'll notice that everything has a price on it, but the price of an object doesn't always reflect what it is worth. Price is what you must pay for something. Value is what something is worth. A million dollar library would be of little value to a group of people who didn't know how to read or write. Yet a small New Testament would be priceless if it were the only Bible available to a group of Christians in an oppressive country.

Many of the things people put high price tags on have very little worth. They may bring pleasure for a while, but the excitement never lasts. The most wonderful things in life are free and are available to everyone. Happiness, peace, security, love, hope, and friendship have no real price, but they make life worth living.

JULY

12

God Never Forgets

Be careful not to do your "acts of righteousness" before men, to be seen by them. If you do, you will have no reward from your Father in heaven. Matthew 6:1, NIV.

The greatest thing a man can do for his heavenly Father is to be kind to one of His children."

Patrick is a very special teenager. In 1990 he attended the Pathfinder teen snow outing at Camp Au Sable in Michigan. On Saturday night a group of the Pathfinders went downhill skiing. Patrick was part of the group.

Mike was also in the group of skiers that night, but Mike had a very hard time getting down the hills. Ten years earlier, when he was 4 years old, Mike was in a car accident. Part of his brain was damaged, so his left arm and leg don't work very well. Mike wanted very much to try skiing, but he kept falling. And when he fell, he couldn't get back up.

When Patrick saw that Mike was having a hard time, he spent the rest of the evening helping Mike get up each time he fell. Instead of enjoying the snow himself, Patrick gave his time to help someone else.

Patrick will probably be surprised to find out that his kindness toward Mike has been recorded in this book. But this is not the only place where his good deed has been written down. Mrs. White says that heaven keeps a book of remembrance. In it all the good things we do are recorded: the words we've spoken in love, the kind deeds we've done, the suffering we've endured, and even the temptations we've resisted (see *The Great Controversy,* p. 481).

Nothing we do out of love for God and others ever goes unnoticed. We may never get credit for the things we do on earth, but we can be assured that Jesus sees everything. And someday He'll reward us in His own special way.

JULY

13

Little Things Matter to Jesus

If you believe, you will receive whatever you ask for in prayer. Matthew 21:22, NIV.

Do you ever wonder whether Jesus cares about the little things in your life?

Jose went to a small church school, and he was the only third grader. All through the school year he kept waiting for another third grader to enroll, but he spent the whole year by himself.

As Jose was leaving school for summer vacation, he came up to his teacher's desk. "Mrs. Johnson, this summer I'm going to pray that Jesus will send a boy to be in my class next year."

"That's a good idea, Jose," his teacher said as she gave him a hug.

But when Jose returned to school in September, he was the only fourth grader. "Should I keep praying for another boy in my grade, Mrs. Johnson?" he asked.

"Of course, Jose. You should always pray about the things that are important to you. But remember, sometimes Jesus doesn't answer all our requests with a yes."

So Jose continued praying for another fourth-grade boy.

In October Mr. Richards, the principal, came into Mrs. Johnson's room before class began. "You're going to be getting a new student tomorrow," he said.

Mrs. Johnson remembered Jose's prayer request. "A boy or girl?"

"A boy."

"What grade?"

"Fourth."

When Jose arrived at school, Mrs. Johnson called him up to her desk. "Jose, we're going to be getting a new student tomorrow. His name is Darren. Do you want to guess what grade he's going to be in?"

"Fourth?" Jose asked.

"That's right. Jesus answered your prayers with a yes."

Darren was the only new student who enrolled that year. Jose never doubted that his new friend was a special gift from Jesus.

JULY

14

Too Good to Be True?

Salvation is not a reward for the good we have done, so none of us can take any credit for it. Ephesians 2:9, TLB.

What would you do if someone offered to give you a dollar bill for only 25 cents? Would you take that person up on the deal, or would you figure it was some kind of trick?

Some years ago one of the TV game shows sent a contestant out on the streets of a big city to find out if people would buy a dollar for a quarter. The contestant approached person after person, offering to give them a dollar bill if they would just give him a quarter. He had to ask 30 people before someone finally agreed to the deal. Almost everyone he stopped thought the deal was just too good to be true.

We're brought up listening to sayings like "No one gets something for nothing," "If it sounds too good to be true, it probably is," and "There's no free ride through life." We expect to pay for everything we get.

Even though the Bible says that salvation is a free gift from God, we often try to do something to earn it. If we get something from God, we expect to pay for it in some way.

On television the other night, one of the commercials promised a free gift to everyone who bought a new refrigerator or freezer from a certain appliance store. Was the gift really free? Of course not. Only those who bought an appliance could have it.

When Jesus offers to save us, there is only one requirement: We must be willing to accept His offer. We don't have to give any money or do any good deeds. We just have to reach out in faith and claim the gift as our own.

Some people feel that once they have received eternal life, they can do anything they want. They believe that they can never become unsaved. But if that were true, then all who become Christians would no longer have the freedom to leave God. They would be prisoners, and that would never do. God wants us to be able to choose whom we want to follow.

If your grandparents give you a new bike for your birthday, they would never ask you to pay them for it. All you would have to do is accept it. But if you didn't take care of it, you could lose it. If you left it parked out in the road, it would end up getting run over or maybe stolen. When we receive eternal life from Jesus, we shouldn't be careless with it. We should show our appreciation by living as Jesus would want us to.

JULY

15

Witnessing Where You Are

These should learn first of all to put their religion into practice by caring for their own family. 1 Timothy 5:4, NIV.

When you think of becoming a "great Christian," what picture comes to your mind? Do you see yourself as a famous speaker, standing in front of thousands as you preach the gospel? Do you see yourself as a missionary going to a remote area of the world to work with people who have never heard the name of Jesus? Do you see yourself as a world-famous doctor who discovers a cure for cancer or AIDS?

One day as Jesus was getting out of a boat, a demon-possessed man came running toward Him. The disciples apparently ran for their lives, but Jesus wasn't afraid. He knew that although the man had no control over himself, he was longing to be free from Satan's power. With just a few words Jesus sent the demons out of the man and into a herd of pigs.

The man was so thankful that he asked for permission to join the disciples and follow Jesus wherever He went, but Jesus had different plans for him. "Go home to your family and tell them how much the Lord has done for you, and how he has had mercy on you" (Mark 5:19, NIV). The healed man had a great mission field right in his own hometown. Jesus needed him to stay home and work right there.

We don't think of our homes as mission fields, but they can be one of the most important places for us to share our faith. At the same time, they can also be the hardest places to witness. When we're at home, we relax. Since we're not trying to make a good impression on our family, our behavior isn't always the best. Many of the things we say and do to the members of our family we'd never think of saying and doing to our friends at school.

If we want to do great things for God out in His world, we must begin by learning to reflect His character right where we are.

Something to think about: Can you name three things that you could do to make your home a happier place to live?

JULY

16

Jesus Never Fails

The Lord will keep you from all harm—he will watch over your life; the Lord will watch over your coming and going both now and forevermore. Psalm 121:7, 8, NIV.

After the farmer and his hired hand loaded the boxes of strawberries onto the pickup truck, the farmer took out his handkerchief and wiped the sweat from his forehead. "Harvey, I've got some repair work to do on the barn. Why don't you go ahead and take this load of berries to the fruit market by yourself?"

"OK, boss," said Harvey as he swung into the driver's seat. "Anything I should pick up in town while I'm there?"

"Why don't you pick up a few more sacks of feed for the chickens? I think we could also use some baling twine."

"All right, I'll see you after lunch," replied Harvey as he started the truck and headed for town.

The sky was bright as the hired man drove along the road. He turned on the radio and listened to the daily farm report. As he neared the city limits, Harvey came to a steep hill that descended right into town. He decided to shift down into a lower gear. As his foot stomped on the brakes, he felt the peddle sag beneath his foot. Instead of slowing down, the truck began picking up speed.

At the bottom of the hill the road curved sharply to the left. Harvey gripped the steering wheel and hung on for dear life. As he careened around the corner, the truck slid sideways. Harvey braced himself. He was sure that he, the truck, and the strawberries were going to flip over. But miracle of miracles, he made it safely around the curve, and as the road leveled off, he was finally able to guide the pickup off the pavement and onto the shoulder.

Shaken, he got out of the truck and walked to the minister's house that was located just down the street. After Harvey had told the pastor about his terrible experience, the minister suggested that they have prayer. "Let's thank the Lord for protecting you just now."

When the minister ended his prayer, he said, "And now I'd like to thank the Lord for protecting me on that same hill when I drove down it yesterday."

"What!" cried Harvey. "Did your brakes fail too when you came down the hill?"

"Why, no," said the minister. "My brakes worked fine when I drove down the hill yesterday, and for that I'm very thankful."

JULY

17

Re-turning Good for Evil

Love is not rude, is not selfish, and does not become angry easily. Love does not remember wrongs done against it. 1 Corinthians 13:5, ICB.

"Forgiveness doesn't change the past, but it does enlarge the future."

That Louis Zamperini ever got to the Olympics was a miracle. That he went as a mile runner was even more of a miracle.

After Louis first started running, he seemed to go from one injury to another. He fractured a hip bone, splintered a knee, broke his ankle—twice, tore ligaments in his legs, and almost lost a toe. But he kept on running and eventually earned a spot on the 1936 Olympic team.

When World War II heated up, Louis set his running career aside and joined the Air Force. During one of his missions his plane was shot down over the Pacific Ocean. For 47 days he drifted on the open water in a raft. Finally he was rescued, but unfortunately he was rescued by a Japanese patrol boat.

Louis spent the next two and a half years in a Japanese prison camp. While there, he suffered beatings and systematic starvation at the hand of the enemy, but he refused to give up and die.

On September 2, 1945, Japan finally surrendered, and World War II came to an end. American troops set about to free all those still held in enemy prison camps. By the time Louis was rescued, he weighed only 77 pounds.

Louis returned to America. After regaining his health, he decided that he wanted to serve others. So he became a missionary. Later he traveled to Japan and with Christian love searched out the guards who had been so cruel to him and forgave them.

Louis didn't allow unfortunate circumstances to turn him into an angry, bitter man. Instead he chose to let go of his right to hate those who nearly killed him.

People who hold grudges damage themselves much more than those they hate. If you are angry at someone, let go of your hate. You really owe it to yourself.

JULY

18

Don't Close Your Eyes

A righteous man may have many troubles, but the Lord delivers him from them all. Psalm 34:19, NIV.

During my first year in college I worked at Terry's, a ladies' clothing store in the Fairplain Mall. Most of the time I worked in the dress department, selling formals and wedding gowns.

At the end of that summer the mall sponsored a weeklong sidewalk sale, and some of us were chosen to work outdoors. Back then, there were few if any indoor malls. So when we had a sidewalk sale, we were out on the sidewalk.

Right before the big sale, we gathered up all the leftover summer merchandise and hung it on racks. On Monday morning we hauled everything outside and set up the cash registers.

The mall's parking lot started filling up, and by noon it was packed. That's when the excitement happened. An older lady who had been looking for a place to park drove past our store. Glancing down one of the parking aisles, she took her eyes off the road, and when she looked up again, she was headed right for one of the parked cars. The next thing we heard was a series of crashes.

Three of us hurried to the parking lot to see if the woman was all right. Mike Ronn, our assistant manager, also came running. "Oh, no," he moaned as he surveyed the damage. The lady had hit not one but seven cars. One of them was a brand-new white Corvette convertible. Mike's car.

I felt so bad for the lady who had caused the accident. She told the policeman that when she saw she was going to hit one of the cars, she tried to slam on the brakes. But she hit the gas pedal instead. When the car shot forward, she covered her face with her hands—and crashed into all seven cars.

When you meet up with a problem, do you react like that lady? Do you cover your face and hope the problem will go away? Or do you face your difficulties? When we try to keep from seeing our problems, they only worsen. If the lady hadn't covered her face, she probably wouldn't have hit as many cars.

We don't have to be afraid when problems come our way. We can face whatever comes, because we know that Jesus is by our side ready to help us.

JULY

19

Honesty Is the Best Policy

The Lord despises every kind of cheating. Proverbs 20:10, TLB.

A few years ago I got picked up for shoplifting.

My husband, Tom, had gotten two new suits at the same store. The blue suit wore very well. But the white one wrinkled every time he wore it. So I called the store, and they told me to bring it in.

"There's nothing wrong with the material," the man said after inspecting the suit. "Cotton just wrinkles more than some of the blended fabrics."

Since there was nothing more to do, I thanked the man for his time and started back for the parking lot. Just as I reached the exit, a man and woman stepped in front of me and blocked the door.

"May we talk with you for a moment?"

"Sure," I said. I thought maybe they were soliciting money for a charity.

"Where did you get that?"

"You mean this suit?"

They nodded.

"This is my husband's." Then it dawned on me. These were store detectives, and they thought I was shoplifting.

"Look at this," I said, pulling out the pants. "See how wrinkled they are? I wasn't very happy with them, so I brought them back to the men's department."

The detectives looked at each other. They didn't believe my story. So I suggested that we go back to the men's department and talk with the clerk.

"She's OK," said the clerk when he saw us. "It's my fault. I should have covered the suit with a plastic bag before she left."

I said goodbye to the store detectives, and they disappeared back into the crowd of people. I wasn't upset at them for stopping me.

Each year people shoplift more than a billion dollars' worth of merchandise in the United States alone. But that's not the only way people cheat stores. They also switch price tags on items. Or they'll wear a sweater once and then return it for a refund.

Stealing from businesses hurts not only stores, but also the other shoppers, for we all have to pay higher prices to make up for their dishonest actions.

If you have a problem taking things that don't belong to you, first ask God for forgiveness. Then either return the items you've stolen, or pay for them. Finally, go to an adult you trust, and ask for help with your problem.

If you don't have a problem with dishonesty, be thankful for a clear conscience.

JULY

20

The Perfect Pattern

This is how we know we are in him: Whoever claims to live in him must walk as Jesus did.
1 John 2:5, 6, NIV.

When we started building our house this summer, I had no idea how much work Tom and I had ahead of us. My father was a builder, but I never paid much attention to what he did. I used to help him sweep out the houses and clean up around the outside. But that was all I knew about building.

Before we started our house, we had to decide where we wanted it. After the stakes were put in the ground, our friend Jim came over with his excavator, and with his giant scoop shovel he dug the hole for our basement.

The next day the cement truck rumbled down our driveway. In less than an hour we had the basement floor and the foundations poured.

After the cement was good and hard, we laid blocks. And we laid blocks. And we laid blocks. It seemed that we'd never get done.

Then came the part I liked the most: framing the house. First we built the subfloor on top of the blocks. Next we started building the walls.

Tom's job was cutting the two-by-fours. No one trusted me with a hammer, so I got to carry the boards from the saw to the construction crew. They laid the boards on the floor and assembled the walls section by section. Then they raised the sections upright and nailed them in place, creating the skeleton of the house.

As Tom cut the boards, he was careful to use the same board over and over again as his pattern. He knew that if he used each newly cut board as a pattern for the next board, we'd have a crooked house. Any error he made in his measuring or sawing would just get worse each time he cut a new board. So he put a big X on his pattern board and made sure that he used it to mark all the others.

Do you realize that you're also a builder? You're building something much more important than a house. You're building a character.

It's good to have heroes whom you can look up to and admire, but you can never use other people as patterns of how you should live. They will never be perfect enough to copy. Jesus is the only example you can safely follow.

What kind of pattern are you following?

JULY

21

Adverse Advice

The plans of the righteous are just, but the advice of the wicked is deceitful. Proverbs 12:5, NIV.

Preston, a brilliant young student, had just graduated from law school. A few days after his graduation, a prominent lawyer from a nearby county invited him to lunch. The two men had a good time getting to know each other. Preston told Mr. Robinson about his work in law school. Mr. Robinson told Preston about some of his exciting cases.

Before they finished their meal, Mr. Robinson leaned back in his chair. "Preston, you have the makings of a good lawyer, but you'll never be successful unless you make some changes."

"What do you mean?"

"Well, to start with, I noticed that you didn't order an alcoholic drink with your meal. If you want to be accepted by the rest of the lawyers, you'll have to take a social drink now and then.

"And another thing," he continued. "I also noticed that you prayed before you ate. You'll have to stop that. If you want to go far in the legal profession, you'll have to forget your religion."

Preston shook his head in disbelief. "But I'm a Christian. How can I pretend to be something else? Why should my beliefs hurt my career?"

"Just trust me," said Mr. Robinson. "I know what I'm talking about. If you want to be a success, take my advice."

Preston didn't argue with the older man, but he refused to listen to Mr. Robinson's advice. In fact, he did just the opposite. Now that he was out of school, he became even more involved with his church.

As the years went by, Preston became a prominent lawyer in his hometown. He was admired not only for his skill but also for his Christian integrity.

It was a little more than 20 years after his graduation from law school that Preston saw the lawyer who had advised him to give up his principles. The older man's face was bloated. His clothes were shabby and ill-fitting.

"Hey, Preston, how about a few dollars for an old friend?" he said. "I need a drink."

Mr. Robinson had followed his own advice, and it had cost him his profession, his peace of mind, and his health.

Many voices in the world offer advice on the best way to live, but there's only one right way—God's.

Something to think about: How can you tell if the advice you hear is coming from God or from Satan?

JULY

22

The Greatest Power of All

Love is patient, love is kind. . . . Love does not delight in evil but rejoices with the truth. It always protects, always trusts, always hopes, always perseveres. Love never fails.
1 Corinthians 13:4-8, NIV.

Corrie ten Boom and her sister Betsie were arrested by the Nazis for hiding Jews in their house during World War II. For their punishment they were taken to a prison camp.

One of the lady guards at the camp was particularly cruel. At times Corrie boiled with hatred against the woman, but Betsie always treated the guard kindly.

Each morning The Snake, as she was called, forced all the woman to stand at attention during the early-morning roll call. No matter how sick a prisoner was, she still had to report.

Throughout the weeks of their confinement, Betsie became progressively weaker. But each morning she and Corrie walked out and stood at attention until they were given permission to return to their barracks.

One morning Betsie was so ill that Corrie had to carry her to line call. As they passed The Snake, Corrie stopped the guard and asked, "Can't I take her back?"

"You know the rules," snapped the guard. "Everyone reports to line call."

Anger boiled up inside Corrie, but she didn't dare say anything, and besides, she knew Betsie would be disappointed with her if she did.

But a few days later, as Corrie carried Betsie out of the barracks, The Snake stopped her. "Take her back to her room."

"But I thought you said—"

"Take her back."

Corrie carried Betsie back to their room and then went out to line call alone.

As soon as everyone was dismissed, Corrie hurried back to see how her sister was doing. Imagine her shock when she entered the room and saw The Snake standing at Betsie's side. The Snake hadn't been inside the barracks for a long time. She, like many of the other guards, knew the women's quarters were filled with lice. So she never came inside.

As Corrie watched, The Snake directed the two hospital workers standing next to her to move Betsie to the hospital, where she could get some treatment.

Even in a concentration camp, love conquered hard hearts.

JULY

23

Thanks a Lot

Let the peace of Christ rule in your hearts, since as members of one body you were called to peace. And be thankful. Colossians 3:15, NIV.

"The best things in life are appreciated most after they have been lost."—Roy L. Smith.

There's Mother's Day and Father's Day and Grandparents' Day. But there's really no special day set aside to thank the other important people in your life.

I wish I could turn back the clock 30 years. I wish I could have just a few minutes with the wonderful lady who taught me how to play the piano. I was only 5 when Mrs. Stoddard, a widow in our apartment house, offered to give me piano lessons. My parents readily agreed, and soon I was spending Wednesday afternoons at her apartment as I learned to play "Grandfather's Clock" and "The Postman" on her grand piano.

But Mrs. Stoddard didn't just give me piano lessons. Every week when I came, she set out a plate of cookies and a glass of milk on the kitchen table. She took me places such as Deer Forest. She taught me how to knit. She bought me Abigail, a handmade prairie doll. She even invited me to stay overnight. I became the daughter she never had.

I took lessons for 10 years, until I went away to academy. During that time she paid for all my music books and never charged me for lessons.

Mrs. Stoddard is not the only person I owe a lot to. There was Mr. Hunt, my junior department leader, who told great stories and took us swimming on Saturday nights. Mr. Burgez, our Pathfinder director, who lived through thousands of verses of "Ninety-nine Bottles of Root Beer on the Wall" as we rode home from campouts. Mrs. Atkinson, my fifth-grade teacher, who played softball with us at recess. And Aunt Julie, whose love I appreciate to this day.

Too often we forget to thank the special people in our lives. We take for granted the kind and helpful things they do for us.

Why don't you take a few minutes to think of three or more adults who have been special to you? Then call them or write them a note and thank them for being your friend.

JULY

24

Fresh Discoveries

Let me understand the teaching of your precepts; then I will meditate on your wonders. Psalm 119:27, NIV.

A worker at the United States Patent Office walked into his boss's office one day and laid an envelope on the desk.

"What's that?" the boss asked.

"My resignation."

"Your resignation?" asked the boss in surprise. "Don't you enjoy your job here?"

"Of course I do, but I don't believe my job is very secure. So much has already been invented that I doubt there will be many new inventions coming along in the future. So I've decided to become a farmer."

The young man was right in one way. Many inventions had already been patented. But he was wrong to think that progress had reached its limit. Little did he realize that after he quit his job many new inventions were yet to be registered with the patent office. Inventions like automobiles, radios, electric refrigeration, and television. He never could have comprehended some of the things people would invent in the future. Things like jet engines, computers, and satellites.

Every day new breakthroughs are being made in the fields of medicine and science. Knowledge seems to be increasing almost faster than we can comprehend it.

And what about the field of religion? Have we learned everything there is to know?

"Why do I have to take Bible classes in academy?" Jack complained to his father as they left academy registration. "I don't think there's much more for me to learn. After all, I've gone to Sabbath school all my life, and I've had Bible classes all though church school."

"I would have to agree with you, Jack, if you were talking about any other book, but the Bible—well, it's different than any other book on earth."

Jack wasn't convinced. "What do you mean, Dad?"

"Well," said his father, "other books can be read a few times, and after that another reading wouldn't give you any new information. But the Bible is like outer space. The more we probe into it, the more there is to discover and study."

Even when we get to heaven, we'll continue to study about God and His love for us. Eternity is a long, long time, but there will always be something new for us to learn.

JULY

25

The Light of the World

But the Counselor, the Holy Spirit, whom the Father will send in my name, will teach you all things and will remind you of everything I have said to you. John 14:26, NIV.

"I just don't get it," said Liz as she and Rachel went to their lockers to get their lunches. "In Bible class today, the teacher talked about God being three Persons in one. I don't understand how that can be."

"That sort of confused me, too," Rachel said as she pulled out her lunch box. "Tomorrow why don't we ask her to explain it?"

So when it came time for Bible class the next morning, Rachel raised her hand. "Miss Howard, could you explain a little more about how God can be three Persons in one?"

"Of course," said the teacher. "We as Christians believe in the Trinity. That is, we believe in God the Father, Jesus Christ the Son, and the Holy Spirit. We believe that God, even though He is one, works as three separate individuals. To understand just how the Trinity works, let's think about the sun.

"First, there's the actual object that we call the sun. It's most like God the Father. Like the sun, God is the giver of life to beings on the earth. He, like the sun, is constant and unchanging. When we begin each new day, we say that the sun rises, but the sun doesn't move. It stays in one place, and the rest of our solar system circles around it.

"The light that the sun sends out is like Jesus. When we look up at the sun, we really don't see it. What we see is the light coming out of the great ball of fire. Jesus is called the 'Light of the world' because He showed us what God is like.

"The warmth of the sun is like the work of the Holy Spirit, the third person of the Trinity. It is He who does the work of the Father. Even after the light is removed for a time, the warmth continues, causing the seeds to sprout and the grass to grow.

"All three come from one source, even though each one has His separate work to do. All three—the sun, light, and heat—are the same sun, but each one depends upon the others. So it is with God the Father, Christ the Son, and the Holy Spirit."

When the teacher finished, she turned to Rachel. "Does that explanation make the Trinity easier to understand?"

"It sure does."

(Adapted with permission from William L. Woodall, *100 Devotions for Boys and Girls* [New York: Association Press, 1957], p. 25.)

JULY

26

God Has All the Answers

If you make the Most High your dwelling—even the Lord, who is my refuge—then no harm will befall you, no disaster will come near your tent. Psalm 91:9, 10, NIV.

In 1738 two missionaries named Daehne and Guettner left their homes in Holland to work among the people in South America. They began working with the Arawak Indians. The Arawak language was not difficult to learn, so the missionaries were soon able to preach to the Arawaks in their own tongue.

At regular intervals Daehne and Guettner made long journeys into the forest, often traveling 300 to 400 miles at a time. They visited areas that had never been seen by White men before. Of course, there were no restaurants where the missionaries could stop when they were hungry. And at night they had to protect themselves from the wild animals by sleeping in hammocks suspended from the trees.

A few days after returning from an especially long journey, Guettner suggested that they make a short trip to a nearby village. Daehne wasn't feeling too good, so he decided to rest instead. Guettner went on without him.

Daehne fixed lunch for himself and then stretched out for a nap on his makeshift bed. But after only a few minutes of sleep, something woke him up.

What's that noise? he thought. *There it is again.*

Looking around the room, Daehne saw a terrifying sight. An enormous snake was sliding down toward him from a shelf near the roof. Before Daehne could escape, the snake dropped on top of him and wound itself around his head and shoulders and began to squeeze tighter and tighter.

Daehne's first thought was *I'm going to die.* His second thought was *I must let Guettner know what happened. I don't want him to think that one of the Arawaks killed me.*

Looking around the room, he spotted a piece of chalk on the table next to his bed. Using all his energy, he freed one of his arms and reached for the chalk. As he began writing on the wall, the Bible verse declaring that believers shall "take up serpents" and not be harmed came to his mind.

It seemed like a message from God. With superhuman strength he grabbed the snake around the neck and squeezed until the reptile loosened its hold. Then he threw it out the door.

No matter what kind of trouble we get into, God never leaves us alone. He has a solution to every difficulty we face. If God could help Daehne escape from the snake, don't you think He can help you overcome your problems?

JULY

27

Keep in Touch

Remain in me, and I will remain in you. No branch can bear fruit by itself; it must remain in the vine. Neither can you bear fruit unless you remain in me. John 15:4, NIV.

We can only stay best friends with Jesus if we keep in touch with Him every single day.

Some people think that if they go to church once a week, they have fulfilled their duty to God. But what God cares about is our friendship with Him.

By spending time with Jesus each morning, we can start our day together with Him. And then if we ask, the Holy Spirit will be our constant companion in all that we do. We never have to lose contact with Heaven, for God's Spirit will be present in our minds. He will be there to give us suggestions on what we should and shouldn't do. He'll warn us when we're walking into danger. And He'll remind us of how important we are to our heavenly Father.

But the friendship isn't one-sided. We can speak to the Holy Spirit too. All through the day we can have Him next to us like an invisible friend with whom we can share our thoughts. We don't need to wait until our evening prayers to speak to God again. He is with us all day long.

When astronauts are sent out into space, NASA keeps in close contact with them through special radios. Even though they are thousands of miles apart, the ground crew and the astronauts flying through space can work together to make sure that the mission is a success.

But during their trip back to the earth, the astronauts momentarily lose contact with mission control. As the spacecraft passes through a certain part of the atmosphere, all radio contact is cut off. For a short time all the people at mission control wait on the edge of their seats until contract is reestablished.

However, we never have to lose contact with Jesus. The Holy Spirit will be with us every second if we invite Him into our lives. But we must keep our radio on and stay tuned for His guidance.

JULY

28

Right or Wrong?

So then, each of us will give an account of himself to God. Romans 14:12, NIV.

Most of us believe that God's laws are important, and we believe that Christians should follow them. But then we come to the hard part. How do we interpret these rules? How do we decide exactly what is right or wrong?

Some actions are easy to judge. We know it's wrong to break into someone else's house and steal a television. And we'd never think of pointing a gun at someone and demanding a wallet. But what if you found a dollar bill lying on the school playground? Would it be all right to keep it? Or would you be stealing? And what about making a copy of a video that you rented from a video store? It's against the law. But . . .

We also know that God wants us to set aside the Sabbath as a special day of worship. So we go to Sabbath school and church on the seventh day of the week. But what about the rest of the day? Is it right to go to McDonald's afterward for lunch? Should we watch TV if there's a really good program on? And what about homework? Would it be all right to study for a test or catch up on the work you missed while you were sick?

How do we decide whether something is right or wrong?

Sometimes people base their decision on what their friends think is all right. Or maybe they check to see if the pastor's family does it. Others say, "As long as I don't feel guilty when I do something, it must be OK."

I'd like to suggest a different way to make your decisions. Try asking yourself a question: If I do this, will it help me become more like Jesus? As we said yesterday, God's goal is to make us more and more like Him. He can't do that on His own. He needs our consent and our cooperation.

When we're trying to decide whether or not we should do certain things, we should try to look at the situation through God's eyes. Will our actions please Him? If the answer is yes, then you're on the right track.

JULY

29

One Second Too Late

As it is, if we had not delayed, we could have gone and returned twice. Genesis 43:10, NIV.

One of the most memorable moments in professional basketball happened June 12, 1990.

It was during the fourth game of the NBA championship finals. The Detroit Pistons were battling to hold on to their NBA title for a second year. The Portland Trail Blazers were doing their best to take it from them.

By the third quarter Detroit stood in front with a score of 83-75. But during the fourth quarter, Portland pushed ahead and regained the lead with five minutes left to play.

As the seconds ticked away, the two teams passed the lead back and forth. During the final moments, Detroit came out on top with a score of 112-109. Just as the buzzer rang out, Portland's Danny Young made a tremendous 45-foot shot.

The crowd held its breath. Did Young throw the ball in time? Had Portland tied the game? Would the game go into overtime?

"No good," declared the officials.

The Piston fans went wild.

Television replays of the last few seconds of the game proved that Danny Young had thrown the ball too late. It didn't count.

Have you ever found yourself losing out because of poor timing?

It's your mother's birthday. You had planned to get her a card, but you forgot. The next time you get to town, you go ahead and buy her one, but you're too embarrassed to give it to her.

You get in trouble at school. You know you should tell your parents, but you put it off. When the teacher phones your mother later that week, you find yourself in hot water for two things: acting up in school and not telling your parents about it. If only you had told them right way.

The teacher assigns a report that's due at the end of the marking period. You keep putting it off. Then the night before it's due, you spend the whole evening at the library. And when you get the paper back with a big red C-, you think *Why did I wait until the last minute to get it done?*

The Portland Trail Blazers lost a championship game because the last basket was a split second too late. Make sure that procrastination doesn't make you lose out in the game of life.

Something to think about: What things do you tend to put off doing?

JULY

30

Making Tracks

Is not this the kind of fasting I have chosen: to loose the chains of injustice and untie the cords of the yoke, to set the oppressed free and break every yoke? Isaiah 58:6, NIV.

"That's strange," Tom commented as we walked toward our school one morning. "The window in Adele's room looks as though it's been pushed out of the frame." He moved closer to investigate. "Oh, boy, I think we've had a break-in."

Sure enough. Tom's desk had been emptied all over the floor.

"Well, my students will be disappointed to find out that my gradebook wasn't stolen," he laughed as he tossed the green book onto the desk. "Whoever broke in was probably looking for money."

The other teachers arrived. We checked the classroom doors and found they hadn't been tampered with. Tom called the police. By the end of the week, the break-in was old news, and we figured that any self-respecting thief would move on to bigger and better things. Wrong conclusion.

Exactly two weeks later, Tom and I arrived at school to find our newly caulked window missing once again. By the third break-in two weeks later, we were on a first-name basis with the police.

We found out that the thief had been making rounds. First he would break in to our school. Then a few days later he'd rob the Catholic church down the road. After that he moved on to the Baptist church across the street. Then he'd start all over again.

Fortunately the police in another county caught him. When he was sentenced to a year in jail, we thought our problems were over. But—

"Oh, no, not again," said Tom when we arrived at school six months later. The window was out again.

Two days later, someone broke into the Catholic church, and that weekend the Baptist church lost more of their sound system.

Do you think the police had any trouble figuring out whom they needed to arrest?

Our burglar's habit of breaking into our school and the churches was so strong that he couldn't stop himself. After an early release from jail, he returned to our area and repeated the same pattern.

To create a habit, we must repeat an action again and again, but eventually it becomes automatic. That's very helpful when we build good habits. But bad habits are hard to break.

If you're battling with some bad habits, don't give up. Ask God to help you. And then begin replacing them with good habits.

JULY

31

Praise the Lord!

Why are you downcast, O my soul? Why so disturbed within me? Put your hope in God, for I will yet praise him. Psalm 42:11, NIV.

Some years ago evangelist Glenn Coon found himself so sick that he could hardly whisper. His problems all started when he got angry with someone who was interfering with his ministry. He ran his angry thoughts over and over in his mind, and then he woke up one morning unable to get out of bed.

Mrs. Coon called Dr. Harry Miller and asked him to stop by. Dr. Miller checked over his patient, and gave his diagnosis. "I can't pinpoint what's wrong with you, Glenn, but you must have picked up a flu bug somewhere. I'll give you a prescription. You should feel better in a few days."

After the doctor left, Elder Coon began to feel guilty. He asked his wife to ask Dr. Miller to come back. "Harry, I'd better level with you," Glenn whispered when the doctor returned. "I know what's wrong with me, and it's not the flu. I've been crabby for weeks now. My bad attitude put me in this bed."

"Well, in that case, you'd better cancel your plans for the next six months."

"Six months?"

"That's right. You're suffering from nervous exhaustion. If you want to get well, you'll need six months of bed rest."

After the doctor left, Elder Coon's mind began to race. How could he just drop his ministry and lie in bed for six months? Why did God let that meddling church member disrupt his work in the first place?

Suddenly he remembered an idea that someone had shared with him years earlier. "We need to educate our minds to give praise to the Lord."

Well, he didn't have anything to lose, and he certainly wasn't going anywhere. So he decided to give it a try. But he couldn't think of one thing to be thankful for. He looked around the room trying to get some ideas.

At last he gave it a try. "Thank You, Lord, for that door, and thank You that it's locked so nobody can poke his head into my room and look at me."

It was feeble attempt, but as he continued, he began to think of all the blessings the Lord had given him. During every waking moment of his day he praised the Lord. And three days later he walked out of the room. He had been completely healed.

The next time you are tempted to complain, remember the power of negative thinking, and try praising the Lord instead!

AUGUST

1

Getting Into Nature

Ask the animals, and they will teach you, or the birds of the air, and they will tell you. Job 12:7, NIV.

One of the most exciting things I've ever done happened some years ago when my husband and I taught in a two-room school in Alpena, Michigan.

It was our first week of school, and after lunch I decided to take my students outside for storytime. They sat on the grass while I read.

"Look what I found," Kevin said, interrupting the story. He held up a yellow-, black-, and white-striped caterpillar.

"That's a monarch caterpillar," said Bethany.

I got a bright idea. "Wouldn't it be fun to see if we could raise some monarch butterflies? Let's look around the yard and see how many caterpillars we can find. Check especially around the milkweed plants. That's what they like to eat."

So the students jumped to their feet and started scouting the area. I couldn't believe it, but by the time we went inside, we had 42 caterpillars.

Eric and Axel went to the storage room and found two aquariums. We put half the caterpillars in one, and half in the other. Connie went outside to gather some small branches for them to crawl on. Kevin collected milkweed leaves for their dinner.

After we had the caterpillars all moved into their new homes, we cut some material and placed it across the opening of the aquariums so our new pets couldn't get out.

Each day we checked the caterpillars to see how they were doing.

"Mrs. Coffee, look at this one," said Billy one morning. We all gathered around the one aquarium to see what Billy was talking about. One of the caterpillars had spun a little silk button on the branch. After clamping its back claws into the button, it had let go with its other feet. By the time we saw it, it was hanging upside down.

It was so much fun seeing these changes close up. We could hardly wait to see what was going to happen to our caterpillars during the next few weeks.

AUGUST

2

More Surprises

In his hand is the life of every creature and the breath of all mankind. Job 12:10, NIV.

Mrs. Coffee, come quick. Something is happening to the caterpillar that was hanging upside down!"

The class and I all jumped up from our seats and hurried over to the table.

"Look at it," said Donna. "It's swinging back and forth."

As we watched, the caterpillar began inflating like a balloon. And then suddenly, *pop!*

"Wow!"

"Ooooh, gross!"

"Neat!"

Everyone had a different opinion about what was going on. The caterpillar had puffed itself up so much, that it split its striped skin. It reminded me of a man trying to take off his coat. As the skin slid up, we could see the caterpillar's green inner body.

The caterpillar continued swinging back and forth, pushing its skin all the way up to where its back feet were clamped to the stick. Then it pinched the skin between two of its rear abdominal segments. At the same time it pulled out a new claw, called a cremaster. This little claw reached out and hooked onto the silk button.

It released the old skin and then jerked violently until it fell to the bottom of the aquarium. The green creature drew itself up tightly. In a few minutes its soft outer skin had hardened into a protective shell, turning it into a chrysalis.

If you've ever seen a monarch chrysalis, you know that it has beautiful gold dots around the top edge. Although we spent a lot of time watching our monarchs while they went through their changes, we were never able to see the gold spots develop. They just seemed to appear instantly.

One by one our caterpillars climbed up to the cloth covering or onto one of the sticks. Pretty soon we had no more caterpillars left to feed. All we could do was wait.

AUGUST

3

New Life

And we eagerly await a Savior from there, the Lord Jesus Christ, who, by the power that enables him to bring everything under his control, will transform our lowly bodies so that they will be like his glorious body. Philippians 3:20, 21, NIV.

My heart dropped when I checked on the aquariums one morning. "Oh, no," I said to my husband. "One of the chrysalises must have died. It's all black. The kids are going to feel bad. Should we throw it away before they see it?"

"No," said Tom. "Leave it there. Maybe that's what's supposed to happen."

"OK," I said halfheartedly.

I'm glad I took his advice, because he was right. The change of color in the chrysalis was proof that the monarch was developing as it should.

A day or two later, Kim made an exciting discovery. "Oh, look, Mrs. Coffee. You can see the butterfly's wing."

Sure enough. The walls of the chrysalis had become so transparent that we could see the orange and black stripes very clearly.

"It won't be long now," added Kevin.

We all became as nervous as expectant parents. After all, we had raised these little creatures.

I will never forget the moment our first butterfly made its appearance. It all started with a sudden crack on the side of the chrysalis. Out pushed a strange-looking insect that looked nothing like the great monarch butterflies I'd always seen.

"Boy, is it ugly," someone said. I had to agree. The butterfly had a swollen abdomen and short, crumpled wings.

"Maybe there's something wrong with it," said Axel. "Maybe it's deformed."

There was nothing we could do but wait and watch.

The butterfly crawled out of its old house and held on to one of the edges. Then it started slowly flapping its short, stubby wings. The more it flapped, the more its wings expanded. And as the wings grew larger, its abdomen thinned out. Within minutes, the strange-looking insect was transformed into a majestic monarch butterfly.

Someday we're going to experience a complete transformation like the monarch's. When Jesus comes, He'll change our old, sinful bodies and give us perfect bodies that will never die.

Won't it be exciting when He comes again and makes all things new?

AUGUST

4

Getting Ready for the Journey

And I heard a loud voice from the throne saying, "Now the dwelling of God is with men, and he will live with them. They will be his people, and God himself will be with them and be their God." Revelation 21:3, NIV.

Our butterflies didn't leave the classroom as soon as they came out of their chrysalises. They stayed in the room for a few hours and exercised their wings in preparation for the big journey they were about to take.

Toward the end of summer, as the days start getting colder, monarchs all across North America begin to head south. The journey is long and difficult. Some butterflies will travel 2,000 miles. The trip takes about two months. Fewer than half the butterflies that start the trip ever reach their destination.

Many go to a tiny section of mountains west of Mexico City. There, during the winter months, tens of millions of monarchs wait for instinct to tell them to return north.

In spring, as the temperatures begin to rise, the butterflies begin to fly back to the Northern states. And the cycle begins all over again. There will be three or four short-lived generations. Then in late summer the last generation of butterflies will migrate south.

When our butterflies were ready to go outside, they flew to the window ledge. The students carefully picked them up and carried them outside, one by one. When the last group was ready to fly away, our whole room went outside and watched them lift off into the sky and begin their trip.

Soon we'll be taking a trip too. We'll fly through the air like the butterflies, but our destination will be heaven. Imagine how much fun it will be to fly through outer space without having to wear a space suit or travel in a rocket! We'll visit places that are far beyond what scientists have been able to see through the giant telescopes.

Like the butterflies, we will not remain at our destination forever, for after a thousand years in heaven, we will return to the earth made new. Here we will live for eternity.

The flight date is getting closer every day. Are you getting ready for the trip?

AUGUST

5

You Can't Tell a Book by Its Cover

The Lord does not look at the things man looks at. Man looks at the outward appearance, but the Lord looks at the heart. 1 Samuel 16:7, NIV.

My father, an antique dealer, loves to fix up old furniture. The things that other people would consider ready for the trash heap, he sees as an exciting challenge. One of the first things I do when I go home for a visit is check the garage to see his latest project.

Last summer Dad came home with a truckload of old furniture. As I watched him unload the different items, one particular piece caught my attention. It was a very plain-looking wooden bench.

"What are you going to do with this?" I asked, pointing to the old bench.

"That deacon's bench?" he asked.

I nodded. "It doesn't look like much to me."

Dad smiled the smile he always gives me when I've said something that reveals my ignorance. "You just wait. That's going to be one beautiful piece of furniture when I get done with it. Come over here; let me show you something."

I followed Dad into his workroom and watched as he brushed paint remover across the back of the bench. After the chemical lifted the old varnish, we wiped it off. And underneath were intricate carvings that the old varnish had hidden. How wrong I had been to judge it so quickly!

It's easy to judge people in the same way.

Mrs. Robbins was a counselor at the high school where I used to teach. The first time we met, all I noticed were her birthmarks. Her entire face was covered with bright-red splotches. But by the end of the year they seemed to have disappeared. As I got to know her, all I saw was her beautiful personality.

Are you quick to judge people by their looks or by the way they dress? Or do you take time to get to know what they're like inside?

AUGUST

6

What About Your Emotions?

In your anger do not sin.
Ephesians 4:26, NIV.

True or false—Christians shouldn't get angry. (Check today's Bible verse for the answer.)

Surprised? All this time you've probably been thinking that it was sinful to get angry. Actually, anger is an emotion, and as counselor Larry Yeagley puts it, "emotions . . . are neither right nor wrong."

We can classify emotions as negative (impatience, anger, disgust, resentment) or positive (joy, love). But not good or bad.

Most people are alarmed by the negative emotions they have. When they feel angry, for example, they think, *I've got to stop feeling like this.*

The best way to deal with negative emotions is to find out what the problem really is.

The school where I teach has a smoke detector. Its job is to warn us if a fire should start. Some months ago the alarm went off. The custodian could have yanked the alarm off the ceiling and thrown it outside so we couldn't hear it anymore. But instead he checked to see why it went off. As it turned out, some food had burned in the oven, causing the kitchen to fill with smoke. We took care of the problem and the alarm turned off.

We should handle our emotions the same way. When we feel afraid, resentful, jealous, or angry, we need to ask ourselves, *Why am I feeling this way?* Maybe you're just tired from staying up too late at night. Or maybe you've been eating too much junk food. Better health habits will often eliminate negative feelings.

At other times you may not be able to identify the real problem. That's when a friend can help. Find someone you can trust, and share your feelings with him or her.

If the problem continues, talk it over with your parents, a teacher, your Sabbath school leader, or your minister. Whatever you do, don't give up. Help is available.

AUGUST

7

We Are His Hands

Go and make disciples of all nations, baptizing them in the name of the Father and of the Son and of the Holy Spirit, and teaching them to obey everything I have commanded you." Matthew 28:19, 20, NIV.

At the end of World War II, many towns in Germany lay in ruins. As a gesture of friendship, many of the American soldiers stationed in the defeated country joined in with the local citizens as they began rebuilding their villages.

In one town, the soldiers first helped the people clear away the rubble. Then they set to work repairing the damaged homes. Their final project was to rebuild the small church that stood in the heart of the village. After rebuilding the stone walls, the workers repaired the roof. Then they started straightening up the inside of the church.

Before the bombing, a statue of Jesus had hung over the Communion table. Now it lay broken all over the floor. The workmen gathered up the pieces and began putting them back together, but when the statue was finally finished, Jesus' hands were missing.

Although the people searched everywhere, the hands were never found. So at the foot of the statue someone carved these words: "I have no other hands than yours."

We are Jesus' hands. We are also His feet and His voice. Whatever good is done on earth must be done by you and me. Jesus could send angels to do His work, but He wants to give us the opportunity to lead others to Him.

We have a big job ahead of us, but we can do it. When Jesus gives an assignment, He also promises to help.

AUGUST

8

When Life's Not Fair

For evil men will be cut off, but those who hope in the Lord will inherit the land. Psalm 37:9, NIV.

Life isn't fair. That's for sure.

My great-aunt smoked cigarettes all her life and lived to be 83. One of the ladies in our church died from lung cancer at 52. She took good care of her body and never smoked.

A minister and his family were hit head-on by a drunk driver. Two of the children died. The mother will never walk again. But the drunk man only broke a few bones.

Policemen struggle to make their house payments while drug dealers eat in the finest restaurants, fly their own private jets, and live in million-dollar mansions.

Somehow we get the idea that only good things should happen to good people. And when we see wicked people getting ahead of us in life, lights flash and a siren goes off in our heads and we say, "Hey, that's not fair!"

God doesn't promise that everything will go well for us on earth. If He protected us from problems, then Satan could accuse Him of bribery.

When I was your age, life went terribly slow. The time between my birthdays seemed more like 365 years than 365 days. But now that half of my life is gone, I look back and say, "Where did the time go?"

A normal life span is about 70 to 80 years. But when you compare it to the billions and trillions of years we'll spend on the earth made new, 80 years seem like a few seconds.

God doesn't promise us protection from problems, but He does promise His love and friendship. He doesn't promise us everything our heart desires, but He does promise us happiness and contentment.

Life on earth will have its ups and downs. But when we think of what God is preparing for us, the hard times down here don't seem so bad.

AUGUST

9

The Heavenly Gardener

He who began a good work in you will carry it on to completion until the day of Christ Jesus. Philippians 1:6, NIV.

Have you ever been to Disney World? If you have, do you remember seeing the plant sculptures during your monorail ride?

Shaping plants into certain forms is known as topiary art. The gardeners at Disney World plant hedges and trees and then train them to grow in various shapes. Finally they carefully trim the hedges so they will look like different Disney characters. Each branch is cut to a precise length, and all unnecessary foliage removed. If the gardeners just started the hedges growing and never cut away the excess branches, we wouldn't be able to tell the characters apart.

Just as trimming is necessary in shaping plants, it is also essential when it comes to shaping characters. God wants to share His character with each of His followers, but in order to do this, He must remove all the sins and bad habits that would keep others from seeing Jesus in us.

Many young people think that as soon as they are baptized, all their problems will go away, but baptism is just a beginning. Once we choose to be part of God's family, He can begin His work of character development.

You may have heard people speak about sanctification. That's a big word used to describe the trimming work that God does in our lives, and this work is something that will go on as long as we live.

When God points out a problem area in our lives, we have two choices: We can let Him work on our characters, or we can ignore Him. The decision is up to us. He'll never force us to change.

If you feel God speaking to you about some changes you need in your life, don't get discouraged. Just remember that He wants to share His perfect character with you. He wants to make something beautiful out of your life.

AUGUST

10

Is Heaven for Every-one?

For the wages of sin is death, but the gift of God is eternal life in Christ Jesus our Lord. Romans 6:23, NIV.

Have you ever thought that maybe God's not completely fair? Have you ever thought that maybe He's being a little too picky because He won't let everybody go to heaven?

Let's pretend for a few minutes that sinners *could* go to heaven. What would life be like for someone who never knew Jesus as a friend? Why, here comes a sinner walking up the streets of gold. Let's ask him. "What's it like to live in heaven?"

"Well, I've been here for three weeks, and I don't know how much longer I can take it. For one thing, I have to cover my eyes everywhere I go. God's glory shines all the time, and it gives me a splitting headache.

"And another thing. I thought we were going to do some traveling when we got up here. So I tried to check out some of the other worlds, but they don't want me around. They find sin repulsive. Shows how much they know about fun!

"It's hard to live in a place like this. All the things I used to enjoy doing were destroyed with Satan. It's depressing to realize I've got to live forever. So I just try not to think about it."

As you can see, Jesus would be unfair if He let sinful people into heaven. He'd be unfair to the perfect beings on the other worlds—they don't want sin to spoil their lives. He'd be unfair to the righteous—He has promised a perfect sin-free environment. And He'd be unfair to the sinful—if He took them to heaven, their lives would be miserable.

It was never God's plan to destroy any of His children. But because our freedom is so important to Him, He allows us to choose our own destinies.

Have you decided where you want to spend eternity? Have you decided to follow Jesus?

AUGUST

11

Being Neighborly

Live wisely. . . . Use every chance you have for doing good. Ephesians 5:15, 16, ICB.

Preach the gospel all the time. When necessary, use words."—Francis of Assisi.

Mike Jordan and his parents lived next door to Mr. and Mrs. Houseman. The Housemans were an older couple, and they enjoyed it when Mike stopped by for a visit.

One afternoon Mike heard Mr. and Mrs. Houseman discussing a problem. "That retaining wall in the backyard is just falling apart," said Mr. Houseman to his wife. "I'm going to have to hire someone to build it back up."

Mike didn't say anything right then, but at supper that night he told his dad about what he'd heard. "Mr. Houseman isn't too well, Dad," he said. "Do you think that we could go over and fix their wall?"

"That's a great idea, son. I'm going to take a few days off from work next week. Why don't we spend a couple of afternoons building that wall back up?"

Mike and his dad had a great time helping their neighbors. When they finally finished the job, Mr. Houseman tried to give them some money. "No, thanks, Mr. Houseman," said Mr. Jordan. "Mike and I did this because we wanted to be neighborly. You folks needed some help, and we were glad to do the work."

"But you spent two days slaving out there in the hot sun. I can't let you work for nothing."

Mike dusted his hands off. "No, really, Mr. Houseman. We don't want any money. We just like helping you out."

Mr. Houseman shook his head as he put his wallet back into his pocket. "Well, people like you are pretty rare. Most people don't care about anyone else but themselves. We're lucky to have you folks for neighbors."

Mrs. Houseman came out with lemonade and cookies for everyone. "You and your son did a wonderful job on that wall, Mr. Jordan," she said. Turning to her husband, she asked, "Lester, you did pay them, didn't you?"

"They wouldn't take a penny, Marian."

"But, but . . ."

Mr. Jordan cut her off. "Mrs. Houseman, neighbors help each other. We were just glad we could be of service."

Mrs. Houseman shook her head. "Well, I just hope that someday I can return the favor. But," she added, "don't expect me to build a wall for you!"

AUGUST

12

Others Are Watching

"You are my witnesses," declares the Lord, "and my servant whom I have chosen." Isaiah 43:10, NIV.

Just a few days after Mike and his father finished repairing the wall for the Housemans, Mike decided to look for a part-time job. He looked through the newspaper ads and checked the bulletin board at the grocery store, but there wasn't much available for a 17-year-old.

Then Mike heard from a friend that Dillon's Hardware needed someone to stock shelves. When he went to inquire about the job, the manager handed him an application. Mike filled it out and then turned it back in to the office.

"We'll call you if we need you," Mr. Fulbright said.

Mike waited to hear from Dillon's, but the phone call never came.

The following week Mike stopped by to see Mrs. Houseman. As they were visiting, Mike told her about his trouble finding a job. "I was really hoping to get a job at Dillon's. I applied there, but I never heard back from them."

After Mike left, Mrs. Houseman got in her car. She drove to the hardware store and headed right for the manager's office. "Jim, I heard that Mike Jordan applied for that job at your store. Why didn't you hire him?"

"Well, Marian, he seemed like a nice enough kid, but I heard that he belongs to a cult."

"A cult! What do you mean?"

"Well, he's a Seventh-day Adventist."

Mrs. Houseman started laughing. "Why, Jim, Seventh-day Adventists are Christians. I've known the Jordans for years, and they're wonderful people. They're always doing nice things for others. Why, just a few weeks ago Mike and his father came over to our house and rebuilt our retaining wall. And they refused to take any money for it."

Mr. Fulbright scratched his head. "I don't know much about the Seventh-day Adventist religion. I guess I misjudged them."

"Well, if you don't hire that boy, you'll be making a big mistake. He's a good, honest worker."

That afternoon Mike got a phone call from Mr. Fulbright, and he started his new job the next day.

Something to think about: What do your neighbors think of you? Do they know that you're a Christian?

AUGUST

13

There's More Ahead!

For the Lord himself will come down from heaven, with a loud command, with the voice of the archangel and with the trumpet call of God, and the dead in Christ will rise first.
1 Thessalonians 4:16, NIV.

While we were in Rome, Tom and I had a chance to visit the catacombs. The catacombs are underground burial places that have been cut out of rock. Some believe that as many as 7 million people are buried beneath the city.

As our guide started our tour, he gave us a warning. "Whatever you do, don't leave the group. There are hundreds of miles of passageways. I have been a guide for 15 years, and I travel only one route. If you get separated from the group, you may never find your way out."

(By then, I thought maybe I should just wait in the bus; I couldn't get lost there.)

Guided only by the faint light that our leader held in his hand, we descended the stone steps into the cold, dark cemetery. The catacombs can best be described as shelves cut out of rock. Dead people were placed on these shelves.

Our guide told us that he had found a few teeth, but since most of the tombs are more than a thousand years old, the bodies have deteriorated and returned to dust.

Inscriptions appear on many of the tombs. In the older sections of catacombs that were used before the time of Jesus, the words often show despair. On many of them were written in Italian the words "Farewell! farewell! forever farewell!"

But after Jesus came personally to earth to deliver the news of salvation, new sayings began to appear over the graves. The assurance of the resurrection had given people hope that there was something beyond life on earth. Over and over appeared the phrases "In Christ," "In Hope," "In Faith of a Glorious Resurrection From the Dead."

And so can it be for us today. When life is painful and sad, we can look forward to eternal life with Jesus. Not only will it be fun and exciting, but it will last forever.

Some years ago there was a popular song that asked the question "Is that all there is?" As Christians we can answer with a loud no, for when our faith is in Jesus, death is only a short rest before our lives *really* begin.

AUGUST

14

Happiness Is—

Now that you know these things, you will be blessed if you do them. John 13:17, NIV.

Some years ago the Ford Motor Company sponsored a contest. They offered a new car to the person who sent in the best definition of the word "happiness."

How would you have defined happiness? Would you have said that happiness is . . .

having lots of friends?
getting good grades on your report card?
making the winning touchdown during a foot ball game?

People look for happiness in different places. Most of the time they believe that *things* will make them happy. So they buy nice clothes, go on exciting vacations, or build large bank accounts.

But happiness is much more than things or a good time. Sure, it's fun to own a Corvette or take a trip to Disneyland. But *fun* is not the same as *happiness*. Fun is what we experience while we're doing something we enjoy. Happiness is what we experience after the event is over. Fun lasts only a short time, but happiness can go on forever.

Some people think God is a real wet blanket because He warns them to stay away from some things they consider fun. There's no doubt about it—sin *is* fun. There's only one problem. When it's all over, we're left with sadness and pain instead of happiness. With sin there's always a price to pay.

So what is real happiness? The contest judges awarded first place to a teacher at Andrews University who wrote: "Happiness is the by-product of helping others."

Happiness is not a goal we can attain if we just try hard enough. Instead, it's one of the benefits we receive when we live an unselfish life. If you want to be a happy person, look for ways to help people. Doing things for others may not always be fun, but it will always bring happiness.

Something to think about: How could you help someone else today?

AUGUST

15

Forgiving As God Forgives

Do not judge, and you will not be judged. Do not condemn, and you will not be condemned. Forgive, and you will be forgiven. Luke 6:37, NIV.

It is better to forget and smile than to remember and be sad."

May Carley was 12 years old when a neighbor came to her father asking for help. The neighbor's mortgage was due, and unless he came up with the payment, the bank would take away his farm. May's father lent the man $1,800, and the farm was saved.

A year went by, but the neighbor never made any attempt to pay back the debt. Instead he came up with an idea of how he could get out of paying back the money. One night as Mr. Carley was driving into town, the drunken neighbor rammed his car into the side of Mr. Carley's car and then drove off, leaving May's father badly hurt. Someone in town heard about the on-purpose accident and drove out to help the injured man. He brought Mr. Carley back into town for medical treatment.

Mr. Carley got out of the car and sat down on the sidewalk while the good Samaritan went looking for a doctor. The injured man, whose condition was critical, was in great pain. And who should come along but the neighbor who had tried to kill him. Instead of apologizing for what he had done, the man kicked Mr. Carley in the face.

Mr. Carley spent a year and a half in the hospital before he finally died, but he never tried to take revenge against the neighbor. In fact, he called each of his five children to his bedside and talked with them separately. "Please promise me," he said, "that you'll never say an unkind word against our neighbor's children. They deserve to grow up as respected citizens in the town they've always lived in, and you'll never be happy if you let hatred stay in your heart."

Only the love of God could give a man that type of forgiveness, and it's only the love of God that can help you forgive the people who mistreat you.

When we forgive people, we do it not because they deserve it, but because God has asked us to.

Something to think about: Are there people in your life whom you need to forgive?

AUGUST

16

Best Friends

Seek the Lord while he may be found; call on him while he is near. Isaiah 55:6, NIV.

Hannah looked out the back window of the car and waved to Rhonda, who was standing on the sidewalk. Father started the car and drove down the street. Rhonda waved until they turned a corner and she lost sight of her friend.

Hannah and Rhonda had been neighbors ever since they were in kindergarten, but all that would change. Hannah's father had been transferred to another company more than 300 miles away. Not only had the girls been neighbors, but they had also been best friends.

"Even though you're moving away, we'll still be best friends forever," promised Rhonda as she helped Hannah pack the day before the move.

"Yeah," Hannah agreed. "I'll never be best friends with anyone else but you."

Although the girls wouldn't be able to see each other very often, they had promised each other to write faithfully. And their parents had agreed to let them call each other once a month.

Two days after Hannah's family settled into their new house, they went to church. Hannah felt lonely during Sabbath school because she didn't know anyone, but at the church potluck she ate lunch with Vicki, one of the girls in the junior department. She found out that she and Vicki would be going to the same school.

That afternoon Hannah told her mother about her new friend. "And guess what! She collects stuffed animals just like I do, and she likes to cross-country ski."

"Well, I'm glad you made a new friend so quickly," said Mother. "I'm sure that you'll find even more new friends after school begins."

And that's exactly what happened. Pretty soon Hannah was so busy with her new friends that she forgot to write to Rhonda, and by second semester, Hannah had stopped calling her old friend.

Have you ever treated your best Friend, Jesus, this way? Have you become so busy with other friends that you don't have time to keep in touch with Him?

Be sure to put Jesus first in your life. Let everything else take second place.

AUGUST

17

Finding Your Value

I praise you because I am fearfully and wonderfully made; your works are wonderful, I know that full well. Psalm 139:14, NIV.

A few years ago I decided that I wanted to learn to play the cello, one of the instruments in the string family. I spent a lot of time learning about stringed instruments before I bought one. I wanted to know what to look for in a cello so I could make a good choice.

One afternoon while talking with a salesman at a well-known music store, I asked why some cellos cost $1,000 and others were more than $200,000.

He walked over to one of the instruments and pulled it from the rack. "Well, the sound of the instrument has some effect on the price, but the most important factor has little to do with the instrument itself. What really determines the value is the reputation of the craftsman who created the instrument. Take this, for example," he said, picking up one of the cellos in the showcase. "This one has a beautiful sound, but it's worth only about $3,000. The man who made it isn't well known, so his cellos don't command a high price. Now, if this were an original Stradivarius, it wouldn't matter if it sounded like a cigar box with strings. Stradivari is the most famous maker of stringed instruments who ever lived. If it had his signature on the inside, it would be worth a fortune—because it is one of his."

So it is with us. Our value does not depend on all the great things we can do, what we look like, or how intelligent we are. We have value because the God of the universe, the greatest craftsman of all time, has created us.

The next time you find yourself questioning your self-worth, just remember that you were made by God and that you're special because you're one of His.

AUGUST

18

Feeding the New Nature

Therefore, if anyone is in Christ, he is a new creation; the old has gone, the new has come! 2 Corinthians 5:17, NIV.

Because we are all born with a sinful nature (tendencies), we cannot choose to do that which is purely right. Even when we do good things, our reasons for doing them may be selfish.

But when we accept Jesus as our Saviour, He gives us a new nature, which desires to do what's right. Then that means that we'll never be tempted to sin again, right? Wrong.

When we accept Him as our Saviour, God does not take away our old sinful nature. If He did, then we would not be free to sin. And to God, freedom of choice is very important. God's kingdom is based on love, and love is only possible when people have a choice. Instead of taking away our ability to sin, God gives us a new nature so we can choose to do right with His power.

Our job is to "feed" the good nature and "starve" the evil one. Everything we do strengthens one of our two natures. That's why our actions are so important. You may have found yourself saying, "Well, it won't matter if I go ahead and sin just this once. After all, it's just a little sin," but there's really no such thing as a little sin because all sin separates us from Jesus.

As our new nature grows, the old one will be crowded out. We won't be free from temptation, but we'll find it easier and easier to say yes to things that are right and no to things that are wrong.

Something to think about: What are some things you can do to starve your old nature? (Example: Stay away from bad TV programs.) What are some things that you can do today to feed the new nature that God has given you? (Example: Study the Sabbath school lesson.)

AUGUST

19

Keep Your Cool

"Temper is such a good thing, that we should never lose it."

Charlie turned off the lawn mower and wiped the sweat from his face. *Just my luck,* he thought. *I have to mow the lawn on the hottest day of the summer.*

He headed into the house and opened the refrigerator door. *Hmmm. There's nothing to drink but milk.* He walked over to the cupboard and found a bottle of 7-Up. Opening the freezer door, he checked the ice cube bin. Empty. So he set the bottle next to some frozen vegetables. *I'll just leave the 7-Up in here until I get done with the lawn. By then it'll be good and cold.*

Two days later Charlie went to the freezer to get a loaf of raisin bread for breakfast. "What in the world?" he said as he stared at the pieces of broken glass lying on top of the frozen vegetables. Then he remembered his bottle of 7-Up. As the pop froze, it started to expand, and finally it shattered the bottle.

People with bad tempers are a lot like the bottle of 7-Up. They can hold in their anger for a while, but eventually they're going to explode.

There's nothing wrong with feeling anger. It's what we do with it that counts. Instead of attacking someone with your fists or your words, do something positive: Pray about it, talk your frustrations over with a friend, or write your feelings down on paper. Physical action can also help you calm down. Go for a walk, play some basketball, or mow the lawn. You could even clean your room. (Wouldn't your mother love that?)

Just make sure that you don't bottle up your feelings!

Better a patient man than a warrior, a man who controls his temper than one who takes a city. Proverbs 16:32, NIV.

AUGUST

20

About Face

A happy heart makes the face cheerful, but heartache crushes the spirit. Proverbs 15:13, NIV.

Back in the early days of America's history, people didn't move around the country as quickly and easily as we do today. Travel was done mostly on horseback.

One day as President Thomas Jefferson and some friends were riding across the country, they came to a river. Days before, a downpour had raised the water to well above its normal level, and the heavy current had washed away the wooden bridge that gave travelers access to the other side.

The only way the men could get across was to ride their horses through the rushing water. The riders and their horses lined the riverbank. One by one they guided their horses through the swift current to the other side.

Finally, it was President Jefferson's turn. Just as he was about to start across, he felt a hand on his arm. He looked down to see a stranger standing next to him. "Please, sir, would you allow me to ride across the river with you? I have no horse of my own."

Jefferson extended his hand to the stranger and helped him mount the horse. Together they crossed the river. As the man was dismounting, someone asked him, "Tell me, why did you ask the president for a ride when you could have asked one of us?"

"The president?" the man asked in surprise. Turning to Jefferson, the man added, "I had no idea who you were, sir. It's just that when I was trying to decide which person to ask, I noticed that a number of the men had a 'No' face. Yours was a 'Yes' face."

What kind of face do you have? When your parents look at you, do they see a "Yes" face when it comes to doing chores around the house? When your teacher looks at you, does he or she see a "Yes" face when it comes to helping out in the classroom?

Better check the mirror and find out what others see when they look at you.

AUGUST

21

No One Will Know

For there is nothing hidden that will not be disclosed, and nothing concealed that will not be known or brought out into the open. Luke 8:17, NIV.

Lila and Sandy attended church each Sabbath, and they went to church school. They also liked to attend the football games at the local high school. Although the games were almost always on Friday nights, they went anyway. After all, the other church members wouldn't know—unless they too went.

Everyone in town believed that the Wildcats would go on to the state championships that year, but it all depended on the last game of the season. Lila and Sandy couldn't miss that game. They huddled in the bleachers with the rest of the fans, screaming their support to the home team. And sure enough, the Wildcats won 23-21.

"Are you going to the championship game over in Detroit?" Lila asked Sandy.

"I wouldn't miss it for anything," Sandy replied. "When is it?"

"I heard someone say it's going to be on Sabbath. That would mean we'd have to miss church."

Sandy shrugged. "I know, but no one has to know about it. After all, this is a chance of a lifetime."

The girls bought tickets to the big game and made arrangements to ride on one of the school buses. Yet they still felt a little uncomfortable. Their parents didn't attend church regularly themselves. So they weren't strict about what the girls could and couldn't do on Sabbath. But Lila and Sandy knew that their teachers and Sabbath school leaders would be very disappointed if they ever found out.

The day of the championship game arrived. The girls got up that Sabbath morning, and instead of going to church they boarded a school bus and rode to Detroit. When they got to the stadium, they found their seats. It felt good to get lost in the crowd. They cheered their team on to victory, and the Wildcats carried home the state championship that year.

The girls heaved a sigh of relief when they got home that night. Their secret was safe.

The next day Sandy hurried out to get the Sunday paper. She wanted to see what the paper had to say about the game. The game made the front page. But what caught Sandy's eye was the big picture that accompanied the article, for it was none other than a close-up shot of her and Lila sitting in the stadium.

When we disobey God, we may think we're doing it secretly, but nothing escapes His view. We may hide our sins, but someday they will be hidden no longer.

AUGUST

22

Mixed-up Values

Eagerly desire the greater gifts. 1 Corinthians 12:31, NIV.

Before the auction that day, I went in early so I could look over all the things that were going to be sold. The items were from an estate of a local chiropractor who had died a few months earlier.

When he was a young boy, the doctor had lost his eyesight. Since he could not see anything, he had turned to music for enjoyment. The items for sale included two trumpets, three accordions, two violins, a trombone, four cellos, an oboe, two saxophones, a bassoon, two clarinets, a xylophone, and some drums. In addition, he had all kinds of stereo equipment, tape recorders, records, and tapes.

What really interested me were six cello bows. I laid them out on the table, and then one by one tried them out on one of the cellos that was going to be sold. After a few minutes, I had an idea which bow I liked best, second best, etc. I wrote down the name of each bow in order of my preference. Then I wrote down how much I was willing to pay for each one, just in case I didn't get my first choice.

After selling a group of brass instruments, the auctioneer picked up the bows and began asking for bids.

My number one choice went for $575. That was a little more than I wanted to pay. So I waited for my second choice. It went for $485. Still too much.

The rest of the bows went for between $500 and $600. That is, all but the last one, which happened to be the bow I liked the least. *Well, maybe I'll be able to afford the worst one in the bunch,* I told myself.

The auctioneer held up the Sarcony bow, and the bidding *started* at $1,000. I couldn't believe my ears. Within seconds people had raised the price to $2,000, $3,000, $4,000, $5,000. *Those people are willing to pay $5,000 for* that *bow?*

"Sold to the man on the right for $5,200," called out the auctioneer.

I went home that day without a cello bow, but I did learn a lesson about life. Many times we overrate the things of this world and underrate what really matters. For example, many people put a lot of value on good looks, money, and popularity, yet they take for granted friends, health, freedom, and salvation.

How is it with you? What do you consider most important? Do you have your priorities in the right place?

AUGUST

23

Lost Treasure

While browsing through a gem collectors' show in Tucson, Arizona, Roy Whetstine came upon a boxful of agates. As he looked at the largest rock, he realized that it wasn't an agate. "What will you take for this?" he asked, holding up the potato-sized stone.

The old rock collector shrugged his shoulders. "I was asking $15 each, but since that one isn't as pretty as the others, I'll take $10."

Whetstine handed the man two $5 bills and hurried for his car. He had a pretty good idea what he had just bought, but to make sure, he took the stone to a gem cutter and had him cut a small hole in it so he could see inside.

Whetstine's hunch was right. He had purchased not an agate, but the largest pure crystal star sapphire ever found. Its appraised value—$2.28 million.

How would you feel if you had been the man who sold the sapphire for only $10? How would it feel to know that you had just lost a treasure you could never get back?

Many young people trade away their self-respect for a few moments of fun. They give in to sexual pressure, and before they know it, they've ended up the loser.

A few years ago I attended the wedding reception of one of the young couples in our church. Linda, a friend of mine, stood next to me while we watched the bride and groom cut their cake. "They're so lucky," Linda said with tears in her eyes. "When I got married I was three months pregnant. I had no choice. I cried through the whole wedding. It was the saddest day of my life."

It's not easy to say no to temptation, but it's always worth it.

Teach me your way, O Lord, and I will walk in your truth. Psalm 86:11, NIV.

AUGUST

24

Where Is Your Treasure?

Store up for yourselves treasures in heaven, where moth and rust do not destroy, and where thieves do not break in and steal. Matthew 6:20, NIV.

"What in the world is Teddy doing?" I asked Tom one morning as I looked out the kitchen window. I could see her digging with all her doggie heart in the alfalfa field behind our house.

Tom and I, curious about what she was burying, walked outside and watched her from behind a tree. "She's burying something," he reported.

"A bone?" I asked.

"No. A piece of bread."

Now, I don't know what she had planned for that piece of bread. I don't think she's ever eaten bread in her life, but she thought it was a great treasure.

We all have things that we treasure. And Marie Spector was no different. Three years ago Marie left her homeland of Israel and moved to Miami, Florida, to start a new life. When she flew to this country, she carried all her valuables in her purse. She planned to open a bank safe deposit box the next day. But within 24 hours, her treasure vanished when a robber grabbed her purse and disappeared into a crowd of people.

Mrs. Spector lost $1,300 in cash and $273,700 in family jewels. None of it was insured.

Nothing we own is completely safe. Possessions can be stolen (as Mrs. Spector found out), lost, or ruined. Or they may just become worthless.

God's answer to the problem of possessions is for us to put them in the one and only safe place—heaven. Instead of spending all our money on ourselves, we are encouraged to put our treasures in heaven. But what does that mean?

When Jesus comes again, all He will take back with Him will be His people. Everything else on earth will be destroyed. So the only way we can put our treasures in heaven is to invest them in people. By giving tithes and offerings, we can help other people know about Jesus.

Maybe someday when you're in heaven, someone will tap you on the shoulder and say, "Thanks for helping send missionaries to my town. They told me about Jesus, and I gave my heart to Him."

Wow, what a great investment!

AUGUST

25

Firsthand Knowledge

These are the Scriptures that testify about me. John 5:39, NIV.

I was standing by the Lincoln Monument in Washington, D.C., when he walked up to me and handed me a carnation. "Any donation you could give would be appreciated," he said with a smile.

I had heard about the Hare Krishna. They're a religious cult that makes money by selling flowers to unsuspecting tourists. Their religion is based on meditation and the belief that people never die. As I see it, they have no need for God, since they believe they are responsible for their own salvation.

"I'm sorry," I said, handing the flower back. "I'm a Christian, and I don't feel I can support the things you believe in."

He didn't let me off that easy. "How do you know we don't believe in the same things?"

I asked him what he believed about death. "Well, we don't really die. We just go on to another body form."

"But that's not what the Bible teaches," I countered. "First Thessalonians 4:16, 17 says that the dead will come up from their graves when Jesus comes again." He didn't say anything, so I continued. "Have you ever read the Bible?"

He stood there for a while, wringing his hands, unaware that he was destroying the bouquet of carnations he was holding. Finally he looked up defensively and said, "Well, I haven't read it myself, but I know somebody who has." With that, he turned around and stalked off, throwing the crumpled flowers into a trash can.

Are you learning about God from firsthand experience, or are you depending on your parents, teachers, or minister to tell you what to believe? It is only through the Bible that we can know the truth, and the only way it'll make a difference in our lives is if we search the Scriptures for ourselves.

AUGUST

26

Being a Friend to the Hurting

Carry each other's burdens.
Galatians 6:2, NIV.

Too many people don't care what happens as long as it doesn't happen to them."

"The day my mother died, I walked out of her room and went to the park to play basketball with my friends." Bill and I were juniors in academy when he told me about his mother's death, which had taken place three years before. "She had had cancer for about two years. Right before Christmas the doctor sent her home. We were all in the room with her when she died.

"I went to school the next day just as if nothing had happened. I guess I didn't want to face up to the fact that she was dead.

"When the news got around at school, the kids didn't know what to say. So they just avoided me. When I walked down the hallway, some pretended I wasn't there. Others turned around and headed the other way so they wouldn't have to face me. If only someone had walked up and said, 'Hey, Bill, I heard about your mom, and I'm really sorry.' If only someone had been there when I needed him."

Suffering isn't something that just happens to adults. People of all ages experience sickness, death, family fights, divorce, physical abuse, and homelessness. You can probably think of at least one person at school who is going through one of these painful experiences right now. How can you help?

The most important thing you can do for those who are hurting is to be their friend. Don't feel that you have to cheer them up and make them forget their problems. What they need most is someone who will spend time with them and listen when they feel like talking.

Sometimes friends may be going through experiences that no one else knows about. Maybe they are being neglected at home. Or maybe they are being mistreated. If you feel that they are in any kind of danger, tell your parents or teacher right away. The sooner someone knows about the problem, the sooner the family can receive help.

AUGUST

27

Doing Things My Way

Alicia and her parents unbuckled their seat belts and picked up their hand luggage. The other passengers on the airplane crowded the aisles. "Let's just wait a few minutes until some of the people get outside," Mr. Gregory suggested.

Alicia looked out the window and across the runway of Gatwick Airport. *I wonder if England will look any different than the United States?* she thought.

At last the aisles began to clear, so Alicia and her parents stood up and started for the exit. After guiding his family through the airport terminal, Mr. Gregory found the luggage pickup area. Once they had retrieved all their bags, they left the terminal and hailed a cab.

The cab driver put their things in the trunk and then started driving them to their hotel. Alicia couldn't believe her eyes. The cab driver was driving down the highway—on the wrong side of the road!

"Mother," Alicia whispered, "we're going down the wrong side of the road."

Mother laughed. "Well, it may be the wrong side in our country, but here in England everyone drives on the left-hand side."

A few weeks ago my students were talking about pizza during lunch. One of them mentioned that in some countries, the favorite pizza topping is fish.

"Oh, gross," said one of the girls. "That's revolting."

"Now wait a minute," I broke in. "We have to realize that people are different. What you and I like may not be what someone else likes. Maybe the people who like fish on their pizza think mushrooms and olives are disgusting."

Sometimes we think that our likes and customs are the only ones that are right. When we feel that way, it's easy to look down on other people who are different instead of appreciating their uniqueness.

The next time you are tempted to judge someone who dresses, looks, or acts differently, thank the Lord that He didn't make us all the same.

And there are different ways that God works in people; but all these ways are from the same God. God works in us all in everything we do. Something from the Spirit can be seen in each person. 1 Corinthians 12:6, 7, ICB.

AUGUST

28

Hidden Sin

Then I acknowledged my sin to you and did not cover up my iniquity. I said, "I will confess my transgressions to the Lord"—and you forgave the guilt of my sin. Psalm 32:5, NIV.

What is that smell? thought my husband, the school principal, as he walked down the hall toward his office. *I wonder if a mouse died in one of the lockers.* Sniffing the air, he followed the scent to locker 43. Opening the door, he glanced through the contents. *Hmmmm. Nothing there but a coat and some books.*

He shut the door, then tried locker 44. Nothing. Next he went to locker 45. As he opened the door, the stench hit him in the face. *What in the world could smell so bad?* he wondered.

Searching through the disorderly contents, he found a lunch sack buried beneath a pile of clothes. Inside was a plastic container filled with something very, very rotten.

Mr. Coffee put a note on the locker door, asking Tina to clean out the contents and get rid of the offending container.

The next day we had our school parties, and at noon everyone went home for Christmas vacation. When we returned to school two weeks later, a horrible smell once again filled the entire hallway. Mr. Coffee searched the lockers again, but found nothing. The plastic container in locker 45 was gone.

The students started complaining about the odor, so I sprayed the hallway with some perfume. It helped a little.

It wasn't until lunchtime that the mystery was solved. One of the teachers went by a storage room and happened to check the wastebasket. Under the discarded papers he found the oozing plastic food container from locker 45.

Mr. Coffee called Tina out of class and had her take the trash container to the dumpster. By the next morning the awful smell was only a memory.

Trying to hide rotten food is like trying to hide sin in your life. The longer you try to conceal it, the worse it becomes. When you have a sin in your life, confess it to Jesus, and let Him remove it. You'll be glad you did. And so will everyone else!

AUGUST

29

The Best Life Insurance of All

You have made known to me the paths of life; you will fill me with joy in your presence. Acts 2:28, NIV.

But I don't want to give my life to Jesus now," said Stacy to Pastor Valdez. "There are so many things that I want to do first. I plan to be a Christian someday, but I'd rather wait until I'm old—after I've had a chance to live a little."

The minister leaned back in his chair and smiled at her answer. "I hear what you're saying, Stacy," he said, "but you've really got it backward."

"Backward? What do you mean?"

"Well, look at it from a purely practical viewpoint. You're 15. What kind of decisions do you have ahead of you?"

Stacy thought for a moment and said, "Well, I suppose I'll have to decide if I'm going to college or not, what I want to do for a job, if I'll get married."

"And whom you'll marry, whether or not you'll have children, what kind of lifestyle you'll adopt, where you'll live, what kind of friends you'll have—"

"OK. So I have a lot of things to decide. What does that have to do with giving my life to God?"

The pastor leaned forward. "If there ever was a time when a person could do without God, and I don't believe there is, but if there was, it would be when you're old and all the decisions have been made. Of all the times in your life, you need God the most right now. He can help you as you make the decisions that will determine whether or not you have a happy life."

A lot of young people feel as Stacy does. They want to do what's right, but they're afraid they'll miss out on a lot of fun.

It's God's plan to give you the best in life. Don't settle for less. Ask Him today to be the Lord of your life. You'll never regret it.

AUGUST

30

Difficulties, the Steppingstones to Success

Whatever your hand finds to do, do it with all your might. Ecclesiastes 9:10, NIV.

It's Monday morning. The teacher is handing back the English test you took on Friday. As you turn over your paper you see a big red D at the top of the page. How do you react?

1. "I just knew I'd mess up. I'm such a dummy."
2. "It's the teacher's fault. If she'd do a better job explaining the lessons, I'd get better grades."
3. "Well, my dad got bad grades in English too."
4. "It looks like I'd better study a little harder next time."

What happens when you fail at something? Do you blame someone else? Do you give up and resign yourself to failure? Or do you learn from your mistakes?

The way you deal with failure will help determine how successful you are in life. If you give in to problems by quitting or blaming others, you'll make very little progress. If you face failure head-on, you can learn from it and come out further ahead.

Thomas Edison was one of the greatest inventors of all times. Once he performed a series of 10,000 experiments using a storage battery. Not one of the experiments worked. When a friend asked him how he felt about failing, Edison said, "Why, I haven't failed. I've just found 10,000 ways that won't work."

Although he met many failures, he was a success because he refused to quit. Edison went on to patent more than 1,000 inventions, including the electric light bulb, the movie camera, and the record player.

Failure is a lot like a mean dog I ran into a few weeks ago. It came around the corner of a building and starting snarling at me. I knew that if I tried to run away, it would chase me. So I folded my arms and started walking straight toward it. When it saw that I wasn't intimidated, it slunk away.

Don't let failure control your life. Stand up to it and be a winner. That we fail is not important—how we handle failure is.

AUGUST

31

First-Class Blessings

Blessings crown the head of the righteous. Proverbs 10:6, NIV.

Mrs. Krieger hugged her son and wiped the tears from her eyes. "Auf Wiedersehen, Johann."

"Don't worry, Mama. I'll be all right. I wish I didn't have to leave you, but America is the land of opportunity. I'll be able to find a good job there, and I'll be able to send you money each month."

The train whistle blew. Johann hugged his mother once more and boarded the train. When Johann arrived in America, he found a job. And as he promised, he began sending money to his mother back in Germany. Each month he went to the bank and bought a bank money order, which is like a check. All his mother had to do was sign her name on the back of the money order. The bank in Germany would gave her German marks, which she could spend in her country.

When Johann received his mother's first letter, he was surprised to find another plea for money. So Johann sent her a larger money order the next time he wrote, but month after month, the pleas for money continued.

One morning as Mrs. Krieger was sitting at her kitchen table eating breakfast a neighbor came by. "How is Johann doing in America?" asked Mrs. Heiss.

"Fine, fine. But he has been gone for six months, and he hasn't kept his promise."

"What do you mean?"

Mrs. Krieger pulled out all the letters Johann had sent. "Before he left, Johann promised to send me money each month, but all he sends me are letters . . . and these little papers."

The neighbor, who could read English, picked up the papers. "Oh, Emily," she said, "Johann has been sending you money. These papers are bank money orders. If you will cash them in, you'll receive German marks."

Sometimes we make the same mistake that Mrs. Krieger did. We ask God to bless us, but when He sends us special blessings, we don't recognize them. We continue to ask, never realizing that He is constantly showing us evidence of His love and care.

Something to think about: What blessings has God given to you today?

SEPTEMBER

1

So Near, but Yet So Far

But he that shall endure unto the end, the same shall be saved. Matthew 24:13.

Jim Peters was a runner. He didn't run just a few miles here and there; Jim was a marathon runner.

Jim entered the British Empire Games of 1954, which were held in British Columbia. He knew the race would be exhausting, but he loved the challenge. When the marathon race was announced, Jim lined up with the other runners. An official held up a starting gun. BANG! The runners shot forward.

Within a short time Jim took over the lead. As the miles flew by, he moved out farther and farther in front of the other runners. During the final moments of the race, Jim was 20 minutes ahead of his nearest competitor.

The crowds went wild as Jim entered the stadium. What a show! What an all-out victory! But instead of sprinting across the finish line, Jim slowed his stride. His body began weaving back and forth, and then he fell to the ground. Friends and teammates screamed their encouragement. "Get up, Jim! Keep going!"

The weary runner stood up and tried to finish the race. But down he went again.

"Come on, Jim!" "You're almost there!"

Again Jim picked himself up off the track and started for the finish line, but again he dropped to the ground. Twelve times he tried to continue the race, and 12 times he fell.

Finally Jim collapsed into his trainer's arms. He never made it to the finish line, which was only 200 yards away. Twenty minute later, James McGhee, the second fastest runner, won the race.

Jim Peters lost the contest because he couldn't make the last 200 yards.

Do you ever find yourself giving up when it comes to spiritual things? Do you start out your day determined to live like a Christian but give up when Satan sends a temptation?

Just like Jim Peters, we must keep going no matter how hard it gets and no matter how many times we fall. As long as we choose to be on God's side, He'll make sure that we come out winners—unlike Jim Peters' tragic experience. We may fall to temptation, but with Jesus' help we can get back up and keep on going. Jim didn't have the energy to reach the finish line, but the Holy Spirit promises to give us all the power we need so that we can.

As long as we keep on running, He'll stay by our side and make sure we receive the crown of life.

SEPTEMBER

2

Nothing Is Too Hard for God

O Lord God! You have made the heavens and earth by your great power; nothing is too hard for you! Jeremiah 32:17, TLB.

Many years ago two strangers stood on a street in Plymouth, England. At midnight the town clock struck the hour. Ten. Eleven. Twelve. Thirteen.

Thirteen?

The two men looked at each other in surprise. "Did you hear that?" asked one.

The other shook his head in wonderment. "It actually struck 13 times. I thought I was hearing things."

The two men went their separate ways. Some weeks later, Captain Jarvis, one of the men, awoke early with a strong impression that he should do something. He got dressed and went downstairs. His groom was standing at the front door with his horse saddled and ready to ride. Captain Jarvis got on the horse and rode off. He had no idea where he should go, so he let the horse take the lead.

The horse and rider eventually arrived at a large town. Captain Jarvis stopped a man on the sidewalk. "Is anything special going on in town today?" he asked.

"There sure is. We're tryin' a man for murder."

Jarvis hurried to the courthouse just as the judge asked the prisoner, "Have you anything at all to say for yourself?"

The prisoner looked up and said, "I have nothing to say, Your Honor, except that I am an innocent man." He went on to tell how he couldn't have committed the crime because he had been in another town when it happened. "I was in Plymouth right at midnight," he explained. "I remember hearing the clock strike 13. In fact, another man and I talked about the strange occurrence. If that man were only here, he could testify that I am telling the truth."

"I'm here, I'm here," shouted Captain Jarvis as he strode to the front of the courthouse. Turning to the judge and jury, he related the remarkable chain of events that had brought him to the courthouse. And he confirmed the man's story. The prisoner was set free.

God has a solution to every problem. No matter what happens, He'll provide a way out of our difficulties. If we trust in Him, He'll see us through even impossible situations.

(Adapted from Kenneth H. Wood, Jr., *Meditations for Moderns* [Washington, D.C.: Review and Herald, 1963], p. 45.)

SEPTEMBER

3

Planning Perfect Moves

Therefore, prepare your minds for action; be self-controlled; set your hope fully on the grace to be given you when Jesus Christ is revealed. 1 Peter 1:13, NIV.

The campers and staff members at Camp Au Sable lined the dock as Chuck Knorr strode out to the end of the diving board. Turning around, Chuck stood on the edge of the board, his back to the water. He held his arms out straight and then closed his eyes. For a few seconds he remained motionless. Then suddenly he jumped away from the board, bending into a pike position before straightening out and slicing through the water with barely a splash.

Chuck was not just any diver. He had been a substitute diver on the American team at the 1968 Olympics in Mexico City. For the next 15 minutes, Chuck gave a diving demonstration to the whole camp. When he was through, we all went into the dining hall for supper.

"What are you thinking about when you close your eyes?" I asked him.

"The dive," he answered. "I run the dive through my mind again and again, concentrating on each twist, turn, and tuck. I have to program my brain so that when I leave the board, my body will automatically make all the right moves."

In other words, Chuck prepared himself ahead of time.

Young people need to prepare themselves, too. Not for diving, but for handling peer pressure. I encourage my ninth and tenth graders to plan ahead of time how they'll handle the different pressures their friends might put on them.

For instance, what would you do in the following situations?

1. You and two other classmates stay at a friend's house overnight. Someone pulls out a pack of cigarettes and lights up one. Everyone else takes a few puffs. Finally the cigarette is passed to you. What would you do?

2. While you are shopping at the mall with a friend, he hides a candy bar in his pocket. "Get one for yourself," he urges. What would you do?

3. A group of your friends make plans to see an indecent movie. You tell them your parents won't let you go. "That's all right," someone says. "Just tell them you're coming over to my house to work on your science project. They'll never know." What would you say?

Don't wait until you're in the middle of a tough situation to decide what to do. Be prepared. Make your plans ahead of time.

SEPTEMBER

4

Time of Trouble—Time of Triumph

The salvation of the righteous comes from the Lord; he is their stronghold in time of trouble. The Lord helps them and delivers them; he delivers them from the wicked and saves them, because they take refuge in him. Psalm 37:39, 40, NIV.

I've always been afraid of the time of trouble. Back when I was in church school, I remember begging Jesus not to come. When I walked to the end of the driveway each night to get the newspaper, I'd be afraid to read the headlines. I was sure I'd see the words PRESIDENT ENACTS NATIONAL SUNDAY LAW.

What scared me the most was the thought of going through persecution. How would I ever be able to handle all that suffering?

Marie Durand, a young French Huguenot, knew all about suffering. In 1730 she, along with other Christians, was sentenced to life imprisonment because she refused to give up her faith in God.

Marie was locked up in the Tower of Constance, a round tower with walls 18 feet thick. Marie was only 15 years old. For the next 38 years Marie remained in the tower. Many of the other prisoners gave up their faith, and as soon as they did, their prison doors were opened, and they were allowed to go free. But Marie refused to recant. She loved God more than she loved her freedom.

The Huguenot library in Paris has one of Marie's letters. In it she says, "God has given us the precious truths of the Bible; to these I must be true and may not prove traitor like Judas." Her life in the Tower of Constance was miserable, but it was her choice. For Marie, losing her friend Jesus was a fate much worse than imprisonment.

If we should live to see the time of trouble, we will have only one choice to make—whether or not we'll be loyal to God. Those who remain on God's side will not have it easy. But they will have God's strength and companionship. No one will force them to stand for what they believe. They will do so because they want to. They could turn their backs on God, but they will remain loyal because staying close to Jesus will be their greatest pleasure.

We don't need to worry about the time of trouble. We just need to get to know our best friend, Jesus.

SEPTEMBER

5

Fault-finders

Accept one another, then, just as Christ accepted you, in order to bring praise to God. Romans 15:7, NIV.

Jeff was an excellent athlete and student. He dressed nicely. He was also very popular with his classmates. In fact, he was elected eighth-grade class president. Jeff went to church school, but on weekends Jeff hated going to Sabbath school. It wasn't that Jeff didn't like Sabbath school, but he was afraid of what might happen to him if he went.

Jeff's mother noticed that every Sabbath morning her otherwise confident, fun-loving son became nervous and short-tempered. He'd drag out of bed, complaining because he had to go to church. He'd get dressed and then five minutes later change his shirt or his tie. He'd comb his hair, making sure that every hair was in place. Then he'd stand in front of the mirror to see how he looked. And he'd ask his family if he looked all right.

Finally Mrs. Logan sat her son down. "Jeff, what's going on? Why is it that every Sabbath morning you become a completely different person? Why is it that you don't want to go to Sabbath school? Why are you so concerned about how you look?"

Jeff hung his head. "You wouldn't understand, Mom."

"Give me a try."

"Well, every week when I walk into our Sabbath school room, there's a group of girls who just wait to make fun of how I look. If I have one hair sticking up or if I have a piece of lint on my slacks, they start pointing at me and laughing out loud."

When Jeff's mother told me this story, I wondered how many hundreds, maybe even thousands, of other young people face the same type of treatment by their peers.

People who don't like themselves are quick to criticize others. In order to raise their own self-importance, they feel they must put down others. But people with a good self-image know that their worth comes from being children of God, and they see others as God's children too.

When people come to your school or your Sabbath school, do you make them feel welcome? Do you accept them just as they are?

SEPTEMBER

6

Know When to Say "When"

Who has woe? Who has sorrow? Who has strife? Who has complaints? Who has needless bruises? Who has bloodshot eyes? Those who linger over wine, who go to sample bowls of mixed wine. Proverbs 23:29, 30, NIV.

Every year at this time, we hear a lot about safe driving. Labor Day weekend is the last vacation most people have before Thanksgiving. So the roads are full of vacationers who want to have one last holiday before school gets into full swing.

The major reason people die in car accidents is drinking. But alcohol doesn't just cause car crashes; it ruins a person's life in many different ways.

Below is a poem written by a 25-year-old prisoner in the Joliet, Illinois, prison:

> The name of every saloon is "bar,"
> Which is a fitting name by far.
> A bar to heaven, a door to hell;
> Whoever named it named it well.
> A bar to manliness, a bar to wealth,
> A door to sorrow and broken health;
> A bar to honor, pride, and fame;
> A door to sorrow, grief, and shame;
> A bar to hopes, a bar to prayer;
> A door to darkness and despair;
> A bar to a useful manly life,
> A door to brawling, senseless strife;
> A bar to heaven, a door to hell;
> Whoever named it named it well.

Weekly Reader magazine asked students between the ages of 9 and 12 if they felt pressured by their friends and classmates to drink alcohol. Nearly half the group said they did. Alcohol is not just an adult problem anymore.

A number of you have been encouraged by a friend to drink, and some of you have given in to the pressure. I would suspect, however, that the majority of you have never been tempted to try a wine cooler, beer, or some other alcoholic drink.

No matter which group you fall into—those who have been tempted, those who have tried alcohol, and those who have never felt the pressure—you can decide today, once and for all, that alcohol won't be part of your life.

SEPTEMBER

7

Becoming Like Jesus

Be perfect, therefore, as your heavenly Father is perfect. Matthew 5:48, NIV.

"I want to welcome all of you to a new school year," said Mr. Rodman as he looked out over the classroom. "For the next 180 school days we're going to have a good time learning a lot of new things." After explaining the grading system, Mr. Rodman asked the students to open their math books.

Andy thumbed through his new book. What he saw scared him. *I'll never be able to do this,* he thought. *This stuff is hard. I just know I'm going to flunk math this year.*

"I'd like you to do pages 4 and 5 today," Mr. Rodman said, interrupting Andy's thoughts. "These pages are just a review of what you learned last year. I'll give you the whole class period to work your problems."

Andy finished the assignment by the time the bell signaled the end of class. He turned in his paper and headed for his locker. "Boy, what did you think of our new math book?" he asked his lockermate, Kirk. "I don't think math will be my best subject this year."

"You did OK in math last year, didn't you?" asked Kirk.

"Sure. But I don't know if I'll be able to handle eighth-grade math. It seems a lot harder than what we had last year."

"Of course it is," said Kirk, "but we don't have to finish the whole book in a week. All we have to do is one assignment each day."

Most projects seem pretty big if we only look at the end product. Learning eighth-grade math seemed impossible to Andy. But as Kirk said, he didn't have to learn it all at once. He just needed to learn one small part each day.

Do you ever get discouraged when you think about becoming perfect like Jesus? It probably seems like an impossible task to change from a sinful person to a perfect person. In the Bible *perfect* doesn't mean "without a flaw"; it means "maturing" and "growing."

Learning math takes time. So does learning to be like Jesus. Being perfect like Jesus means becoming like Him a little more each day. Perfection doesn't happen all at once. It happens one day at a time.

SEPTEMBER

8

Controlling the Flames

So, if you think you are standing firm, be careful that you don't fall!
1 Corinthians 10:12, NIV.

Soldier Dave Roever surveyed the Vietnamese jungle ahead of him. He'd have to clear a path so the others could get through. He stood up in the boat and reached for a hand grenade. Drawing his arm back, he started to hurl the grenade into the thicket ahead of him. Right at that moment an enemy soldier aimed his gun at the object in Dave Roever's hand and pulled the trigger. The bullet shattered the grenade, setting it off only six inches from Dave's face.

White phosphorus sprayed over Dave's body, ignited, and turned him into a human torch. Dave jumped into the swamp, but the flames kept burning, even under water. Only copper sulfate can quench phosphorus.

By the time the medics reached Dave, he had lost nearly 40 percent of his skin. As soon as possible, the Army moved Dave to a hospital, where he began the long process of healing.

The doctors decided to do some further surgery on Dave. So two weeks after the accident, he was wheeled into the operating room. The anesthesiologist put him to sleep, and the operating team got ready to begin the operation. The doctor took his knife and made an incision. Instantly Dave's internal organs burst into flames. Some of the white phosphorus from the hand grenade had worked its way inside Dave's body, and as soon as the phosphorus mixed with the oxygen in the air, it set Dave on fire again.

Sin acts the very same way in our lives. Like the phosphorus, it waits inside us. We aren't even aware of its presence, but at any minute it can burst into flames and hurt us.

We can never feel confident when it comes to handling sin on our own. We can never say that we've overcome this or that sin forever. Because just when we begin to feel confident enough to let down our guard, Satan attacks us, and we lose the battle.

Our only hope is to ask Jesus to fight our battles for us. When He's directing our lives, we can have confidence when it comes to overcoming sin. Not because of our own strength, but because of His.

SEPTEMBER

9

Making the Grade

When a wise man is instructed, he gets knowledge. Proverbs 21:11, NIV.

Today I want to give you some inside information. Since school has just started, I want to pass along some secrets on how you can become popular with your teachers. After being a teacher for 18 years, I have a pretty good idea what makes them tick.

First, get enthusiastic. Don't moan and groan every time your teacher gives an assignment. Be thankful that you have the opportunity to learn.

Second, ask questions. Don't be afraid to speak up when you don't understand. Oh, sure, it's embarrassing to show your ignorance in front of the class, but the question you ask is probably the one the others would ask if they had the courage. Remember: Ask a question and look like a fool for a moment; refuse to ask a question and remain a fool for the rest of your life. (Warning: Don't ask lazy questions. Don't ask for information that you could get by reading the directions.)

Third, don't miss class. My mother had a wonderful way of making sure I didn't miss school when I was young. Whenever I came downstairs in the morning and complained of a stomachache or a sore throat, she listened patiently. Then she said, "Well, if you're going to stay home today, we'll get some things done around the house. First you can clean the bathroom. Then we'll start the wash. While that's going, you can vacuum the carpets, and . . ." When she got that far I was usually miraculously healed and halfway dressed for school. Of course, there are times when you should stay home, but don't use "sickness" as an excuse to take a vacation and watch TV. Schoolwork is twice as hard when you're behind the rest of the class.

Finally, do your assignments on time. When you keep your work up-to-date, you'll get better grades and have a better attitude toward school.

If you give these ideas a try, I guarantee that your teachers will be glad to have you in their classroom. And you'll find yourself enjoying school a lot more.

SEPTEMBER

10

Poor Sports

Therefore, my dear brothers, stand firm. Let nothing move you. Always give yourselves fully to the work of the Lord, because you know that your labor in the Lord is not in vain.
1 Corinthians 15:58, NIV.

Back in 1894 professional baseball was just catching on as a national pastime. The world champion team that year was the Baltimore Orioles.

Baltimore was in Boston playing the Red Sox. As the Orioles were coming to bat in the third inning, Baltimore's legendary third baseman, John McGraw, ended up in a fistfight with Boston's third baseman.

One by one players from both sides jumped up from their benches and joined in the skirmish. The fans, not wanting to be left out, turned on each other, and soon 3,500 spectators were trading punches in the stands.

In the middle of the brawl, the fans sitting in the 25-cent bleacher seats noticed a strange warmth beneath them. Jumping up from their seats, they learned that someone had set fire to the stadium.

Finally the fights on the field ended, and the teams went back to their places and continued to play—in spite of the fire that continued to blaze. By the time the fireman managed to extinguish the inferno, the blaze had destroyed 170 buildings, caused $300,000 worth of property damage, and left 2,000 people homeless. All because of a baseball game.

There's something about being in a crowd that pushes people into doing things they'd never do alone. Maybe that's why so many young people get into trouble with someone else. They become less fearful of the consequences when they know that someone else will be there to share the blame, and they rationalize their actions by thinking, "Well, if Gary does it, then it can't be all that bad."

Don't let the crowd tell you what to do. Be your own boss. Think for yourself, and learn to stand for what is right no matter what other people decide to do.

SEPTEMBER

11

Deadly Joke

Let not my heart be drawn to what is evil, to take part in wicked deeds with men who are evildoers. Psalm 141:4, NIV.

The U.S. Coast Guard received the call about 7:00 p.m., Friday, July 6, 1990. "A boat—it's sinking. You've got to hurry."

"Where? Where is it?" the guardsman asked the young caller.

"In Lake Erie, about 18 miles from Lorain, Ohio."

Immediately the Coast Guard crew jumped into action. Starting their cutter, they shot through the water toward the reported accident. Little did they know that the phone call was a joke—a joke that would soon turn into a tragedy.

A short time later the Coast Guard received another call. This time from an adult. "We need help fast," the caller said. "I'm out in my sailboat near the harbor. I just saw a young boy fall from the break wall into the water."

"I'll have someone there as soon as possible," replied the officer, "but the rescue team just went out on another call."

After searching in vain for the sinking boat, the rescue team realized the call had been a hoax. By then it was too late to help Daniel Perez. The 14-year-old boy drowned in the harbor.

Whoever called in the false alarm to the Coast Guard probably just wanted to have a little fun. The prankster didn't realize the "fun" would contribute to someone else's death.

Just last week the papers told of another calamity that happened for the sake of a little fun. Some young people made a scarecrow out of old clothes and some stuffing. Carrying the "body" to a highway overpass, they tied a string around it and then lowered it to the road below.

Twenty-eight-year-old Tracey Pearson didn't know it was a dummy. She thought someone was standing in the middle of the road. As she swerved to avoid hitting the "person," she swerved off the road into a ditch. Her car rolled over, and Tracey was thrown to the ground. She was pronounced dead at the McLaren General Hospital.

There's nothing wrong with having fun, but if we aren't careful, our fun can turn into disaster.

Don't spoil your good times with years of regret. Play it safe.

SEPTEMBER

12

Loving Others—Loving God

I tell you the truth, whatever you did for one of the least of these brothers of mine, you did for me. Matthew 25:40, NIV.

Wherever there is a human being, there is a chance for kindness."

Sixteen-year-old Todd Hunt attends Northeast Middle School in Comstock, Michigan. He goes to a regular school, but Todd is not a normal teenager. He has cerebral palsy, and his mind is equivalent to that of a 4-year-old.

When he was 15, Todd read his first sentence: "The man had a cat."

People of all ages often feel uncomfortable around those with handicaps. Years ago people with mental retardation were chained to walls and treated worse than animals. Now society realizes that retarded people have feelings just like everyone else, and that they deserve to be treated with respect and dignity.

Todd's parents were worried when their son started taking classes at a regular school. How would the students treat Todd? Would they pick on him or just ignore him?

Well, Todd's classmates totally surprised the Hunts. They didn't pick on Todd or reject him. They accepted him and made him feel like part of the group. When they found out that he never got any phone calls after school, they organized a calling plan. Each student in Todd's class chose a day to call him. Now every night Todd gets a short phone call from one of his friends.

And during basketball season, when Todd goes down to the floor to shoot baskets during breaktime, the other kids cheer for him.

Being accepted by his peers has helped Todd in a number of ways. After his first month at Northeast, Mrs. Hunt noticed a number of changes in her son. "He started walking better and standing straighter. His mind is improving too. He speaks more clearly, and now he can talk with adults as well as other kids."

Todd's class at Northeast Middle School has learned to accept Todd despite his handicaps. They've learned that although people may be different, they still need to feel like they belong.

Although Todd has benefited a lot from the kindness of his classmates, they too have gained something from knowing him. They've learned how to love and accept someone who is different. And in so doing, they've given a great gift to their heavenly Father.

SEPTEMBER

13

Set Your Sights High

And whatever you do, whether in word or deed, do it all in the name of the Lord Jesus, giving thanks to God the Father through him.
Colossians 3:17, NIV.

Thomas Lipton left home when he was 15 years old. With only $8 in his pocket, he said goodbye to his native Scotland and headed off to America in search of fame and fortune.

After working at odd jobs for a number of years, he returned to Scotland, and on his twenty-first birthday he opened the first of a chain of food stores. Later he began a career as a tea merchant. Soon he was one of the richest men in the world. Although Thomas had accomplished his goal of fame and fortune, he still had one nagging ambition—he wanted to become the captain of the fastest racing yacht in the world. He wanted to win the America's Cup, the most prized trophy in yacht racing.

At great expense he built one of the fastest yachts that ever sailed. Then he brought the *Shamrock* to America for the boat race. He lost. Not one to give in to defeat, Lipton decided to build a brand-new boat—one even better than his first *Shamrock.* So again he poured his time and money into his second yacht. Again he sailed to America. And again he lost the race. Five times, with five different *Shamrocks,* Thomas Lipton tried to win the America's Cup and lost.

Although Lipton never did win the race, he did win the respect and admiration of the American people, for each time he lost the race, he had nothing but praise for the winners. He never complained or felt sorry for himself. He accepted his losses like a true sportsman.

In the quest to capture the America's Cup trophy, Lipton put his whole heart into his goal. He gave of his time and his money—investing more than $5 million. Some people may say he was silly to get so involved in boat racing. But the point is that he set a goal for himself, and he put all his energies into reaching that goal.

Do you have a goal that you're excited about? Is there something that you would like to accomplish before the end of the year? before you graduate from high school? by the time you're 30?

I hope you've set some goals for yourself. People with goals enjoy life more than those who just slide through life without direction. Those who have a purpose in life live life on purpose.

Something to think about: What would you like to accomplish in the next few months? by summer vacation?

SEPTEMBER

14

Meeting Others' Needs

And the Lord's servant must not quarrel; instead, he must be kind to everyone. 2 Timothy 2:24, NIV.

Back in the old days, before cars came into being, horses were the "wheels" of most Americans. If you wanted to go somewhere, you either threw a saddle on your horse or harnessed the horse to a buggy.

One day in St. Louis two riders guided their horses through the city streets to the town market. The men both dismounted and tied their reins to a hitching post. The owner of the black horse left to do his shopping, but the pinto's master set down a bag of oats for his horse. Then he hurried off to the market.

The pinto buried his nose in the sack of grain and began munching contentedly. As he lifted his head, he noticed that the black horse was eyeing his oats longingly. Before long the black horse started neighing to his companion.

The horse with the feed neighed back, which must have been his way of inviting the other fellow to help himself.

After receiving permission to share the oats, the black horse moved toward the bag of feed, but his reins were just too short. Try as he might, he could get only within three feet from the bag. The pinto noticed the problem. Stepping closer to the bag, he began pushing it with his nose until the other horse was able to reach it. After a friendly nose-rub of greeting, the two horses finished the oats together.

Horses aren't the only animals that display kindness. Prince was a shepherd dog that lived on a large farm. He spent most of his time walking alongside the farmer as he plowed the fields with his team of horses.

After finishing the work for that day, the farmer turned the horses loose in a small field near the road. As they grazed, the horses noticed a bundle of cornstalks that had fallen off the farm wagon on the other side of the fence. The horses leaned over the fence and strained to get the stalks, but try as they might, they just couldn't reach them.

Prince, who had followed the horses into the field, watched them for a while. Then he trotted off to a place where one of the fence boards had broken off. After squeezing through, he ran to the bundle of stalks, grabbed them in his teeth, and dragged them back through the hole in the fence. After placing the stalks in front of the horses, Prince stood by, wagging his tail as he watched his friends enjoy their meal.

If animals can find ways to be kind to each other, shouldn't we?

SEPTEMBER

15

A Voice From Heaven

The angel of the Lord encamps around those who fear him, and he delivers them. Psalm 34:7, NIV.

John, would you like to work for me this summer?" asked Mr. Granger, John's teacher, as they were walking out to recess. "I'm going to build a house, and I could use you on my construction crew."

"That would be great," said 14-year-old John. "I'll ask my parents and see if it would be OK with them."

John's parents gave their permission.

Of course, since John was the new guy, and also the youngest, he became the crew's "gofer." But he didn't mind it. Mr. Granger paid him $4 an hour, and the work was fun.

John brought "mud" to the block layers as they put up the basement walls. He helped pour the cement floor. And he worked alongside the other men as they built the walls of the house.

One morning as the crew prepared to work on the roof, Mr. Granger sent John down to work in the basement. "Pick up all the scrap wood and throw it in the cardboard barrels. Then sweep the floor."

John found the broom and began working. He swept everything to the middle of the room, right beneath the stairwell. As he bent over to pick up a handful of wood, he heard someone call his name.

Now, John wasn't one to answer the first time he was called, but something impressed him to respond immediately to the voice. "Yeah?" he replied as he stood up. Just as he looked in the direction of the voice, a heavy four-by-four came hurling through the opening in the floor, missing his nose by less than an inch.

I could have been killed, he thought. Racing up the ladder, John made his way to the roof of the house. "Hey, who called my name just now?"

The men looked at each other and shrugged. "We didn't say anything," said Dan. "Why?"

"Well, someone said 'John,' and when I looked up, one of those four-by-fours flew right past my face."

Mr. Granger and the rest of the crew followed John back down to the basement. "Well, it looks as though someone special came to your rescue today," said John's teacher as he picked up the piece of wood.

"You mean my guardian angel?" asked John.

Mr. Granger nodded.

The crew returned to the roof and left John in the basement. As he picked up the rest of the litter on the floor, John realized that he wasn't alone. He looked up and smiled. "Thanks, angel," he said softly.

SEPTEMBER

16

Fatty, Fatty, Two-by-Four

Pleasant words are a honeycomb, sweet to the soul and healing to the bones. Proverbs 16:24, NIV.

The children gather around Nola, the chubby little girl who has just transferred from another school. Locking arms, they begin chanting, "Fatty, fatty, two-by-four. Can't get through the kitchen door."

Paul picks up his math assignment and takes it to the teacher's desk. Janet watches Paul as he walks past. "Look at him," she says out loud. "He walks just like an ostrich." The rest of the class hears the comment, and a few laugh. Paul's face turns red, and he hurries back to his desk.

Priscilla walks through the lunchroom, looking for a place to sit. As she sets her tray down at one of the tables, Shane elbows the boy sitting next to him. "Hey, look who's going to sit with us. It's good old pizza face." Priscilla runs to the restroom and buries her face in her hands as she sobs. Why does she have to be the only person in the whole school with bad acne?

Have you ever been on the receiving end of a put-down? Have you ever given someone a put-down?

Yesterday at noon I heard Anne make fun of Clint's ears. I asked her to come into the hall, and we talked about what she had just done. "But Mrs. Coffee," she said, "I was just kidding. Clint knows that. We tease each other all the time."

"But there's teasing, and there's teasing," I replied. "It's one thing to joke around about someone's new haircut or a funny thing a person says. But when you poke fun at others' physical features, you can hurt them deeply, because they really can't do much to change."

"But I didn't mean anything by it," Anne persisted.

"I know you didn't, but it still hurts."

I went on to tell Anne about a friend of mine who still remembers a comment someone made more than 25 years ago. "One time this kid I didn't even know called me Big Nose," she reported. "I don't why he did it, but ever since I've been sensitive about my nose. Down deep inside I know my nose isn't large, but I'm still embarrassed about it."

When you're tempted to make fun of someone, put yourself in that person's shoes. Why not give a compliment instead?

SEPTEMBER

17

Piggyback Across Niagara

But I trust in you, O Lord; I say, "You are my God." My times are in your hands; deliver me from my enemies and from those who pursue me.
Psalm 31:14, 15, NIV.

On June 30, 1859, Jean Gravelet, better known as Blondin, conquered Niagara Falls. Stretching a tightrope 160 feet above the deadly current, he crossed from one side to the other in only five minutes.

But Blondin didn't stop there. He continued to cross the falls in different ways. Once he carried a chair across and then sat on it when he reached the middle. Another time he stood on his head. During one night crossing, the only light Blondin had was from train headlights. And then when he reached halfway across the wire, he had the lights turned off. He finished his trip in complete darkness. At other times he walked the tightrope blindfolded or on stilts.

One of his most daring journeys across the falls involved a man named Henry Colcord. Blondin announced to the world that Henry would ride on his back and the two of them would cross Niagara together.

On the day of the crossing, nearly a million people showed up to watch the daredevil and his passenger. Henry jumped up on Blondin's back and then put his feet into the special stirrups that Blondin had built for the occasion. And across the tightrope they went.

After they had traveled about 100 feet, Blondin decided he needed a rest, and he told Henry to get down. Of course Henry wasn't too crazy about the idea, and he refused. Blondin explained that if he didn't get down, they both might fall into the water. So Henry dismounted.

After a few minutes, Blondin told Henry to climb back up. Then they continued as the crowd watched in silence. Halfway across the wire, Blondin started to run, and he didn't stop until he had reached the other side.

Blondin was declared the world's most daring man, but poor Henry was never the same again! It took a lot of courage for Henry Colcord to put his trust in Blondin, for the tightrope walker was human, and one mistake could have sent both men to their death.

We have Someone much greater than Blondin in whom we can put our trust, and He cannot make a mistake. Jesus asks us to put our lives in His hands. He promises that if we trust Him in every area of our lives, He'll make sure that we reach our destination—heaven.

SEPTEMBER

18

Swapped for a Horse

The knowledge of the secrets of the kingdom of heaven has been given to you. . . . Whoever has will be given more, and he will have an abundance. Matthew 13:11, 12, NIV.

The night raiders slunk through the darkness. Peeking through the window of the little shack, they saw the slave woman sitting at a table. Kicking the door open with his boot, one of the men rushed into the room and grabbed the lady. A baby cried out in the corner. Another of the raiders grabbed it, blankets and all. Then as silently as they came, the men disappeared with their stolen goods into the night.

When Moses Carver woke up the next morning, he discovered that one of his slaves and her child had been kidnapped. Harnessing a horse, he rode off to town in search of the woman and her baby. He sent word out that he wanted to buy back his slave. Some time passed before he was in contact with the raiders, but by then they had gotten rid of the slave woman, although they still had the child.

Moses agreed to give the men one of his horses if they would let him have the baby. They agreed. So Moses and his wife, Susan, took the sickly baby boy into their home and raised him.

Most people at that time wouldn't have seen much value in the frail slave child. After all, a slave's worth was measured in the amount of work he or she could do for the master, but God had plans—big plans—for the little boy traded for a horse.

The Carvers taught little George to read and write, and they encouraged him when he showed a great interest in plants and other forms of nature.

Many schools would not accept Black students, so George didn't begin attending school until he was 11 years old. For the next 20 years George worked hard to be able to pay for his education. He studied hard, too, and his knowledge about plants grew along with his love for them.

After completing college, George began teaching at Tuskegee Institute, an industrial and agricultural college for Black students. He also continued his work in research and became one of the world's great scientists. Tomorrow we'll learn about some of the things George discovered.

When God looks at us, He doesn't see us as we are. He sees us what we can become with His help. He knows that each of us has great potential.

God took a weak, sickly, little slave child and used him to bless the world. What could He do with you, if you'd give Him your life?

SEPTEMBER

19

The Sky's the Limit

Serve wholeheartedly, as if you were serving the Lord, not men, because you know that the Lord will reward everyone for whatever good he does, whether he is slave or free. Ephesians 6:7, 8, NIV.

"There is no limit to the usefulness of the one who, putting self aside, makes room for the working of the Holy Spirit upon his heart, and lives a life wholly consecrated to God."—E. G. White.

Instead of using his knowledge as a way of becoming rich, George Washington Carver used it to bless others. He taught the farmers in the South to use their land more effectively by rotating crops and using fertilizer.

Then the boll weevil hit Alabama, destroying almost all the cotton. So Dr. Carver encouraged the farmers to grow peanuts and sweet potatoes instead, but that brought on another problem. By using Dr. Carver's ideas, the farmers had been able to produce large crops of peanuts and sweet potatoes, but although the supply had increased, the demand was the same. People could eat only so many peanuts and sweet potatoes, and the farmers' crops began to rot in the fields.

Dr. Carver decided to look for new ways to use the crops, but he didn't work on his own. He turned to the Lord for help. He asked, "God, what is a peanut, and why did You make it?" God answered his question by showing him 285 different products that could be produced from the peanut—cheese, ink, shaving lotions, soap, shampoo, synthetic rubber, and face powder, just to name a few. Carver also found 118 different ways to use sweet potatoes.

George had many opportunities to make money on his ideas and inventions, but he preferred to share his knowledge instead of selling it. Helping people was more important to him than making money.

Dr. Carver's salary at Tuskegee was only $1,500 a year. But when offered well-paying jobs elsewhere, he always turned them down. Thomas Edison, the great inventor, tried to get Carver to work for him, but George replied that God wanted him to stay at the institute. Even when offered a salary of $100,000 a year, Carver turned it down.

In George Washington Carver, God saw someone who was willing to serve others.

God took a poor, orphaned little slave child and turned him into one of the greatest minds of the century. What, do you suppose, He could do with you?

SEPTEMBER

20

The Angel Who Would Be King

We have not received the spirit of the world but the Spirit who is from God, that we may understand what God has freely given us.
1 Corinthians 2:12, NIV.

Back a long time ago Lucifer, the highest angel in all heaven, wanted to be like God. But his great dreams ended up spoiling the whole universe.

You may have wondered just what was so wrong about Lucifer's wanting to become like God. After all, isn't that what you and I should be trying to do? Shouldn't all Christians make it their goal to grow more and more like Jesus every day?

Read the following passage found in Isaiah 14:13, 14. See if you can determine just what Lucifer's goal was. "You said in your heart, 'I will ascend to heaven; I will raise my throne above the stars of God; I will sit enthroned on the mount of assembly, on the utmost heights of the sacred mountain. I will ascend above the tops of the clouds; I will make myself like the Most High' " (NIV).

Lucifer was not contented with his position in heaven. Although he was given leadership over all the other angels, he wanted more authority. But God could not give him any more because Lucifer was just a created being.

Lucifer's problem was that he wanted God's power, but not His character. Lucifer got his priorities mixed up.

We can never be like God when it comes to intelligence, strength, or authority. Just like Lucifer, we, too, are created beings. But when God lives in us through the presence of the Holy Spirit, we can be filled with His character. And that's how we can become like God.

Every morning we need to ask for the presence of the Holy Spirit in our lives. When we open our hearts and minds to Him, He will speak to us and help us make the right choices. He'll encourage us when we're having a bad day. And He'll help us reflect God's love to the people around us.

SEPTEMBER

21

Who's Better?

May he give you the desire of your heart and make all your plans succeed. Psalm 20:4, NIV.

When I was younger, my sister Karen and I didn't get along very well. I remember one afternoon that we spent coloring some pictures. Quite sure of myself, I threw out a challenge to her. "I bet I can color better than you."

"Bet you can't," retorted Karen. So we grabbed our crayons and declared an artistic war.

When we finished our pictures, we went looking for someone to judge our masterpieces. "Which picture is better?" we asked Mom, who was making a pie for supper.

"Why, they're both nice, girls," she said.

We kept pressing for a decision, but Mother wisely refused to choose between the two pictures.

She didn't want us to compare ourselves with each other. She wanted each of us just to do her best.

Dr. Arne, a famous composer from England, was placed in a similar position when he was called upon to choose a winner between two competitive singers. The men, who considered themselves accomplished vocalists, came to the composer and asked him to listen to them and then decide who was better.

When both had finished, Dr. Arne turned to the first and said, "I believe that you're the worst singer I've ever heard in my life!"

"Then," exclaimed the other man clapping his hands in joy, "that means I am the winner."

"I hardly think so," said Dr. Arne. "You can't sing *at all!*"

Whenever we compete in order to beat someone else, we always end up losers in the end. For if the other person beats us, our self-esteem hits bottom. And if we do manage to outdo the other person, we lose our humbleness, and pride takes over.

If you want to compete, compete with yourself. Work to make progress, not to surpass someone else. Set your own personal goals, and then have a good time reaching success.

SEPTEMBER

22

Bullets to Medals

Weeping may remain for a night, but rejoicing comes in the morning.
Psalm 30:5, NIV.

Have you ever doubted God's ability to turn something bad into something good? Have you ever gotten yourself into a situation that you thought was hopeless?

More than 200 years ago the Russian general Rimniksky Suvarov found himself in a seemingly hopeless situation. He and his men, while in the middle of a battle, had been completely outnumbered by the enemy.

Suvarov's men realized that they were headed for defeat. "We have fallen into the enemy's hands," they said.

Suvarov saw things differently. Turning to his soldiers, he threw out a challenge. "Why not say 'The enemy has fallen into *our* hands'?"

Confident that they could win the battle, the general ordered his men to advance, and Suvarov's forces succeeded in defeating the opposing army. After capturing the enemy's citadel, the general sent his soldiers to search out all the ammunition that had been stored there. He took the lead bullets, melted them down, and then remade them into medals for his men. So the lead that was intended to kill Suvarov's soldiers became their badges of honor.

Jesus does the same for us. When Satan sends hardships and troubles our way, Jesus turns them into blessings. What Satan sends to hurt us, Jesus uses for our good.

Just today I talked with a friend who grew up in an abusive home. All her life she wondered what good could come from the beatings her mother used to give her, but during the past week she's seen how God can turn her "bullets" into "medals."

"I find God bringing other abused people into my life," Joan said. "My cousin Esther just moved back to this area in order to mend a broken relationship with her abusive mother. As she talked about how hard it was to forget the past, I knew how to encourage her. As we ended the conversation, Esther said, 'Joan, you'll never know how helpful you have been. It's so good to be able to talk to someone who understands what I have gone through.' "

You may not have been abused, but you probably have had some sad times in your life. Don't become discouraged. Jesus can turn these painful experiences into blessings. Just trust Him.

SEPTEMBER

23

Would You Pass Inspection?

The city does not need the sun or the moon to shine on it, for the glory of God gives it light, and the Lamb is its lamp. . . . Nothing impure will ever enter it, nor will anyone who does what is shameful or deceitful, but only those whose names are written in the Lamb's book of life. Revelation 21:23-27, NIV.

During the summer Tom and I spent in Japan, I became fascinated by the bonsai trees. Bonsai (bone-sigh) trees are miniature trees that stand between two inches to three feet high.

I had a number of souvenirs that I planned to take back to Michigan, and I planned to get a bonsai right before we left. But Tom talked me out of it, and I'm glad he did.

When we flew back to the United States we had to go through customs, a place where inspectors check your luggage. As the man at customs went through our things, I asked, "What would have happened if I had brought a bonsai back with me?"

"I would have confiscated it and destroyed it."

"Why?"

"Because plants and dirt can carry insects that could harm crops grown in the United States. For the good of everyone, we can't take chances." He went on to explain that in the early 1800s gypsy moths were not found in our country, but in 1868 someone coming from France accidentally brought them to Massachusetts. Now the moth has begun to spread through a number of states, destroying forest, shade, and fruit trees wherever it goes.

Right now customs officials are doing their best to make sure that the medfly doesn't become widespread in the United States. For if it does, it could cost taxpayers hundreds of millions of dollars in control costs and increased food prices.

Our country is doing all it can to protect its citizens from the dangers of harmful insects. That's why officials won't allow vacationers to bring in plants and fresh foods.

When Jesus comes again, there will be a number of things that He won't allow in heaven: selfishness, laziness, pride, dishonesty, unclean words and thoughts, unthankfulness, murder, rebellion, and disobedience.

For the sake of those who will live eternally, He must keep out everything that would cause pain and unhappiness. But Jesus isn't just interested in our eternal life. He cares about us even while we're living in a sinful world. That's why He gives us guidelines on how we should live right now.

Something to think about: If you had to pass through customs inspection before you entered heaven, what would the inspector need to remove?

SEPTEMBER

24

The Greatest Sacrifice

So Christ was sacrificed once to take away the sins of many people; and he will appear a second time, not to bear sin, but to bring salvation to those who are waiting for him. Hebrews 9:28, NIV.

Many people have seen *Praying Hands* by Albrecht Dürer, but not many know the story behind the painting.

Five hundred years ago Albrecht and his friend Franz Knigstein were struggling to become artists. Their studies took so much time that they had very little time to earn money for food and housing. So they talked it over and came up with a plan. One of them would continue his art studies full time, and the other would work to support them both.

When they cast lots, Albrecht won. "But don't worry," he assured Franz. "When I am done learning, I will come back. Then you can go to art school, and I will earn a living for both of us."

After a number of years Albrecht returned home, ready to keep the promise he had made to Franz. But it was too late. For by then Franz's hands had become stiff from the hard physical work he had been doing. He could no longer control a paintbrush as he had when he was younger. He had made a great sacrifice so that Albrecht could reach his dream.

Albrecht continued to work as an artist. One day he found Franz kneeling in prayer. Albrecht quietly picked up some paper and began sketching Franz's hands. From that drawing came *Praying Hands.*

We have a plaque of the praying hands in our living room. Whenever ever I see it, I think of Albrecht and Franz. But I also think of Jesus. In my mind I see Him in the Garden of Gethsemane with His hands pressed together in prayer. I try to imagine what it must have been like as He made the decision to sacrifice His life in order to save me from eternal death.

Someday we'll see Jesus' hands, and on them will be the scars left by the nails that hung Him on the cross.

Praying Hands reminds us of the great sacrifice Franz made so that his friend Albrecht could become an artist. Jesus' scarred hands will remind us through all eternity of the sacrifice He made so that we could become His friends.

SEPTEMBER

25

The Perfect Solution

I have set you an example that you should do as I have done for you. John 13:15, NIV.

Today I'd like to give you a little quiz. You know how teachers just love to test their students. Well, I'd like to find out how you'd react to some different situations. Answer the questions truthfully.

1. In the middle of the year, a new student joins your class at school. Randy doesn't dress very nicely, and sometimes comes to school with a dirty face and greasy hair. The other kids make fun of him behind his back. One day you receive an invitation to his birthday party. After checking around at school, you find out that your friends also got an invitation, but they aren't going to the party. What do you do?

2. Pete is a bully. He especially likes to pick on younger kids. One day you see him push one of the first graders off the monkey bars. A few days later he throws the softball at one of the girls and hits her in the head (and then laughs about it). A few innings later he intentionally trips you as you're rounding third. You slide through the dirt on your face. What would you do?

3. Juan has trouble with math. You're the best student in the class. So naturally he asks you for help, but you need the time to get your own work done. What are you going to do the next time he comes to your desk for help?

It's not always easy to decide what you should do, is it?

Now I would like you to read through the questions again. This time ask yourself, "What would Jesus do?"

♦ ♦ ♦

Did you answer any of the questions differently the second time?

Back when I was in academy I read a book titled *In His Steps*. It tells the story of a group of people who decide to pattern their lives after Jesus. Whenever they have a decision to make, they ask themselves, "What would Jesus do?" That one little question completely changed their lives.

There are times when I have a hard time making decisions. When that happens, I ask myself, "What would Jesus do?" It's amazing how quickly I can decide when I see the problem through His eyes instead of my own.

Why not try it and see how it works for you?

SEPTEMBER

26

Keep On Keeping On

Do you see a man skilled in his work? He will serve before kings. Proverbs 22:29, NIV.

Toby the turtle lived in Mr. Rice's garden. Toby loved to eat Mr. Rice's red, ripe tomatoes. Mr. Rice didn't mind Toby helping himself once in a while, but the turtle made quite a pig of himself, and practically destroyed the whole tomato crop.

Not wanting to destroy the turtle, Mr. Rice took Toby for a ride and dropped him off near a nice woods about a mile and a half from the garden. "At last our tomatoes will be safe," said the man to his wife.

But two weeks later Mrs. Rice found a turtle sampling their tomatoes again. "I'm sure that's Toby," she said to her husband.

Mr. Rice didn't believe it, but he decided to try an experiment. He cut a little mark on the turtle's shell. Then he took it to the same woods a mile and a half away.

Again Mr. and Mrs. Rice found a turtle in their garden within two weeks, and this time it had a mark on its shell.

So Mr. Rice picked up Toby and took him a few miles away in the other direction. That time he didn't return. A year later, however, when the tomatoes were just beginning to ripen, guess who showed up? Toby.

"All right, Toby, I guess we're going to have to take some drastic measures," he said to his four-footed uninvited guest. "I'm going to take you so far away that you'll never find my garden again."

So Mr. Rice drove Toby across the Delaware River to a friend's house that was five miles beyond the river. Before he let him go, Mr. Rice made a few more marks on Toby's shell.

Fours years passed, and Toby was all but forgotten—until Mrs. Rice found Toby back in the garden eating tomatoes again. To return to Mr. and Mrs. Rice's tomato patch, Toby had either crossed the bridge or swum the river.

The Rices tried one more time to find Toby a new home. They took him for another ride, six miles in a different direction. This time it took Toby only two years to make his way back to his favorite eating spot.

Do you give up when things get tough? Or do you persist until you've accomplished what you've set out to do?

Just think what you could achieve if you had Toby's determination. Don't let a turtle show you up. Go for it!

SEPTEMBER

27

Impossible but True

They were longing for a better country—a heavenly one. Therefore God is not ashamed to be called their God, for he has prepared a city for them. Hebrews 11:16, NIV.

Do any of you play the flute? If so, you owe a debt of gratitude to Theobald Boehm, a German musician who is known as the father of the modern flute.

Back before 1835, flutists had a terrible time playing certain scales. The fingering was awkward, if not impossible. So Boehm set about to design a flute that could play easily in all keys. When he was satisfied with the finished product, Boehm traveled to London and Paris to introduce his new flute to the music world. While in Paris he stopped to see the great composer Rossini. He hoped that Rossini would give his approval to the new instrument.

When Boehm arrived, Rossini was shaving in his dressing room. So Boehm pulled out his flute and began to play all types of scales, arpeggios, and trills in one key and then another. Then he dashed off the scale of D-flat, which had been one of those "impossible" keys.

Rossini burst out of his dressing room, his face covered with shaving cream, and cried out, "You cannot play that!"

"But I am," said Boehm calmly.

"I don't care if you are," retorted the composer furiously. "It's utterly impossible."

Rossini's response reminds me of how we sometimes feel about heaven. God may have promised us that heaven is going to be a big improvement over earth, but it still seems impossible.

I have to admit that I have a hard time imagining what heaven will be like. I mean, what are we going to do for billions and billions of years?

Just because we don't have heaven all figured out, we shouldn't assume that life there will be dull. We shouldn't take Rossini's attitude and say, "If I can't visualize something, then it just can't be."

Whenever Jesus takes something away, it's always because He has something better for us. So when He comes to take us away from this earth, you can be sure that what He has waiting is going to be fantastic!

SEPTEMBER

28

Beyond Our Wildest Dreams

But in keeping with his promise we are looking forward to a new heaven and a new earth, the home of righteousness.
2 Peter 3:13, NIV.

How would you feel if your mother woke you up this morning and said, "Instead of going to school today, I want you to just have fun. Do whatever you feel like doing. This is your day."

Would that be great or what?

Well, that's what I imagine heaven to be like. Let me explain what I mean. You see, every day we live we spend most of our time maintaining. We sleep because our bodies get worn out and tired. We eat because we'd die without proper nutrition. We take a shower because we get dirty.

But there's more. We pick up our rooms (at least some of us do) because they get messy. We take out the trash because it starts piling up and giving off a strange smell. We wash our clothes because they get dirty.

Do you get the idea?

What would it be like to have all your time for fun? No chores, no school, no body hygiene. Just fun. Every day. All day. For ever and ever.

Well, that's what I believe it's going to be like in heaven.

I can imagine some of you saying, "But Mrs. Coffee, what am I going to do after I've gotten tired of riding a lion or going deep-sea diving without gear?"

Now let me ask *you* a question. How many visits would it take to Disney World and Epcot Center before you got bored? My guess is that you could spend hundreds of hours wandering around the Magic Kingdom and Epcot Center and love every minute.

If a man-made amusement park built on swampland in Florida could entertain you for days and days, think how much fun you could have in a God-made amusement universe!

Heaven is beyond our wildest dreams. Singer Keith Green once pointed out that God spent just six days creating our earth, but He's been working on heaven for thousands of years.

Won't it be exciting to walk through the gates and see heaven for the very first time? I don't know what God has ready for us up there, but I can hardly wait to find out. How about you?

SEPTEMBER

29

A Killing Fortune

It is for freedom that Christ has set us free. Stand firm, then, and do not let yourselves be burdened again by a yoke of slavery.
Galatians 5:1, NIV.

A fool and his money are soon parted."

Have you ever seen people lining up in stores as they wait to buy lottery tickets? Many people believe that their lives would be completely happy if they could just win the big jackpot.

Youssouf the Terrible Turk didn't play the lottery, but he did win a fortune. The 300-pound wrestler came over to the United States from Turkey in search of fame and fortune. He soon became the most popular wrestler in the business.

People from all over the country flocked to see him crush his opponents, one after another. Youssouf was truly a man of strength. But he had one weakness. He loved gold.

Back when the Terrible Turk competed on the wrestling mat, gold coins were part of the American currency, and each time Youssouf won a match, he insisted that his share of the winnings be paid in gold. He accepted nothing but gold. As soon as he was paid, Youssouf would stuff his gold coins into the leather money belt that he always wore around his waist.

One day Youssouf suddenly announced that he was retiring from wrestling and moving back to his native land. He didn't need to compete any longer. He had all the gold he wanted. So Youssouf the Terrible Turk boarded a large steamship and headed for Turkey. Around his waist he carried his money belt filled with gold.

On the second night out, the ship ran into violent weather. Water started filling the boat, and it began to sink. Passengers fled to the upper deck. The ship's crew lowered lifeboats into the water.

Clutching his precious money belt, which was strapped around his waist, Youssouf ran across the deck. Fear showed in his eyes as he searched for a way of escape. Spying a lifeboat adrift on the water just a few feet from the big ship, the strong man dived into the ocean. But as Youssouf started to swim for the small boat, the weight of his gold coins pulled him below the waves, and he was never seen again.

Youssouf made gold his god. And it destroyed him. That's what always happens when we don't put God first in our lives.

Something to think about: Is there anything in your life that's pulling you down today?

SEPTEMBER

30

We Are Weak, but He Is Strong

All the people were amazed and said to each other, "What is this teaching? With authority and power he gives orders to evil spirits and they come out!" Luke 4:36, NIV.

Joe Greenstein, a man who lived in Brooklyn, New York, once offered $1,000 to anyone who could copy the feats of strength that he was able to do. In case you're interested in taking him up on the offer, here's a list of Joe's accomplishments. He

—shattered a dog chain fastened around his chest.

—drove a spike through 28 layers of sheet metal and a 2-inch board all at once with his hand.

—bit a spike in half with his teeth.

—bent a steel rod in half with his bare hands.

—twisted a horseshoe into a W.

Not bad. Especially when you consider that Joe was 82 at the time.

The type of strength Joe had does impress people, but physical strength has its limits. When it comes to fighting Satan and sin, the mightiest strongman and the weakest kindergartner are in the same boat. We may want to give up sin, but in our own strength we'll always fail. We just don't have what it takes to defeat the power of temptation. If we did, then Jesus could have stayed in heaven. If we were capable of handling our own sin problem, then He wouldn't have had to die for us.

All we can do is choose who will have control over our lives. If we choose Jesus, then He'll put in us a hatred for sin. He'll give us a change of attitude. On the other hand, if we don't choose to follow Jesus, we will be doomed to be Satan's slaves. And we'll have no other choice but to lead a life of sin.

Don't think that you must clean up your life before you come to Jesus. Don't wait until you've gotten rid of your bad habits before you give your life to Him. Because without Him, you're helpless when it comes to fighting sin. You could be as physically strong as Joe, but you and every single other human being are still totally helpless in the battle against sin.

Satan is a spirit being, and only another spirit being can fight him away from us. When he begins to tempt you to do something wrong, call on God for help. He'll take over and send Satan on his way.

OCTOBER

1

Weak Support

Rain came down, the streams rose, and the winds blew and beat against that house; yet it did not fall, because it had its foundation on the rock. Matthew 7:24, 25, NIV.

When architect Sir Christopher Wren revealed his plans for an unusual church dome that he was designing, he received severe criticism. "It'll never work," other architects cried. "If it doesn't have more support, it'll surely fall down."

Finally the people responsible for building the church gave in to public opinion. "Put in two supporting pillars," they ordered Wren.

The famous architect angrily objected. "I know what I'm doing. There is absolutely no reason to use pillars." The church leaders wouldn't back down, so Wren had to add the pillars. End of discussion. Sir Christopher Wren reluctantly did as he was told. He knew the pillars weren't necessary, but if they wanted pillars, then he'd give them pillars.

Fifty years passed. The dome needed to be repainted, so workmen set up scaffolding and crawled to the top of the dome to begin their touch-up work. Only then did the world discover that the pillars Wren had been forced to add did not reach the top. They were short by two feet. Everyone had assumed that the pillars went all the way up, but in fact, they supported nothing.

Do you remember the song about the foolish man who built his house upon the sand? The song came from a story that Jesus told about two builders who chose different foundations for their homes. The wise man built his on rock. When the rain came down, the house stood firm. The foolish man set his house on sand. After a good cloudburst, his foundation gave way and his house collapsed.

The houses represent our lives. The foundations represent whom or what we trust in.

Foolish people build their lives on things like good looks, power, wealth, and intelligence. And, like the pillars in Wren's church, everything appears to be fine, but when serious problems arise, the foolish people find out that their supports are worthless.

Those who build their lives on their trust in God will never be disappointed, for no matter how bad the storms of life may get, God will never let them down. Their Foundation is sure.

OCTOBER

2

I've Got the Joy, Joy, Joy, Joy

The joy of the Lord is your strength. Nehemiah 8:10, NIV.

When I was a little girl, my grandpa taught me a very important lesson. We were seated at the kitchen table when Papa asked me a question. "What is happiness, Renee?"

I thought for a few seconds and then answered, "It's a good feeling a person gets."

Papa smiled. "That's exactly right. All are looking for happiness, but not many will ever find it. Do you know why?"

I shook my head no.

"Well, that's because they don't know how to spell it."

Right then I decided that my grandpa wasn't very smart. I was only in the third grade, and I could spell *happiness.*

"Papa, almost anybody can spell *happiness.*"

"Not really," he said. "Many people think they know how to spell it, but they don't. For instance, some spell it m-o-n-e-y. Others spell it p-o-w-e-r. But there is only one way to spell it."

He drew three letters on a piece of paper. "J-O-Y. That's how you spell happiness. What's the first letter, Renee?"

"J."

"That's right. And the J stands for Jesus. He deserves first place in our lives. Next comes the O, which stands for others. At the end comes Y, which stands for you. When we put Jesus first in our lives, other people second, and ourselves last, we'll have the happiness that we're looking for."

When Jesus becomes Lord of our lives, He helps us feel good about ourselves. And only when we feel good about ourselves can we care about others.

Putting ourselves last doesn't mean that other people are more important that we are. It just means that instead of focusing on ourselves, we'll be looking for ways to show kindness to the people around us.

If you find yourself missing out on happiness, check to see how you're spelling it.

OCTOBER

3

Expert Advice

Ask the former generations and find out what their fathers learned. . . . Will they not instruct you and tell you? Will they not bring forth words from their understanding? Job 8:8-10, NIV.

We can always learn something from our own mistakes, but it's a lot smarter to learn from somebody else's."

A few years ago my husband and I bought a van. When we first saw it, we said, "That's just what we need." Boy, were we wrong!

If we had been smart, we would have done a little more checking before we became the proud owners of a cream and white VW van. We should have checked some magazines that give advice on which cars are good and which aren't. But we didn't. Unfortunately we relied on our own judgment rather than the judgment of people who know a lot about cars. For the next three years the van spent most of its life in the repair shop. It seemed that the more money we spent in repairing it, the more the van broke down.

One day as I was thumbing through the special automobile issue of *Consumer Reports,* I saw a page entitled "Cars to Avoid." Curious, I checked to see if our van was listed. Sure enough, there it was, right down to the exact year and model.

I tell you this story to illustrate the folly of not taking the advice of people who know more than you do.

The worst result to come out of our experience with the van was that we wasted a lot of money on it, but bad decisions often result in much more serious results. The decisions you are making today will help shape the rest of your life. Right decisions will lay a foundation for a successful and happy life, but wrong choices could destroy the dreams and hopes you have for your future.

That's why God gave you parents. Not to take away your fun or make life miserable, but to help you avoid the troubles that lie ahead. Parents have lived a lot longer than you have, and they've seen much more of life. Besides, they've made plenty of mistakes themselves, so their advice is pretty valuable.

Why not learn from their mistakes instead of making your own?

OCTOBER

4

Happy on the Outside, Crying on the Inside

My soul is downcast within me; therefore I will remember you. Psalm 42:6, NIV.

Doctor, my life is a mess. I can't sleep or eat. I worry all the time. I don't even want to be around my friends anymore. And when I'm like this, they don't want to be around me, either. I feel so bad that sometimes I wish I could just lie down and die. Is there any hope for a person like me? Can you help me find a reason for living?"

It was easy for the doctor to see that the patient was suffering from deep depression. "I'll do everything I possibly can to help you," the doctor replied. "First, I'd like to give you a routine checkup. We need to find out if a physical problem might be causing you to feel so depressed." So the doctor checked the patient carefully, but he couldn't find a single thing wrong with him. The man was in excellent physical shape.

After scribbling some notes on the man's chart, the doctor turned to him and said, "I'm going to give you a prescription that you must follow carefully. I think you need to get your mind off yourself. So tonight I want you to forget your problems and have a good time.

"There's a circus in town this week, and the clown act is wonderful. Why don't you go to the circus and learn to laugh again? If anyone can lift your spirits, Grimaldi the Clown can."

The patient shook his head sadly. "I'm afraid that won't work," he replied.

"And why not?" asked the doctor.

"Because I *am* Grimaldi the Clown."

Every night Grimaldi put on a happy face and went out to entertain his audience, but his happy face was just painted on to cover the sadness he felt down in his heart.

Could there be boys or girls at your school who also wear painted-on smiles? Is it possible that some of the biggest classroom clowns are just pretending to be happy? Could they really be lonely and sad?

We can't fix all the bad things that happen to people, but we can be kind to others. We can smile and be friendly. We can let people know that we care about them.

OCTOBER

5

Eternal Choices

By faith Moses, when he had grown up, refused to be known as the son of Pharaoh's daughter. He chose to be mistreated along with the people of God rather than to enjoy the pleasures of sin for a short time. Hebrews 11:24, 25, NIV.

Some years ago, Charrington's was one of the largest breweries in England. Fred Charrington belonged to the wealthy family that owned the beer company. His father looked forward to having Fred on the staff someday, but something happened to change the direction of Fred's life.

Through the friendship of a local pastor, Fred became a Christian. Right away he felt a need to follow Jesus' example of service. So he and a friend started a school for the children in one of London's slum districts.

One evening as Fred and his friend were leaving the school, they saw a poor, ragged woman walk to the bar across the street. Her two small children cowered at her side as she stood at the door begging her husband for some money for food. But the drunken man only shoved his wife down the steps and went back to his drinking.

Fred looked up and saw a sign with the Charrington name in big gold letters hanging in the front window of the bar. *I will never have anything to do with the Charrington Brewery again,* he vowed to himself.

The next morning Fred announced to his family that he wanted no part of the family business. Fred's decision was not an easy one, for it cost him a yearly income of $200,000 and his share of the business, which was worth more than $1 million.

But money wasn't the only thing that Fred lost. He also lost the love and support of his family. They treated him as though he were dead.

Fred moved to Stepney Green, one of the poorest parts of east London. There he turned his efforts to the temperance work. Instead of working in a company that produced beer, he did all he could to encourage people to stay away from alcohol.

Times were hard for Fred. He had very few worldly goods. But he was happy. And his conscience was clear.

Like Moses, Fred chose to give up worldly pleasures so he could follow God. Would you have done the same if you had been in his place?

OCTOBER

6

Wanted: Men and Women

Blessed are all who fear the Lord, who walk in his ways. Psalm 128:1, NIV.

"The greatest want of the world is the want of men [and women]—men who will not be bought or sold, men who in their inmost souls are true and honest, men who do not fear to call sin by its right name, men whose conscience is as true to duty as the needle to the pole, men who will stand for the right though the heavens fall."—E. G. White.

Fred Charrington's family thought that within time he would come to his senses and return to work for the family brewery, but Fred remained true to his beliefs. He wanted no part of a business that brought nothing but pain and suffering to the people who supported it.

One day Fred's mother ventured to the shabby apartment house where Fred was living. She missed her son and wanted to see how he was doing. She was shocked at Fred's poor living conditions. Hurrying home, she called a local store and had them deliver some furniture to his apartment.

Fred's father, on the other hand, only grew angrier and angrier at his son. In a final show of displeasure, the older man called his lawyer and told him to remove Fred's name from his will.

Neither his mother's kindness nor his father's anger could change Fred's attitude toward the family brewery business. Fred continued to stand for Christian principles. He continued to fight against drinking.

Years later when Fred's father lay dying, he sent a messenger to Fred's apartment. "Your father wants to you to come home right away," the messenger said.

When Fred walked up to the family mansion, a servant ushered him into his father's room. "Hello, Father," said Fred nervously.

Mr. Charrington didn't say anything for a while, but when he turned to his son, Fred could tell that the anger was gone. "You were right, Fred," the old man said softly. "You chose the better way of life."

When we live according to God's principles, other people may treat us unfairly. They may make fun of us and even hurt us. When we follow the Bible, life won't always be easy, but it will always be the better way of life.

OCTOBER

7

Passing On the Blame

[Satan] was a murderer from the beginning, not holding to the truth, for there is no truth in him. When he lies, he speaks his native language, for he is a liar and the father of lies. John 8:44, NIV.

When the townspeople of Freiburg, Germany, heard the approach of the war planes the night of May 10, 1940, they didn't pay much attention. There was no reason that the enemy would want to bomb Freiburg. It contained no soldiers or ammunition warehouses.

But suddenly bombs peppered the sky as the planes unloaded their destructive forces. People screamed as explosion after explosion tore apart the quiet little town, destroying buildings and many lives.

The next day Adolf Hitler announced to the world that the Allied forces had broken their promise not to harm open cities. "Five German bombs will fall for every enemy bomb," he vowed, and he set about to keep his promise. Nazi war planes flew into the Netherlands and destroyed Rotterdam. Next they moved on to England, where they bombed Dover, Portsmouth, London, and Coventry before Hitler's reign of terror ended when he committed suicide on April 30, 1945.

It was some time before the truth finally came out. It was not the Western Allies who had bombed Freiburg in 1940. The German air force had destroyed the town. Field Marshall Hermann Goring, one of Hitler's righthand men, had ordered a bombing raid on Dijon, France, but the planes had gotten lost in heavy fog. Thinking they had reached their destination, they dropped the bombs, only to find out later that they had bombed one of their own cities. Not willing to admit the mistake, Hitler and Goring covered up the blunder and blamed the Allies. Then the two used the incident to help justify the brutal attacks that followed.

Do Hitler's actions remind you of someone else who is at work destroying people today? When bad things happen to people, Satan tries to convince them that God is responsible for all the trouble in the world. He says, "If God really cared, do you think He'd let that happen?" Or he tries to get us to believe that God sends troubles to punish us for disobeying. Insurance companies even label certain disasters as "acts of God." What a bunch of lies!

Only when officials studied the records at the Institute for Current History at Munich, Germany, did they find out the truth about who had bombed Freiburg. The only way we can learn the truth about Satan is to study the Bible.

OCTOBER

8

Mind Pollution

It is better to heed a wise man's rebuke than to listen to the song of fools. Ecclesiastes 7:5, NIV.

"What is wrong with Rachel?" Father asked Mother as he came downstairs for breakfast. "I asked her if she wanted a ride to school this morning, and she ran into her bedroom and slammed the door."

Mother set the cereal boxes on the table and poured the orange juice. "I have no idea."

"Well, maybe she's just in a bad mood. Let's give her some time and see if things improve."

So they dropped the subject for the time being. But when 12-year-old Rachel's attitude continued to get worse, Mr. and Mrs. Young decided to get to the bottom of the problem.

"When did you begin to notice the change in Rachel?" Mr. Young asked his wife as they were talking one evening.

"About a month ago, I think."

"What happened a month ago that might have brought on Rachel's change?"

Mrs. Young thought back. "Well, she had her birthday about a month ago."

"That's right. We gave Rachel a new clock radio."

"The radio. H'mmm. I wonder if the radio could be the source of her problems," said Mrs. Young. "Rachel doesn't listen to music during the day, but she wakes up to music every morning. I think I'm going to do a little checking tomorrow to see what she hears when the radio comes on at 6:30."

So the next morning Mrs. Young peeked in Rachel's room right as the clock radio came on. It took only a few seconds of listening to realize that the music Rachel was starting her day with was hard rock.

That evening Rachel's parents talked with their daughter about her change of attitude, and they told her about their concern for the type of music she was listening to.

"Well, Mom, when I got my new radio, I didn't change the dial. That's just the music that came on."

"Then let's try an experiment," Father suggested. "Why don't you choose another station—one that plays some soft, quiet music. Then see how you feel after hearing that when you wake up."

So Rachel tried what her father suggested, and what a difference the calm music made! Within a few days her parents started seeing some changes, and within a few weeks she was back to being her happy, cheerful self again.

OCTOBER

9

For Your Information

The fruit of righteousness will be peace; the effect of righteousness will be quietness and confidence forever. Isaiah 32:17, NIV.

Does it matter what kind of music you listen to? Does music affect your attitude, just like it affected Rachel's?

Before you brace yourself for a lecture about the evils of rock music, relax. My purpose is not to tell you all rock music is bad. What I would like to do today is just give you an idea of how music affects people. After attending a seminar by musician Wolfgang Stefani, I learned a lot about the power of music on the body.

First off, let's talk about noise.

When I visited the FBI Building in Washington, D.C., I watched one of the agents do some target practice. Before he picked up his gun, he put on a special headset to protect his ears from the loud noise.

Have you ever been at an airport and watched one of the ground crew direct a plane to its parking space? Did you notice that he or she wore ear protectors?

Noise is a big problem. Different countries have passed laws to control noise in the workplace because so many are having to retire early because of deafness. Noise is measured in decibels. For instance, a normal conversation runs at about 60 decibels. A vacuum cleaner, at about 90 decibels. Most people could listen to vacuum noise for about eight hours before it began to damage their hearing. But a circular saw running at 100 decibels will cause damage in less than one hour.

Noise is one of the problems with rock music. Can you guess how loud the music is at rock concerts? Sometimes it's as high as 130 decibels. This means that a listener can listen only for three to four seconds before hearing damage results. You may not go to rock concerts, but do you ever wear headphones when you listen to music? Then you may be listening to music that is as high as 115 decibels.

When Sweden's navy was trying to detect a Russian submarine that had ventured into an unauthorized area, they called on their youngest sailors to man the monitoring devises. They chose them because they needed men with good hearing to pick up the submarine's signals. But the young sailors failed to hear the sub, and it got away. Later the navy found out why the sailors had not been able to detect the submarine. Every one of them had hearing damage caused by the music they had been listening to.

Do you value your ability to hear? If so, you may want to turn down the volume of your stereo.

OCTOBER

10

And the Beat Goes On

For the breath of the ruthless is like a storm driving against a wall and like the heat of the desert. You silence the uproar of foreigners; as heat is reduced by the shadow of a cloud, so the song of the ruthless is stilled. Isaiah 25:4, 5, NIV.

Another important element of music is rhythm.

Pretend that you have a toothache. Your mother drives you to the dentist's office. How do you feel as you get out of the car and walk into the waiting room? You'd like to run in the opposite direction—right?

Well, as you take your seat to wait your turn, you happen to notice two things: the dentist office odor and the music. Can you hear that music in your head? It's probably something like "Moon River" or a song from *The Sound of Music*. Most people call it elevator music. It's no accident that dentists play light, quiet songs. They know that most of the people sitting in the office are nervous. They also know that soft, easy-listening music helps calm people down.

What if you walked into the dentist's office and heard some heavy metal music blaring through the speakers? You'd get so uptight that you'd probably be ready to pull out your tooth yourself.

Rhythms really have a strong influence on our bodies and how we feel. In fact, of the five basic elements of music, rhythm (or beat) affects us the most.

Our bodies have their own sets of internal rhythms, and these rhythms can be changed by the music we listen to. Musical beats can affect the blood pressure, digestion, pupil dilation, brain waves, hormone production, pulse, breathing, and the electrical impulses of the skin.

For instance, each minute our hearts beat about 60 to 90 times. But most rock music rhythms are between 180 and 240 beats a minute, which is about three times faster. When we hear fast music, our hearts begin to race.

There's nothing wrong with a strong rhythm. The problem comes when the beat doesn't let up. Strong, fast rhythms are often used in places such as Haiti and Africa, where devil worship is practiced. At the highest point, the drums beat between seven and 12 times a second. When the brain rhythms reach eight beats a second, the people lose control of their bodies, and the devil takes possession of them. It is during those times that people will do things like cutting their bodies with knives or walking through fire.

Rhythms are very powerful—for good and for bad. What is your music doing to you?

OCTOBER

11

Following the Crowd

Will you keep to the old path that evil men have trod? Job 22:15, NIV.

Have you ever heard of the processionary caterpillar? It seems that these little creatures like to follow one another.

Once a man decided to see just how long they would march behind each other. So he took a large flowerpot and set it on a table. He placed a number of the caterpillars on the edge of the pot and watched to see what they would do.

They started inching along the rim, one after another, each one following the one ahead. Hour after hour they marched along. The man decided that by then they must be tired and hungry. So he placed some food inside the flowerpot to see if he could tempt them to break rank, but the little creatures just kept parading around and around.

The caterpillars never stopped. They kept inching along, following the leader. After a few days the caterpillars grew so weak that they could hardly move. They needed rest. They needed food. But not one broke away from the crowd. Instead they all died.

Do you ever act like a processionary caterpillar? Do you insist on following the crowd, even when the crowd is going nowhere?

Some students don't study because their friends don't value good grades. Instead of setting goals for the future and learning all they can, they follow the crowd that is going nowhere in life.

Do you ever act like a processionary caterpillar? Do you join in with your friends even when the things they're doing are self-destructive? Do you set aside your values in order to be accepted? Do you participate in things that dishonor God and make you lose your self-respect?

None of the caterpillars were willing to break away and go after some food, and so they all died. If only one had been willing to change direction, maybe the others would have followed.

It's not easy to break away from the group, but sometimes it's the right thing to do. Do you have enough courage to stand alone?

OCTOBER

12

Running Ahead of God

The troubles of my heart have multiplied; free me from my anguish. . . . Guard my life and rescue me; let me not be put to shame, for I take refuge in you. Psalm 25:17-20, NIV.

Mrs. Swane buried her face in her hands. "What are we going to do?" she moaned. "The house needs a new roof. Last month the furnace needed repair. When are the problems ever going to end?"

Her house was nearly 100 years old, and it constantly needed repairs.

"Sell it and get something smaller, something newer," friends suggested. But Mrs. Swane had lived there all her life. The house had belonged to her family for three generations—her grandfather had built it. Selling the house would be like selling a member of the family. No, she couldn't do that.

But how could they ever afford to pay for the repairs? The Swanes were both retired, and they had little money in their savings account.

Instead of praying about the problem, Mrs. Swane continued to worry about it. One night as she was lying in bed, she got an idea. *No, I couldn't possibly do that,* she said to herself. But as she continued to think over her options, her idea seemed to make sense: she could burn down the house.

I know that burning down a house is against the law, she thought, *but I'm going to have to do it. I can't sell the house to someone else. But we can't afford to live here, either. Yes, we'll just have to burn it down. That way we can collect money from the insurance company and buy a new house.*

So Mrs. Swane began to make plans on how she would burn down her house. What about all the things they had in the house—family pictures, good china dishes, books, and furniture? If she took the family possessions out of the house ahead of time, she could save them from being destroyed, but the firemen would suspect arson if the burned house contained no personal property. No, she'd have to let most of her things burn in the fire, but she'd save out her most valuable keepsakes.

Although her conscience bothered her, Mrs. Swane decided that she'd have to go through with her plans. Tomorrow.

God has a solution to every problem we face, but sometimes we don't bother to ask Him for His advice. Like Mrs. Swane, we decide to handle our problems on our own. But instead of solving our problems, we just create more.

Did Mrs. Swane burn her house down? You'll find out tomorrow.

OCTOBER

13

Up in Flames

For I will forgive their wickedness and will remember their sins no more. Hebrews 8:12, NIV.

The sky was still black when the Swanes woke up. Mrs. Swane dressed quickly, while her husband went to the garage for the cans of gasoline.

As she waited for her husband to return, Mrs. Swane walked through her beloved house, stopping for a moment at each room. The last room she visited was the playroom, where her two sons had spent many happy hours.

"I'm back," Mr. Swane called from the kitchen.

Without a word the Swanes each picked up a can and started through the house, pouring gasoline over the wood floors.

"Now?" asked Mr. Swane.

Mrs. Swane could only nod her head yes.

Mr. Swane pulled a lighter from his pocket. Picking up a newspaper, he lit one edge. "Run!" he yelled as he threw the burning paper into the living room.

The gasoline exploded into flames. The house went up like a torch. By the time the fire department arrived, the house was beyond help.

The fire investigation went smoothly, and the Swanes received a check from their insurance company. *We're going to get away with it,* Mrs. Swane told herself.

The Swanes may have fooled the investigators, but they couldn't fool their consciences. The guilt and remorse for what they had done began to disrupt their lives completely. In fact, their grief became so intense that they finally began attending a grief seminar.

After a few meetings they shared with Pastor Edwards what they had done. "We can't keep the money, Pastor," they said. "But if we try to give it back, we'll probably end up in prison."

The pastor contacted the insurance agency for them. After hearing their story, the company promised to forgive the Swanes if the insurance check was returned.

They now live in a little house trailer. They have very few possessions, for most everything was destroyed in the fire. But the Swanes have peace of mind.

If you are carrying guilt for something you have done wrong, don't wait to make things right. Confess to Jesus what you have done.

OCTOBER

14

Jumping to Tragic Conclusions

But we are hoping for something that we do not have yet. We are waiting for it patiently. Romans 8:25, ICB.

"The secret of peace is trust."—John Figgis.

People do senseless things when they think there's no hope for the future.

A man in Detroit, Michigan, believed he had Lyme disease, an infection transmitted by ticks. He didn't go to a doctor to find out; he just diagnosed himself.

So when his wife took sick, he assumed that he had passed on the disease to her, and also assumed that they both were going to die.

According to the Detroit *News*, the man became so desperate that he decided to end their lives. First he shot his wife as she was sleeping. Then he turned the gun on himself and committed suicide. In the note found by police, the man wrote that the murder-suicide was the only way out of their awful situation.

The sad part of the story is that Lyme disease isn't contagious or fatal. If diagnosed in time, it can be treated with antibiotics. And even if one doesn't receive treatment, he or she is not doomed to die.

The poor man acted very much like the children of Israel. Each time they faced an obstacle, they lost all hope. Instead of waiting to see what the Lord was going to do to solve their problem, they thought the worst.

One of my favorite passages is found on page 330 of *The Desire of Ages*. It says: "Our heavenly Father has a thousand ways to provide for us, of which we know nothing. Those who accept the one principle of making the service and honor of God supreme will find perplexities vanish, and a plain path before their feet."

Even if we can't see a way out of our problems, God is already at work solving them for us. All we have to do is trust Him, and the more practice we get, the easier it will be to trust Him the next time.

OCTOBER

15

Never Say Never

As the heavens are higher than the earth, so are my ways higher than your ways and my thoughts than your thoughts. Isaiah 55:9, NIV.

Do people ever ask you what you want to be when you grow up? People used to ask me that when I was in school. I always said, "I haven't decided yet, but I know one thing—I'll never be a teacher or a secretary." Boy, did I have to eat my words! When I graduated from college, I had a major in secretarial science and minors in education and business. To this day I don't exactly know how I ended up as a teacher, but I think God had something to do with it.

It's hard to remember back to the time when I laughed at the idea of becoming a teacher. I don't know why I was so against teaching because I love being a teacher.

So what does this have to do with you? Well, do you ever say things like—

"Why should I practice the piano? I'll never play it when I get older."

"Learning English is a big waste of time. What difference does it make whether or not I speak correctly?"

"Study my Sabbath school lesson every night? I don't care about learning what went on thousands of years ago. All I care about is right now"?

"The nature classes at summer camp are sooooo boring! Why can't I just take craft classes?"

You're young, and the person you are today is not the person you'll be five years from now. And the person you are when you're 20 will not be the person you'll be when you're 35.

Because you'll do a lot of changing as you grow up, it's a good idea to take advantage of as many opportunities as you can. You may not be interested in some things right now, but give yourself a few years, and who knows—maybe you'll find yourself enjoying things you used to find uninteresting.

This is especially true when it comes to spiritual things. I remember learning what seemed like thousands of memory verses at Sabbath school, Vacation Bible School, and church school. At the time I didn't see much value in all that memory work. Now that I am older, I'm thankful that I tucked away those words of God in my mind.

God has a special plan for your life if you're willing to cooperate with Him. When a new opportunity comes up, take advantage of it. It just might be part of His design for your life.

OCTOBER

16

Crime and Punishment

No discipline seems pleasant at the time, but painful. Later on, however, it produces a harvest of righteousness and peace for those who have been trained by it. Hebrews 12:11, NIV.

How do you react when your parents have to discipline you because you have done something wrong? Have you ever resented their interference in your life?

During lunchtime at school Steve, one of my students, was telling his friends how his father had punished him for disobeying. "First Dad told me, 'Steve, this is going to hurt me more than it will hurt you.' Then he grounded me for a whole month." Steve shook his head. "I don't know how *he's* feeling, but all I know is that *I'm* the one who can't ride his motorcycle for four weeks."

Steve was right. His father wasn't the one who'd lost his privileges, but that didn't mean that his father wasn't feeling bad about what had happened.

I know as a teacher that at times I'm tempted to let a student get away with something he or she shouldn't be doing. It would be so much easier just to pretend that it wasn't happening. But I know that if I don't correct the student, the problem will just get worse.

Eli had a problem with discipline. No doubt he loved his sons, but for some reason he didn't correct them when they disobeyed. When Hophni and Phinehas grew up, they became priests, but their rebellion against God brought disgrace on the priesthood. Eli did not do his job as a parent, and God eventually had to let both sons reap what they'd sown.

Parents have an enormous responsibility to God and society. Your parents have been entrusted with the life of another human being—you. And although you probably don't appreciate it when they resort to discipline, it's the most loving action they can take.

Something to think about: If children were never corrected by their parents, what type of persons would they grow up to become? Would you want one or more of such people as your friends? marriage partner? employees? or boss?

OCTOBER

17

Looking to Jesus

Let us fix our eyes on Jesus, the author and perfecter of our faith. Hebrews 12:2, NIV.

Chet attended a small one-room country church school. Chet always wished there were more kids in his school, but he never thought of leaving and going to public school. Especially when he had a teacher like Mr. Dawson.

Mr. Dawson was the neatest person Chet had ever known. He had a way of making school a fun place to be. He also shared Chet's love of sports, and he had a great sense of humor. Best of all, he was a dedicated Christian.

But Chet noticed a change in Mr. Dawson right after spring vacation. Mr. Dawson wasn't his usual happy self. Chet found out why a few days later.

On Friday just after the dismissal prayer, Mr. Dawson asked the class to sit down. He said he had an important announcement to make. "I really have enjoyed teaching you students," he began. "But I won't be coming back on Monday morning."

Chet couldn't believe his ears. Mr. Dawson wasn't coming back? The students sat in stunned silence as Mr. Dawson continued. "I have resigned from my teaching position. My wife and I are getting a divorce."

Someone in the back of the room began to cry.

"I just want you to know that I care about each one of you very much, and I'll never forget you. You'd better go now. Your rides are waiting."

Chet got out of his seat and shuffled toward the exit. As he walked by Mr. Dawson, he tried to say something, but the words wouldn't come.

When Chet broke the news to his mother, Mrs. Christy put her arm around her son. "It's hard when people you care about let you down, isn't it?"

Chet nodded. "I just can't believe it, Mom. How could he get a divorce? He always told us that marriage was forever. Doesn't he believe that anymore?"

"Chet, Mr. Dawson is human just like the rest of us. You probably thought he was perfect, but he isn't. No one but God is, and that's why we can't look to other people as our examples." Mrs. Christy paused, then continued. "People are always going to disappoint us, but God will never let us down. We must build our faith on our relationship with Him, no matter what others do."

"I'll never forget Mr. Dawson, Mom," said Chet. He sat for a few moments, then added, "Let's pray for him tonight at worship."

OCTOBER

18

Our Hope Is in Christ

May the God of hope fill you with all joy and peace as you trust in him, so that you may overflow with hope by the power of the Holy Spirit. Romans 15:13, NIV.

Chet and his classmates missed their teacher. They kept hoping to see the familiar red van sitting in the parking lot, but they never saw Mr. Dawson again.

The school board hired a new teacher. Mr. Clark was OK, but he just wasn't Mr. Dawson.

Within a few weeks Chet's sorrow at losing his teacher turned to anger. "I hate him," he muttered one evening as he was helping his mother.

Mother looked at Chet in surprise. "Hate who?"

"Mr. Dawson."

"You're pretty angry, aren't you?"

"Yeah. How could he let us down like that?"

Mother didn't reply right away, but then she turned to Chet and said, "When you were just a baby, our church had a minister whom we all loved. But at church board one night he announced that he was resigning. He no longer believed the teachings of the Adventist Church.

"For a short time afterward I began to wonder whether or not he was right. After all, he was a minister. He knew the Bible. So I decided to restudy all our beliefs—you know, the ones printed on the back of the bulletin. Well, when I was done, I felt even more convinced that God was using Adventists for a special work."

"But how could a minister do something like that?" asked Chet.

"Remember when I told you Mr. Dawson was just human? Well, even ministers can make mistakes."

"But if a minister and a teacher just give up everything they used to believe in, is there any hope for me? They know so much more about God."

Mrs. Christy disappeared into the living room and then returned with a small book in her hand. "When our minister left the church, someone showed me this passage, and it helped put my mind at ease: 'Many a star that we have admired for its brilliancy will then go out in darkness. Chaff like a cloud will be borne away on the wind, even from places where we see only floors of rich wheat' " (*Testimonies,* vol. 5, p. 81).

"So you see," continued Mrs. Christy, "some of our very important church leaders will turn their backs on what they used to believe in. That is one of the signs that we're getting closer to Jesus' coming.

"But as long as we invite Jesus into our lives every day, Satan will not be able to break *our* friendship with God. So there is hope for you and me."

OCTOBER

19

Handi-capped but Not Held Back

We who are strong ought to bear with the failings of the weak and not to please ourselves. Romans 15:1, NIV.

A few months back I mentioned Mike, the handicapped boy who wanted to learn to ski. Today I'd like to tell you more about him.

Mike is one of the ninth graders in our school. When he was 4 years old, he was in a bad car accident. For 56 days he lay in a coma. Although he didn't die, life changed dramatically for Mike.

Not only was he paralyzed on his left side, but he also suffered brain damage. For 11 years he experienced seizures. By the time he was 14, he had seven or eight seizures a day. About this time Mike started to think about going in for his sixth operation.

The doctors explained that the operation had its good points and its bad points. There was a good chance that the operation would end his seizures. The bad news was that the operation would destroy some of Mike's eyesight.

It has been a year and a half since Mike's brain surgery. He did lose some of his sight, but the seizures stopped. If they don't return during the next six months, the doctors feel quite sure that Mike will not have to worry about them for the rest of his life.

One of the benefits of being seizure-free is that Mike doesn't have to take so many different medications. Before, he always felt tired and confused. Now he has so much energy that he seems to be busy every minute of the day.

Brain injury is just one of many different handicaps that people must learn to live with. There are also blindness, paralysis, deafness, muscular dystrophy, and cerebral palsy, to name some of them.

Some of you may have some disabled students in your school, or you may live near someone with a handicap. If you don't spend much time with handicapped people, you may feel uncomfortable when you are around them.

There are two important things to remember. First, you won't catch what they have. So you don't need to worry about being with them. Second, disabled people may look and act different, but they share the same feelings, hopes, and dreams that we all do.

If you have some handicapped young people in your area, don't miss out on an opportunity to become their friend. Don't let their differences get in the way.

And how should you treat people with some sort of physical problem? The same way you'd want to be treated if you were in their shoes.

OCTOBER

20

Rising Above the Obstacles

We also rejoice in our sufferings, because we know that suffering produces perseverance; perseverance, character; and character, hope. Romans 5:3, 4, NIV.

"What happens *to* you is not nearly as important as what happens *in* you."

If you were to meet me, you probably wouldn't guess that I have a handicap. I have bad eyesight. In fact, if my glasses fall off my nightstand, I have to ask Tom to find them for me. I'm that blind, but most people don't know about my disability because I wear contact lenses.

Some people can't read. Others are shy. And what about the people who are crippled by fear or a poor self-image? My guess is that everyone has at least one problem that could be considered a handicap. We can't always do something to get rid of a flaw or weakness, but we can and should learn how to cope with it.

Mike has refused to sit around and feel sorry for himself. He doesn't let his disabilities stop him from enjoying life. Mike is an active Pathfinder with the South Haven Mariners. He goes on all the activities his club sponsors. But when the subject of a 50-mile bike trip came up, some people doubted that Mike could participate. After all, he is paralyzed on his left side. How could someone pedal a bike 50 miles with only one good leg? It's hard enough with two good legs!

But Mike decided from the beginning that he was going to join the rest of the Pathfinders on the bike trip. So his parents bought him a three-wheeled bike, and a friend built a special attachment that would secure Mike's left foot to the pedal.

On the day of the bike trip Mike lined up at the starting point with the rest of the Pathfinders. He knew that he had only eight hours to complete the 50 miles, but he was confident he would make it, for he knew that many of his friends from school and church would be praying for him throughout the day.

The first part of the trip went well, but toward the end the road became hilly. So the other Pathfinders took turns pushing Mike up the inclines.

Although every muscle in his body ached, Mike never thought of giving up. As he crossed the finish line, his friends and family cheered him for his accomplishment. His mother looked down at her watch. He had made it in exactly eight hours.

Mike is truly an amazing young man.

OCTOBER

21

Picky, Picky

Taste and see that the Lord is good; blessed is the man who takes refuge in him. Psalm 34:8, NIV.

I've never known anyone like Jeffrey. He must have been the pickiest eater in the whole world. His mother, a wonderful cook, would fix all sorts of great things for supper, but Jeff would eat a peanut butter sandwich.

Jeff's mother worried about her son's lack of appetite. "I don't know what to do," she said. "I'm afraid he's going to get sick if he doesn't start eating better."

Once when Jeff was 6, he came over to our house for Sabbath dinner. While I was fixing the food, he and I made a list of the things he liked to eat. When we were all done, Jeff had a list of only 12 things.

What was worse, not only did Jeff not like to eat most foods, but he didn't like to watch other people eat them, either. If he saw someone eating spinach, he started to gag. He even gagged when his mother scraped off the plates before washing them.

I was a little worried about what would happen when Jeff started first grade. What would he do when other kids brought things in their lunches that he didn't like? Would his teacher have to put him in a corner so he wouldn't get sick?

Fortunately Jeffrey's food interests grew. He decided that man could not live on peanut butter alone, so he started trying things like lasagna, burritos, and egg rolls. And he found out he liked them!

It's the same way with spiritual things. Sometimes we look at spiritual food (Bible study, prayer, witnessing, and worship) and say, "No, thanks. That doesn't appeal to me." So we limit ourselves to just Sabbath school and church. We don't take the time to sample the other ways of getting to know Jesus better.

Other people make the mistake of sampling spiritual things only a few times before they give up. They try reading the Bible or having evening worship just once or twice, and when nothing very exciting happens, they say, "Well, that sure was a waste of time. I might as well watch TV."

It takes time to develop a taste for new foods. It also takes time to develop a taste for spiritual things. Each time you study your Bible, pray, share with others, or participate in worship, the easier it will be. And after a while you'll find yourself enjoying the things of God.

OCTOBER

22

The Day of Disappointment

The Lord says, "I am the one who comforts you. So why should you be afraid of people?" Isaiah 51:12, ICB.

How would you feel if Jesus were scheduled to come today? Would you be wondering what you were going to get for Christmas? Would you be concerned about your favorite football team's record for the season? Would you be studying for your weekly spelling test? Of course not! Every waking minute you'd be wondering if you were ready.

On October 22, 1844, thousands of people expected Jesus to appear before the end of the day. After studying prophecies in Daniel, they were convinced that the end of the world was only hours away.

A week earlier, one of God's faithful workers, Charles Fitch, had died. His wife and children attended his funeral but felt little sadness. After all, Jesus would raise her husband and their father back to life in just a few days.

Many people had left their crops in the fields and given away their possessions.

The Adventists (those who believed in Jesus' second coming) gathered in groups and waited for the first glimpse of Jesus coming through the clouds. And they waited. And waited. And waited.

When October 23 dawned, they faced another day on sinful earth. The children whose father had died realized that they were not going to be reunited as a family as soon as they had expected. The people who had not harvested their crops sadly trudged off to the fields to try to salvage some food for the winter. But disappointment was not the only hurt the Adventists suffered. They also experienced the pain of ridicule and rejection from their neighbors and families.

Many Adventists began to wonder if God even existed.

October 22, 1844, became known as the Great Disappointment. Because of His great power and creativity, God brought something good out of that difficult time. While many believers gave up their trust in God, others decided to find out what had gone wrong. So they dug deeply into the Scriptures. They found out that only God knows the day and hour of Jesus' coming. They learned about the important work going on in the heavenly sanctuary. They discovered that God's special day of rest is Saturday.

Out of this intense Bible study the Seventh-day Adventist Church was eventually formed. God used the Great Disappointment to give His people a special message that they could share with the world.

OCTOBER

23

It's a Cold, Cold World Out There

For surely, O Lord, you bless the righteous; you surround them with your favor as with a shield. Psalm 5:12, NIV.

"All that glitters is not gold."

I must have been about 10 years old when I went to my first circus. And I was impressed. We watched a man being shot out of a cannon. Next came the lion trainer and the tightrope walker. Then the beautiful lady on the high trapeze who performed death-defying tricks in her elegant red satin costume. Between acts the clowns ran around the ring, performing their comedy routines. With all the excitement, I forgot to eat my popcorn.

After the show was over, Mother led me around behind the tent, back where the circus people lived.

I wish she hadn't. The clowns had no time for children. They were busy wiping off their painted-on smiles. Their silly antics in the big tent were nothing but an act. The trapeze lady stood by a travel trailer. Coughing, she eagerly inhaled a cigarette. Gaudy makeup covered her aging face. I'd seen enough. The magic was gone.

When we look at non-Christians, we often have the same experience. We see the outside, which appears exciting and desirable, but if we could only get beyond the phoniness, we'd see how empty they are inside.

Some time ago I heard an evangelist tell about the great interest people had in attending his Revelation seminars. "They're coming from everywhere," he said. "We aren't having a hard time getting the people of the community to attend the seminars. Our problem is that the people in our churches aren't interested in helping out."

"Why is that?" I asked.

"They don't feel a need," he said, shaking his head. "They don't know what life is like out there."

He went on to explain how he had grown up in a non-Christian home. "You can't imagine what it's like to live without God. It's awful. I know what my life used to be like, and I know what I have now. I want to tell the people out there that there is hope. That there's a reason to live."

Instead of envying the world and its so-called freedom, we can be thankful for what we have as Christians.

OCTOBER

24

Dress for Success

Stop judging by mere appearances, and make a right judgment. John 7:24, NIV.

Old Mrs. Twomley leaned back in her hospital bed and stared at the ceiling as Nurse Kelly came breezing in. "Good morning, Mrs. Twomley."

"Good morning yourself!" barked the old woman.

Miss Kelly smiled as she checked Mrs. Twomley's pulse and recorded it on her chart. "It looks like it's time for your shot, Mrs. Twomley."

"That may be true, but I want a real nurse to give it to me."

"I *am* a real nurse," replied Miss Kelly.

"For all I know, you might be a janitor. I want a real nurse in a real uniform and nurse's hat. I'm not letting just anybody give me a shot."

The old woman was stubborn. Back when she had been a nurse, everyone in her profession wore the same thing: a special dress, a hat, and white hose. She wasn't used to the hospital's new relaxed dress code.

Mrs. Twomley had a point. Uniforms do help us identify a person's profession. A uniform lets you know that the person walking into the cockpit of the airplane knows how to fly. A uniform lets you know that the man holding the ticket pad has the right to pull you off the road if you're driving too fast.

When we were in Japan, it seemed that almost everyone wore a uniform. All the students wore uniforms, the looks of the uniform depending on which school they attended. The men working for the electrical company wore bright yellow, and would you believe, the ditchdiggers wore white!

Just as uniforms say something about the people who wear them, so our appearance says something about us. Whether or not the message our appearance gives is true doesn't matter. People still form opinions about us by the way we look. If you dress neatly, then others are likely to see you as careful and self-respecting, but if you look sloppy and dirty, people will label you as a careless person with little or no self-esteem.

What do people see when they look at you? Are your clothes clean and neat? Is your hair combed, and are your teeth brushed? Do you smell nice? And even more important, do you look like a personal representative of Jesus? Would people be able to look at you and tell that you're a Christian?

OCTOBER

25

If Only

The Lord our God is merciful and forgiving, even though we have rebelled against him. Daniel 9:9, NIV.

If only I hadn't cheated on my math test . . ." "*If only* I had picked different friends . . ." "*If only* I'd listened to my parents . . ." "*If only* . . ."

All of us have regrets that make us feel guilty. We'd probably all like to start life over again and do some things differently. But we can't. We need to go on with life. Sometimes that's hard when we feel so guilty for what we've done.

Satan is very, very clever. He has two lies about sin that he uses on us at different times.

Before we've done something wrong, Satan says, "Hey, what's the big deal? So you sin a little. It really won't hurt you that much. You can always stop if you want to."

After we've listened to him for a while, we start to see things his way. So we walk right into sin, and *wham!* All of a sudden, Satan's whole attitude changes. "Look what you've done, you terrible person!" he whispers. "Why, you're so disgusting that even God doesn't want you. You might as well give up trying to be a Christian, because you're hopeless."

Although Satan may be convincing in his lies, don't believe him.

First off, one sin *does* matter. Every time we disobey God, we're going to be hurt in some way. But on the other hand, when we do give in to temptation, we can't accept Satan's second lie, either. Our situation is not hopeless. Instead of sitting around and hating ourselves, we need to go to Jesus and let Him take away our guilt. The longer we hold on to sin, the more damage it does.

A few years ago a minister we know drove 100 miles out of his way to be able to pay for some candy he'd stolen when he was a 7-year-old child.

The store had changed owners several times, so the present owner was not the man John had stolen from. But John still gave the man $2 to pay for the Snickers bar he'd shoplifted. The candy bar had cost only five cents back then, but John wanted to repay with interest.

When he told me about his experience he said, "I don't know why I waited so long to make the thing right. For 30 years I carried guilt for what I'd done, and it made me miserable. But boy, did I feel great when I walked out of the store!"

OCTOBER

26

A Friend Close By

The Lord himself goes before you and will be with you; he will never leave you nor forsake you. Do not be afraid; do not be discouraged. Deuteronomy 31:8, NIV.

Doug," said the doctor quietly, "the tests are conclusive. You have leukemia."

Thirteen-year-old Doug leaned back in his hospital bed, his mind whirling. He and his parents had suspected leukemia, so this wasn't exactly a shock. But there was something so final about the doctor's words. There would be no more pretending. Doug would have to face the facts.

Doug's father broke the silence. "Is there anything we can do? Can he be cured?"

"Well, Mr. Ingram, with leukemia there's a lot more hope than there is with other forms of cancer," explained Dr. Corbin. "If Doug is willing to go through three years of chemotherapy, he'll have a good chance of recovery, but we can't promise anything. We have no way of knowing just how well the medication will work. I suggest you talk it over together and decide what you want to do."

After the doctor left the room, Doug's parents pulled up chairs next to their son's bed. "Well, what do you think, Doug?" Father asked.

"I'll try anything, Dad."

"You realize that chemotherapy will make you very sick. It won't be easy," Doug's mother added.

"I know," said Doug, shaking his head. "But I want to get better. I want to live. I'll take my chances with the chemotherapy."

"I'm proud of you, Doug," said his dad. "Your mother and I will do all we can to help you. As Mother said, it won't be easy—for you or for us—but we'll do all we can to help."

Doug gave a weak smile. "I guess you'd better tell Dr. Corbin that we want to go for it."

Doug didn't feel sorry for himself. He faced his problem with courage and determination. He knew that he had a skilled doctor who would be there to help him with his treatments. And he knew that he had two loving parents who would be by his side.

You may not be facing a life-threatening illness, but in the days and weeks to come, you'll need courage to deal with the problems that will come your way. Like Doug, you don't have to face your trials alone. You have people who care about you. And you have a heavenly Father who loves you more than you can imagine.

Don't be afraid of what tomorrow might bring. Take courage. You're not alone.

OCTOBER

27

Problems or Opportunities?

You have granted him the desire of his heart and have not withheld the request of his lips. You welcomed him with rich blessings and placed a crown of pure gold on his head. Psalm 21:2, 3, NIV.

Some people blame God when bad things happen to them. They say, "If God is so loving, then why would He let something like this happen to me?" When Doug found out about his leukemia, he didn't blame God. He knew that sometimes bad things just happen. Problems are part of life.

Do you ever feel that since you're part of God's family, you shouldn't have to face trials and disappointments? Do you feel that your relationship with God should protect you from anything unpleasant?

Pretend for a moment that tomorrow when you go to school, your teacher makes an announcement: "All students whose parents are teachers don't have to do any more homework."

You'd probably say "Unfair!" And you'd be right. Why should students be excused from doing their homework just because they are related to teachers? The reason we do homework is that it helps us learn and it prepares us for life.

It's the same way with problems. Expecting God to protect Christians from all unpleasant circumstances would be like excusing teachers' kids from their homework. Neither would make a whole lot of sense.

Problems are not all bad. In fact, if we have the right attitude about them, they can be wonderful opportunities for us.

Here are just a few ways problems can work for you. They can help you—

realize how much you need God's help.
learn to trust God.
see how hurtful sin is.
find a better way of living.
enjoy the good times even more.

I know from experience that the biggest improvements in my life have come about because of problems. I am a better teacher because of problems. I am a happier person because of problems. And I am closer to God because of problems. Were the problems worth it? Of course!

When you give your life to God, He can turn every single problem into an opportunity and make you a winner.

OCTOBER

28

Someone Understood

For we do not have a high priest who is unable to sympathize with our weaknesses. . . . Let us then approach the throne of grace with confidence. Hebrews 4:15, 16, NIV.

By the time Doug's parents got ready to leave the hospital that evening, Doug was feeling pretty good. At last the weeks and months of wondering were over. The doctors knew what was wrong with him. And there was hope. The three years of chemotherapy wouldn't be easy, but it just might destroy his cancer.

Doug's parents kissed him goodbye and started out the door of the hospital room. "Hey," called Doug, "since I'm a sick person, don't you think I should have some flowers in my room?"

"Good idea," laughed Mr. Ingram. "We'll see what we can do."

That night Mrs. Ingram called her sister to tell her about Doug's diagnosis. "And you wouldn't believe what he said as we were going out the door. He said, 'Since I'm a sick person, don't you think I should have some flowers in my room?' "

Doug's Aunt Rita laughed. "That sounds like Doug, all right. I'll order the flowers tomorrow."

So the next morning Aunt Rita called a florist. "I need a nice get-well bouquet for my teenage nephew."

The clerk wrote down the information, and then Aunt Rita added, "I really hope you'll do an extra-special job on his flowers. You see, Doug found out just yesterday that he has leukemia."

When the flowers were delivered to Doug's room that afternoon, Doug eagerly opened the card that was attached. "Hope you'll be well soon. Love, Aunt Rita," it read. Doug was just about to put the card on the table next to his bed when he noticed another card taped to the other side of the vase.

I wonder who that's from? he thought. Opening the envelope, he pulled out a handwritten note.

"Dear Doug,

"I just heard that you have leukemia. I had leukemia when I was 7. I'm 23 now. Don't give up. You can make it too.

"Love,

"Laura Grimes."

Of all the flowers, cards, and letters Doug received while he was in the hospital, none meant as much to him as the one from the young lady at the flower shop. Laura knew what he was going through.

When you face a problem, remember that Jesus understands. He knows what you're going through. But He also knows that you can make it, for He'll be right there at your side to see you through.

OCTOBER

29

Friend or Foe?

Live in peace with each other. . . . Make sure that nobody pays back wrong for wrong, but always try to be kind to each other and to everyone else.
1 Thessalonians 5:13-15, NIV.

Have you ever noticed how hard it is for some people to get along with others? If you have a hard time getting along with certain kids at school or a brother or sister, then you know what I'm talking about.

Ned and Marty had that problem. One minute they were friends, the next minute, enemies. No one ever knew what to expect from them. One day they'd be walking along the countryside enjoying each other's company. The next day they'd be at each other's throat, fighting right in the middle of town.

Why didn't their parents or teachers do something? you're probably wondering. Well, you see, Ned and Marty weren't people. They were dogs. Ned was a Newfoundland; and Marty, a mastiff.

One day the two enemy-friends decided to see what was happening down on the waterfront. Together they trotted out to the end of the pier. After watching the boats skimming by, the dogs started a friendly tussle. But the tussle soon turned into a full-fledged fight. Tempers flared and teeth started snapping. Ned grabbed at Marty and they began rolling on the cement. Before they realized what was happening, both Marty and Ned fell off the pier and into the deep water below.

The cold water snapped them out of their angry mood, and the fight stop instantly. All the dogs could think of now was to get back to shore as quickly as possible.

Ned, the Newfoundland, was an excellent swimmer. He paddled to the shore and then hurried back to the pier. As he stood there shaking himself off, he looked out over the water for Marty.

But things weren't going too well for Marty. He couldn't move through the water as well as Ned had. He struggled with all his might to reach the shore, but he made little progress. Finally his strength gave out, and as Ned watched from the pier, Marty started to sink.

When Ned saw his friend go under, he jumped into the water and swam to Marty's side. Grabbing him by the collar, Ned held Marty's head above water and dragged him to shore.

Although the two dogs had battled back and forth before the incident at the pier, they never did after that. They learned that fighting only causes problems.

OCTOBER

30

War of the Worlds

The end of all things is near. Therefore be clear minded and self-controlled so that you can pray. 1 Peter 4:7, NIV.

Fifty-five years ago tonight Americans all over the United States turned on their radios and listened to after-dinner music as they read their evening newspaper.

Suddenly the music faded as a radio announcer broke in with a news bulletin: "At 20 minutes before eight, central time, Professor Farrell of the Mount Jennings Observatory, Chicago, Illinois, reported observing several explosions of incandescent gas occurring at regular intervals on the planet Mars. The spectroscope indicates the gas to be hydrogen and moving toward the earth with enormous velocity. Professor Pierson, of the observatory at Princeton, confirms Farrell's observation and describes the phenomenon as 'like a jet of blue flames shot from a gun.' "

At that point the announcer returned the audience to the music being played at the Meridian Room of the Park Plaza Hotel in New York City.

The people listening to the announcement didn't think too much about it. But when the announcer broke in once again, they realized that something frightening was taking place. It seemed that some large object from space had hit the earth. No one knew exactly what it was. It was quite a while before America understood what was going on. A spaceship of Martians had landed on earth!

Soon reports were coming in from all over. The country was being attacked by aliens. The world was about to end. Americans everywhere panicked. Some people fell to their knees and confessed their sins to God. Others, afraid of what was coming, ran for their lives.

Then the radio station announced that the radio play *The War of the Worlds* would continue after a short intermission. The whole thing had been and was a drama.

How would you feel if you thought the world was about to end? Would you be afraid? Or would you be excited?

As Christians we don't have to worry about how the world will come to an end. The Bible tells us clearly that Jesus will bring an end to all things when He comes again.

Our world will not be destroyed by aliens or even by World War III. It will be destroyed by the brightness of Jesus' coming.

OCTOBER

31

Who Are You Watching?

My dear children, you belong to God. . . . God's Spirit, who is in you, is greater than the devil, who is in the world.
1 John 4:4, ICB.

Around Halloween time Satan gets a lot of attention. Television stations feature a lot of horror movies. People dress up in weird costumes and go trick-or-treating. In some places the police and fire departments are on patrol all night, fighting the fires arsonists set all over town. October seems to be the time when America likes to focus on evil. So what are Christians supposed to do, ignore what's going on and forget about Satan?

Before I answer that question, I'd like to tell you a story. The *London Sporting Magazine* told of a clever fox that found a way to catch some turkeys that were roosting high in some Scotch fir trees near a farmyard.

Each night the fox would stand under the trees and look up at the turkeys, which were completely out of his reach. There was absolutely no way for him to climb up there and grab his dinner. He had to think of a way to get them to come down to him. So he started to scratch the ground underneath the trees. That got the turkeys' attention. They all looked down to see just what was going on below. When they noticed the fox on the ground, they decided to keep their eyes on him. There was no telling what that crazy fox might do.

The fox then started running in circles around the trees. The turkeys kept their eyes on him as he went round and round. Soon the birds became confused and dizzy. Suddenly one of the turkeys fell to the ground. The fox stopped his circling, grabbed the bird, and killed it. Then he started circling the trees again until another turkey fell from its perch. Satisfied with his catch, the fox slunk off into the woods with his meal.

Satan is just like the fox. He wants our attention, for if we start looking his way, we'll take our eyes off Jesus. We need to realize how powerful Satan is, but we don't need to fear him. As long as we're on God's side, we have nothing to worry about. Satan has already lost the great controversy. And his time is just about over.

No matter what Satan does to try to get your attention, ignore him. Don't be a turkey. Keep your eyes on Jesus.

NOVEMBER

1

The Pity Party

Why are you downcast, O my soul? Why so disturbed within me? Put your hope in God, for I will yet praise him, my Savior and my God. Psalm 42:5, 6, NIV.

Kyle's health problems started the day he was born. A premature baby, he spent the first weeks of his life in the hospital. Then before he started school he developed allergies and asthma. Once he started school it seemed that he came down with every illness imaginable.

"I'm so sick of being sick all the time," he said to his mother one night.

"I made an appointment for you with Dr. Kraner tomorrow for your allergy shot. Maybe he can suggest something for your cold."

When Kyle walked into Dr. Kraner's office the next day, the doctor could tell that something was troubling Kyle. "How are you feeling, Kyle?"

"Terrible, just plain terrible!" Kyle shot back. "Why do I have to get sick all the time?"

The doctor sensed right away that Kyle's problem was not his poor health, but his self-pity. "Listen, Kyle, I have a few house calls to make when I'm done here. Why don't you come along with me?"

"OK," said Kyle. "I don't have anything better to do." A few minutes later Dr. Kraner and Kyle left the office in the doctor's car.

The first patient they saw was a young woman suffering from a spinal disease. She had no control over certain muscles and was often in great pain, but instead of complaining, she showed her two visitors the typewriter she was learning to use.

Next they visited a blind boy who was busy weaving a rug. "How does it look?" he asked.

The final visit was with a lady paralyzed on her right side. She visited with them while she prepared supper for her husband and two small children.

As he sat in Dr. Kraner's car on the way home, Kyle thought about the people he had met that afternoon. "Dr. Kraner, were you trying to tell me something by bringing me along?"

The doctor smiled and nodded his head. "Did you learn anything?"

"I sure did. I guess I've been feeling sorry for myself all these years because I have a few problems, but mine are nothing compared to what other people have to go through."

"What are you going to do about it?"

Kyle thought for a moment. "I'm going to stop feeling sorry for myself and start concentrating on all the things I *can* do. The pity party's over."

NOVEMBER

2

Winners and Losers

Your hands made me and formed me; give me understanding to learn your commands. *Psalm 119:73, NIV.*

Keith is always the last person chosen when he plays baseball at school. Every day he lines up against the gym wall with the others. Every day he watches the team captains compete for the good players. Every day he hears someone say, "You can have Keith. We don't want him." Keith feels like a big loser.

Wendy looks through the newest issue of *Seventeen.* Beautiful models line the pages. She can't help noticing their stylish clothes, perfect hairstyles, and flawless complexions. Wendy walks over to the mirror on the bedroom door. Looking at herself, she notices her skinny legs and dull blonde hair. Wendy hates what she sees.

Ben opens his report card. All D's. *What a dummy!* he says to himself. *I may as well quit school.*

Why is it that most people feel unhappy with themselves? Poor self-esteem isn't a problem everyone is born with. It's something that happens over time.

For example, in a class of 20 kindergarten students, about 16 of them feel good about themselves. By the time this group reaches fifth grade, only 4 of the 20 like themselves. When this class finally gets to twelfth grade, only 1 student out of the 20 has good self-esteem.

Why does this happen?

We start forming opinions about ourselves when we're very young. We notice that we're shorter than everyone else. We're also weaker and less intelligent, and we aren't very coordinated. As we compare ourselves with adults, we begin to wonder if we have any value at all.

When we're young, our families usually help us feel worthwhile even though we're small. But as soon as we start getting to know people outside our home, we find that not everyone thinks we're so great, and we begin to wonder if maybe they are right after all.

Anytime we compare ourselves with others, we're going to feel discouraged. There will always be someone who is better looking, smarter, or more popular. We need to be thankful that we are who we are. We need to be the best that we can be.

NOVEMBER

3

Pulling Together

Be of one mind, live in peace. And the God of love and peace will be with you. 2 Corinthians 13:11, NIV.

Just as Mr. Gaines turned into his driveway, he saw his neighbor Mr. Shultz struggling to get a large trunk through his front door. Always happy to help someone in need, Mr. Gaines parked his car and jogged across the lawn. "Wait a minute, Carl, and I'll help you with that trunk."

"Boy, am I glad you came along," said Mr. Shultz. "I thought I was going to have to wait until my son got home from football practice."

Mr. Gaines squeezed through the door and got on the other end of the trunk. "OK, ready," he called out.

The two men set themselves to the task and worked with all their might. But within a few minutes they were totally exhausted. And the trunk had moved only a few inches.

"Give me a few seconds to rest," said Mr. Gaines as he leaned over trying to catch his breath. "What do you have in this trunk, anyway?"

"Just a bunch of old books."

"Well, let's try again. I think we can get them out of the house this time."

"Out?" said Mr. Shultz. "Why, I've been trying to get them *in!*"

That's what happens when people are pushing or pulling in different directions.

Some years ago during an ocean cruise, the recreation director organized a mini-Olympics for the guests on the boat. The tug-of-war was scheduled for the second day of the event.

The captains of the two teams chose their participants carefully, but it was obvious that the one team had the bigger and heavier members. When the tug-of-war was announced, the rest of the passengers lined up like fans at a baseball game. Then to everyone's amazement, the side with the smaller people won. Nobody could understand it, so the director ran a second test. The same team won again.

Later the truth leaked out. The lighter side had met secretly during lunch and practiced pulling together. The other side may have been heavier, but they had never learned to work together.

Just think what people could accomplish if they stopped trying to do their own thing and learned to pull together.

(Adapted with permission from Archer Wallace, *The Field of Honor* [New York: Abingdon-Cokesbury Press, 1949], pp. 53, 54.)

NOVEMBER

4

The Missing Piece

For in Christ all the fullness of the Deity lives in bodily form, and you have been given fullness in Christ, who is the head over every power and authority. Colossians 2:9, 10, NIV.

Let's set up the card table and start that new puzzle we got," Mother suggested as she and Tonya were doing the supper dishes.

"OK," said Tonya. "And let's build a fire in the fireplace and make some hot chocolate."

Tonya quickly finished drying the dishes and started the hot chocolate. Mother set up the card table and built a fire. After dumping all the puzzle pieces out onto the table, Tonya and Mother separated out the edge pieces and put the border together. Then they began working on the inside pieces.

By 9:00, they were almost done. That's when Scott, Tonya's brother, decided to join in. Everyone grabbed a handful of pieces and took turns putting them in place.

"OK, who's got the last one?" asked Tonya, looking at Scott.

"Not me," said Scott holding his hands up in self-defense.

"Are you sure?" Tonya didn't trust her brother. The previous time they had put a puzzle together, he had hidden a piece under the couch so that he could put in the last piece himself.

"No, really, I didn't hide a piece this time."

So they all got down on hands and knees and checked over the floor and peered under the furniture for the missing piece. They even pulled the cushions out of the sofa and chairs. But nothing turned up.

"I guess we just got a puzzle that isn't all here," said Mother.

"Boy, it's sure a letdown to work that hard and then not have all the pieces," added Tonya. "That makes the puzzle kind of worthless."

"Oh, not at all," Mother laughed. "In fact, I think we can learn a lesson from our puzzle."

"What?" asked Scott.

"Well, the puzzle is like your life. There are many different things that make you the person you really are—your personality, character, abilities, looks, goals, friends, etc. All these things are part of you, and they're all important.

"But if you don't have God in your life, you won't be complete. You'll always feel like something is missing. You may try to fill the emptiness with other things, but they just won't work."

What about your life? Does God have a place in your life?

NOVEMBER

5

Invisible Barrier

Perseverance must finish its work so that you may be mature and complete, not lacking anything. James 1:4, NIV.

"We can do anything we want to do if we stick to it long enough."—Helen Keller.

I once saw a movie in which a group of fish acted like some people I know. The fish—plain brown trout—were released into a large aquarium. A few hours later a man dropped in some minnows for the trout's supper. During the next few days the fish were fed the same way, but about a week later things changed. The man shooed the fish to one side and then separated the tank down the middle with a large piece of glass. Next he added some minnows on the side opposite the trout.

The trout spied their dinner and swam right for the minnows. But *boink!* the trout hit their noses on the glass. They tried again, and the same thing happened. The frustrated fish continued to try to get at the minnows, but the glass kept getting in their way. The fish became so discouraged that they eventually stopped trying to go after the minnows. After the glass was taken out of the tank, the trout still didn't try to catch the minnows. Even when the minnows started swimming right past their heads, the discouraged trout just ignored them. They never again tried to satisfy their hunger, and they ended up starving to death. All because they'd had a few bad experiences.

Do you ever act a little "fishy"? Are you ever tempted to give up when things don't come easily? If you do poorly on a test or two, do you quit studying? If you don't make friends easily, do you spend all your free time by yourself? If you can't play basketball very well, do you quit practicing your free throws?

Don't assume that just because you aren't a success right now, you can't become one in the future. Don't be like the trout. Keep pushing toward your goal.

NOVEMBER

6

Beware! Thin Ice!

Set a guard over my mouth, O Lord; keep watch over the door of my lips. Psalm 141:3, NIV.

"Come on, let's go sliding!" Tim called to his friend Chad. "The lake is almost all frozen."

"Just a minute. Let me ask my mom if I can go," said Chad. He ran back to the house and found his mother folding laundry. "Mom, can I go sliding on the lake with Tim?"

"Are you sure the ice is solid enough?"

"It's fine. Can I go?"

"Well, I suppose so, but be sure to stay away from the soft spots. I don't want you falling in."

"I'll be careful; I promise," said Chad.

Chad grabbed his sled, and the two boys started down the snow-covered road together. When they arrived at the lake, they walked around a few minutes just to check the ice. "Well, there are a few spots that aren't frozen, but I think it'll be OK for us to go ahead and slide," said Tim.

"Yeah, as long as we stay away from the thin ice we'll be safe."

The boys had a great time skimming across the ice, but after a while, Jim decided he wanted to do something a little more exciting. "Let's see how close we can come to the edge."

"I don't know . . ." said Chad. "I promised my mom that I'd be careful."

"Oh, we won't fall in. We'll just see how close we can get." So the boys started playing chicken. One would slide toward the edge. Then the other would see if he could slide a little closer.

"You won't be able to beat me this time," laughed Tim as he sat confidently on his sled.

"Just watch me." Chad threw himself on top of his sled and shoved off toward the edge, but he slid across the ice a little faster than he had planned. Instead of stopping near Tim, he zipped right past him and into the freezing water.

Some boys and girls like to play close to the edge with the words they say. They may not use four-letter words or think they are taking the name of the Lord in vain, but they use what I call "vegetarian" swear words, like *gosh, gee whiz, golly, jeez, heck,* and *shoot*. Words like these make it easier for them to slip over into using worse swear words or foul language.

Christians should honor the Lord in their words and actions. Watered-down swear words may not be as bad as some words people use, but do you think it's appropriate for those who have Jesus living in their hearts?

NOVEMBER

7

The Inside Is What Counts

Your beauty should not come from outward adornment. . . . Instead, it should be that of your inner self, the unfading beauty of a gentle and quiet spirit, which is of great worth in God's sight. 1 Peter 3:3, 4, NIV.

The first time Tina stepped onto the academy campus, she captured the attention of all the male students. There was no doubt about it—Tina was gorgeous. Her long blonde hair shimmered just right. Her complexion was perfect. She even had naturally pink cheeks. And her clothes—well, every time she walked into a room, she looked like a model. In other words, Tina looked like a dream date.

During the first week of school, 20 boys asked her to go with them to the skating party. She finally decided to go with Randy, the senior class president. The other 19 accepted defeat and vowed to get a date with her the next weekend.

Randy was excited to think he'd be able to spend some time getting to know Tina better, but at the skating party Tina wasn't very much fun. She skated only once. The rest of the evening she sat on the sidelines combing her hair and watching everyone else have fun. Randy decided his first date with Tina would be his last.

The following weekend Tina got 15 invitations to the hayride. This time she went with Quinn, the Student Association vice president. The same thing happened. She went to the hayride, but she just sat on the hay and acted very bored. Quinn checked her off his list too.

As the weeks went by, Tina's popularity dropped steadily. By the time the Christmas banquet rolled around, not one fellow asked her for a date.

Tina's outside appearance may have been very attractive, but she was not a beautiful person on the inside. She spent a lot of time fixing her hair and choosing just the right clothes. But she neglected her personality and character, and eventually people didn't even want to be around her.

It's important to take care of your outside appearance by keeping your hair neat and clean, caring for your skin, and wearing attractive clothes. But make sure that you don't forget to look for ways to be beautiful on the inside, too, for what's inside counts more.

Something to think about: What do you spend more time on—your outside appearance, or the person you are on the inside?

NOVEMBER

8

Family Trees

Whoever acknowledges me before men, I will also acknowledge him before my Father in heaven. Matthew 10:32, NIV.

"Look, Mrs. Coffee!" said Missy as she stopped me in the hallway at school. "Look at what my grandma got for me!"

Missy reached into her locker and pulled out a personally signed picture of Burt Reynolds.

"Where did your grandma get that?" I asked.

"She wrote to him and asked for it. You see, my grandma is Burt's aunt, so that makes him my relative, too." Missy was very proud that she was related to a famous Hollywood star.

It's always fun to find out whom we're related to, especially if we can trace our roots back to someone famous. You can be sure that if we do find an important person in our family tree, we're going to want our friends to know about it.

You may be thinking, *All the people in my family are just ordinary. I'm not related to anyone special.*

But you're wrong. You're related to the most outstanding, most wonderful, most famous Person who has ever lived—Jesus.

You probably won't be able to find Jesus in your family tree, but you are part of His family if you've given your heart to God. For if God is your Father, then Jesus is your friend and brother.

Now I want to ask you some personal questions. Are you eager to let your friends know that you're related to Jesus? Would your friends know by the way you act at school and at home that you're part of God's family?

You can't show people an autographed picture of Jesus to prove that you are related, but there are other ways to show that you know Him. You can bow your head and close your eyes during prayer. You can treat others with kindness, even when they aren't kind to you. You can get involved with singing during worship. And you can do your best in your home and school responsibilities.

When Jesus comes back again, He'll be coming for His family members. Will you be a part of that group?

NOVEMBER

9

Step Into the Sunshine

Your sun will never set again, and your moon will wane no more; the Lord will be your everlasting light, and your days of sorrow will end. Isaiah 60:20, NIV.

Maybe you're lucky enough to live in a place where the sun always shines. If you are, then you won't understand how depressing it can be to go for days and days without sunshine.

I live in Michigan, and my state is known for being overcast and dreary during most of the winter months. In some months we may have only seven or eight days when the sun actually breaks through the cloud cover.

Recently researchers have discovered that the lack of sunlight makes some people very depressed. While most people learn to cope with the dark winter months, those with SAD (seasonal affective disorder) have a hard time getting through each winter day.

Sunlight definitely has an effect on my students. When the days are bright and sunny, my class is more likely to be cheerful. When the weather is dreary, the mood in my room usually turns dark, especially when we've had a whole week of cloudy weather. Certain students become short-tempered, everyone feels tired and listless, and brains don't function as well. On days like that I wish I could fly the whole school to sunny Florida for a week at Disney World.

I have a feeling that the Bible writers knew how important sunlight is in our lives, for they often described the Lord as a light.

When the sun isn't shining outside, I feel like something important is missing from my day. I get the same feeling when I don't have my special time with Jesus.

As we get closer to Jesus' second coming, sin will seem to almost completely shut out God's light, but Jesus' presence will continue to brighten the lives of those who love Him. Although terrible things will happen all around us, He will give us peace, courage, and hope for the future.

You may not have a bright, sunny day today, but you can invite Jesus to bring His light into your life today.

NOVEMBER

10

Who Loved Mother the Most?

The one who obeys me is the one who loves me. John 14:21, TLB.

Herbie, Rita, and Janet tiptoed down the hall to Mother's room. "Surprise!" they called out.

"We brought you breakfast in bed," said Herbie as he placed the tray carefully on the bedspread.

"Oh, this looks so good!" Mother said as she surveyed the tray. "Scrambled eggs, orange juice, and a doughnut."

"And the orange juice is freshly squeezed," added Rita.

Janet pulled out an envelope and handed it to her mother. "Here's a card from all of us."

Mother opened the card and read, " 'To the best mother in the world. We love you.' "

"Well, what brought all this on?" Mother laughed.

"Oh, nothing. We just wanted to do something special for you," Janet explained.

"Well, after I enjoy my breakfast, I'm going to try to sleep a little longer. The baby was up most of the night, and I'm worn out. Would you all help me out by doing some chores this morning?"

"Sure," the three answered.

"OK, then. Herbie, would you clean up the garage before you go out to play? You left some of Dad's tools out when you were working on your bike last night. Rita, it's your turn to weed the garden. And Janet, would you please start the wash for me?"

"Don't worry, Mom," said Herbie. "We'll take care of everything."

With that the three left Mother alone to eat her surprise breakfast in peace. Herbie went right out to the garage, but before he got started with his job, Joey, his best friend, stopped by. "The guys are going to play some softball. Want to come?"

"Sure," said Herbie. Without thinking, he grabbed his bike and followed Joey down the street.

Rita hurried out to the garden and started pulling weeds. After just two rows she decided to go inside for a drink, and before she knew it, she was curled up in the easy chair enjoying a new book.

Janet separated the laundry into piles and put the first load into the washer. She noticed that they had made quite a mess in the kitchen when they prepared Mother's breakfast. After cleaning off the counters, she ran water into the sink and started doing the dishes.

All three children claimed they loved their mother, but who do you think loved her the most?

NOVEMBER

11

Don't Lose Control

"But I will restore you to health . . . ," declares the Lord. Jeremiah 30:17, NIV.

One of the scariest moments in my life was the day my husband and I boarded a plane and flew to England. I had never been in an airplane before, and I must admit that I was nervous.

I did pretty well getting from the waiting area to the plane, and I stayed calm all through the routine safety instructions. But when the engines started racing, so did my heart. Looking out the window, I watched the scenery whiz by as we taxied down the runway. Then came the most frightening moment of all—when the plane left the ground and started ascending into the clouds. It felt as though a giant hand was pressing me back into my seat.

Just yesterday I was talking to one of the teachers at our school. She said she refuses to get on an airplane. She's not alone in her feelings. Thousands of people are terrified of flying.

Although several large airplanes crash each year, most people continue flying. But what would happen if each *week* a jumbo jet went down? Would you be afraid to fly? How about if a jumbo jet crashed *every single day*, killing 450 people each time? I think I'd find some other way to travel. If 450 people died each day from plane accidents, you can be sure that society would insist that something be done immediately.

Approximately 1,350 people die in the United States each and every day from—plane accidents? No—smoking. Yet we don't see people getting too upset about the problem.

No doubt some of you have already tried smoking. If you have, I hope you've decided that you don't ever want to do it again. Smoking is very addictive. We hear a lot about the dangers of taking drugs, but did you know that the nicotine in cigarettes is more addicting than most hard drugs? Patients at a drug rehabilitation center in California were asked which was easier to quit—cigarettes or drugs. Almost all of them said it was easier to give up drugs.

No one can keep you from smoking, but *you* can choose to stay away from cigarettes.

Cigarette companies spend millions of dollars on advertising to find new customers to replace the nearly 500,000 American smokers who die each year. They try to convince us that smoking will make life more enjoyable.

Say no to cigarettes. Let someone else enjoy the fun of bad breath, yellow teeth, and smoker's cough.

NOVEMBER

12

Friends to the End

A friend loves at all times. Proverbs 17:17, NIV.

"Onion head, onion head!" A group of boys crowded around 17-year-old Mitch. Pointing to his balding head, they continued their cruel taunts. "Hey, I think we have one of those endangered species in our midst. Isn't he a bald eagle—the national bird?" laughed one.

Mitch gritted his teeth and hurried into the school. His tormentors laughed as they watched him go. "See you around, Cue Ball," someone called out.

Mitch wished that they'd just leave him alone. It wasn't easy looking different from everyone else, but Mitch couldn't do anything about it. When the doctors first diagnosed his leukemia, Mitch didn't realize how much his life would change.

Before he had gotten sick, Mitch had played varsity football, but now after losing 90 pounds, he could hardly walk to class. He had gotten used to the weakness and nausea, but he could never get used to the names some of the kids were calling him. If they weren't pointing out how skinny he was, they were making fun of his bald head.

But not all the students treated Mitch unkindly. After football practice one afternoon, one of the players asked the other members of the team to stay for a few minutes. "I don't know if you realize it or not, but some of the kids have given Mitch a hard time about losing his hair," he explained to the group. "He never complains about it, but I hear their comments when we change classes. I think we need to do something about it. What do you say?"

"Count me in," agreed one player.

"Me too," said another and another.

"What are we going to do?" someone asked.

"Well, here's my plan . . ."

When Mitch came to school, he couldn't believe his eyes. Neither could the rest of the student body. Every single member of the football team, including the coach, had shaved his head completely bald. And until Mitch's death three months later, all the members of the team continued to shave their heads. It was their way of standing by their dying teammate. It was their way of saying that they cared.

NOVEMBER

13

The Big Catch

"What a catch!" exclaimed John Napoli as he surveyed the salmon that filled his fishing boat. "There must be at least $3,000 worth of fish here!"

Turning his boat toward San Francisco Bay, he started for home. By the time he was within two miles from the bay, he had been forced to slow down to almost a crawl because of the thick, heavy fog.

Suddenly he heard people screaming for help.

Running to the edge of his boat, John peered down into the water. He couldn't believe his eyes. All around him were people bobbing in the water and shouting for help.

Sometime earlier, the U.S.S. *Benevolence,* a Navy hospital ship, had been rammed by another large boat. The passengers on the Navy vessel had stayed aboard as long as possible, but as the boat sank beneath the waves, they were forced to leap from the ship.

As the fog began to lift, John could see hundreds of people fighting for their lives. Without a second thought, he turned his salmon boat into a rescue ship.

He steered his boat toward a group of survivors and began to pull them in one at a time. As his boat filled up with people, he realized that he was running out of room. So he started throwing his salmon overboard. Asking God for strength, John returned to the task of rescuing the survivors. Soon he had a dozen people on board. Then two dozen. Then 35 . . . 50 . . . 63 . . . and finally 70. And by the time he had finished, his entire $3,000 catch had disappeared back into the ocean.

Do you remember the song "Fishers of Men"? In that song Jesus invites us to work along with Him to rescue people who are drowning in sin. He wants everyone to know that there's plenty of room in God's family for all who will trust Him with their lives. Eternal life is His free gift to all who will accept it.

Won't you help get the word out that Jesus saves?

"Come, follow me," Jesus said, "and I will make you fishers of men." Matthew 4:19, NIV.

NOVEMBER

14

Use It or Lose It

Go to the ant, you sluggard; consider its ways and be wise! It has no commander, no overseer or ruler, yet it stores its provisions in summer and gathers its food at harvest. How long will you lie there, you sluggard? When will you get up from your sleep? Proverbs 6:6-9, NIV.

Too many people make cemeteries of their lives by burying their talents."

Some years ago St. Augustine, Florida, was the scene of a tragic story. For many years the area fishermen on the shrimp boats shared their catches with the sea gulls living near the water's edge. The birds never learned to fish because they could always count on getting free meals from the men on the boats. And since the birds felt no need to catch their own food, they didn't teach their babies to fish, either.

When the shrimp boats moved to a different port, they left behind a large flock of lazy birds that didn't know how to take care of themselves. There were plenty of fish for the gulls to eat, but the birds had never learned how to find their own food. So they sat along the shore starving to death, because they'd never learned to work.

The sad predicament that these birds got themselves into can happen to any creature that expects to get something for nothing. Students who are content to just get by in their studies and those who cheat on their tests are like the birds that never learned to take responsibility for their own lives. Instead of putting some effort into learning, such students choose to take the easy way out.

When I was in academy, one of the girls in my grade took the easy way out. When our teachers gave us assignments, Heather would wait until all her classmates were done with theirs. Then she'd copy the answers from her friends' papers. When the teachers handed out quizzes or tests, Heather would "borrow" answers from the people sitting around her.

Heather graduated from academy, but when she went on to college, she just couldn't do the work. She dropped out after one year. Her laziness finally caught up with her.

If we don't use our abilities, we lose them. Students lose their intelligence if they avoid opportunities to learn. Athletes lose their skills if they don't train continually. Musicians lose their mastery if they don't practice regularly. We will never get out of life any more than we put into it.

NOVEMBER

15

A Loving Destruction

I take no pleasure in the death of the wicked, but rather that they turn from their ways and live. Ezekiel 33:11, NIV.

How could a loving God destroy the wicked at the end of the earth?

I was driving down the highway to a writer's meeting when I noticed something lying on the outside edge of the pavement, right on the white line.

Oh, the poor little dog, I thought. *It got a little too close to the road, and someone hit it.*

Just before I passed the little beagle, I saw something that made me catch my breath. The dog was still alive. I hit the brake pedal and whipped my car over to the shoulder of the road and backed up.

Getting out of my car, I walked slowly toward the dog. It heard me coming and turned its head in my direction. "Oh, puppy," I said softly, "you poor little thing. I want to help you. Don't be afraid."

I waited for her to snarl at me, but her big brown eyes just watched me expectantly. I crouched down and held out my hand to her. She made a little whining sound. Reaching out, I stroked her head and told her that I was going to help.

And I did try. I went to a house nearby and asked if they might know whom she belonged to. They didn't. So I asked them to call the police and have someone pick up the dog. Then I went back to the little beagle.

I stroked her head and talked softly to her. She tried to move away from the cars and trucks that sped so close to where she lay, but her back was broken. After waiting with her for 20 minutes, I realized that no one was coming to help.

Somehow I picked her up and laid her on the front seat of my car. Then I drove to my uncle's house and told him what had happened. "Uncle Harry, would you put her out of her misery? I can't stand to see her suffer any longer."

He walked out to the car with me and checked the dog over. "You're right. Her back is broken. Let's move her to the backyard."

We slid a floor mat under her and carried her behind the house. Uncle Harry got his gun, and it was over in a few seconds.

I went back to my car and cried. I had wanted so much to help her get better, but I couldn't. All I could do was end her suffering.

When God finally destroys the wicked, He'll not do it out of anger—He'll do it out of love. He will let them die so they never have to suffer again.

NOVEMBER

16

The Impractical Practical Joke

Every prudent man acts out of knowledge, but a fool exposes his folly. Proverbs 13:16, NIV.

A knock at the classroom door interrupted Mr. Phillips' history lecture. "Mr. Phillips, there's a phone call for you in the office," said a voice from the hall.

Perfect timing, thought John as he watched his teacher leave the room. John slowly opened his desktop a few inches and peeked inside. Lifting up a box of colored pencils, he found what he was looking for—his heavy-duty all-purpose rubber band.

Next John tore a sheet from his notepad. Then he folded it until he had a nice fat paper wad. With both hands hidden inside his desk, he slid the rubber band over his fingers and put the paper wad in position. John turned around and aimed the missile at Rick's head. "Psst," he said, trying to get his friend's attention.

Just as Rick looked up, John let go of the paper wad. "Ehhhhhhhhhh!" Rick screamed as he dropped out of his seat onto the floor.

Mr. Phillips came running into the room. "What's wrong?"

"I didn't mean to hurt him," John sobbed. "It was just a little joke. I didn't mean to hit him in the eye."

"In the eye!" Mr. Phillips dropped down to Rick's side. "Just hold on, Rick," he said. "I'll call your mom, and we'll have her take you to the emergency room. You're going to be OK. Just try to relax."

Soon Rick's mother came rushing into the classroom. Mr. Phillips helped the injured boy to his feet and led him to the car.

For the rest of the morning John slouched in his desk, wishing he could disappear. The other students stared at him with silent disapproval. They were tired of his childish pranks.

Right before lunch Rick walked into the room. A large patch covered his right eye. Everyone expected Mr. Phillips to give the class a lecture on the danger of playing tricks on other people. But he didn't. He didn't need to. Rick's bandaged eye said it all.

NOVEMBER

17

Plug Into the Power

His divine power has given us everything we need for life and godliness through our knowledge of him who called us by his own glory and goodness. 2 Peter 1:3, NIV.

Here, honey, I got that power strip you wanted."

"Thanks a million, Dad," said Danielle. "Now I can get my computer set up. I've got an English assignment I need to print out before class tomorrow."

Danielle took the special extension cord and hurried to her bedroom. Because there was only one electrical outlet in her room, she hadn't been able to set up her new computer and printer.

After taking the computer and the printer out of their boxes, Danielle arranged everything on her desk. Then she joined the different parts together with special cables. Finally she plugged the electric power cords into the power strip.

"At last," she said happily. "Now I can get some work done."

Danielle pulled her chair out and sat down in front of the computer. She turned it on, but nothing happened.

Oh, great. It's not working. Just my luck. I probably got a defective power strip.

"Daaaaad!" she called out.

"What's the problem?" her father asked as he walked into the room.

"The power strip isn't working."

"What do you mean?"

"I plugged all the cords into it, but the computer won't start. Should we take the power strip back and get a new one?"

Dad got down on his knees and checked the new extension cord. "I see your problem," he laughed. "You got so busy plugging in the cords from the computer and the printer that you plugged the end of the power strip into itself." He separated it and plugged it into the electrical outlet in the wall. Instantly the computer started up, and the monitor turned on.

Have you ever made a mistake similar to Danielle's? When you're trying to accomplish something, do you ever try to rely on your own power?

Whether we're trying to overcome temptation or finish a difficult assignment, we need to ask God for His help. There's no reason to try to go it alone, because when we plug into His power, we'll always have success.

NOVEMBER

18

One Day at a Time

Therefore do not worry about tomorrow, for tomorrow will worry about itself. Matthew 6:34, NIV.

If you trust, you don't worry; if you worry, you don't trust."

Kenneth Wood in his book *Meditations for Moderns* tells about a clock that had a problem. One day, as the story goes, the clock began to worry about all the work that it would face during the coming year.

If I tick twice every second, that means I'll have to tick 120 times a minute, thought the clock. *And if I tick 120 times a minute, I'll have to tick 7,200 times each hour. In just one day I'll have to tick 172,800 times.* The thought was almost more than the clock could handle.

That means in one year I'll tick 63 million times. In five years I'll tick 315 million times.

At this point the clock fell off the shelf and landed on the floor in a dead faint, but a few minutes later it woke up. *There's no way that I can tick 63 million times,* it said as it picked itself up from the carpeting. *But I do have the strength to tick one more time. So that's what I'll do. I'll just tick one more time.*

So the little clock went ahead and took life one tick at a time. It went on to keep steady time, not for five years, but for more than 25 years.

Do you ever find yourself worrying? Do you worry about your grades? your popularity? your appearance? your health? your parents? your money or lack of it?

Worry is not only unproductive—it's also destructive. It takes away today's happiness, and it can even make you sick. If you find yourself worrying a lot, try this assignment for one week:

Each time you begin to worry about something, write it in a notebook. Wait for two weeks. Then take out the notebook and read through your list of worries. You'll be surprised to find out that few, if any, of your fears ever came true.

God wants us to live our lives one day at a time. There's no need to be worried about what might happen tomorrow or the next day. Since God is in control of your tomorrows, you don't need to worry about them today.

NOVEMBER

19

He Answers Before We Call

Before they call I will answer; while they are still speaking I will hear. Isaiah 65:24, NIV.

During World War II an American bomber ran out of fuel while on a mission over the Pacific Ocean. The crew had no choice but to land on a nearby island. Since the island belonged to the enemy, those aboard knew that it was just a matter of time before they would all be captured and hauled off to a prison camp.

But the chaplain didn't give up hope. He began praying that help would come. The airmen respected the chaplain's faith, but they didn't think prayer was going to do them any good. As far as they were concerned, they were doomed. But the next day they changed their minds.

Early that morning, just before the sun came up, one of the crew awoke suddenly. He had a strong feeling that he should go down to the beach and walk along the shore. He tried to go back to sleep, but the feeling would not go away. So without awakening the others, he got up and walked down to the beach. When he got there, he found a huge drum of aviation fuel riding the waves of the incoming tide. Shouting, the airman awakened the rest of the crew. Everyone ran down to the beach to see what the racket was all about.

"Look what just washed in!" the airman exclaimed. "Don't just stand there; let's get this thing on shore."

The men jumped into the water and helped roll the drum out of the water and over to the stranded plane. It took no time at all before they had the bomber refueled. Clamoring aboard, the men started up the engines. Soon they taxied down the beach and felt the thrill of takeoff as they climbed toward the clouds.

Later the mystery of the floating fuel became known. The drum had been part of a cargo of fuel that had been dumped off a barge after the boat had been bombed by the Japanese. All the other drums had been lost. This one container had floated past 25 islands and traveled almost 1,000 miles before it washed up on the shore of the island where the men were stranded.

NOVEMBER

20

Clever Disguises

He prays to God and finds favor with him, he sees God's face and shouts for joy; he is restored by God to his righteous state. Job 33:26, NIV.

Have you ever tried to disguise your voice? No matter how hard you try, it still sounds like you. What about your handwriting? Have you ever tried to send a letter to a secret pal? The only thing that works for me is to write left-handed, but even then what I write still resembles my normal handwriting.

A famous thief once came up with what he thought was a foolproof way of stealing without getting caught. From past experience he knew that if he left any fingerprints at the scene of the crime, he'd be picked up before he could leave town. The Federal Bureau of Investigation already had his fingerprints on file.

So he set about to get rid of his fingerprints. He removed the top layer of skin from his fingertips. "That should do it," he bragged to his friends. "From now on they'll never see my fingerprints again. I can help myself to anything I want, and the police won't know who did it."

His clever plan didn't work. As the skin healed, his fingerprints grew right back.

You can change the color of your hair and style it differently, and if you're a male, grow a mustache and a beard. But no matter what you do to change your appearance, you'll still look like you.

The Bible says that it is impossible for a leopard to change how it looks. Then it adds that it is just as impossible for sinful people to change their characters.

You may be able to put on your best behavior when a special guest comes for dinner. You may be a perfect angel when the minister or the teacher visits your home, but eventually you'll go back to acting like your old self.

Real changes happen only when Jesus changes us from the inside out. When we grow in our love for the things of God, we'll want to be different. Our selfishness will be replaced with a desire to be like Jesus.

The thief couldn't get rid of his fingerprints. The leopard can't lose its spots. And people can't change their characters. But God's friends will receive brand-new hearts.

NOVEMBER

21

Holding High God's Banner

We will shout for joy when you are victorious and will lift up our banners in the name of our God. Psalm 20:5, NIV.

Have you ever sung the song "I'm in the Lord's Army"? There's no doubt about it. We *are* soldiers in a war—the most important war the universe will ever know: the war between good and evil, between God and Satan. Each day we must reenlist. Each day we must pledge our loyalty to one side or the other.

During the Civil War, the Sixteenth Connecticut Regiment had almost been wiped out at Plymouth, North Carolina. Sensing that they would soon have to surrender to the enemy, the commander called together his remaining men. "As much as I hate to say it," he began, "I feel that we have no choice but to surrender to the enemy. But before we do, I have one request to make." Walking over to the regiment's flag, the commander ripped off the blue shield that identified his group. "The enemy may take us captive, but they will never have the opportunity to dishonor our flag."

After cutting apart the shield, he handed a piece to each of his men. "Guard your part of the shield with your life. If you feel yourself coming close to death, pass it on to one of your fellow soldiers. When the war is over, bring your piece back to Connecticut, and we will reassemble our banner."

Several of the men died in the prison camp, but they all kept their promise. When the war was over, the survivors returned to their home state, carrying with them the precious scraps of the shield.

As Christians we have a responsibility to guard the banner of God. Everything that we say and do brings either honor or dishonor to His cause. No matter how fierce the battle becomes, we must not let the enemy cause us to bring disgrace on the name of Jesus.

The Civil War flag of Sixteenth Connecticut Regiment can be seen today in the Hall of Battle Flags in the state capital, Hartford, Connecticut. But, more important, is the banner of God's love on display in your life today?

NOVEMBER

22

Where Do You Put Your Trust?

No one who believes in Christ will ever be disappointed. Romans 10:11, TLB.

Elizabeth stopped her best friend as they walked up the steps of the church. "I can't believe it, Camille. My husband is going to take me on a cruise for our anniversary! I've heard that the ship is the largest one ever built. And talk about luxury! Why, some of the richest people in the world have already booked passage! And to think we've got tickets! I know it will be a trip I'll never forget." Elizabeth was right. The cruise from England to New York City would end up being an event she could never erase from her memory.

The *Titanic,* considered to be the greatest ship ever built, left England on April 10, 1912, with approximately 2,200 passengers aboard. The crew, hoping to break the record for a trans-Atlantic crossing, set the boat at full speed.

The designers of the *Titanic* created it to be not only beautiful but also safe. In fact, it was advertised as being unsinkable.

As the ship sped along, a lookout kept watch, searching the water for icebergs. The crew members were well aware that icebergs were common in the North Atlantic at that time of the year. On the fifth night of the trip, the lookout shouted an alarm. "There's an iceberg coming up about one mile ahead."

The crew turned the ship sharply to one side. Because it was plowing through the water at such a high speed, they weren't able to steer clear of the berg. If the *Titanic* had hit the iceberg head on, little damage would have been done to the ship. But it struck the iceberg sideways, and the great ship started to take in water.

Within three hours, more than 1,500 people lost their lives. Only 705 survived. The great "unsinkable" ship sank to the bottom of the ocean on her very first voyage.

More than 2,200 people put their complete faith and trust in a ship they believed would carry them safely to their destination, but it failed them.

People put their trust in many things: money, investments, power, position, success, other people, and even themselves. But they will always end up disappointed.

The only place we can put our trust without disappointment is in God. Get to know your heavenly Father. He never fails.

NOVEMBER

23

He Just Wouldn't Listen

But if you do warn the wicked man and he does not turn from his wickedness or from his evil ways, he will die for his sin. If he had taken warning, he would have saved himself. Ezekiel 3:19; 33:5, NIV.

One morning after washing and waxing his red Corvette convertible, Charlie decided to go for a ride. "Let's see how you run after your bath," he said to it as he patted the sports car on the hood.

Charlie jumped into the driver's seat and started the engine. After turning on the radio, he backed out of the driveway. He drove slowly down the country road, because he didn't want to get his car all dusty, but as soon as he entered the highway, he started picking up speed.

Charlie looked around. He didn't see any police cars. So he pressed the pedal to the metal and let the Corvette burn up the road. Just as he came over the first rise in the highway, he saw a blue patrol car at the bottom of the hill.

Charlie hit the brakes, but just as he passed the police car, Charlie heard a siren. He looked in his rearview mirror. Charlie pulled off the road and waited. The policeman walked up to his car and asked for his driver's license and car registration. "Mr. Spense, I clocked you at 15 miles per hour over the speed limit, but I'm just going to give you a warning this time. Do yourself—and everyone else—a favor and slow down."

Charlie smiled as he slipped his driver's license back into his wallet. "Thank you, Officer. You can count on me."

The very next day as Charlie was on his way to work, he was stopped again—by the same policeman. "Well, Mr. Spense, I guess we meet again. I'm afraid I'll have to give you a ticket this time."

Charlie bristled. "Why do you guys have to pick on innocent citizens all the time? Why don't you go out and fight the real criminals?"

"Mr. Spense," said the policeman, "we're just trying to make the roads safe for everyone. The speed limit is 65, and that's the law. We don't like giving people tickets, but it's the only way we can get people to slow down."

When Officer Feeley told me about Mr. Spense, he said that the man continued to get speeding tickets. Each time Mr. Spense protested the unfair treatment, but he finally stopped speeding—after he ran his car into the back of a semi and died from a broken neck.

NOVEMBER

24

Winning Words

A gentle answer turns away wrath, but a harsh word stirs up anger. Proverbs 15:1, NIV.

Some years ago the United States Navy conducted research to find out which tone of voice the commanding officers should use when giving orders to sailors. One thing the Navy learned was that the men usually responded in the same tone of voice that they heard coming over the telephone or intercom. For instance, when someone shouted an order, the sailors shouted back. When the order was spoken in a quiet voice, the men answered back quietly.

Have you ever noticed that people usually treat you the same way you treat them?

Recently I drove to town to have a wedding program printed. I asked the lady at the printshop to run 100 copies. When she handed me the finished product, I realized that something was wrong. "Oh, no," I said, "the back page is upside down!"

The lady went over to the printer and told him what had happened. He came stalking to the counter, his face clouded. "Listen, lady, that's exactly how the paper was handed to me," he said. "It's not *my* fault it's upside down."

"You're right," I said. "It's not your fault. It's mine. I'm sorry. I handed you the papers in the wrong order. I guess I'll just have to have the program copied again. I'll pay for all 200 copies."

The man's face relaxed, and he took the papers from my hand. "I've got another order going right now, but I'll have your program done soon. And don't worry about paying for the ones done wrong. There'll be no charge for them."

I couldn't believe how quickly his attitude changed when I took the blame for the mistake. I'm sure if I'd gotten angry at him the end results would have been very different.

When people get angry at us, we don't have to respond in the same way. Instead, we can take control of the situation.

Why not try an experiment? The next time someone speaks to you in an angry or impatient voice, answer calmly. See if a quiet answer will turn away the other person's anger.

NOVEMBER

25

Everyday Pleasures

All 10 were in the same predicament. All 10 had been forced to leave their families. And all 10 were dying. When they heard about Jesus coming to town, they decided to see if He would help. After all, they had nothing to lose. Things couldn't get any worse.

As Jesus was walking toward Jerusalem, the 10 men ran after Him. Because of the rules about leprosy, they kept their distance, but they called out to get His attention. "Jesus, have pity on us!"

"Go and show yourselves to the priests," Jesus instructed them.

As they started running for town, they looked down at their skin. They were healed! Ten men saw their diseased bodies instantly healed. Ten men received a new lease on life. But only one man came back to Jesus to thank Him.

Have you ever thought, *Boy, those other nine men were sure ungrateful. If I'd been healed of a deadly disease like leprosy,* I'd *have shown my appreciation to Jesus?*

It's sad to think that the nine men didn't take the time to express their thanks to their Healer, but don't we sometimes forget to thank God for what He's done for us? Don't we too often take His gifts for granted?

It's easy to get excited about the new things that we get for our birthday or at Christmas. But what about the everyday things that we often take for granted, because they're always around?

Pretend for a moment that you and your family decide to take a boat ride one afternoon. When you're far from shore, a storm comes up. Fortunately, your father sees a little island in the distance and maneuvers the boat over to it.

For one whole week you live on the island, surviving on the picnic lunch you'd brought along and the wild fruit you find growing everywhere. After seven days someone in a Coast Guard cutter sees a fire you have made and rescues you.

What ordinary things would you miss during your week's stay on the island?

When we take time to appreciate the things God has given us, we get more enjoyment out of life. Every day of our lives should be a day of thanksgiving.

It is good to say, "Thank you" to the Lord, to sing praises to the God who is above all gods. Psalm 92:1, TLB.

NOVEMBER

26

20/20

Now all that I know is hazy and blurred, but then I will see everything clearly, just as clearly as God sees into my heart right now. 1 Corinthians 13:12, TLB.

"The leaves! Oh, they're so pretty!" I stood outside the eye doctor's office and looked at the tree across the street.

After I'd failed a vision test at school, my parents took me to Dr. Ticknor. He checked my eyes and prescribed my first pair of glasses. When I put them on, a whole new world opened up to me. Thanks to the glasses, I realized that a tree wasn't just a green blob. Trees had individual leaves that caught the sunlight as they fluttered in the breeze.

When eye doctors check a person's vision, they rate it with a number such as 20/35, which means that what the patient can see at a distance of 20 feet, someone with perfect eyesight can see at 35 feet. The goal is to bring a person's defective eyesight as close as possible to 20/20. But that can't be done unless the patient wears the prescribed glasses.

One day I received a phone call from the high school down the street. A number of the students from our junior academy were enrolled in their after-school driver's education class. The driver's ed teacher informed me that one of the girls from our school had just failed the eye exam. It turned out that her vision was 20/200. In other words, she couldn't see much of anything.

"And to think I've let her practice driving for three weeks," he said. "Tell her she can't come back to class until she gets glasses."

Molly refused to wear glasses, so she had to drop out of driver's ed. She chose to live with poor vision.

While not all people need to wear glasses to see better, we all have a type of eyesight that needs improving—spiritual eyesight. Spiritual eyesight is the ability to see (understand) the things of God.

Our physical eyes generally grow weaker over time, but the more we use our spiritual eyes, the stronger they become. We can sharpen our spiritual vision by reading the Bible, praying, and following God's instructions. The more time we spend with God, the better we'll get at seeing what He wants us to do.

Eyeglasses can open up a whole new world to a person with poor eyesight. But even more important is the spiritual eyesight you can have if you just take the time to exercise it every day.

NOVEMBER

27

Perfect Vision

No eye has seen, no ear has heard, no mind has conceived what God has prepared for those who love him.
1 Corinthians 2:9, NIV.

"Boy, I sure hope Jesus doesn't come until after I graduate from academy," said Sandy as she and her friends were finishing the Bible assignment in the school library. The textbook chapter they were studying talked about the signs of the Second Coming.

April shut her book and shoved it into her backpack. "I know what you mean. I've always had dreams of getting married someday and being a mother—you know how much I like little kids. I've always hoped that Jesus would wait until I'm at least 40 years old."

Ty looked up from across the table. "I thought I was the only one who felt that way," he said, "and it makes me feel guilty. We're supposed to pray for Jesus' soon return, yet sometimes I almost feel like praying that He won't come while I'm young."

April nodded. "It's hard to get all excited about heaven when you've never seen it. At least we know what to expect down here on earth."

"Well, it's not that I don't want to go to heaven," Ty continued. "It's just that there are so many things I want to do before life on earth is over. It's easy for older people to talk about how great it would be for Jesus to come. They've already lived their lives, but my life is still ahead of me."

Have you ever felt like Sandy, April, and Ty? Do you find yourself hoping that Jesus will put off His coming? If you do, don't feel guilty. Like April said, it's hard to get excited about something you've never seen. Although things aren't perfect here on earth, we've at least learned to adapt. We can't imagine any other way of living.

And that's the problem. Because our spiritual eyesight isn't a perfect 20/20, our picture of heaven is fuzzy and distorted. And what we "see" doesn't always look that appealing, but the more we study the Bible and the more we come to know Jesus, the better heaven will look. We'll realize that the best the world has to offer is nothing in comparison with what Jesus is preparing for us.

But even more than that, when we get to know Jesus as our best friend, we'll want to be with Him. We'll be excited about heaven because that's where He is.

NOVEMBER

28

The Face on the Side of the Mountain

And we, who with unveiled faces all reflect the Lord's glory, are being transformed into his likeness with ever-increasing glory, which comes from the Lord, who is the Spirit.
2 Corinthians 3:18, NIV.

"We are shaped and fashioned by what we love."—Goethe.

Nathaniel Hawthorne tells the story of Ernest, a young boy who grew up looking at the Great Stone Face. The Great Stone Face is a group of rocks that when seen from the valley, appear to look like the face of a man.

For as long as he could remember, Ernest was fascinated by the stone face, which jutted from the side of the mountain. Whenever he looked at it, he felt inspired to be a better person.

Legend claimed that someday a baby boy would be born who would grow up to look just like the Great Stone Face. Ernest hoped that someday he would be able to meet the special man.

One day excitement filled the entire village. "He's here!" the people said. "The man who looks like the Great Stone Face is here!"

Ernest could hardly believe that he was about to see the man he'd been waiting to meet all his life. But when Ernest caught sight of the man everyone was talking about, he was disappointed. For the man did not have the upright character that was so evident in the face high on the mountain. No, he was definitely not the one Ernest had been waiting for.

Years passed. Ernest continued to look at the Great Stone Face, which seemed to watch him from the top of the mountain. The townspeople continued to seek out the great man who would come to their village. Finally Ernest grew to be an old man, and one day as he was speaking to the townspeople, the sun shone on the Great Stone Face.

"Look!" someone said, pointing. All eyes turned to the face on the side of the mountain. "Why, the Great Stone Face—it looks just like Ernest!"

And so it did. After watching the face for so many years, Ernest had come to look just like it.

When we keep our eyes on Jesus, we too will change. The more we see His beautiful character, the more we will become like Him.

The secret to developing a Christlike character is to know Jesus so well that you speak His words, think His thoughts, and do His deeds.

Something to think about: Do others see Jesus in you?

NOVEMBER

29

By Design, or by Default?

Watch and pray so that you will not fall into temptation. Matthew 26:41, NIV.

When you have to make a choice and don't make it, that is in itself a choice."—William James.

The students in the computer class slid into their seats as the 1:00 p.m. bell rang. Mr. Patterson opened his book and asked the class to turn to page 27. "Today we're going to learn about the term *default*. Instead of telling you what it means, I'd like to show you. But first you'll need to boot up your word-processing program."

The class turned to their computers and followed the teacher's instructions. "Now," continued Mr. Patterson, "type your name on the screen. When you're finished, press F7 to exit. At the bottom of your screen you should see this." He held up a sign with the words *Save Document? (Y/N) Yes.* "Your computer is asking if you want to save what you've just typed. Instead of typing in *yes* or *no,* just hit the Enter key and see what happens."

The class followed the instruction. Ted raised his hand. "It's asking me to name the file I'm saving."

"That's right. You didn't have to tell the computer to save what you've typed, because the default is *yes*. The default is the automatic response that the computer will make unless you tell it differently. The only way to stop the computer from saving what you've keyed in is to type *no.*"

Our lives are a lot like the computer. We too have automatic responses. Because we've been born sinful, it's natural for us to do evil. Unless we make a conscious choice to say no when we're tempted, we'll end up sinning.

Don't lose out on eternal life by default. When you're faced with temptation, ask God to give you the power to say no.

NOVEMBER

30

When God Opened Another Door

In his heart a man plans his course, but the Lord determines his steps. Proverbs 16:9, NIV.

When Robert was a young man, his goal in life was to be a great pianist, and he was well on his way to becoming one of the most famous of his day. As he practiced he noticed that his third fingers, because of their extra tendons, were clumsy and hard to control. Robert's hands were no different than yours or mine, but he felt he had to do something about the problem. "If I could just correct the problem, I could play even better," he told his friends.

So he began experimenting with different devices and eventually came up with an invention he was sure would work. When attached to the hands, the gadget kept his third fingers from moving so they didn't interfere when he used his other fingers.

Instead of helping his playing, Robert's device crippled a finger on his right hand. His career as a master pianist ended abruptly. For a while Robert was so depressed that he lost interest in life. But whenever God shuts one door, He always opens another.

One day Robert had an idea. "I can't play music anymore, but I can *write* music!" And that's exactly what he did. He turned his energies into composing piano solos, and his wife, Clara, who was already a concert pianist, performed the music he wrote.

Today Robert Schumann is considered to be one of the greatest piano composers of all time. Had he continued as a pianist, his talent would have ended with his death, but through his compositions he continues to bless each new generation of pianists, who discover the beauty of his songs. What Robert considered to be the worst thing that could happen to him turned out to be a great opportunity for him to express his musical talent in a different way.

If God should close a door on one of your dreams, take a look around you. He's probably opening another just around the corner.

DECEMBER

1

Eternal Life: Choice—Not Chance

Believe in the Lord Jesus, and you will be saved. Acts 16:31, NIV.

"You mean that some of the people in our church won't be saved when Jesus comes?" Steve asked in surprise.

During Bible class we had been discussing the parable of the wheat and the tares found in Matthew 13:24-30. As the story goes, after the farmer had planted his crop, an enemy sneaked in and planted tares (weeds) in the same area. At the time of harvest, the farmer asked his servants to separate the tares from the wheat. The wheat was then taken into the barn, while the tares were destroyed.

I explained to the class that the story represents the end of the world when the angels separate the church members into two groups: the Christians and those who just tried to look like Christians.

That's when Steve spoke up. "I don't understand it," he continued. "I always thought that if a person became a church member and attended church, he would be saved."

Many people have the same opinion. They believe that by doing the right things they can meet God's requirements.

It's good to keep God's laws, but doing the right things won't ever save us. Our salvation is not determined by what church we attend, what day we worship on, or even how much we know about God and the Bible. The only way we can have eternal life is to ask Jesus to save us. When we do this, Jesus will take away our sins and give us His righteousness. But He doesn't stop there. He also wants us to have a new life. He wants to free us from our sinful habits and replace them with His love and kindness.

Have you asked Jesus to be your Saviour?

DECEMBER

2

Sisters and Scars

Therefore, as we have opportunity, let us do good to all people, especially to those who belong to the family of believers.
Galatians 6:10, NIV.

I don't know what I would do without my sister Karen. We're the best of friends. However, our relationship was very different when we lived together under one roof. Let me give you just one example.

Karen's favorite pastime was bug collecting. She loved to sift through the contents of our basement window wells to see what creepy, crawly treasures she could find. On one of her hunting expeditions, she made the mistake of using my cat's water dish for a bug depository. When I discovered what she had done, I marched out of the house, picked up the dish, and dumped out the bugs.

"You dummy!" screamed Karen. Jumping up, she yelled a few death threats and came running after me. I ducked inside the house and pulled the glass door shut behind me.

Karen, who had a temper problem back then, didn't bother to open the door. She smashed through headfirst.

Hearing the commotion, Mother came up from the basement. "What's going on here? I'm sick and tired of—"

What she saw wasn't a pretty sight. Most of the broken glass covered the hall floor. The rest of it was stuck in Karen's face.

Now, 25 years later, Karen still has a scar on her chin. Every time I see it, I am reminded of the cat's dish episode.

It's hard for me to imagine how we could treat each other the way we did back then. Today Karen is one of my closest friends. We would do anything for each other. All the rivalry, teasing, and selfishness have been replaced by respect and love.

I tell you this story because I want you to know that there is hope for you and your brothers and sisters.

Mother used to say, "Someday you girls will be the best of friends." I didn't believe her—but she was right.

Why not practice being friends with your brothers and sisters while you're still young? Then maybe you can avoid some of the scars that result from unkindness.

We were driving down the expressway when we saw the dog. "Oh, look at that poor thing," I said to Tom.

A German shepherd had wandered out onto the median that ran between the four lanes of traffic. There it stood, confused, wondering which way to go. Suddenly it bolted toward our side of the highway, hoping to escape the frightening vehicles that whizzed by on both sides. We held our breath as the dog ran out in front of the traffic. An approaching truck driver blew his horn and scared it back to the grassy median. The dog hung its head and wandered over to the other side of the highway and began trotting alongside the pavement.

Tom shook his head. "No matter which way he turns, he's going to get hit. I wonder where he came from and how he ended up in the middle of the highway."

As we got closer, we noticed a broken chain hanging from the dog's collar. Apparently he had run away, thinking (to the extent that a dog can think) that breaking away from the restricting chain would make him free. However, his supposed freedom had put his life in danger, and unless someone rescued him, the dog wouldn't live to see another day.

Some of us are like that dog. We have the wrong idea about restrictions. We think that rules take away our happiness. We're sure that if we could just be free to do whatever we wanted, life would be great. Satan used this temptation on Eve, and he's using it on us today.

God knows that freedom requires restrictions. So He gave us the Ten Commandments. He will never force us to obey them, but we'll never know what it means to be free unless we do.

DECEMBER

3

Freedom of Restrictions

Then you will know the truth, and the truth will set you free. John 8:32, NIV.

DECEMBER

4

Switched Price Tags

Do not love the world or anything in the world. If anyone loves the world, the love of the Father is not in him. 1 John 2:15, NIV.

The story is told of a group of boys who decided to break into a local hardware store. In the middle of the night they secretly entered the building. When they got inside, they didn't steal money from the cash register or help themselves to the merchandise. Instead they began switching the price tags on all the items.

In the morning when customers came to make their purchases, they found thumbtacks selling for $17.95, and paintbrushes for 25 cents a pound. Lawn mowers were priced at $1.49, and the flyswatters were a real buy at $199.99.

Satan has played a similar trick on our society. He has carefully switched the price tags on our values. The customers at the hardware store weren't fooled by the phony prices, but most of the world has been tricked into valuing the wrong things.

Consider the following.

God wants us to love our neighbors as we love ourselves. The world tells us to forget about everyone else and "look out for Number One."

God tells us to lay up treasure in heaven. The world tells us that the more things we buy, the happier we will be.

God says that true freedom comes from obeying Him. The world claims that we're free only when we push aside all restraints and do what we feel like doing.

Are you letting the world tell you what is worthwhile? Do you find yourself being pressured into accepting the values that are portrayed by worldly music, television, and movies?

Our actions are influenced by what we value. Study the Bible so you'll know what things have true worth. Don't be fooled by phony price tags.

DECEMBER

5

Sins and Sin

Great peace have they who love your law, and nothing can make them stumble. Psalm 119:165, NIV.

We have the idea that sin is something we do—stealing a car, cheating on a test, lying to our parents. We think that if we could just stop doing these things, we'd have it made.

From the fifth to the tenth centuries a Christian group called the stylites decided to put this idea into practice. They spent their lives sitting on top of tall poles. They reasoned that by sitting up there, they could avoid sin.

Being exposed to the public eye probably did keep the men from sinning. There aren't many bad things a person can do while seated up in the air on a platform, but public exposure didn't take care of the real problem. It didn't protect them from *sin*.

Sin is not the same as sins. *Sins* are the outward expression of what's already gone on in our minds. *Sin*—a mental separation from God—is the real problem.

To better understand these two words, let's look at Harry. Harry is on the FBI's most-wanted list. He's committed about every crime there is. Harry's life is full of many sins.

One day the police close in on him and make the arrest. The judge throws the book at Harry and sentences him to 99 years in prison. Because Harry is such a dangerous criminal, he must spend the rest of his life in solitary confinement.

Harry now finds himself in an place where committing crimes will be next to impossible. He can't lie, murder, or steal because there's no one else around he can do this to, but does that make Harry a righteous person? Of course not. Even though Harry can't practice his sins, he's still sinful because his attitudes and thoughts are still the same.

If you want to become more like Jesus, take your eyes off the things you do wrong. Start concentrating on getting to know Him as your Saviour and Friend. When your mind is filled with love for the Lord, He will live in you and replace your sinfulness with His own perfect character.

DECEMBER

6

How Much Do You Trust God?

But my righteous one will live by faith. Hebrews 10:38, NIV.

The story is told about a man who suspended a heavy cable across Niagara Falls. After checking its connections, he climbed to the top of the wire. Ever so carefully he began inching his way across as the deadly waters surged below him.

By then a large crowd had gathered. They held their breath as the daredevil moved along the swaying wire. When he reached the other side, he started back—only this time he pushed a wheelbarrow in front of him!

A large cheer went up from the spectators as he returned safely to their side of the river.

"How many believe I can do it again?" asked the daredevil.

All raised their hands.

"This is wonderful," he replied as he smiled at the people. "Since all of you believe I can do it again, who will be the first to sit in the wheelbarrow and go across with me?"

Every hand went down. Their faith in his ability ended when he asked them to put their belief into action.

The belief (or trust or faith) that Jesus wants us to have is more than just recognizing that He is God. The Bible says that the devils believe and tremble (James 2:19). Their belief is similar to that of the people watching the man walk across the waterfall. The people in the story recognized that the man was what he claimed to be—a wonderful tightrope walker—but they refused to believe he could be trusted with their lives.

Dr. A. Graham Maxwell suggests that true belief in God involves three steps:

1. Believing in what God says.
2. Accepting what He offers.
3. Doing what He wishes for the rest of eternity.

Those who have this type of faith in God are the kind of people who will feel comfortable in heaven.

DECEMBER

7

He Always Brings the Victory

But thanks be to God! He gives us the victory through our Lord Jesus Christ.
1 Corinthians 15:57, NIV.

When we trust God and can praise Him for whatever comes into our lives, He always brings victory. He may bring victory by changing our circumstances, or He may bring victory *in* those circumstances.

Joni Eareckson Tada was only 17 years old when her life changed forever. While swimming with some friends, she dived into shallow water and hit her head on the bottom. The accident paralyzed her from the neck down.

At first, people encouraged Joni to pray and ask God for a miracle. But as time went by, she realized that God was not going to change her circumstances. Instead, He would give her victory in her circumstances.

Since her accident, Joni has written a number of books, made several record albums, learned to paint by holding a brush in her mouth, starred in a movie, spoken to audiences around the world, and organized a ministry for people with handicaps.

Recently she told an interviewer that becoming paralyzed was probably the best thing that could have happened to her. Being disabled has been very difficult, but it has forced her to use her talents and attempt things she never dreamed she could do.

Have you ever ridden in a vehicle with bad shock absorbers? My dad had an old Ford pickup that he used around our farm. Every once in a while he used it to drive my sister Karen and me to school. As long as the road was smooth, our ride was uneventful. But a bad stretch of pavement was enough to set our teeth rattling, and when it came to bumps and ruts, the shocks offered no protection at all. The old pickup would hit those bumps just right, and presto, Karen and I would be soaring up in the air, sometimes hitting our heads on the truck roof. (That was before the days of seat belts.) A trip down Cleveland Avenue right after the spring thaw was like riding to town in a trampoline.

Some people's lives are like that—they do fine as long as everything goes smoothly, but as soon as problems appear, the ruts in life throw them off balance.

When we learn to praise God for everything that happens, we'll be able, like Joni, to find victory in all circumstances. And life will stay in balance, no matter what the ride is like.

DECEMBER

8

Treading on Danger-ous Ground

Be self-controlled and alert. Your enemy the devil prowls around like a roaring lion looking for someone to devour. 1 Peter 5:8, NIV.

The story is told about an old circus lion that was waiting patiently for its evening meal. The animal feeder came by the cage, opened the door, and tossed in a live chicken. The chicken caught sight of the lion and squawked in terror as it fluttered around the cage. But the lion didn't move a muscle. After a while, the hen began to calm down. The lion acted as though the bird weren't even there. Smoothing her ruffled feathers, the chicken decided explore her new home.

Running along the bars, the chicken checked the view from all four sides. Then she decided to get a better view of the sleeping king of the jungle. Clucking softly to herself, she inched forward. The lion yawned but made no move to grab her. The hen, now more confident than ever, strutted right up to the lion's face to get a closer look.

"Clu—"

It was over in a second. It never failed. Given time, the chickens always lost their fear and eventually walked right into the trap. The lion finished dinner, roared its appreciation, and stretched out for another nap.

Do you find yourself acting like the chicken and intentionally placing yourself on dangerous ground? Has your curiosity led you over to Satan's territory?

While in Europe, Tom and I climbed the Leaning Tower of Pisa. If you've ever seen a picture of it, you know that (1) it's very tall, and (2) it's on its way to falling over. When you walk along the side that tilts downward, gravity tries to pull you over the edge. (A number of people have fallen to their death from the tower.)

While most of us stayed very close to the center supporting wall, some tourists walked out to the very edge and looked over. Instead of keeping a safe distance from possible destruction, they tried to see how close they could get to the edge.

When Satan tries to lure you into his territory, run the other way. Don't even give him a chance.

DECEMBER

9

Warning: Coming Destruction

While people are saying, "Peace and safety," destruction will come on them suddenly, . . . and they will not escape.
1 Thessalonians 5:3, NIV.

A few days after we saw the Leaning Tower of Pisa, Tom and I walked on the streets of one of the eeriest places on earth—the city of Pompeii. More than 200 years ago people began digging out this ancient Italian city that had been buried for so many hundreds of years. Why did Pompeii suddenly disappear from the face of the earth?

In A.D. 62, about 30 years after Jesus went back to heaven, a strong earthquake badly damaged much of Pompeii, but the people went about rebuilding their city and went on with life. Seventeen years later, in A.D. 79, four days of strange weather conditions prompted the people to suspect another earthquake might occur. Some, remembering the way previous earthquakes had damaged the city, moved to their country homes; others remained in town. They all made the mistake of interpreting the present situation by what had happened in the past.

When Mount Vesuvius suddenly erupted, spewing hot ashes, stones, and cinders on Pompeii, escape was nearly impossible. For two days the volcano poured its contents onto the city, leaving Pompeii buried under as much as 20 feet of pumice and ashes.

Like the inhabitants of Pompeii, most people today don't get too excited over warnings about the end of the world. They base their beliefs on the past—"It never happened before, so why worry?"

There have always been skeptics. Of all the world's inhabitants, only eight boarded Noah's ark. Only four escaped from Sodom. Only the Christians who followed Jesus' instructions fled Jerusalem before Rome destroyed it. More than 1 million Jews died, and the Romans took 97,000 captives (*The SDA Bible Commentary,* vol. 5, p. 499).

As we see the warnings that signal the end of the world, most people carry on as though life on earth will never end. Like the people of Pompeii, they don't suspect the coming destruction.

Are you preparing for the Second Coming? What do you think is the biggest obstacle you face in being ready to meet Jesus face-to-face?

DECEMBER

10

The Sin God Can't Forgive

Neither death nor life, neither angels nor demons, neither the present nor the future, nor any powers, neither height nor depth, nor anything else in all creation, will be able to separate us from the love of God. Romans 8:38, 39, NIV.

Have you ever wondered whether God has given up on you? Have you ever wondered whether you've committed the unpardonable sin? It's a scary thought to think that God may have walked away from you, but it's a thought that people of all ages battle with.

Drew stayed behind after his Sabbath school leader dismissed the rest of the juniors at the end of the lesson study. "Mr. Warren, how do people know if they've committed the unpardonable sin?" he blurted out.

Mr. Warren was a bit surprised at Drew's question. "What brought up that question?"

"Well, before my family came to church today, we had worship at our house. My dad read in Ephesians a verse that says, 'Do not grieve the Holy Spirit' [Ephesians 4:30, NIV]. I asked him what that means, and he said that when people refuse to listen to the Holy Spirit, He will eventually leave them. When that happens, the people can't be saved. They're doomed, I guess."

"Does that thought bother you?" asked Mr. Warren.

"Yeah, I guess it does. I know that the Holy Spirit speaks to me through my conscience. But I don't always do what He tells me to do, and I know I have a lot of sin in my life."

"So you're afraid that you may have said no so many times to the Holy Spirit that He's left you. Is that what you're saying?"

Drew hung his head. "That's what I'm afraid of."

Mr. Warren picked up his Bible, turned to John 6:37, and read, " 'All that the Father gives me will come to me, and whoever comes to me I will never drive away' [NIV]. You see, Drew, Jesus will never turn us away. He'll always forgive us when we're sorry for what we've done. The unpardonable sin is a sin that is never confessed to Jesus. He can't forgive us unless we ask Him to."

Have you ever worried that maybe God has rejected you because you haven't been able to overcome some of the sins in your life? Remember that God loves you. Instead of worrying about all the things you do wrong, think about Jesus. When your eyes are on Him, you'll begin having victory over your problems.

DECEMBER

11

Money, Money, Money

Whoever loves money never has money enough; whoever loves wealth is never satisfied with his income. Ecclesiastes 5:10, NIV.

Hetty learned to love money from the time she was a child. I suppose that most people enjoy money, but Hetty—well, it became the most important thing in her life.

When Hetty's father died, he left his daughter nearly $1 million in cash, plus $4 million in various properties and investments. Through careful investments, Hetty continued to build her financial empire. She became so consumed by the love of money that she became its slave.

Hetty became convinced that her father and aunt had been poisoned by their enemies and that her life was in danger too. So when she went to town, she would take a different route than before and sometimes hide in doorways to throw her enemies off track. Rumor has it that she would also make up her bed and then sleep underneath it on the floor. If anyone tried to break in to kill her, they'd think she was out of town.

When she had to travel short distances, Hetty rode around in a carriage built out of a henhouse. On long-distance train rides she rode standing up in the baggage car, because the fare was cheaper.

Every morning Hetty sent her son to town for a newspaper. After checking the financial section to see how her investments were doing, she would send him back to town to sell the paper to someone else.

She ate cold oatmeal because she didn't want to waste fuel heating it. And when her son hurt his leg, she spent so much time searching for free medical care that his leg finally had to be amputated.

When Hetty died, she left behind an estate valued at nearly $100 million. The money went to her daughter, who was just as greedy as she was.

Although Hetty Green became one of the richest women in America, she never learned to share with others. She could have built hospitals, libraries, or churches, sponsored students through college, provided housing and medical care for the poor, or built parks. She could have helped thousands of people. But she just helped herself to more and more money.

There's nothing wrong with earning and spending money, but when it becomes the most important thing in our lives, we can never be happy.

Put God first in your life, and then you'll be able to enjoy money without it controlling you.

DECEMBER

12

Facing the Bears

So do not fear, for I am with you; do not be dismayed, for I am your God. I will strengthen you and help you; I will uphold you with my righteous right hand. Isaiah 41:10, NIV.

"If we fear the Lord, we don't need to fear anything else."

When we lived in northern Michigan, it was not uncommon for people to see black bears in the woods near our town. One morning our pastor put on his jogging shoes and went for a run in the woods behind his home. As he turned a corner in the path, he came face-to-face with a big black bear. He said that he just did a quick about-face and headed back in the direction he had come from.

Yesterday I heard on the radio that black bears really aren't fierce. In fact, they're cowards. The announcer recommended that if you happen to wake up some morning and find a black bear checking out your campsite, you should jump up, raise your arms, scream, and throw stones. The bear will get the message, and it'll soon be on its way.

Do you expect to meet up with any bears today? I'm not talking about the furry kind with sharp teeth. The bears I'm talking about can be the town bully, a teacher you don't get along with, a tough assignment, or a health problem.

If you run into one or more of those bears, you need to treat them just like you would a real bear. I'm not suggesting that you throw stones and scream at your English teacher or at the people you don't get along with. What you need to do is to stand up to the problems and not let them scare you.

Every morning when I have my quiet time with God, I read over a number of Bible texts and other quotations that I have found especially helpful. One of my favorites is found in *Christ's Object Lessons,* page 173: "If we surrender our lives to His service, we can never be placed in a position for which God has not made provision."

We can rest assured that when we have to deal with the bears in our life, we don't need to be afraid. We aren't alone. God has promised to be with us no matter what situation we get ourselves into, and He always has an answer to our problems.

DECEMBER

13

Reaching Behind Bars

In a remote village in Japan, the keeper of the prison received a portion of the New Testament. At that time, only certain parts of the New Testament had been translated and printed in the Japanese language. The man wasn't interested in reading the Bible, so he gave the portion to one of the intellectual prisoners who was serving time for murder.

One night a fire broke out at the prison. It was a perfect opportunity for the prisoners to make their getaway. Guards surrounded the prison, rifles at the ready, but no one tried to escape. Instead of running to freedom, the men stayed and helped put out the fire.

The authorities were totally bewildered. Why would the prisoners want to stay around to help when they could have easily run away to freedom? The director of the prison ordered a full investigation. He was going to get to the bottom of the mystery.

After a thorough inquiry, the authorities learned that something strange had happened to the prisoners. After reading the Bible, the scholarly murderer had accepted Jesus as his Saviour, and the first thing he did was to tell the other prisoners about his newfound faith. By the time the fire broke out, the men in the prison had also come to believe in God. The power of God's love had kept them all inside the prison when they had had a chance to escape.

After learning about the great change that had taken place in the murderer's life, the prison officials decided to let him go free. They didn't see any reason to keep him behind bars when he was no longer a threat to society. But when he was told about his freedom, the man turned it down. He chose to stay at the prison so he could continue to bring a new way of life to his fellow prisoners.

Now the Lord is the Spirit, and where the Spirit of the Lord is, there is freedom. 2 Corinthians 3:17, NIV.

DECEMBER

14

Ignorantly Rich

With me are riches and honor, enduring wealth and prosperity. Proverbs 8:18, NIV.

In May 1901 the Dutch steamship *Tambora* ran onto a submerged reef and sank off a small island in the East Indies. The people on the island rowed out to the ship the next day to see if there were any valuables they could salvage. One of the men arrived after all the good things had been claimed. He had to settle for a bundle of wet colored paper. After he dried out the paper, he decided to use it to cover the inside walls of his hut.

A few months later a Chinese merchant stopped on one of his regular visits to the island. In times past the merchant had done some trading with the islanders. The man who had found the colored paper looked over the merchant's goods. "I'd like some needles and a couple of spools of that thread."

"What do you have to trade?" asked the merchant.

"I have no money, but I have something that you'll like. I have a fine large fish bone."

"A fish bone? I don't have much use for a fish bone," huffed the merchant.

"But you must see it. Come to my hut."

So the merchant followed the man to his simple home. As they entered the hut, the merchant's eyes almost popped out of his head when he saw the colored paper on the man's walls. The colored paper that the national had found was Dutch money. The man who thought his most valuable possession was a fish bone actually had $40,000 worth of Dutch bank notes plastered on his walls. The man on the island was living in the middle of a small fortune, but the money was really worthless until he recognized its value.

Do you realize that you're living in the middle of some wonderful treasures too? And chances are that you, like the West Indian, don't recognize their value.

Do you have good health? Do you have a family who loves you? Do you have a clear mind? Do you have a home and regular meals? Do you have friends? Then you have a vast fortune too.

How does it feel to be rich?

DECEMBER

15

And the Choir Sang On

Do not be afraid or discouraged because of this vast army. For the battle is not yours, but God's. 2 Chronicles 20:15, NIV.

The time: 850 B.C.
The place: The land of Judah.

The Moabites and the Ammonites had decided to attack the people of Judah. After comparing the size of their combined armies with Judah's army, they knew they had the upper hand, but just to be sure, they enlisted the help of the Meunites.

King Jehoshaphat, the king of Judah, could have panicked. Instead, he turned to the Lord and asked what he and the people should do. God assured the king that the battle was not man's, but God's. Then Jehoshaphat, instead of organizing the soldiers, was impressed to put together a choir and set them out in front of the army of Judah. (How would *you* have liked to wear a choir robe instead of a weapon to battle? But that's just what happened.) The singers took the front positions and led the army of Judah into battle.

As soon as the choir began to sing praises to God, something strange happened. The Moabites and Ammonites turned against the Meunites and destroyed them. Then the Moabites and Ammonites turned on each other and fought until they had wiped themselves out. The people of Judah never had to raise a hand to defend themselves.

After the dust had settled and the choir had finished its last song, Judah had only one job to do—gather up all the riches and jewels left by the dead soldiers. (And that job was so big that it took three days.)

It's good to praise God after He has given us victory, but it takes real faith to praise Him before we can see the final success. When you're tempted to give in to discouragement or fear, just remember that God wants to help you fight your battles. He will help you just as He helped the people of Judah. Praise Him for what He is going to do, and then watch Him give you the victory.

DECEMBER

16

Big, Bigger, Biggest

For you are a people holy to the Lord your God. The Lord your God has chosen you out of all the peoples on the face of the earth to be his people, his treasured possession. Deuteronomy 7:6.

Have you ever stood in a crowd of people and felt like a nobody? Sometimes it's easy to feel so small and unimportant that you wonder if God even knows you're alive. After all, there's a big universe out there. And when I say *big,* I mean *BIG.* Consider the following facts.

1. The sun, which is the closest star to the earth, is 93 million miles away. If you had a rocket that could travel 1,000 miles per hour, 24 hours a day, it would take you more than 10 *years* to get from earth to the sun.

2. Our next-closest star is 26 million million miles. That's almost 300,000 times farther away than the sun. Traveling in our same rocket to this star would take about 3 million years.

3. Our galaxy, the Milky Way, measures approximately 600,000 trillion miles across. It would take our rocket nearly 70 billion years to travel across it.

4. There are millions, perhaps even billions, of other galaxies.

5. The most distant objects that can be detected from earth are quasars. Astronomers believe they're a type of galaxy that gives off large amounts of radiation. Some are a trillion times brighter than the sun. Some quasars are more than 10,000,000,000,000,000,000,000 (10 sextillion) miles from the earth. To travel this distance would take our rocket 1,000 trillion years.

Do you feel a little small? Well, don't get discouraged. We may be a tiny speck in the universe, but we are very special to God. "Every soul is as fully known to Jesus as if he were the only one for whom the Saviour died. . . . He cares for each one as if there were not another on the face of the earth" *(The Desire of Ages,* p. 480).

The universe may be a big place, but God's love for you is even bigger!

DECEMBER

17

Turning Negatives Into Positives

Do your best to present yourself to God as one approved, a workman who does not need to be ashamed and who correctly handles the word of truth.
2 Timothy 2:15, NIV.

Get your papers. Get your papers right here." Ben walked up and down the streets of Chicago, shouting his sales pitch to the people walking by.

Life wasn't easy for Ben. When his friends were sitting in their nice, warm classrooms, Ben was standing on the cold street corner trying to earn some money, and what he earned didn't go for new clothes or a bike. His money bought food for his family.

One afternoon as he was carrying his papers under his arm, he saw a beautiful lady coming his way. "Want to buy a paper, lady?" he asked.

"Humph," sneered the lady. "I wouldn't buy a paper from a dirty little boy like you."

The woman's words stabbed at Ben's heart. He turned in embarrassment and didn't sell another paper that day. As he ate his supper that night, all he could think about were the lady's cruel words: "I wouldn't buy a paper from a dirty little boy like you."

Am I really that dirty? he thought. Getting up from the floor, he walked to the only mirror in the house. As he saw his reflection in the mirror, he realized that the lady was right. He *was* dirty.

The next morning when Ben got ready to start his day, he took a bath and clipped his fingernails. He combed his hair and made sure that his clothes were neat and clean. Then he put on his coat and hurried to pick up his newspapers. As Ben walked up and down the street selling his papers, he noticed that people seemed to be friendlier. In fact, his papers sold so fast that he ran out of them two hours earlier than usual.

Years later Ben became the owner of a large business in Chicago, and strangely enough, he credits his success to that unkind lady. "I'd never be where I am today if she hadn't pointed out how dirty I was. She helped me see that a person's appearance is important. And when I began taking pride in my appearance, I also learned to take more pride in my work. Instead of being angry that she put me down, I'm thankful."

It isn't very pleasant when people find fault with us, but often we can gain something from their criticism. When someone points out one of your problem areas, don't get discouraged. Use the criticism to improve yourself.

DECEMBER

18

Be True to Yourself

Who may climb the mountain of the Lord and enter where he lives? Who may stand before the Lord? Only those with pure hands and hearts, who do not practice dishonesty and lying. Psalm 24:3-5, TLB.

"A person's true character is shown by what he would do if he knew that no one else would ever find out."

It's one thing to be honest when you know someone is watching, but it's another thing to be honest when you could be dishonest and get away with it.

Back in 1925 Bobby Jones was playing in the U.S. Open golf championship with Willie Macfarlane. It was the final round, and the score was close. Each stroke could mean either victory or defeat for the players.

Bobby stepped up to the ball, moved his feet into position, and got ready to swing. But in so doing, he accidentally touched the ball with his club. The ball barely moved. In fact, no one else noticed what had happened. But Bobby did.

Turning to the official, Bobby said, "You need to penalize me one stroke. I moved the ball."

"I didn't see anything," admitted the official. "Are you sure?"

"I'm sure."

So the scorekeeper charged an additional stroke to Bobby's score, and Bobby and Willie continued their game, which ended in a tie at the end of 18 holes.

During the second playoff round, the men were tied again, but on the final stroke of the game, Willie Macfarlane beat Bobby by one point.

If Bobby had let his little slip go by, he would have won the U.S. Open. He could have rationalized that since the ball really didn't travel anywhere, it shouldn't be counted as a stroke. But honesty was more important to him than winning. Bobby could have ignored his conscience and gone home with the prize money, but instead he went home with his integrity.

Although Bobby Jones didn't win the 1925 U.S. Open, he came back to win it in 1926, 1929, and 1930. He also won the British Open in 1926, 1927, and 1930.

It isn't easy to be honest. But it always pays in the long run.

DECEMBER

19

Gross Gifts

A man who lacks judgment derides his neighbor, but a man of understanding holds his tongue. Proverbs 11:12, NIV.

When I was in grade school, the Christmas gift exchange day was one of the most exciting days of the year. We all tried to keep secret whose name we had drawn.

You've probably gotten some good gifts and some not-so-good gifts during the years. I remember getting some bubble bath from a classmate one year. That was a big disappointment for a tomboy like me.

I always find it interesting to watch my students' reactions when they open their gifts during the Christmas party. One certain gift exchange remains in my memory today, although it happened 16 years ago.

At the time, my husband and I were teaching in a two-room school. Instead of exchanging gifts among the students in each room, we put the names of all the girls in the school in one pile and all the boys' names in another. Then we had the students pick someone to buy a gift for.

On the day of the party, both groups met in my classroom for games and refreshments. We saved the gift exchange for the very last event of the day. I started the gift chain by picking out a gift from under the tree. It was for Darren, so I handed the present to him. Then Darren got up and found the gift he'd gotten for Dean. Dean gave a present to Kevin, and so on. When the boys were all done, the girls started.

Mr. Coffee got out his camera and took pictures while the students unwrapped their presents. Then we went around the room, and each person showed what he or she had gotten and told who had given the present.

When it was Lynn's turn, she held up a little six-inch baby doll. "I got this doll from Diane," she said, holding it up. "Thanks, Diane," she added.

Third grader Diane beamed that Lynn was so happy with the gift, but I knew that down deep inside, Lynn was disappointed. Lynn was a very grown-up eighth grader, who had no interest in playing with dolls, yet she didn't let her feelings show. She didn't want to hurt the younger girl's feelings.

How do you react when someone gives you a gift you really don't like? Are you a gracious receiver?

If you receive a disappointing gift this Christmas, you can at least be thankful that someone cared enough to give you a present. If you can't be excited about that gift, you can still appreciate the thought behind it.

DECEMBER

20

Too Soon

But among you there must not be even a hint of sexual immorality, or of any kind of impurity, or of greed, because these are improper for God's holy people. Ephesians 5:3, NIV.

Now, you're sure you'll be all right?" asked Mrs. Clampton as she put on her coat.

"Mom, I'm 12. I can stay by myself for a few hours." Jo Ellen handed her mother the car keys. "If anyone comes to the door, I just won't answer it."

Mrs. Clampton hugged her daughter. "I'll call if I can't get back by 8:30. I'm not sure what the roads are going to be like. Now don't forget to finish your homework, and be sure to do the dishes."

Jo Ellen watched her mother walk out to the garage. "At last," she said. Jo Ellen hurried to the Christmas tree in the living room. "I'm not going to wait any longer," she said to no one in particular. "Christmas is a whole week away, and I'm tired of trying to guess if Mom got me the tape recorder I wanted for Christmas. I'm going to find out."

Kneeling by the tree, Jo Ellen dug through the pile of brightly wrapped presents until she found the one covered with the candy-cane paper. "This is the only one that's the right size for a tape player."

She placed the gift in front of her and took a deep breath. She'd never done anything like this before, and her conscience bothered her. "Well, I won't really look at the gift. I'll just see if it's what I think it is," she said, trying to rationalize her actions.

Jo Ellen slowly peeled back the tape so she wouldn't rip the Christmas wrapping. Sure enough. The big black letters on the box read Panasonic Dual Cassette Player/Recorder. *Great, that's just the one I wanted,* she thought. *Now I'll just wrap it back up, and no one will ever know what I did.*

Setting the present back where she'd found it, Jo Ellen started to go to the kitchen to do the dishes, but then she looked at the rest of the gifts under the tree. "It probably wouldn't hurt to see what's in that little one from Grandma." And before she knew what was happening, Jo Ellen had opened every single present with her name on the outside.

By the time December 25 arrived, Jo Ellen didn't even care about opening her gifts. All the excitement was gone, and there was nothing she could do to bring back the fun she'd known in past Christmases.

Someday you'll probably get married, and the love you'll share with your marriage partner is like a present. Open it too soon, and you'll give away something that can never be replaced. If you wait until you get married, you won't be disappointed.

DECEMBER

21

Prison Doors

The Lord sets prisoners free, the Lord gives sight to the blind, the Lord lifts up those who are bowed down, the Lord loves the righteous. Psalm 146:7, 8, NIV.

Harry Houdini was probably the most famous magician the world has ever known. He was also an expert escape artist. Houdini let people lock him in heavy chains, and within minutes he'd be walking around free. He also let people put him in a strait-jacket and hang him from a rope by his feet. Somehow he freed himself from that predicament, too. He went so far as to boast that he could escape from any jail cell in less than one hour.

The warden of a new prison in the British Isles took him up on his challenge. "You'll never be able to get out of my prison," he said.

"We'll see about that!" replied Houdini.

Of course the newspaper reporters heard about Harry's newest stunt, and they were all there the day he was scheduled to make his big breakout.

After Harry waved to his audience, he entered the prison cell. The door slammed behind him. As soon as the warden and the guards left the cell block, Harry pulled out a 10-inch piece of flexible steel that he had hidden in his belt. He walked over to the massive door and began picking the lock.

Five minutes went by. Harry was still working. Ten minutes. It was taking a lot longer than he had expected. *I should have been out by now,* he thought.

The clock continued to tick off the minutes. Harry began to get nervous. Would he ever get free? Sweat popped out on his forehead. An hour had gone by.

Frantic, the great Houdini worked faster and faster. The stress was almost more than he could handle. Finally after two hours, he dropped to the ground in utter exhaustion, and as his body fell against the iron door, it swung open. It had been unlocked the whole time.

Does Satan ever make you feel like his prisoner? Does he tell you things like "You're hopeless; you can never change" or "You have no right to go to God; He doesn't want to help someone like you. You're mine now"? If he tries to bluff you, don't listen to him. He knows the door is unlocked. But as long as he can hide the truth from you, he can keep you as his prisoner.

When Jesus died, He broke Satan's power. All you have to do is accept Jesus as your Saviour. Then He'll come into your life and free you from your evil habits and desires.

Will you stay in Satan's prison—or will you walk out into a new life of happiness and freedom?

DECEMBER

22

Pretty Packages

But those doing right come gladly to the Light to let everyone see that they are doing what God wants them to. John 3:21, TLB.

Angela surveyed the mound of brightly colored presents lying under the Christmas tree. *Which one should I choose?* she thought. The Pathfinders had decided to exchange Christmas gifts, but instead of buying new things for each other, they were to bring handmade presents.

"Attention, everyone," called out Mr. Hansen, the Pathfinder director. "It's time for the gift exchange."

After the Pathfinders took their places on the floor, Mr. Hansen pulled out a cardboard box. "Inside this box are 30 slips of paper with a number written on each one. The person who gets 1 will choose a gift first. Then 2 will go next, and so on. Now remember, the gifts for girls are on the right."

When Angela's turn came, she reached in and pulled out number 3. *Oh, boy, this is my lucky day,* she thought.

"Oh, no," Sandy moaned as she looked at her number. "I'm last."

Preston had number 1, so he went first. He looked over all the presents and picked a large square box covered with shiny red paper and a big white bow.

Valerie went next.

Then Angela got up and quickly took the present she'd had her eye on—the one decorated with real candy canes.

By the time Sandy got her present, the only one left was a package wrapped in newspaper. Angela felt sorry for her friend.

Mr. Hansen looked around to make sure everyone had a present, then he said, "All right, kids, open your gifts."

Paper and ribbons flew through the air as the Pathfinders ripped open their presents. Angela found a counted cross-stitch picture inside her box.

A crowd stood around Sandy. Angela leaned over to see what everyone was looking at. "Isn't it beautiful?" Sandy said as she held up her gift, a photo album covered with soft pink material and trimmed with lace and dainty colored ribbons.

"I'm sorry I didn't wrap it with nice paper," apologized Holly, "but we ran out of wrapping paper."

"Oh, that's OK," said Sandy. "Who cares what the outside looks like when what's inside is so beautiful?"

Isn't it the same when it comes to people? What we look like on the outside isn't half as important as what we're like on the inside.

DECEMBER

23

Gifts Galore

When I was young, I loved going shopping with my mother. I always found dozens of things I couldn't live without. "Would you buy this for me?" I'd beg.

Mother always had the same answer. "Wait until Christmas."

I'm sure glad God doesn't ask me to wait until Christmas. He gives me blessings all through the year.

Below are the letters of the alphabet. See if you can think of a special gift from God that starts with each letter. (You may use single words or phrases.)

a—fresh *air*

b—

c—

d—

e—

f—

g—

h—

i—

j—

k—

l—

m—

n—

o—

p—

q—

r—

s—

t—

u—

v—

w—

ex—

y—

z—

Isn't God good? Let's thank Him for His wonderful gifts to each of us.

I will sing to the Lord all my life; I will sing praise to my God as long as I live. Psalm 104:33, NIV.

DECEMBER

24

Giving to All God's Creatures

I lie down and sleep; I wake again, because the Lord sustains me. Psalm 3:5, NIV.

Hey, Mom, where's the wrapping paper?" Becky called from the bottom of the steps.

"I think Brian left everything in the basement."

"Well, I'm going to go to my bedroom and wrap a few more gifts. I'll set the table as soon as I'm done."

Becky hurried to her room and shut the door behind her. She didn't want her snoopy brother finding out what she'd gotten him. As she wrapped her gifts, Becky looked out the window. *I'm so glad we got snow for Christmas,* she thought. Becky always looked forward to winter. She loved skating and sledding, and as far as she was concerned, the only Christmas worth having was a white Christmas.

Gathering up the presents, she carried them to the Christmas tree and then went into the kitchen. As she walked past the sliding glass door in the dining room, she saw something run into the barn.

What was that? she thought. As she stood looking out the window, the animal came back out of the barn. "Why, it's a dog," she said softly. "Oh, the poor thing. He looks half starved."

The dog moved slowly down the driveway. Its ribs stood out under its mangy-looking coat.

Becky hurried to the door. "Here, doggy. Here, boy."

The dog's head jerked up. Turning, it caught sight of Becky. Becky clapped her hands lightly. "Here, boy."

The dog lowered its head and slinked off behind the toolshed.

Mrs. Forrest walked into the kitchen to check on supper. "Who are you talking to?" she asked.

"There was a big black dog out by the barn. He looks as though he hasn't eaten in days. May I give him some food?"

"Go ahead. I think Uncle Marty left a few cans of dog food when he and Sparky were here at Thanksgiving. They're in the basement."

Becky found the food. She spooned out a can onto a big paper plate and set the food by the back door. "Merry Christmas, doggy," she said.

Something to think about: During the cold months, food is often scarce for wild animals. What food presents could you give to the creatures that live near your home?

DECEMBER

25

He Came to Speak Our Language

"Don't be afraid!" he said. "I bring you the most joyful news ever announced, and it is for everyone! The Savior—yes, the Messiah, the Lord—has been born tonight in Bethlehem!" Luke 2:9-11, TLB.

"Wake up, Brian," shouted Becky as she pounded on her brother's bedroom door. "It's Christmas morning!"

Brian lifted one eyelid and squinted at his alarm clock. Six o'clock. "Ohhh, it's so early," he groaned.

Becky stuck her head into the room. "Hurry up, slowpoke. It's time for worship. Grab your robe."

Brian inched out of bed. After putting on his robe, he lumbered on down to the living room.

"Becky, that black dog is out there by the barn again," said Mother, who was standing by the kitchen window.

Becky joined her mother at the window. The dog lay shivering underneath the hay truck. Becky found another can of dog food. As soon as she opened the back door, the black dog ran off again. She set the food on the porch and then joined her family in the living room. "Well, at least he ate the food I gave him last night," she said as she flopped down on the couch. "Maybe if we keep putting out food, he won't be so afraid of us. I just wish he could understand that we want to help him."

"Too bad you don't know dog language," Brian mumbled.

Dad picked up his Bible and turned to Luke 2. "You've got a point, Brian. If we could just communicate with the dog, we would tell him that we're his friends, but since he can't understand our language, he thinks we're his enemies. God faced a similar problem when He tried to tell people how much He loves them.

"Adam and Eve knew God as a friend, and so did many others. But as time went on, people got mixed up. They began blaming God for all the bad things that happened, and soon they saw God as the enemy.

"In order for us to know the truth about God, Jesus left heaven and lived on earth. Through His words and actions He was able to communicate to us just how much God cares about us."

"And that's what Christmas is all about, isn't it?" added Brian.

"Exactly," said Dad.

DECEMBER

26

It's All in the Packaging

I am not ashamed of the gospel, because it is the power of God for the salvation of everyone who believes. Romans 1:16, NIV.

When we spent a summer in Japan, we were very fortunate that generic packaging hadn't caught on over there yet. Since we couldn't read Japanese, we had to look at the pictures on the front of cans and boxes in order to determine what was inside.

We did pretty well—most of the time. I remember one day when we bought a can of fruit cocktail. After eating supper, I opened the fruit for our dessert. The fruit turned out to be baked beans.

I don't know about you, but I'm not attracted to food packaged in generic labels. I like brightly colored pictures on the front of the things I buy at the grocery store. Boxes with black and white lettering make me doubt the tastiness of what's inside. I've had people tell me that generic food isn't any different than regular name-brand items, but I have my doubts.

When telling other people about what their church believes, I've heard some young people put their church in a generic wrapper. "Well, we can't dance or go to movies. We go to church on Saturday, and then we have to sit around the house until sundown. We can't eat unclean meat, smoke, or drink. And caffeine is out too."

Be honest. If you heard someone describing his or her church like that, would you want to join it? I sure wouldn't. I think I'd run the other way.

Now let's see what a teenager could say to put an attractive label on our church: "I'm a Seventh-day Adventist. We're interested in keeping healthy, so we avoid unclean meat, cigarettes, alcohol, and caffeine. We also set aside the seventh-day Sabbath as a special day to worship God and be with our families. And because we want to do only things that bring honor to God, we are careful about what we read and what we watch on TV."

Doesn't that sound a lot more positive? Both descriptions give the same basic information, but the second makes our church appealing. I'd be interested in a church described in those terms.

I hope that the next time you tell someone about your church, you'll throw out the generic labels and show that person just how attractive the Seventh-day Adventist Church really is.

DECEMBER

27

Aban-doned

Though my father and mother forsake me, the Lord will receive me. Psalm 27:10, NIV.

"Please, ma'am, would you take care of my baby until I can find some work?"

Miss Mary, an elderly woman, looked up from her knitting at the young girl standing on the steps of the broken-down porch.

"You want to leave your baby with me?" the woman asked.

"Yes, ma'am. I'm hoping to find work picking fruit. Will you watch him a day or two?"

"Why, I suppose I could," said the lady. "A little boy?"

The girl nodded and handed the baby to the stranger. "I'm mighty obliged, ma'am. I couldn't find anyone to take care of Darrell, and I've got to find work."

"Well, don't you worry. I've raised a couple of children in my time. Little Darrell and I will get along just fine. He'll be right here when you get back."

With that, the young mother took one more look at her baby and then turned and walked away. Miss Mary leaned back in her rocking chair and hummed a lullaby to the little child who lay sleeping in her arms.

Why would that girl just hand her baby over to me? she thought. *Surely there must be a friend or relative who could look after him for a few hours.* Miss Mary didn't know that the young girl had no one else to turn to. The father of the baby wanted nothing to do with her or the child. He was already married and had a family of his own. Miss Mary enjoyed her time with the baby.

By evening, she began to worry. "Where's your mother, little man?" she asked as she warmed up the baby's bottle. Darrell just looked up at her with his dark brown eyes. "Well, mother or no mother, I'm going to feed you and put you to bed. I just hope your mother gets back pretty soon."

Three days went by, but Darrell's mother did not return. Miss Mary began asking friends if they knew of the young girl who had asked her to baby-sit. As the days turned into weeks and the weeks into months, Miss Mary realized that Darrell's mother was not going to return. She had abandoned her child.

Although Darrell's mother deserted him, God never left him alone. During the next few days I'd like to tell you about how God worked in the life of this homeless little boy.

DECEMBER

28

Homeless and Alone

I will live with them and walk among them, and I will be their God, and they will be my people. . . . I will be a Father to you, and you will be my sons and daughters.
2 Corinthians 6:16-18, NIV.

Miss Mary became the only mother Darrell ever knew. She accepted him into her home and raised him the best she could, but when Darrell was only 7 years old, Miss Mary became very sick. One day she called Darrell to her side. "Honey," she said, "I don't have much to give you, I'm just too poor."

The little boy understood what she was trying to say.

Miss Mary put her arm around him. "But I want to give you something that is more valuable than all the money in the world." The old woman opened a drawer by her bed and pulled out a small New Testament. "Here, Darrell, take this Bible. I want to give you Jesus."

When Miss Mary died, her sister took Darrell into her family for a while, but Darrell never had a real home after that. He was moved from home to home. Six months at one place. A few weeks at another. By the time he was 13, Darrell was tired of being shifted from one place to another. So he packed up his few belongings and set up a home for himself under a bridge.

Since he had no money and no job, Darrell had to make do. After school he walked along the Florida highways and streets in search of pop cans. He'd sell the cans and use the money to buy food. When it got dark, he'd stand outside the local convenience store and do his homework under the fluorescent lights.

Most of the students in Darrell's class at school made fun of him, for Darrell didn't always smell too good. He had to take his baths in the river. He washed his clothes there, too. If the other children had known that Darrell was homeless, they probably would have treated him more kindly, but they had no idea that he was on his own.

Although Darrell had asked Jesus to come into his heart when he was 9 years old, he often wondered if God really cared about him. "Why do I have to live like this?" he cried out to God. "Why did my mother leave me? Why can't I have a home like everyone else?"

Every time he questioned God, God's only answer was, "Trust Me. I have everything under control." God didn't explain everything to Darrell, but He promised to take care of him.

When you're sad and lonely, can you have faith that God has everything in control?

DECEMBER

29

A Happy Ending

But they do not know the thoughts of the Lord; they do not understand his plan. Micah 4:12, NIV.

The gem cannot be polished without friction; no man can be perfected without trials."

For a while Darrell blamed God for his miserable life. He even began to wish he'd never been born. But the Holy Spirit continued to speak to Darrell's mind, and one day he decided to stop looking at all the problems he had. Instead, he began to look to Jesus.

Darrell's circumstances didn't change, but his attitude did. For the first time in a long time, Darrell felt that life was worth living. He no longer felt angry at his mother for leaving him. He realized that if he hadn't come to live with Miss Mary, he might never have come to know about Jesus.

Darrell graduated from high school and went on to college. Today he is a dynamic minister, serving the God who brought him through all his trials. Not long ago Darrell was the featured speaker on a special Christmas television program. During the program he told of his life and how God had taken care of him. A few days later he received a phone call from a stranger. "You don't know me, but I saw you on television the other day. And I believe that I know your father. You look just like him."

Sure enough, the lady who called did know Darrell's father. When Darrell found out that his father was in the hospital, he flew to see him. What an exciting time the two men had meeting each other for the first time! But the most exciting event of Darrell's whole life happened when he was able to tell his father about Jesus, for Darrell's father was not a Christian. As the two visited together, Darrell's father came to trust Jesus, and he asked Him to come into his life.

Today Darrell is very thankful for the things he had to go through. Even though he didn't understand at the time why God allowed certain things to happen, he now sees that God was able to turn every problem into a blessing.

When life doesn't make sense to you, you don't need to worry, for God has everything under control. Just trust Him to work things out in His own time and way.

DECEMBER

30

Keep on Track

Teach me your way, O Lord; lead me in a straight path. Psalm 27:11, NIV.

The old trapper slung his pack over his shoulder and strapped his snowshoes onto his boots. Pushing the door open, he trudged out of the cabin and headed across the snow that blanketed the ground outside.

Town was a full 15 miles away, but Trapper Hank was used to walking long distances. After reaching the halfway mark to town, Hank noticed that the sky was beginning to cloud over. *Snow,* he thought. *I'd better get moving. I don't want to get caught in a storm.*

Pushing himself even harder, he increased his speed and moved even faster across the frozen ground, but he wasn't fast enough. Before he could reach the safety of Pigeon Hollow, large snowflakes began dropping from the sky. Soon Hank could see nothing in front of him but a swirling wall of white. The familiar trail to town was now hidden by new-fallen snow.

Where am I? he wondered. *I can't tell which direction I'm heading in.*

After making a few wrong turns, Hank began to worry. He knew that if he got lost in the snow, he would freeze to death. Hank strained to see through the blinding snow. If he could only see a light. To Hank's relief he caught sight of some tracks just ahead. *I must be close to town,* he decided. *I'll just follow the tracks, and I'm sure they'll get me there safely.*

With renewed energy, Hank hurried on through the storm, following the tracks carefully. But when he saw a second set of tracks, he realized that he was just walking in a circle, following his own tracks. Fortunately for Trapper Hank the snow stopped soon afterward. If it hadn't, he may never have found his way to safety.

Jesus has given us a path to follow as we journey through life. By reading the Bible and following its instructions, we can find the way to heaven. Satan does his best to keep us from seeing clearly the way God wants us to walk. He likes to get us off the path. The only way we can keep from getting sidetracked is to study God's Word every day. When we stay close to Him, we'll never lose sight of the path.

The Bucky Stone Books
by David B. Smith

Making Waves at Hampton Beach High (book 1)

Hampton Beach High isn't ready for a kid who stands up for his convictions. But Bucky Stone isn't afraid to be the first. Things begin to change at his public school—one person at a time. Paper, 127 pages. US$4.95, Cdn$6.20.

Showdown at Home Plate (book 2)

It's late Friday afternoon during the championship game, and every eye is on Bucky. Should he take his turn at bat or be true to his conviction not to play on Sabbath? Paper, 126 pages. US$4.95, Cdn$6.20.

Outcast on the Court (book 3)

When Bucky makes the basketball team, he discovers he has what it takes to help lead the Panthers to victory. But winning won't come easy. Not with his fiercest opposition coming from his own coach and team. Paper, 143 pages. US$4.95, Cdn$6.20.

Bucky's Big Break (book 4)

Bucky couldn't imagine life being interesting without sports, but he did expect it to be safer. He was dead wrong. His new position as a bank teller opens up all kinds of possibilities for his future—but that's only if he has one. The next customer in line is banking on becoming rich quick. And this guy's got a gun! Paper, 126 pages. US$4.95, Cdn$6.20.

Look for book 5 in the Bucky Stone series.

To order, call **1-800-765-6955** or write to ABC Mailing Service, P.O. Box 1119, Hagerstown, MD 21741. Send check or money order. Enclose applicable sales tax and 15 percent (minimum US$2.50) for postage and handling. Prices and availability subject to change without notice. Add 7 percent GST in Canada.